# THE PRINCIPLES OF ETHICAL REASONING

## Ethics and Policing in a Civil Society

Bruce D. Bjorkquist

Prentice Hall

Toronto

**Canadian Cataloguing in Publication Data**

Bjorkquist, Bruce D., 1942–
    The principles of ethical reasoning : ethics and policing in a civil society

Includes bibliographical references and index.
ISBN 0-13-092625-6

1. Police ethics. I. Title.

HV7924.B56 2002        174'.93632        C2001-930039-5

0-13-092625-6

Vice President, Editorial Director: Michael Young
Editor-in-Chief, Softside: David Stover
Acquisitions Editor: Sophia Fortier
Marketing Manager: Sharon Loeb
Associate Editor: Meaghan Eley
Production Editor: Sherry Torchinsky
Copy Editor: Susan McNish
Production Coordinator: Trish Ciardullo
Page Layout: Jansom
Interior Design: Julia Hall
Cover Design: Amy Harnden
Cover Image: PhotoDisc

3 4 5    05

Printed and bound in Canada.

# Contents

## Chapter 3:   Prescriptive Ethics: Establishing Norms of Conduct in a Civil Society   44

## Chapter 4:   Codes of Conduct: Examining the Ethical Standards of a Civil Society   66

## Chapter 5:   Principles: Identifying the Basic Ethical Concepts of a Civil Society   89

## Chapter 6:    Goodness: Preventing Harm and Doing Good in a Civil Society    112

## Chapter 7:    Equality: Treating Others Impartially in a Civil Society    135

## Chapter 8:   Justice: Treating Others Fairly in a Civil Society   158

## Chapter 9:   Truth: Being Honest and Having Integrity in a Civil Society   182

## Chapter 10:  Freedom: Making Ethical Choices in a Civil Society    206

# List of Situations

# List of Media Watch Boxes

# Preface

Twenty-five years ago I taught my first course in ethics at Conestoga College. Each year since then, ethics has been one of my assigned courses in both semesters of the school year. Over those many years I have used a great variety of textbooks, many of which were extremely well written. More often than not, however, they were written by university professors for university classrooms. In university settings, students are most likely to take ethics in their second or third year, after completing one or more preliminary courses in philosophy. The textbooks presumed as much.

The great majority of students who have entered my classrooms for the study of ethics have not had the benefit of an introductory philosophy course. Though bright and enthusiastic, they often found the textbook intimidating. The theoretical orientation, technical terminology, and conceptual complexity were not, I'm convinced, beyond their intelligence levels, but they were beyond their experience. So much of what we had to get at was shrouded in technical language and an array of competing theories.

Gradually, I found myself providing my classes with handouts that I had prepared. As these were simpler in style and focused on the essentials of an issue, students responded more favourably to them than they did to the assigned text. Needless to say, the years have generated a fair number of such handouts. Eventually, the idea of a text written in a simple manner and focused on the needs of my college students took shape. The introduction of the Police Foundations program into Colleges of Applied Arts and Technology was the catalyst in the process that has resulted in the book you are now reading.

Throughout, I have tried to present information in a simple, conversational style. Where necessary, I have used technical terms but have, in each case, provided clear definitions or explanations so that terminology does not become a hindrance to learning. Examples, too, I have chosen carefully with a view to facilitating comprehension. Moreover, in each chapter I have provided situations for discussion and debate that are based on real-world events. Descriptions of those real-world events are always included so that classes can compare their own views to what happened in real life. Student responses to the cases that I have included have always been positive.

In adopting a relatively simple and practical approach to the book, I have kept references to a minimum, and most of these are to either newspaper or magazine articles. This is in keeping with making the book accessible to persons who are interested in ethics but not necessarily in scholarly research. Once again, the hope is that this approach will provide relatively easy access to the world of ethics and show, further, that ethics is very much the stuff of everyday life. It is to be found all around us, not just in the writings of famous philosophers.

In summary, I have written a book for college students that I hope will encourage students and teachers alike to learn more about ethics and its applications to our personal and professional lives. I hope that ethics classes will be exciting places to be as teachers and students together explore what ethics is all about. The respectful exchange of ideas and points of view on ethical issues can be a most rewarding experience for both students and teachers. In that regard, I trust that this book will serve us all very well.

In addition to making the study of ethics enjoyable, the book must, I believe, have a practical benefit for both individuals and police services. While this book is primarily a book about ethics in policing, it addresses issues of a personal nature as well. Chapter 9 on Truth, for example, discusses honesty in policing. However, it also addresses honesty in school and marriage. The same principles that we use to make ethical decisions in policing are used to make ethical decisions elsewhere in our lives, school and family being only two such places. In addition to serving us well in the classroom, then, my hope is that it will serve us well in policing and in our personal lives as we make our moral choices.

## AN OUTLINE OF THE BOOK

Chapter 1, Origins, is not, as one might assume, about the history of ethics. Rather, it is about why we have ethics. It is about the logical, not historical, origins of the subject. In order for people to meet their basic needs in life while working in harmony with others, certain principles must be adhered to. These are the principles of ethical reasoning that are essential for life in a civil society. Chapter 1 describes our needs as humans and then proceeds to show how a civilized satisfaction of those needs requires ethics and, of course, the law. The first chapter, then, explains the logical origin of ethics and describes the context in which we make our ethical choices, namely, that of a civil society.

Chapter 2, Analytical Ethics, underscores the fact that ethics is all about critical thinking and informed choices in a civil society. To think critically is a skill beneficial to all areas of our lives, including ethics. After distinguishing among different dimensions of ethical inquiry, the chapter describes certain perennial questions that inevitably arise in the field. It then concludes with some very practical guides to critical thinking. In particular, there are sections on critical thinking, the PRINCIPLES Model, and the DECIDE Process. The Model and Process are two conceptual tools designed to assist in understanding moral issues and making ethically defensible choices. Also, at this point, the principles of ethical reasoning—goodness, equality, justice, truth, and freedom—are introduced in a preliminary fashion.

Chapter 3, Prescriptive Ethics, describes two broad approaches to making moral or ethical choices. An understanding of these two approaches is very important in that individuals will be better able to understand their own ethical positions. Moreover, both approaches continue to influence ethical decision making today, both personally and professionally. The influence of both utilitarianism and duty ethics on policing, for example, is evident and illuminating. Later chapters highlight these influences in specific situations, such as the need for non-discriminatory treatment of citizens or the use of deception in police investigations.

Chapter 4, Codes of Conduct, first discusses ethical codes in general, emphasizing the relationships among ethical values, ethical principles, and the ethical norms that comprise the codes. The United Nations Universal Declaration of Human Rights and the Canadian Charter of Rights and Freedoms are societal codes in that they have application to very large numbers of people, whole societies. In contrast, professional codes are ethical codes that have much more limited application, namely, to the members of a particular profession, like policing. An overview of the Ontario Police Services Act, Code of Conduct, and three codes of the International Association of Chiefs of Police are presented. Reference to all of these codes continues throughout the rest of the book as various issues are addressed.

Chapter 5, Principles, describes and explains each of the five principles of ethical reasoning. First introduced in Chapter 2 and referenced in Chapters 3 and 4, important concepts associated with these fundamental principles are now offered in detail. These are the principles without which civil societies cease to exist. These same principles, when ignored or abandoned by individuals, make ethical conduct impossible. Ethics is all about the application of these five principles to the choices we make personally and professionally. Each of the remaining chapters of the text is devoted to one of these principles. The principles of ethical reasoning become the organizing principle for all that follows.

Chapter 6, Goodness, begins with the simplest rules that can be derived from the principle: "Don't harm" and "Do good." From these simple beginnings, the chapter proceeds to examine the lethal use of force in self-defence, the challenging issue of euthanasia, and the sensitive issue of abortion. Each topic is concerned with issues of goodness. Killing in self-defence harms the person killed, but the harm can be ethically justified under strict conditions. Does assisted suicide constitute a harm or does it bring goodness to a person? Is abortion the harming of a human being or not? If it is, can it ever be justified? In the consideration of each of these topics, all relevant principles, not just goodness, are introduced as necessary.

Chapter 7, Equality, begins by stating the principle as a positive and a negative duty, the simplest norms to come from the principle: "Treat others as equals" and "Don't discriminate." After citing instances of the principle in various codes of conduct, its application to racism and sexism are explored. Next, patriotism and family favouritism are discussed, with issues related to professional favouritism following. To what degree, if any, can we favour our professional colleagues in the exercise of our duty? To what degree, if any, can we favour friends? Can such discrimination in favour of someone be ethically justified? If so, how?

Chapter 8, Justice, starts with the duties "Be fair to others" and "Don't be unjust." It then proceeds to distinguish various forms of justice—social, criminal, enforcement, legal, and penal, for example—and addresses issues relevant to each of them. Two competing views regarding the nature of punishment in general are analyzed before turning to the specific issue of capital punishment. Once again, the relationship of justice to the other principles is underscored as specific aspects of issues are addressed.

Chapter 9, Truth, follows next. From the basic duties "Don't deceive" and "Tell the truth," we proceed to questions about lies, falsehoods, and simple mistakes. We note that there are good lies and bad lies, and we distinguish between them. The importance of confidentiality in policing is reviewed before issues of honesty in school, marriage, and policing are examined. What are good lies and bad lies in these contexts? How, for example, is police deception in investigations justified? Who is responsible for any such justification? Who can authorize it? When it comes to the truth, what is the proper relationship of those in police services to the civil society that they serve? All of these questions are examined, and ethically defensible answers are proposed.

Chapter 10, Freedom, like the other chapters, begins with a statement of the basic duties associated with the principles: "Don't coerce others" and "Respect the choices of others." These are the basic duties expressed as simple rules. The freedom principle has, in fact, been an important part of each of the preceding chapters, starting with Chapter 6. Ethics, of course, is always about choices. How much individual freedom, for example, is ethically justifiable in a specific situation? Preliminary considerations then give way to the topics of pornography, sexual offenders, and prostitution.

# IMPORTANT FEATURES OF THE BOOK

**Learning Outcomes**  Each chapter begins with a clear statement of learning targets followed by an introductory section designed to capture reader interest.

**Chapter Summaries**  Concise summaries of the various topics in the chapter follow the presentation in each chapter. These are provided as a review, but they can also be used by readers as introductory overviews of the chapter.

**Mastering the Material**  Each chapter includes a number of items designed to test the reader's comprehension of key ideas. Along with chapter objectives, they can be used to identify learning targets before reading the chapter. After reading the chapter, they can serve as tests of comprehension. Readers who can complete these items without consulting the text should do very well on chapter quizzes and tests. Teachers may want to use some of them as test items.

**Key Terms**  Key words in each chapter are highlighted in bold and appear in the Glossary at the end of the book.

**Situations**  Case studies based on real-world incidents punctuate the text. Early chapters have one situation each, but later chapters have several. Teachers can borrow from later chapters if they feel inclined to do more case studies in the early going. A list of situations allows for easy borrowing or locating of the various cases.

**Critical Thinking: The PRINCIPLES Model**  First introduced and explained at the end of Chapter 2, the model is reviewed piecemeal in each of the subsequent chapters. These sections provide a reminder and a review of this conceptual tool.

**Critical Thinking: The DECIDE Process**  Also introduced in Chapter 2, this companion tool to the PRINCIPLES Model is also reviewed in each of Chapters 3 through 10. Together, the PRINCIPLES Model and the DECIDE Process can serve as powerful tools for understanding moral issues and making ethically defensible choices.

**Media Watch: Ethics in the News**  Many of these newspaper or magazine articles describe the real-world events upon which particular situations for discussion (above) are based. This allows for discussion of different points of view in the classroom as well as the opportunity to see how others handled things in the real world.

**Readings and References**  Readers wishing to explore a given subject further will find detailed information on publications related to each chapter at the end of the book.

**Appendices**  Each of the key documents that are referenced repeatedly in the book appears in its full form in the appendices. These include the two societal documents: the Universal Declaration of Human Rights and the Canadian Charter of Rights and Freedoms; and the professional codes of ethics from the police services: The Ontario Police Services Act, Code of Conduct, the International Association of Chiefs of Police Law Enforcement Code of Ethics (1957 and 1991), the Law Enforcement Code of Conduct (1989), and the Canons of Police Ethics (1957 and 1991).

**Teacher's Guide**  A teacher's guide with suggested teaching strategies, answers to the Mastering the Material items, and a bank of test items accompanies the text.

# Acknowledgments

I wish to thank the many students with whom I have worked over these many years, particularly those of the Police Foundations program at Conestoga College. For your patience with me, your willingness to listen, to think, and to offer your views, I thank you. For your challenges to my own thinking, offered in the spirit of mutual learning, I am especially grateful.

I also want to thank my professional colleagues and dear friends who are a constant source of encouragement. Good colleagues and good friends provide both inspiration and information. Nobody should have to teach in isolation. I don't, and that fact is a great strength to me as I continue to try to get it right in the classroom. It continues to be a strength to me as I now try to get it right in print. Among those many colleagues, I want to note especially Bob Bamford. Our discussions, both on sea and land, with respect to Beauty, Truth, and Goodness have been excellent. Also, thanks for the laughter. To the cops in my life—Carolyn Harrison, Al Hunter, Dave Stewart, and Brent Walker—I offer special thanks. You are probably unaware of the help that you have been to me. Thank you.

While I could mention many professors who have taught me over many years, I'll limit myself to one. Professor Jan Narveson of the University of Waterloo has been an inspiration to many students, including me. Through his lectures, writings, and stimulating discussions, he has made me think about ethics and the principles of ethical reasoning. As I think of him, I think also of Thomas Hobbes, David Hume, John Stuart Mill, and Immanuel Kant whose ideas live on. Thank you.

Pat Dockrill, Emmett Hogan, and Rebecca Volk reviewed an early version of the manuscript and offered both encouragement and very valuable suggestions. I have acted on many of your ideas and am confident that this text is much better as a result. I thank each of you for your thoughtful reviews.

Thanks are also due to David Stover, Sophia Fortier, Susan Ratkaj, Sherry Torchinsky, Meaghan Eley, and Susan McNish, at Pearson Education for their guidance and suggestions. Thank you.

Finally, I thank Janet, Sonia, and Sara, to whom I dedicate this second book. Together, over many years, we have sought to be good to one another. I think we've done very well.

Bruce Bjorkquist
Doon, Ontario

## chapter one

# Origins: Exploring the Role of Ethics in a Civil Society

## LEARNING OUTCOMES

After completing this chapter, you should be able to

- Describe three important aspects of human nature
- Distinguish between survival needs and social needs
- Discuss nature's role in the satisfaction of basic human needs
- Distinguish between civilized and uncivilized ways of satisfying human needs
- Describe three characteristics of a civil society
- Provide a working definition of ethics and closely related terms

## INTRODUCTION

In all likelihood you are reading this book because you hope to become a police officer. Before you picked up this text, you undoubtedly knew that there is a great deal to learn if you want to serve and protect the public as an officer in a police service. Such service can be both a rewarding and a demanding career. Traffic control, crowd control, criminal investigation, civil and criminal law, proper use of firearms, and the appropriate use of force are only a few of the many aspects of policing that prospective officers must study. In addition to these subjects and many others, there is ethics.

What is ethics and why is it an important part of your program of studies? The answer to that question will occupy us throughout this book. Ethics is important for many reasons and, hopefully, its importance will become very clear as we study the various topics that follow this introduction. Ethics is important for everyone, but it is particularly important for those who aspire to professional positions within society. Police officers, like doctors, nurses, and other professionals, are expected to carry out their duties in an ethically responsible manner. Ethical conduct is what, in part, makes the career a demanding one. It is also what makes it rewarding.

Toward the end of this chapter we will offer a formal definition of ethics. For the moment, however, let's say that **ethics** is the study of right and wrong in human relationships. Since human relationships include both our personal and professional lives, virtually all of our experiences have an ethical dimension to them. The manner in which we relate to our spouses, children, and neighbours, for example, is the subject of ethics. But so, too, is the manner in which a professional police officer handles an arrest. Our study of ethics will involve us in both the personal and professional aspects of our lives. There are many different ways in which we can begin this important subject. Let's start by considering the following situation.

| SITUATION 1.1 | Police Fundraiser |
| --- | --- |

Imagine that you are a rookie police officer and you are going to attend your first Police Association meeting. Senior officers, including your constable coach, have encouraged you to get involved because decisions are going to be made regarding the raising of funds. The money raised will be used to fight crime by lobbying elected officials to support the following causes: the restoration of capital punishment, the toughening of the Young Offenders Act, and the increasing of police services budgets.

The motion that comes before the membership is as follows: "The Association will hire telephone fundraisers to solicit donations to Operation Fight Crime. Donors who give $100 or more will receive gold stickers for their vehicle windshields. Donors of $50 to $99 will receive silver windshield stickers. Donors who give $20 to $49 will receive bronze windshield stickers. All windshield stickers will bear the words 'I Support the Police.'"

Will you vote for or against the motion? Why?

Thoughtful consideration of this situation raises a number of important questions. All of them are relevant to our study of ethics. The situation requires that you think through a number of issues. What personal principles, for example, will guide your thinking as you decide what to do? What values of the Police Association underlie the motion? Are your values in agreement with those of the Association? Would the implementation of Operation Fight Crime break any rules of professional policing?

Consider, further, the relationships that are involved in this situation. First, there is your relationship to your coach. What if she is a strong supporter of the motion? How will that affect your vote? Should it affect your vote? What if the vote is an open vote involving a raising of hands. Would you raise your hand to vote no after she has raised hers to vote yes? What about the other officers present? How will your vote affect your relationship to them? Let's leave this situation now and continue with our preliminary remarks about ethics. We will have occasion to refer to the situation again as we proceed further in our study.

One way to begin to understand what ethics is all about is to consider certain aspects of human nature and what we need to do to have a fulfilling life. Initially we might be put off by this approach because, admittedly, we humans are very complex creatures. A little reflection, however, will show that despite our complexity there are certain basic characteristics that are shared by virtually all human beings. These characteristics can be very useful in helping us understand what ethics is and why ethics is so important. In this chapter we will explore these basic human qualities as we begin to answer the question, "What is ethics all about?"

The key to understanding what ethics is all about is to focus on the fact that ethics, as we noted above, has to do with relationships between and among people. Our moral choices in life are made in the context of a network of relationships. For example, we live in families and communities, we work in organizations and institutions, and we are members of society. Understanding some fundamental aspects of society and how it functions provides us with the social context in which relationships exist and ethical choices are made. In particular, we will do well to understand the functioning of what we will call a civil society.

We will return to the subject of civil society after we have reviewed some basic characteristics of individual human beings. What, we need to ask, do all individuals have in common? What, especially, do we have in common that can help us to understand what ethics is all about?

# HUMAN NATURE

Many writers have, over the centuries, attempted to describe human nature. Poets, sages, and scientists have written much on the subject—a subject that isn't free of controversy and debate. Despite disagreements about human nature, there are many indisputable facts. The field of psychology has undertaken to provide an objective description of many of these. In this section we will describe briefly certain characteristics that are relevant to answering the question we raised above. We'll begin by considering three aspects or dimensions of human nature: our capacity to think, feel, and act.

## Human Beings Are Rational Beings

The scientific classification of human beings places us in the genus *hominidae,* of which there is only one species, namely, *homo sapiens,* the intelligent ones. While many question the ultimate intelligence and wisdom of the human species, there is no questioning the fact that we are rational beings. Psychologists refer to this rational dimension of human nature as the **cognitive dimension**. We humans are cognitive beings, reasoning beings.

Included in the cognitive dimension are all kinds of intellectual abilities and activities. We think, we reason, we remember, we make decisions, and we solve problems. Despite the many mistakes and poor judgments that we make, there are countless examples of the intelligence of our species. It is our ability to think and reason that has led to the designation *homo sapiens*. Our sophisticated cognitive functioning sets us apart from and, in some sense, above the other animals. This is not to argue that we are always right and never make mistakes. Clearly we make many mistakes. And clearly we do so all too often.

Nevertheless, our cognitive abilities are a true wonder of nature, and we should be proud of this capacity to think. Except for a very few unfortunate human beings, we all think and reason on a daily basis. Our ability to reason and solve problems gets us through many of the challenges of life. We will see later that the human capacity to reason is at the heart of ethical ways of solving life's problems.

Reasoning, among other things, involves the use of general principles to arrive at conclusions about particular situations. Simply put, **principles** are basic ideas. The subject of this book is, as you know, the rational principles that give meaning to discussions in ethics and provide moral guidance for our actions. We will have much to say about the cognitive aspects of ethics as we proceed. In the Police Fundraiser situation that we looked at above, among other things it is important to identify what principles are guiding the project. Are they sound principles, for example, and do they square with commonly accepted principles of ethical conduct?

We humans are rational beings who use basic principles in virtually all areas of our lives. In ethics we explore the use of such principles in discussing, establishing rules for, and judging human conduct. In other words, the cognitive dimension of ethics involves the study of the basic ideas that humans use to decide what is right and wrong in human relationships. In Chapter 2 we will devote ourselves to an examination of certain key aspects of human reason as they apply to ethics. In particular, we'll examine the role of logic in ethical argumentation and debate.

## Human Beings Are Emotional Beings

In addition to being rational beings, we are emotional beings. Psychologists refer to this feeling dimension of our nature as the **affective dimension**. Our species is marked by a wide variety of emotions and moods and, at the level of the individual, virtually all humans experience the basic feelings: happiness, sadness, anger, disgust, surprise, and fear. An individual who doesn't have these experiences or has dysfunctional exaggerations of them is considered to have an emotional disorder, suffering from one or another of the emotional illnesses that have been identified by contemporary psychiatry.

One aspect of our emotional experience that has received a great deal of attention in our time is empathy. **Empathy** is, simply put, feeling what another person is feeling. In other words, when humans identify with the feelings of others, they have empathy for others. We need to note, very clearly, the significance of empathy for the moral life. I like to refer to empathy as the "moral feeling" or the "ethical feeling" because it is essential for moral conduct.

If people have no empathy for others, they can do the most hurtful things to them. They can do these harmful things because the perpetrators do not feel what their victims feel. Psychopaths and sociopaths, for example, lack empathy for other people, and this absence of fellow feeling often leads to anti-social behaviour. We will return to this subject later. For the moment, we note the importance of empathy, a critical aspect of our emotional life and our moral life as human beings.

Because we are emotional beings we desire some things more than other things. We feel, for example, that our family is more important than our material possessions. Because we feel more or less intensely about different things in our world, we place a higher value on some things than we do on others. We are emotionally connected to our friends in ways that we are not with mere acquaintances or strangers. Consequently, we value time spent with friends. The same amount of time is given neither to acquaintances nor to strangers. Generally speaking, they are of less value to us than our friends are.

We can define a **value** as whatever a person or group feels strongly about. Our values, then, are the things that are most important to us in life. Included among the many things that are important to us is the way in which others treat us. Ethical or moral conduct is an important part of our individual value systems. Each of us as an individual has such a **value system** comprising all the things that we feel strongly about in life. In passing, we should note that groups also have value systems. We will have much to say about both group values and individual values as we proceed with our study of ethics. We've already touched on this subject in the Police Fundraiser situation presented above.

The motion that we considered reflects the values of those who framed it. Often, in organized groups, motions reflect the values of the group's leaders, its executive officers. If the vote passes, then the membership is expressing its support for the values that underlie the motion. If you vote yes because you believe in the goals of the motion for the restoration of capital punishment, for example, then your personal values prompt you to support the group's values. You and the group, no doubt, feel strongly about those goals. In other words, you place high value on them. If you vote no, however, you must feel differently about either the goals or the means of achieving them.

The fact that we are emotional beings is significant for our understanding of ethics. In this section we have underscored the point that feelings underlie both empathy and values. Ethical conduct is impossible without empathy, and a complete understanding of ethics is impossible without a clear view of values and their role in ethical decision making. Further examination of the role of feelings in ethics lies ahead of us as we continue to attempt to answer the question, "What is ethics all about?"

## Human Beings Are Acting Beings

We have just pointed out that human beings are both rational beings and emotional beings. In addition, we are acting beings. The expression "acting beings" may bring to mind images of the theatre. In using this label for the third dimension of human nature, however, we are not referring to the human ability to play a part in a movie or play. Rather, the label has been chosen to capture what many psychologists simply call behaviour. Another expression for the **behavioural dimension** is the **psychomotor dimension**. What do we mean by the behavioural or psychomotor dimension?

The answer is really quite simple. As human beings, we have certain sensory experiences, we have certain feelings, and we have certain thoughts. For example, Joe feels hungry, he sees an apple across the room and knows what it is. All of this prompts Joe to act. He gets up from his chair, walks across the room, picks up the apple and eats it. His feelings and thoughts have led Joe to act. His behaviour in this example is very simple. He gets up, walks a short distance, picks up an apple, and eats it.

Let's return to the Police Fundraiser situation to illustrate the same point. In that case, the thoughts and feelings of individuals prompt an action, either the raising of the hand to say yes or the raising of a hand to say no. As cognitive beings, we think issues through using basic principles to arrive at conclusions. As affective beings, we feel more or less strongly about different things. As acting beings, our thoughts and feelings motivate our actions or behaviours. All three dimensions of human nature play vital roles in ethics. We will explore moral values, moral principles, and moral conduct in order to understand what ethics is all about.

Human beings, we have been saying, are acting beings who regularly take action on the basis of their feelings and thoughts. Putting it slightly differently, we regularly translate thoughts and feelings into actions. Interesting, and extremely important for our understanding of ethics, is the fact that humans regularly make judgments about the actions of others. Our actions are frequently judged by others to be appropriate or inappropriate. They are judged to be good or bad, right or wrong. We, of course, also make such judgments about the conduct of others.

The judgment that an action is right or wrong is often a moral or ethical judgment. Much of this book will be an examination of how such judgments are made. Additionally, we will examine the reasons we give for our actions. For the present, we simply note that groups establish rules of conduct that specify for members of the group the actions that are expected or forbidden by the group. The written and unwritten rules of a group are called **norms**. These norms form a code of conduct for members of the group and identify actions that are acceptable and unacceptable to the group.

As acting beings, then, humans can expect that certain of their actions will be judged to be right, while other actions will be judged to be wrong. The most important norms of the group will identify those actions that the group will not tolerate. The most important rules of a group are called **mores** (pronounced more-rays); the least important are called **folkways**. The mores of a group usually include prohibitions against lying, stealing, murdering, and other actions that are very disruptive of group life. Often they are written into laws. The folkways of a group usually include rules associated with fashions and etiquette. Interestingly, the rules forbidding the harming of members of one's own group, killing them, for example, may not necessarily extend to the harming of persons from other groups.

## BASIC HUMAN NEEDS

The feeling and reasoning human individual that we have described above always acts to satisfy certain basic human needs. A **need**, of course, is something that we require for survival or some other very important reason. These basic needs are the topic of the present section of this chapter. We will study two basic categories of needs, namely, survival needs and social needs. It is important, however, to keep in mind the various points made in the preceding section as we now consider these human needs and their satisfaction. The discussion of how human needs get satisfied will follow later in this chapter.

### Survival Needs

Every individual must satisfy certain fundamental needs in order to survive and thrive in life. The basic human needs essential for the survival of the individual human being are called, appropriately, **survival needs**. Sometimes referred to as **physiological needs**, these are the needs of the human body, which, if not satisfied, will result in death.

One obvious survival need is the need for food. If the human body does not receive certain essential nutrients, death will ensue. Water, too, is essential to life. Another need that is sometimes taken for granted is oxygen. If deprived of oxygen for even a short while, brain function ceases and death occurs. Human beings also require shelter from the forces of nature and, sometimes, from other humans.

A simple but important point about survival needs must be underscored here. All human individuals have the same survival needs. Regardless of one's race, colour, gender, or social status, all humans want to survive and thrive. Survival needs are universal. When there is an abundance of food, water, and shelter, it is relatively easy for individuals to satisfy their needs without interference from others. When supplies are short, however, or if some individuals get greedy, it can be a very a different story.

## Social Needs

Having briefly reviewed the basic survival needs of humans, we turn now to the second category of needs, **social needs**. Here we note three basic needs which, if not satisfied, will not result in the death of the individual but may cause serious frustration and upset for the individual. We will also see how the attempt to satisfy these needs can quickly lead to conflict between and among individuals.

Most people need to experience love and a sense of belonging. These love and belonging needs are called **affiliation** needs. To affiliate with others is simply to associate or connect with them. We are born into families where the first connections are made. The child, yet unaware, is welcomed into an association of people that we call a family. Mother, father, and siblings initiate the connection that will be critically important for the infant.

Later, the growing child will seek out many groups with which to affiliate, and the need for this connection with others will be met in hundreds of different ways as the individual matures into adulthood. Except for a few hermits, most human beings have a need to affiliate with others. We are, as the ancient philosopher Aristotle once said, social animals. This simple fact, we will find, is critically important for a proper understanding of our subject, ethics.

To what degree, for example, did the desire to belong to the Police Association and to be accepted by one's constable coach play into your vote on the Police Fundraiser motion? Affiliation needs are often met through association with one's fellow workers. We all want to belong. Will affiliation needs, we need to ask, override our responsibility to act on conscience? Or, will affiliation needs keep us from honestly arguing against a motion and those who have brought it forward? Toward the end of our study we will return to these kinds of questions when we consider the so-called blue wall of silence and the issue of whistle-blowing.

Another important social need is the need for **achievement**. The need to achieve is, of course, the need to succeed at something. It may be to go somewhere, to produce something, or to become someone. In our time we talk about high achievers and low achievers. While this distinction may be important for certain purposes, it should not hide the fact that virtually all humans need to achieve in some way or another. The levels of achievement may well be very different for different individuals. If you are committed to a career in policing and are successful, then many of your personal achievement needs will be met within the field of police service.

The need for power has been identified as a third important social need of human beings. You may immediately think of very passive persons that you know, and argue that they don't have this need for power, a need to dominate others. A clearer understanding of what is meant by power, however, may help at this point. **Power** is the ability to influence others in desired directions. Given this definition, we note that power doesn't necessarily equate with dominance or manipulation. Those are possible ways of exercising power, but so are kind and caring ways of influencing a situation.

The definition of power given above is neutral. Power, by definition, is neither good nor bad in itself; it is just influence. How influence is used, however, immediately raises ethical questions. Will power be used for good or for ill? In the Police Fundraiser situation, will the Association's power be used for good or for harm? The goal of fighting crime seems like a worthy one, a good end. Are the means to achieving that end, it must be asked, open to an abuse of power? Would the lobbying of elected officials by the police constitute an abuse of power? Ethical questions like these arise whenever people attempt to meet their needs in a social context. Needs satisfaction and ethical questions go hand in hand.

As we noted in our consideration of survival needs, questions arise as to the manner in which individuals will attempt to satisfy their needs. With affiliation, achievement, and power, it is very easy to see how the interests of one person might conflict with those of another. The satisfaction of these very important needs is a constant source of ethical concern as individuals compete to ensure that their personal needs are met. It is also easy to see that failure to satisfy one's social needs might make it difficult or impossible to satisfy one's survival needs. If you don't have the earning power of a job, for example, it may be very difficult to satisfy your survival needs.

## HUMAN DESIRES

We have been examining human needs, describing some of them, and raising questions about their satisfaction. We must try now to make a distinction between needs and desires. A **desire** is something that we want but don't necessarily need. It is quite easy, in many cases, to argue that a person has a real need when the person's survival is at stake. If the need is not met, the person will suffer serious harm or even death. Our need for food, water, and oxygen are clear needs.

Consider, however, a situation in which an officer has met his need for power and achievement by climbing the institutional ladder, becoming an inspector within a police service. Does his wish to climb to an even more prestigious position, that of chief, for instance, constitute a need, or is it merely a desire? He won't die by not climbing higher, but he may well be stifled in his personal development. When is a need truly a need and when is it merely a want or desire?

Take a more modest example. Many of us who didn't have air conditioned cars at one point in our lives told others at the time that we didn't really need it. After all, we said, hot days are relatively few in this part of the world. Air conditioning is not, we continued, a necessity; it's a luxury. We didn't need it. Later, having bought a car with air conditioning and having used it on a number of occasions, our view of the matter changed. Having experienced air conditioning, would we willingly buy another car without it? It's not very likely that we would. Yesterday's luxury has become today's necessity. When is a need truly a need and when is it merely a want, a desire?

This question is a difficult one, and one that I'm not sure that I can answer clearly. Raising the question, however, is very important in itself. Later in our examination of ethics we will note situations in which people argue for the right to meet a basic need of one sort or another. Will we be able to clearly determine whether they are presenting a real need or simply something they desire, a luxury, in fact? Is private property, for example, a basic right or a basic need? Many will argue that it is. Isn't it possible, however, to conceive of a world in which all land is publicly owned and each individual has only a right to use of the land, not the land itself? Is private ownership of property a basic need or merely a desire?

## NATURE'S SUPPLY

Earlier in our discussion of survival needs, we alluded to the fact that nature doesn't always provide the conditions in which all members of a community can easily meet their basic survival needs. We return to this point now to note that often Mother Nature's supply is scanty. Famines, for example, are reported somewhat routinely in different parts of the world. Water supplies are contaminated and made useless in various places. Hurricanes, typhoons, floods, and earthquakes render the satisfaction of basic needs impossible in many circumstances.

Even when nature does provide an abundance of food and water, we sometimes find that the actions of some human beings make it difficult or impossible for others to meet their survival needs. Human control of food and water supplies has long been a critical element in warfare. If you can contaminate or divert your enemies' water supply and prevent them from getting food, you are on your way to victory. This example, drawn from war, makes an important point as we begin our study of ethics. Even when Mother Nature provides an abundance of basic necessities, some humans may create shortages for their own reasons.

How do human beings satisfy their basic needs when nature isn't bountiful? How do we satisfy our basic needs when others interfere with our supplies of food and water? How do we satisfy survival and social needs when either nature or other humans prevent us from doing so easily? How, indeed, do we try to satisfy our basic needs when nature has provided a bountiful harvest and we live in a free society where no one is wilfully preventing us from meeting our basic needs?

Generally speaking, there are two basic ways in which humans have attempted to satisfy their basic needs and wants. One is a civilized way that promotes co-operation and builds a community based on the principles of ethical reasoning. This civilized way is the way of ethical or moral needs satisfaction. It is also the way of rational norms and the rule of law.

The other way is an uncivilized way that promotes conflict and destroys community by pitting individual against individual in a struggle for survival where might makes right. This uncivilized way is the way of unethical or immoral needs satisfaction. It is the way of the outlaw who puts his self-interest above the interests of others.

In the next section we will explore these two ways—the civilized and the uncivilized—in greater detail. In so doing we will arrive at a preliminary answer to the question, "What is ethics all about?"

## SATISFYING HUMAN NEEDS

In the middle of the seventeenth century in England, a political philosopher named Thomas Hobbes wrote a book called *Leviathan*. It was a book in which he attempted to describe the human condition in situations where there is no central authority and no rule of law. He called this condition "the state of nature" and argued that in the state of nature human life is "solitary, nasty, short, and brutish" (Hobbes, 1962, p.100).

Without a strong government to enforce the rules of civilized society, he believed, anarchy would prevail. Without an authority to control the actions of individuals, cunning and power would be used by each person to satisfy his or her own needs without regard for the needs of others. Life would be a jungle where the fittest would survive in an all-out battle against all competitors. In such a state, he said, there is "no society" and only "continual fear and danger of violent death" (Hobbes, 1962, p.100).

Hobbes' view was that human individuals were **egocentric,** considering only their own interests. Individuals would use cunning and power to try to ensure that they would prevail against their enemies and, in the process, satisfy their own needs. In order for social chaos to be avoided, Hobbes argued, each individual would have to give up his or her particular claim to the bounty of nature and enter into a social contract with the other members of society. The government would have the power to keep everyone in place, ensuring that civilized behaviour would replace the violence of the jungle.

Hobbes was arguing, of course, that individuals must give up certain rights to a higher authority, a government, in order to achieve security in the face of their enemies. The government would ensure that peace and order prevailed and that all citizens would have a reasonably fair chance to satisfy their basic human needs. In order for citizens to agree to enter into a social contract of this nature, the government would have to operate on the basis of some rational principles that would guarantee a somewhat equal share of nature's bounty to all citizens.

The important point here is that the government would have to make decisions based on basic values and principles that are reasonable and fair. If a government doesn't subscribe to certain rational and ethical principles, it will use its power and cunning in a self-serving manner and look after its own members and supporters only. It will do violence to other citizens, using its power to satisfy itself, giving little or no regard to the welfare of others. Unfortunately, many dictators do just that. Power is the name of their game. In democracies, too, governments all too often seem to act in their own interests as opposed to the interests of the citizenry.

If a government doesn't subscribe, however, to rational and ethical principles to some degree, it invites the wrath of its citizens. In fact, it invites the wrath of its own members, one against the other. Only brute force and fear tactics can keep a government in power if it doesn't operate on the basis of some rational and moral principles that ensure the welfare of its people. A central authority must ensure order by virtue of its power, but any government that enforces laws that are unfair to its citizens invites social disorder, anarchy, and chaos. The rule of law is most likely to succeed when the law is just.

## THE NATURE OF A CIVIL SOCIETY

**Civil societies** have three essential attributes. They are democratic, pluralistic, and committed to the rule of law.

The first essential feature of civil societies is that they are democratic in nature. By **democratic**, of course, we mean that the members of society freely choose their representatives. There are different forms of democracy, but all of them, in one way or another, place ultimate authority in the hands of the people. The political party that receives the most votes from the people becomes the government for a designated period of time, after which another election is held. Provisions allow for governments to be removed from office if they fail to maintain the support of the people. Elected representatives are accountable to the electors, those who choose them.

The second essential feature of civil societies is that they are pluralistic. A **pluralistic** society is one composed of different groups that have a variety of different interests. No single group—political, racial, or religious, for example—has all the power within a civil society. Power is shared and balanced. Pluralistic societies are sometimes referred to as multicultural or multiethnic societies. What allows such societies to function is the fact that, despite differences, members are committed to rational rules established through democratic processes.

The third essential feature of civil societies, then, is that they are committed to the **rule of law**. Societies based on the rule of law function according to rational rules that are binding on all members of society. In other words, in civil societies nobody is above the law. This rule of law, it should be noted, is a relatively recent development in the history of human societies.

In civil societies the elected representatives of the people are responsible for, among other things, the creation of new laws and the amending of existing ones. This responsibility is called legislative responsibility; the elected members, when they change or create laws, are referred to as **legislators**. In a civil society, legislators who make the laws are not above the laws that they make.

To be effective, the laws in place at any time require persons to enforce them. Within a civil society, the **police** have that responsibility. They are agents of the government and, as such, they ultimately answer to the people. The expression "police service" captures this particular point. Police officers serve the members of a civil society by ensuring that there is compliance with the laws of the society. As enforcers of the law, the police are not above the laws that they enforce.

The Police Fundraiser situation raises many interesting and important ethical questions. One question has to do with the relationship of the police to the democratic processes of a civil society. Individual officers, like all citizens, have the right to vote in elections. Does an association of police officers, however, have a right to endorse particular candidates? Could the freedom of candidates to express their personal views be compromised by association lobbying that is perceived to be intimidating? What is the ethically appropriate relationship between the police and elected officials in a civil society?

These kinds of questions were raised in the public mind when the Toronto Police Association initiated Operation True Blue (Canadian Press, 2000). The Association began to solicit public donations, acknowledging contributions with a window sticker to be displayed on the donor's vehicle windshield. The money raised was to be used to promote law-and-order issues. City officials, politicians, and the public criticized the Association program, eventually forcing its end. Many saw the program as a threat to the democratic process, and some politicians felt intimidated by it. Others raised questions as to the expectations of donors. Would they demand a favour in return if, for example, they were pulled over for speeding? Still others wondered whether the impartiality of officers would be compromised, giving breaks to donors and tough justice to others.

The rule of law also requires fair hearings to ensure that lawbreakers are punished and that innocent persons are not. This responsibility in a civil society falls to the **courts**. The courts, of course, consist of judges, juries, lawyers, and others whose responsibility it is to ensure that justice prevails. Once again, those who serve society in the courts are not above the law. A judge, for example, is bound by the law as much as any other citizen is.

Finally, the rule of law within a civil society requires agents of government who are responsible for punishing and correcting offenders. **Correctional officers**, like police officers, are agents of the government. They do not decide who deserves punishment, nor do they decide what punishment to mete out. They simply administer the prescribed penalties according to the law. Corrections officers, like all other members of a civil society, are not above the law.

We have noted that legislators, police, the courts, and correctional officers all play key roles in a civil society, and we have underscored the fact that none of them is above the rule of law in a free society. Let's express this critical point in yet another way before proceeding to look at the nature of law. For a civil society to function properly, those who fulfill these key roles must understand the limits of their responsibility, limits that are defined by law. These legal limits, it should be noted, are established on the basis of the principles of ethical reasoning.

## THE NATURE OF LAW

Consider, for a moment, what the law is. The **law** of any society consists of the rules in force in that society at any given time. The critical point is that the law of any group is a reflection of what the government at the time decides are the best rules to have in place. It doesn't matter whether the government is democratic or autocratic, elected or not—whatever the government decides is law, is law.

In a democratic society like our own, we are accustomed to challenging existing laws when we feel that they are poor laws. Democratic societies by their very nature encourage public debate about the law. In autocratic societies, people also criticize what they consider to be poor laws, but they usually do so only in private, fearing the authorities. Regardless of the type of society and regardless of the particular laws in place, the laws are likely to be criticized by someone. Why is this the case?

Existing laws are criticized because individual citizens and different groups of citizens have different values and value systems. In the matter of abortion, for instance, on the one hand some citizens value a woman's right to make her own choices more than they value the life of the unborn. In contrast, other citizens place greater value on the life of the unborn than they do on a woman's right to choose. Every society has disagreements among its members as to what a particular law should allow or forbid.

When individuals and groups discuss and debate their differing positions in a rational manner, they are engaging in ethical discussion and debate. When legislators discuss and debate the substance of a new law, they too are engaging in ethical or moral discussion. Debates occur, of course, because legislators usually have different feelings as to what is most important. They have different values and value systems. For example, the ongoing debate about the purpose of imprisonment—Is it primarily for punishment or primarily for rehabilitation?—is an ethical debate. People with different values, operating on rational principles, arrive at different conclusions. Each wants the law to reflect his or her point of view because that's what he or she feels is most important.

When you arrived at the Police Association meeting to consider the proposed motion regarding the Police Fundraiser, if the discussion and debate that preceded the vote was democratic and rational, then the debate was an ethical debate. If members freely expressed their different points of view, and if they used their values and principles to arrive at what they considered to be the right action for the association to take, then the debate was an ethical one. Such debates are essential in a civil society.

## WHAT ETHICS IS ALL ABOUT

In this chapter we described individual human beings as thinking and feeling beings who act in accordance with their thoughts and feelings. These actions are often directed toward the satisfying of basic human needs, both survival and social. Moreover, we raised the question as to how these needs can be met, given the fact that nature often fails to provide adequately for everyone, and that some humans sometimes keep others from getting their share of nature's supplies. Two different ways were identified.

## The Civilized or Ethical Way

The **civilized way** or **ethical way** of attempting to satisfy one's basic needs is to co-operate with others on the basis of some common values and principles, seeking the welfare of all concerned. This way understands and respects the law in general, while remaining ready to challenge any specific law that seems unfair to some or all group members. Any challenge to existing law, however, will be made through ethical discussion and debate. In other words, the challenge to the existing rules is conducted in a civilized manner. The civilized person tries to do what is right and good and tries to avoid what is wrong and bad. This is the way a civil society functions.

In a civil society, police officers are both guardians of the people and guardians of the principles that a civil society is founded on. Both goals, the protection of persons and the protection of principles, are worthy ones. Those who serve and protect as peace officers in civil societies belong to a noble profession. They are worthy of the highest respect when they carry out their responsibilities in accordance with the law and the fundamental ethical principles of a civil society.

Notice, now, how the Canons of Police Ethics, Article 2, address the point of the preceding paragraph: "The first duty of law enforcement officers, as upholders of the law, is to know its bounds upon them in enforcing it. Because they represent the legal will of the community, be it local, provincial, or federal, they must be aware of the limitations which the people, through law, have placed upon them. They must recognize the genius of the Canadian system of government which gives to no individual, groups of people, or institutions, absolute power, and they must insure that they, as prime defenders of that system, do not pervert its character."

## The Uncivilized or Unethical Way

Unfortunately, many people fail to live by the norms of civilized life. The **uncivilized way** or **unethical way** of attempting to satisfy one's basic needs is, of course, the way of deceit and treachery. Persons who act in uncivilized or unethical ways do whatever they can to get whatever they want. They act without concern for the rights and welfare of others. Common thieves have no concern, for example, for the hard work of the homeowners whose homes they enter by stealth. They take what they want, and their only concern is a concern about getting caught. They are outlaws.

Many members of civil societies obey the law because they understand and value civilized life. Others may obey the law primarily out of fear. Regardless of the reason for obedience, most citizens are law-abiding. The law-abiding members of society are the ones who ensure that police services are in place to protect against the actions of the uncivilized. They and the police are partners in the protection of people and civil society itself. The strongest societies are those in which citizens and police see one another as partners in the protection of freedom and the rule of law.

## Ethics Defined

After this lengthy review of human nature and needs, we can now offer a definition of ethics and answer our original question, "What is ethics all about?" **Ethics** is the study of the values and principles that generate the norms that specify what is right or wrong conduct in human relationships in a civil society. In any study, the purpose is to understand the subject under investigation. In this book, ethics is our subject.

We will be attempting throughout to understand what ethics is all about. Bit by bit, we will explore and try to understand the many aspects of this very important subject. As with this chapter, we will have to discipline ourselves to move slowly and deliberately in order to achieve our goal. To assist us in our beginning, let's look at a number of other definitions, each of which focuses on an important aspect of our study.

## Ethical Values Defined

In our examination of values earlier in this chapter, we noted that a value is whatever a person or group feels is important. We pointed out that each individual or group values many things and some things more than others. The sum total of values that an individual or group has is called a value system. Within all value systems there are values that relate to right and wrong conduct between humans, and values that do not. Honesty, for example, is an ethical or moral value because it has to do with how we relate to other human beings. All human beings have some ethical or moral values within their overall value system.

**Ethical values**, then, are the values that generate the principles of right or wrong that are applied to human relationships in a civil society. Remember that values arise because humans are affective beings. We have an important emotional dimension, and it is this feeling dimension that gives us our values, including our ethical or moral values. We feel strongly that some forms of behaviour are morally acceptable—honesty, for example. We also feel that other forms of conduct are not. Cheating, for instance, is wrong. We feel that it is morally unacceptable. The study of ethical values is critical to our overall understanding of ethics.

## Ethical Principles Defined

In order to communicate our ethical values to others, we need appropriate concepts and words with which to convey our moral feelings. Similarly, to discuss and debate what we perceive to be an unjust law, we need to present our ideas clearly. The cognitive counterparts of ethical values are ethical principles. By *principles* we mean the basic ideas upon which other ideas are built.

**Ethical principles,** then, are the basic concepts (ideas) that underlie what is considered right or wrong conduct in human relationships in a civil society. Throughout our study of ethics, we will be examining these principles of ethical reasoning. That is, we will be identifying and explaining the basic concepts associated with right or wrong conduct in human relationships. The study of ethical principles is a critical part of the overall study of ethics.

## Ethical Norms Defined

We pointed out earlier in this chapter that values and principles generate norms of conduct. If, for example, we value honesty, then the rational principle of honesty is used to establish the rule "No cheating." Norms, of course, are rules. Here, ethical norms are those associated with right or wrong conduct in human relationships. Cheating hurts relationships.

No one wants or likes to be cheated. It's not surprising that every civilized community has a rule that forbids cheating members of the community. It's interesting that some communities devoted to cheating others, the Mafia for example, will not tolerate cheating within the Mafia community. A deal's a deal even for the Mafioso. Don't try to cheat the boss or other members. You'll pay big-time.

We can define **ethical norms**, then, as the rules that specify what is considered right or wrong conduct in human relationships in a civil society. We will examine many specific rules of conduct as we proceed in our study, and we will also examine some ethical codes. A **code**, of course, is a collection of rules. Much of ethics is about what people should or shouldn't do in their relationships with others. Also included in ethical norms are many rules that stipulate what we must or must not do. Ethical norms will occupy a lot of our time in our study of ethics. Should we, for instance, restore capital punishment in Canada? Should young offenders be treated as adults? These and many other questions are questions about the ethical norms of our society.

## Ethical Conduct Defined

When individuals act in order to satisfy their needs, their conduct may or may not be consistent with the ethical norms of the group to which they belong. If their actions are consistent with the ethical norms of their group, then their conduct will be described within the group as ethical. If, on the other hand, they satisfy their needs by acting contrary to the established ethical norms, their conduct will be described as unethical.

**Ethical conduct** is conduct that is consistent with the norms that specify what is right or wrong in human relationships in a civil society. This simple but important definition rounds out our preliminary look at the origins of ethics. Like the other definitions in this section, it directs us to another key aspect of our study of ethics, the judgment of actions as ethical or unethical. Such judgments are made regularly by the members of all societies. Ethical conduct is, of course, the basis of civilized life within a community,

Such judgments, we might add, are necessary. If someone rapes somebody in order to satisfy a need for sex or power, the rapist and the rapist's action will be judged to be wrong. It violates a basic norm of civilized life. Because the action violates the norm, it is judged to be unethical conduct. Civilized groups will not and cannot allow such actions to go unpunished. **Unethical conduct** is conduct that is not consistent with the norms that specify what is right or wrong conduct in human relationships in a civil society. No civilized group can condone unethical conduct within its midst. Unethical conduct is destructive of civilized life in a community.

## CHAPTER SUMMARY

After offering a preliminary definition of ethics, the study of right and wrong in human relationships, we drew attention to the fact that ethics is an important part of both our personal and professional lives. We then presented a situation in which a new officer attends a police association meeting for the first time. We noted that the issue under consideration at the meeting evoked several ethical questions.

A look at our nature as human beings revealed that we are cognitive, affective, and behavioural beings. In other words, we think, feel, and act. All three of these dimensions of human nature are important for an understanding of ethics and the making of ethical choices. Ethical principles result from thinking about moral matters. These principles are an aspect of our cognitive dimension. Ethical values, on the other hand, are a part of our feeling or affective dimension. Feelings and thoughts, we saw, inevitably result in actions. Our actions are part of our behavioural dimension. Norms or rules of conduct specify what constitutes ethical behaviour and what does not.

Human beings who think and feel use their thoughts and emotions in their efforts to satisfy certain basic human needs. Human survival requires the satisfaction of basic needs such as water, food, and air. If we don't satisfy these needs we die. In addition to survival needs, human beings have three social needs. The need to affiliate with others is the need to connect with others socially. The need to achieve is the need to succeed at something or to become someone. The need to exercise power is the need to have an influence on people and events. Affiliation, achievement, and power needs are the three social needs.

People can attempt to satisfy their needs and desires in either of two ways. They can try to meet their needs in a civilized way or an uncivilized way. The civilized way is the way of ethics and the law. This is the way of co-operation and compromise that is based on rational principles, the principles of ethical reasoning. These ethical principles provide the foundation for the laws of a civil society. The uncivilized way is the way of the outlaw. It is the way of the criminal. It is the way of the unethical or immoral.

Civil societies are based on freedom and the rule of law. They are democratic societies in which citizens give up a certain amount of freedom in order to achieve a degree of security, a security that allows members to pursue the satisfaction of their needs and desires, respecting others who would do the same. In such societies, laws may be challenged provided that the challenge is made through rational discussion and debate. Regardless of one's agreement or disagreement with an existing law, members of a civil society obey the law until it is changed, if it is changed.

We concluded the chapter by providing definitions of the following: *ethics, ethical values, ethical principles, ethical norms, ethical conduct,* and *unethical conduct.*

## MASTERING THE MATERIAL

Now that you have read this chapter, use the following guides to ensure that you have mastered the material.

## Human Nature

1.  What is a rational being?
2.  Define *cognitive dimension.*
3.  Identify five cognitive abilities.
4.  Define *principle.*
5.  To what dimension do principles belong?

6. Define *affective dimension*.
7. Identify several affective experiences.
8. Define the following: *empathy, values, value system*
9. What is the behavioural dimension? What is another name for the behavioural dimension?
10. To what dimension do codes of conduct apply?
11. Define the following: *norms, mores, folkways*

## Basic Human Needs

1. What two things in human experience lead to action?
2. Define *survival needs* and provide three examples.
3. What is another name for survival needs?
4. Define *social needs* and identify three of them.
5. Define the following: *affiliation, achievement, power*

## Human Desires, Nature's Supply, and Satisfying Human Needs

1. What is the difference between a need and a desire?
2. Identify two sources of food shortages.
3. Describe the civilized way of satisfying needs.
4. Describe the uncivilized way of satisfying needs.
5. Define *egocentric*.

## The Nature of a Civil Society and the Law

1. Define *civil society* and identify the three essential characteristics of a civil society.
2. With respect to the law, describe the role of the following:
   (a) a legislator
   (b) a police officer
   (c) the courts
   (d) a correctional officer

## What Ethics Is All About

1. Define the following: *ethics, ethical values, ethical principles, ethical norms, code, ethical and unethical conduct*

| Media Watch: Ethics in the News 1.1 | Aggressive police tarnish their cause |

If they are not careful, police associations in Ontario are going to do more damage to the police profession than anything a wily criminal could do. At least one association is shooting its own members in the foot by damaging their reputation for fairness and neutrality.

Consider the latest tactic of the Toronto Police Association. The 7000-member association has launched a fundraising campaign dubbed Operation True Blue. The money is supposed to be used to support law-and-order issues, such as tougher laws for juveniles. Even if the association's issues are in the public interest, this fundraising tactic is questionable because police officers should maintain a respectful distance from the lawmaking process. Their association should not be perceived as a lobby group for the public—or the police, for that matter.

Whatever validity the campaign has is negated by the fact that contributors are given windshield decals that indicate the level of their donation. A $100 donation is worth a gold decal. The association intends the decal merely to acknowledge support, but surely police officers know better than anyone that some citizens will make donations with the hope that the decals will keep them out of trouble if they are stopped for a minor offence.

Police, who have a difficult job at the best of times, do not need the added aggravation of dealing with people who expect a favour because they have contributed to the association's bank account.

This campaign comes at a time that other police associations, including the one in Guelph, have taken unusually aggressive positions. The Guelph association held a secret ballot late last year on the leadership of Chief Lenna Bradburn despite the fact there was no evidence that she was either corrupt or not carrying out the duties expected of her by the police board.

Fortunately, the police association in Waterloo Region has avoided getting into these quasi political issues. For that, the residents of the region should be thankful. A good image is a tool police officers cannot afford to toss away.

Source: *Kitchener-Waterloo Record*, January 27, 2000, A8.

| Media Watch: Ethics in the News 1.2 | Toronto police union under fire |

TORONTO—The controversial head of Toronto's police union came under fire Wednesday for a fundraising scheme that solicits money from the public to target unfriendly politicians.

While national civil libertarian groups fretted over the potential abuse of power, Craig Bromell, the president of the Toronto Police Association, bragged that he's setting a precedent for other Canadian police unions to follow.

Lawyers, politicians, activists and concerned members of the public stood shoulder to shoulder at a jammed meeting Wednesday of the Toronto Police Services Board to complain about the union's actions.

Even Toronto police Chief David Boothby publicly expressed his outrage, denouncing the union for what he called unethical behaviour. "Quite frankly, they've really crossed the line," Boothby said.

The furore is over a fundraising drive called Operation True Blue in which the union has hired telemarketers to call people and ask for money.

The police force opposes the action and worries that the public is left with the impression police are on the phone drumming up funds.

Depending on the size of the cheque, donors get windshield stickers that show exactly how generously they've supported the police union fundraising drive.

"We find it very disquieting," said Alan Borovoy, of the Canadian Civil Liberties Association, which has demanded Ontario's solicitor general put an immediate stop to the campaign.

"The idea of police soliciting funds from the general public is inherently intimidating.

"Those who are solicited will believe that if they say no, they will get less protection than they need and harsher treatment than they deserve."

Part of the controversy over the fundraising drive is how the money will be used. Bromell said it will go toward promoting the association's position on the Young Offenders Act, parole regulations and penalties for criminals.

He will also use a portion of the funds to promote and oppose political candidates.

He denied previous reports that the money will be used for private investigators even though he's made it well known the union has and will resort to such measures to defeat politicians who question police policy.

His threats had several board members shaking as they presented their views at Wednesday's meeting, saying it was "political suicide" to speak out against Bromell.

"Let me tell you I feel intimidated today," said Coun. Anne Johnston.

"You're taking your political life in your hands coming here and adding yourself to the list of people who will be politically targeted in the next election."

Toronto Mayor Mel Lastman, who is investigating the legality of the campaign, convinced the board to give him a week to negotiate.

Source: *Kitchener-Waterloo Record*, January 27, 2000, A3.

# Analytical Ethics: Thinking Critically about Ethical Issues in a Civil Society

## LEARNING OUTCOMES

After completing this chapter, you should be able to

- Explain the analytical dimension of ethics
- Discuss the relationship of ethics to the law
- Describe the relationship between ethics and religion
- Explain the relationship between ethics and determinism
- Define four key ethical terms
- Explain several aspects of the role of logic in ethics
- Identify and explain three faulty appeals
- Identify and explain two forms of faulty sampling
- Identify and explain four forms of faulty reasoning
- Describe the PRINCIPLES Model and the DECIDE Process

# INTRODUCTION

In Chapter 1 we described three important dimensions or aspects of human nature. We started with a discussion of the cognitive dimension, the dimension that includes all of the rational activities that humans engage in. Among those rational activities is critical thinking. **Critical thinking** means actively seeking to understand, analyze, and evaluate information or an argument. We also described the affective dimension, the realm of human emotions, feelings, and moods. Last, we described the behavioural dimension, pointing out how human thoughts and feelings motivate human behaviour. We described these dimensions because each one of them is essential to understanding ethics and ethical conduct among humans.

Thinking critically about ethical issues, of course, is the subject at hand. In this chapter we will study this important aspect of the field of ethics. Each dimension plays a critical role in ethics and, therefore, each requires our attention and understanding. In order to understand ethics and make ethical choices most effectively, we need to be familiar with all three of these areas of ethics. Ethics, you will recall, is the study of the values and principles that generate the norms that specify what is right and wrong conduct in human relationships within a civil society. In keeping with the theme of this chapter, we might say that ethics is critical thinking applied to the principles and values associated with moral conduct in human relationships.

The **analytical dimension** of ethics refers to that part of ethics that, among other things, analyzes the meaning of words and the logic of ethical arguments. You will recall that critical thinking involves the analysis, comprehension, and evaluation of ethical issues. When we do analytical ethics, we will be concerned with the definition of ethical terms and the soundness of ethical arguments. The **descriptive dimension** is that part of ethics that investigates the facts associated with a particular moral issue. If, for example, we get the facts with respect to an issue like child pornography, we will be doing descriptive ethics. Descriptive ethics is always about the way things actually are in the world, not the way that they should be. The third dimension of ethics is the **prescriptive dimension**, that part of ethics that states what is or is not considered ethical conduct within a particular group. Prescriptive ethics states the way people should act. It states the ideals of human conduct.

# ANALYTICAL ETHICS

What is analysis? To answer this question, let's take a simple example with which you, no doubt, are familiar. If we do a chemical analysis of water, we discover that water is composed of two parts hydrogen combined with one part oxygen, hence the formula $H_2O$. Whenever we analyze anything, we break it down into its basic parts to better understand the object under study. **Analysis**, then, is the process of identifying the component parts of a subject. Analysis is essential in the field of ethics just as it is in chemistry and virtually all other areas of human endeavour.

When we discuss and debate moral issues with a view to determining what is right or wrong, it is essential for us to analyze both the meaning of words and the logic of arguments. If two people are not using words in the same way, then they are likely to talk past one another. If faulty reasoning goes undetected, then invalid conclusions are likely to be offered as truth. To think about moral issues, to discuss them intelligently, and to make good personal choices in moral matters, we need to analyze the language and logic of the issue at hand. **Analytical ethics**, then, is the part of ethics devoted to the analysis of the language and logic of ethical debate. Consider for a moment the meaning of the word *adultery* and the following situation.

| SITUATION 2.1 | Bahamian Vacation |
| --- | --- |

Constables John and Jane Brown, who were married to each other eight years ago in a civil ceremony, are spending a winter vacation in the Bahamas. On the second day of their vacation, they meet Mike and Mary Smith, another married couple, who are also vacationing at the same resort. After supper one evening, the discussion turns to sex. The Smiths admit to being swingers and ask the Browns if they'd be interested in swinging. The Browns have talked about swinging several times in the past and both have expressed some interest in it. They retire to their room to discuss the offer in private. About an hour later, they return to the lounge where they agree to swing with the Smiths. John and Mary go to the Smiths' room, where they have sexual intercourse. Mike and Jane go to the Browns' room and do the same. They spend the night with their new and temporary partners, and then meet for breakfast in the morning. The next day, the Browns and the Smiths each fly on separate flights to their respective homes.

What is adultery? What exactly do you have to do to commit adultery? Has anyone committed adultery in this case? Has anyone done anything morally wrong in this case? Consider carefully, think critically, and be prepared to explain your answers to these questions.

The Bahamian Vacation situation provides us with a somewhat provocative case to consider and analyze. Opinions, no doubt, will differ from person to person regarding the morality of the swingers' actions. I have introduced this situation in order to give us an opportunity to make a number of observations about analytical ethics. The situation is intended to encourage critical thinking about the meaning of *adultery* and the issues raised by the questions asked at the end of the scenario.

Throughout our study of ethics we will be doing analytical ethics. Each major topic, like capital punishment or pornography, will require an analysis of the language used and the validity of the arguments put forth. Our analysis of the word *euthanasia,* to give another example, will reveal four different meanings for the one word. When we investigate those topics, we will do the detailed analysis required to be informed and to make good moral choices. For the moment, however, we will provide a summary of some key issues in the area of analytical ethics. A careful analysis of the arguments in each of these issues will help us to better understand what ethics is all about.

## ETHICS AND THE LAW

Toward the end of Chapter 1 we made reference to civil societies and the importance of ethics and the law for those communities. We defined the *law* as the rules in force in a society at any given time. The expression "in force" means, of course, that the government is prepared to employ whatever force is necessary to apprehend, prosecute, and punish those who break the rules. Civil societies, we noted, employ police forces to ensure compliance with the law.

Consider for a moment the introduction of a new law within society. Before a new law comes into effect, especially in democratic societies, there is often an intensive debate about the pros and cons of the proposed law. That debate is an ethical debate. People of different political persuasions have different values and, consequently, some will support and others will oppose the legislation. The debate will involve facts and principles, no doubt, but it will also hinge on the differing values of the debaters.

Sometimes, long-established laws come under criticism by members of society. When this occurs, the debate that ensues is also an ethical debate. Once again, people with differing values will take different views of existing laws. Arguing on the basis of ethical principles, they will try to change the existing law to coincide with their personal values. Others will argue for the status quo.

Since values change from time to time, it is not surprising that some old laws become outdated. In this sense, ethics is fluid. Individual values and group values do change. Such changes are the source of what some will call moral progress. At any given time, others will call it moral regress, a step backward. What, by way of example, would you call the actions of the swingers on vacation? Does their freedom to engage in new sexual arrangements constitute moral progress or moral regress?

Especially important for our purposes is the distinction between ethics and the law. They are not necessarily the same. When certain societies legalized slavery, for example, some members of those societies argued that slavery was immoral and ought not to be legal. Their claim was that the existing law was unjust, unethical. Unjust laws, they continued, should be abolished. Eventually, over a long period of time, slavery was outlawed. Many would point to this evolution as an example of moral progress.

We cannot, as this example shows, take the view that an action that is legal is necessarily right from an ethical point of view. Nor can we automatically assume that something that is illegal is necessarily wrong from a moral point of view. What is legal may square with moral standards, but it may not. Laws against murder, for example, seem to be consistent with basic moral principles and values. But what about a law that makes doctor-assisted suicide a crime? Today, doctor-assisted suicide is illegal in Canada, but many Canadians believe that the practice is ethically justifiable. They argue that an action that is illegal is, in fact, a morally correct action, at least under certain circumstances.

Now, with respect to ethics and the law, what can we say about our swinging vacationers, the Browns and the Smiths? Assume for the moment that swinging is illegal in the Bahamas. If it is illegal under Bahamian law, some readers will argue that it isn't necessarily immoral. What consenting adults do sexually in private, these people will argue, is morally defensible despite the fact that it is against the law. In contrast, others will maintain that such sexual activity is both illegal and immoral. Now, for the sake of argument, assume that swinging is legal in the Bahamas. If it is legal in the Bahamas, these same people will argue that it should not be legal. In their view, swinging is morally wrong and the law should reflect that fact.

What can we learn from all this? The key point is that what is legal isn't necessarily right from an ethical point of view. Moreover, what is illegal isn't necessarily wrong from an ethical point of view. In our study of ethics and ethical issues, then, we will want to know what the law is with regard to any particular topic, such as prostitution. We mustn't, however, assume that the law is right from a moral point of view. Ethical debate is always appropriate. It's part of the analysis of the existing rules of any community.

## ETHICS AND RELIGION

Every religion has rules of conduct that its adherents are expected to follow. Some of these norms have to do with obligations to a god or gods (**religious duties***). Others pertain to ceremonial or ritual practices (**ritual duties**). Still others state the adherents' duties to their fellow human beings (**social duties**). These latter duties are the ones that are of most importance to us in our study of ethics. Throughout our examination of the field of ethics, we will be concerned with social duties. Our study will not, however, be based on religious belief.

One of the questions asked in analytical ethics is, "What is the connection between religion and ethics?" Let's start with a view that some people have taken with respect to this question. Some have argued that a person has to be religious in order to be moral. These people argue that belief in a god or gods is essential to the moral life. Are they correct? A number of arguments would support the view that they are not.

### Ethical Atheists

First, the existence of ethical atheists who conduct themselves in morally acceptable ways is sufficient to show that you don't have to be religious to be moral. The moral atheist doesn't lie, cheat, steal, or murder. Such behaviour demonstrates that moral conduct isn't necessarily based on religious belief. It is also important to note that some religious people behave in unethical and immoral ways toward others. Some have committed terrible offences against others in the name of their religion. Being religious doesn't guarantee that one will behave ethically toward one's neighbours. And, of course, it doesn't mean that one won't.

### The Existence of God

A second reason to answer the question in the negative is that the existence of a god or gods is a matter of belief, not knowledge. In other words, some people believe that there is a God, but they are unable to provide convincing proof of God's existence. If the existence of God is unproved, then religious persons are requiring that faith or belief in a divine being, not knowledge, is a prerequisite for being moral. But surely this is asking too much of non-religious people. In addition to believing in the existence of God, religious people often claim to know, sometimes in great detail, the will of their God.

### Human Authorities

The previous point leads naturally to a third point. All the major world religions look to sacred writings, or holy books, to discover the will of God. That is, they turn to sacred texts to find the moral commands of their God. Inevitably, however, some human authority like a pope, a mullah, or a rabbi has to interpret the holy writings and explain the will of God to the faithful. This requires that people now put their trust in a human authority in order to find out what is morally required. The rule forbidding adultery, for example, comes from a sacred book written thousands of years ago. For centuries, human authorities within the world's religious traditions have forbidden adultery and have spiritually enforced compliance with the rule.

## Contradictory Claims

A fourth argument follows from the previous one. Different religious traditions offer conflicting prescriptions for the moral life, each claiming that God is the source of their moral teachings. A classic case of this is to be found within one major world religion, Christianity. Faithful Roman Catholic Christians are forbidden to have abortions. Many faithful Protestant Christians, in contrast, may make their own personal choice about abortion with the blessing of their religious tradition. The same God, in this case, would seem to be giving conflicting moral advice within the same tradition. If one looks to other religious traditions around the world, it is not difficult to find more examples of conflicting prescriptions.

## Logical Priority

A famous Greek philosopher introduced a fifth argument centuries ago. Plato, in his dialogue *Euthyphro*, argued that ethics and religion were logically distinct from one another (Plato, 1961, p.178). What he meant was that morality is logically prior to religious experience. One could only recognize, for example, a voice as the voice of God if one knew in advance what God was like.

Plato asked, "If God commands us to do something, does God command it because it's right? Or, is it right because God commands it?" In the first case, if God commands something because it's right, then morality exists independently of God. In the second case, if something were right solely because God commands it, then we would not be morally obligated to obey the command. It would lack moral authority. God could, for example, command us to kill innocent children. Would such a command from God, asks Plato, make it right to kill innocent children? Plato said no, such a command would lack moral authority.

In this section we have looked at a number of important points regarding the relationship between religion and ethics. Our purpose has not been to criticize religion or religious people. By arguing, as we have, that a person doesn't have to be religious to be moral, we have tried to show that religion cannot provide an ethical foundation for *all* humans. We will show later that another foundation for human ethics is available, a foundation based on human reason. This base can serve both religious and non-religious people alike. Indeed, it does so even when people don't recognize it.

## ETHICS AND ETHICAL RELATIVISM

"When in Rome do as the Romans do." This popular saying can serve as an introduction to the issue of ethical relativism. The expression implies, of course, that Rome has its rules and that they are different from the rules of other communities. Right and wrong are different in different places. **Ethical relativism** maintains, first, that morality differs from time to time and from place to place. Second, it maintains that no group is entitled to judge the morality of another group. In recent times the notion that morality is relative has become very popular. Ethical relativism seems to promote tolerance and respect for differing cultures and their moral standards.

Without doubt, it is the emphasis on tolerance and respect that seems to have won ethical relativism a large number of followers. A careful analysis of ethical relativism will show, however, that the position is subject to a number of fatal criticisms. It is an approach to ethics that sounds good at first, but one that reveals flaws upon closer inspection. We need to examine relativism as it is applied to different groups but also to different individuals. Let's begin with relativism applied to groups.

## Cultural Relativism: Ethical Relativism Applied to Groups

**Cultural relativism**, first of all, implies that there are no universal moral standards shared by all groups and cultures. Ethics and morality, according to this form of relativism, are relative to the different cultural values and standards of each group. As noted above, cultural relativists argue further that no group should judge another group. Every group should be tolerant of every other group. In arguing that every group should be tolerant of others, however, cultural relativists are really espousing a universal principle. That principle is the one that says we all ought to be tolerant and non-judgmental of other cultures. Cultural relativism is self-contradictory, then, when it insists upon universal tolerance of other groups. Self-contradictory positions do not make very good foundations for the moral life.

Note further that if cultural relativism were correct, we would not be able to criticize any other society or group. Take, for example, the case of slavery noted earlier. Cultural relativism would forbid any criticism of slave-owning societies by other societies. Indeed, if one extends the idea of relativism to any group different from one's own, it would be inappropriate to criticize, for example, a group that attacked your own group for no good reason. Such a consequence, from what at first appears to be a reasonable position, shows cultural relativism to be untenable. As a relativist, one could never make moral criticisms of groups other than one's own. We could never, for example, condemn slavery, genocide, or any other evil practices that might occur in groups other than our own.

## Individual Relativism:
## Ethical Relativism Applied to Individuals

So far, our analysis of relativism has focused on groups. The relativist approach has also been applied to individuals. **Individual relativism** maintains that ethics and morality are relative to each individual human being. Each individual has his or her own morals, and morals differ from one person to another. It maintains, further, that no individual should judge the moral behaviour of another individual. We hear individual relativists say, for example, that if a person *thinks* that something is right, then it *is* right for that person. Or we hear them say that if a person *feels* that something is right, then it *is* right for that person.

On the relativist view, if the Browns and the Smiths—the swinging vacationers—feel that swinging is right, then swinging is right. If they think it's right, then their thinking makes it right. Ethics, on the individual relativist view, is different for each person. If, as you read the situation earlier in this chapter, you judged their actions to be morally wrong, according to relativism you had no right to do so. On the individual relativist view, the fact that the couples felt it was right made it right. No one is entitled to criticize them or their actions.

The problem with the individual relativist position becomes very clear if the swinging couples decide to steal various items from the hotel in which they are staying. If they feel that stealing is right, on the individual relativist view, stealing is right. No one should criticize or judge them. Moreover, if a rapist at the hotel feels that rape is right for him, then it is right. If individual relativism is correct, we cannot criticize swingers, thieves, or rapists. Surely individual relativism is misguided. Tolerance of the behaviour of a person cannot extend to actions that are clearly and wilfully hurtful to others.

Careful analysis of individual relativism reveals its subjectivity. Right and wrong, according to this view, are determined solely by what each individual thinks or feels, not by any objective or universal standard. Because it makes individual feeling the standard for determining right and wrong, individual relativism is also called **subjectivism**. On this view, criticism of the most morally outrageous actions would be inappropriate. There would be no objective basis for judging individual acts to be right or wrong; consequently, praise and blame would make no sense.

On the individual relativist view, we could not hold others accountable for their actions. If a person thinks or feels an act is right, according to individual relativism, that makes the act right. As with the group version of relativism, individual relativism proves itself to be indefensible as a moral point of view. We'll return to this subject in Chapter 3 where we will further examine individual ethical relativism under the heading of Emotivism.

In Chapter 4, we will examine **ethical universalism**, a point of view that argues that there are universal ethical values and principles that all civilized communities and individuals have in common. In contrast to relativism, universalism maintains that human beings in different communities have similar natures, similar needs, and similar values. From these universal values arise universal principles common to all civilized communities and all civilized individuals. These values and principles provide objective standards upon which ethical judgments can be made.

## ETHICS AND DETERMINISM

An important question in analytical ethics is whether human beings have free will or not. Those who argue that human beings have no freedom of choice are called determinists and their view is called **determinism**.

The topic is an important one because the concepts of responsibility and accountability only make sense if people have free will to make choices. Determinists take the view that all things in the universe are caused by external forces. For every effect there is a cause, they say, and there are no uncaused causes. Human beings fall within the natural order and, as such, we and our actions are effects of the forces of nature.

## Free Will?

Think of a newly born infant. Its physical makeup is the result of its parents' sperm and egg uniting. Genetically, the infant is determined by its DNA code, a code provided by its parents. The child is their product. Think further of this child. Initially it cannot talk or think. It makes no sense to speak, at this early stage, of the child's making choices or exercising its free will. As it matures it is constantly being shaped by external forces in its environment, primarily by its parents. They nurture the child to whom they gave life. At what point could this child, determined by a genetic code (nature) and the forces of culture (nurture), acquire a free will or the freedom to make personal choices?

## Hard Determinism

**Hard determinists** argue that the child never acquires this freedom. Throughout its life, like all other things in nature, external forces determine what the child will become. Hard determinists get their name from the fact that they are convinced that free will is a fantasy.

They take the very hard (strong) view that the forces of nature determine our actions, not some mystical free will. For hard determinists, there is no such thing as free will.

If the hard determinists are correct, however, then the ethical concepts of responsibility and accountability make no sense. Both concepts imply that persons are free to make choices and, consequently, that people can be praised or blamed for their actions. If people do not make free choices, if they *cannot* make free choices, then praise, blame, responsibility, and accountability are meaningless. Why would we, for example, blame someone for actions over which they have absolutely no influence? If hard determinism is correct, then ethics and morality make no sense.

## Soft Determinism

Recognizing the importance of praise, blame, responsibility, and accountability in both ethics and the law, **soft determinists** adopt a less stringent view of determinism and freedom. Like the hard determinists, the soft determinists believe that there are no uncaused events in the universe. Where they differ from their stricter brothers and sisters, however, is in their view that included among the many causes in the universe is human choice.

Human beings, according to the soft determinists, are determined in many ways. Humans are, however, unique in the universe in that they have limited freedom of choice and, therefore, act as causes along with all the other causes in the universe. Because they have free will, they can be praised for good actions and condemned for bad actions. Humans who have free will are responsible creatures who are accountable for their freely chosen actions. Because they take the view that human beings have limited freedom to choose, these determinists are called soft determinists. They take a less strict view of determinism than do the hard determinists.

The view of the soft determinist is compatible with ethics and morality. The concepts of praise, blame, responsibility, and accountability make sense on this view. Traditional views of both ethics and the law assume that people make free choices for which they can be praised or punished. In the next section, we will see how the concept of free will underlies our basic understanding of concepts like moral and immoral. To say that a person did a bad thing implies that the person had a choice to do so. Similarly, to say that a person did a good thing implies that the individual made choices for which he or she is responsible. The law, of course, also implies that individual human beings are free to make choices.

In assessing the actions of the swinging couples, the Browns and the Smiths, we assume that they freely chose to swing. If they chose freely, then it makes sense to say that they are morally responsible for their actions. On the same assumption, we can meaningfully argue that their actions are morally acceptable or that they are not. If, however, we assume that they did not choose freely, then it makes no sense to praise or blame them for swinging. Swinging, we might say, was beyond their control; their actions were not free but determined. Ethics and ethical judgments require the assumption that people choose freely and, therefore, are responsible and accountable for their actions. Once again, the law makes the same assumption.

## ETHICS AND KEY ETHICAL TERMS

Having reviewed the matter of determinism and free will, let's note how some very basic ethical terms imply that human individuals are moral agents who are free, responsible, and accountable. Four ethical terms deserve our attention. They are key terms that we will use repeatedly as we discuss the various moral issues presented in this book. You will quickly notice that there are parallel concepts and words in the field of law. Before analyzing the four key words, let's clarify what we mean by a "moral agent."

## Moral Agents

We human beings are unique among all animals in that we are capable of understanding and choosing. We have both the capacity to know and the capacity to make choices. Unlike other animals, which act upon instinct, we make choices based on our understanding of a particular situation. These two elements—knowledge and choice—distinguish human beings from all other creatures. A **moral agent**, then, is a being that is capable of knowing the difference between right and wrong and is capable of making choices. Moral agents can, of course, choose to do what is morally right or they can choose to do what is morally wrong. Whatever choices they make, moral agents are responsible and accountable for their actions.

In ethics we often say that a particular action, like lying, is immoral or unethical. Sometimes we use the simple words "bad" or "wrong" to mean the same thing. At other times we will describe an action as ethical, good, or right. Let's analyze the meaning of the key ethical terms *moral, immoral, amoral,* and *non-moral.* For ease of presentation, I'll use these particular words and avoid repeating their synonyms.

## Moral

The first term to consider is the term ***moral.*** What is implied in the common use of the word *moral?* When we say that a person's actions are moral, we mean that the individual knows the difference between right and wrong, and freely chooses to do what is right. There are two key parts to the meaning of the word: knowledge and choice. To say that a person acted in an ethical manner, we mean that the person knew right from wrong and chose to do what is right.

## Immoral

The second key term to consider is the word ***immoral***, the opposite of *moral*. We can readily see that the same two elements are at the heart of the meaning of *immoral*, just as they were at the heart of its opposite. When we say that someone's actions are immoral, we mean that the individual knows the difference between right and wrong, and the individual chooses to do wrong. Once again, the word *immoral* implies both knowledge and consent. Actions are judged to be wrong or bad, morally speaking, if a person knew that the action was wrong but wilfully did it nevertheless.

## Amoral

A third key term is the word ***amoral***. Sometimes we know that an individual did something that was hurtful to another, but we recognize that the perpetrator didn't know what he or she was doing. For example, imagine that a person suffering from some serious mental illness kills a person while in a delusional state. While the individual clearly did the killing, the circumstances are taken into consideration and we conclude that the perpetrator didn't know what he or she was doing or that he or she acted under a compulsion. Such people are "out of their minds," we might say.

In cases like this, where offenders lack knowledge of their acts, and of the consequences of their acts, we say that the action is amoral. In court, the person might be declared not guilty by reason of insanity. The actions of very young children, the seriously mentally challenged, and the mentally ill are considered to be amoral, not moral or immoral. If a human being is judged incapable of understanding the difference between right and wrong or is incapable of choosing freely, then we consider his or her actions to be amoral, not moral or immoral.

## Non-Moral

The last of the four key terms that we need to consider is the word ***non-moral***. We use this word to describe things and the actions of animals, both of which are beyond the realm of ethical or moral conduct. A tree, a car, and a pencil are all in themselves incapable of acting morally or immorally. They are not, to put it differently, moral agents. We place animals into the same category. If a bear mauls a camper to death, we are saddened and may kill the bear to prevent further attacks. We don't, however, hold court and decide whether the bear was morally responsible for the camper's death. Animals, because they operate on instinct, are not considered to be moral agents. Like things, we consider animals to be non-moral beings.

The key terms *moral, immoral, amoral,* and *non-moral* give us a certain insight as to our understanding of the moral life and the ethical judgments we make about human actions. As we noted, the basic concepts of knowledge and free choice underlie the meaning of these words. It should not surprise us to see, later, that freedom is one of the fundamental and essential principles of ethics.

## ETHICS, LOGIC, AND CRITICAL THINKING

We said at the beginning of this chapter that analytical ethics involves the analysis of both language and logic. Having looked at a number of key issues in analytical ethics in the sections above, let's now discuss briefly the role of logic in our thinking—particularly in our moral thinking. **Logic**, of course, is the science of correct reasoning. As in all other areas of human experience, so too in ethics, clear and critical thinking is essential to making decisions and solving problems effectively. **Critical thinking** is logical thinking that analyzes, evaluates, and makes judgments about the truth or correctness of statements and arguments. The review of logic that follows will help us to think clearly and critically about moral issues.

Let's start with a simple example. If I asked you to draw a square circle, what would you do? In all likelihood you would accuse me of talking nonsense. That response would be most appropriate. In my request, the concept of a square is incompatible with the concept of a circle. In other words, I'm being illogical. My request for a square circle is self-contradictory. When we are logical in our conversation and our arguments, we abide by fundamental rules of correct reasoning. When we depart from these basic rules, we become illogical.

Sometimes a person's illogical arguments or statements are obvious, as is the case in my example. At other times, however, the lack of logic in a conversation may not be so obvious. For this reason, we need to examine the analytical aspect of ethics in order to be able to detect logical errors, whether they are our own or those of others. We need to take arguments seriously and determine whether they are sound or not. Critical thinking in ethics is as important as it is in any other area of life.

Two types of reasoning or arguing are important in ethics and all other human study. One type is called deductive reasoning and the other is called inductive reasoning. Both are important to understand. You use both types, no doubt, in your own reasoning, even if you are unaware of the fact. Let's take each in turn.

## Deductive Reasoning

First, what is deductive reasoning? **Deductive reasoning** is logical reasoning that moves from *general* statements that are true to a *particular* conclusion that is true. If the premises (statements) of the argument are each true, and the deductive steps are valid, then the conclusion will be true. The entire sequence of reasoning constitutes a sound argument. The thinker has moved from general truths to a particular truth by deduction. Sherlock Holmes and many other detectives, both fictional and real, are famous for their deductive reasoning. Given certain general truths, detectives draw specific conclusions. The butler did it, for example.

Look at the following example of deductive reasoning.

Example 1
(1)  All mothers are female.
(2)  Mary is a mother.
(3)  Therefore, Mary is a female.

The first premise is a general statement that is true. Assume that the second premise is true as a matter of fact. From these true premises we can deduce the third statement that is a particular statement that we know to be true. In other words, sound deductive arguments yield conclusions about which we can be certain.

Consider another example.

Example 2
(1)  All swingers are adulterers.
(2)  The Browns are swingers.
(3)  Therefore, the Browns are adulterers.

If the first two premises are true, then the conclusion is true and certain. An important part of the analysis of the Bahamian Vacation situation, however, had to do with the truth of the first premise. In other words, is the first premise true or is it false?

Notice the following argument, which sounds almost the same as the argument in Example 1, but, in fact, is significantly different.

Example 3
(1)  All mothers are female.
(2)  Mary is a female.
(3)  Therefore, Mary is a mother.

In this argument, the first premise is the same as it was in the first example, and it is a general truth. Assume that the second premise is true as a matter of fact. Note that in the second premise the word *female* has replaced the word *mother*. This difference makes it impossible for us to know the truth of the conclusion by simple deduction. Mary, a female, may or may not be a mother. From the argument alone, we don't know. The conclusion may or may not be true. Unsound arguments leave us in a state of uncertainty.

Now notice the following argument, which sounds similar to Example 2. It is, however, significantly different.

Example 4
(1)  All swingers are adulterers.
(2)  The Whites are adulterers.
(3)  Therefore, the Whites are swingers.

If we assume that the first two premises are true, we cannot *know* that the conclusion is true. It may or may not be true.

Deductive reasoning is an important part of logical argument. But, as two of our examples illustrate, we have to be very careful about the validity or soundness of arguments. In other words, we need to think critically about the arguments of others as well as our own. Deductive reasoning is one form of reasoning. Let's now look at another.

## Inductive Reasoning

The second type of reasoning that we need to be familiar with is inductive reasoning. Even though you may not be familiar with the expression "inductive reasoning," you have no doubt used this type of reasoning on many occasions. It is the type of reasoning that scientists frequently use in their pursuit of general truths (laws) about the universe. **Inductive reasoning** is logical argument that moves from *particular* statements to *general* statements.

The famous scientist Isaac Newton was said to have discovered the law of gravity when he noted that apples in an orchard always fall downward to the ground. He never noticed one flying off in an upward direction or sideways, for example. What Newton noticed is that apple number one fell to the ground, apple number two did the same, and so did all the apples that he ever observed. From a series of truths about particular apples, he arrived, by inductive reasoning, at the general truth expressed in the law of gravity. Indeed, he was able to arrive at a general truth that went far beyond apples. The law of gravity applies to all objects, not just apples.

Below, in summary form, is the inductive process that Newton used to arrive at the general conclusion expressed in the law of gravity.

(1)  Apple #1 fell downward toward the earth.
(2)  Apple #2 fell downward toward the earth.
(3)  Apple #3 fell downward toward the earth.
(4)  All apples (objects) fall downward toward the earth.

Inductive arguments, good scientists will tell you, do not result in the absolute certainty that sound deductive arguments yield. Nevertheless, conclusions frequently have such a high level of probability that, for all practical purposes, the conclusion is beyond doubt. Only a fool, for example, would doubt the truth of the law of gravity.

Sometimes people offer deductive and inductive arguments that are not valid. In any area of life, but especially in ethical discussion, we need to ensure that our arguments are sound and that the conclusions we draw are true. In the paragraphs that follow, we will identify some logical fallacies or errors that are commonly made. Hopefully, we will be able to ensure that our arguments and those of others are valid arguments that lead to conclusions that are true.

# FAULTY LOGIC OR UNCRITICAL THINKING

Critical thinking requires that we avoid basic errors in reasoning. These errors in reasoning, or faulty logic, take many forms. In this section we will note several of the most common errors. We'll review these errors in three categories: faulty appeals, faulty sampling, and faulty reasoning.

## Faulty Appeals

When debating an issue, individuals may appeal to an authority, popular opinion, or someone's status in support of their position. Such appeals may or may not be valid. If an appeal is invalid, we call it a faulty appeal. Being logical in the discussion of ethical issues involves, among other things, avoiding faulty appeals. Three appeals are often faulty appeals.

First, appeals to authority can be problematic. An **appeal to authority** involves trusting that a particular authority is knowledgeable and will make true statements about the issue in question. If a person appeals to an *inappropriate* authority, then that person's claims become suspect. For example, appealing to a famous movie star in support of your position on capital punishment is valid only if the movie star is a recognized authority on the death penalty. If one appeals to a legitimate authority, that authority is much more likely to provide the truth than a person who lacks expertise in an area or is biased. The truth about smoking, for example, is more likely to be told by the Canadian Medical Association than it is by a tobacco manufacturer. We need to ensure that the authorities that we invoke in our arguments and debates are legitimate authorities, not inappropriate ones.

Another type of appeal is **appeal to public opinion.** In this case, one appeals to the views of the public in support of one's argument. If, for example, someone argues that General Motors cars are the best cars because most people in town own GM cars, the argument may or may not be valid. Even if it is true that the majority in town own GM cars, that fact doesn't mean that GM cars are the best cars. We do well to note that in the past the vast majority of people on the planet believed that the earth was flat. Appealing to public opinion did not make the earth flat. The public was wrong. When we appeal to public opinion, we need to proceed with caution. The public is sometimes right on an issue, but it is not always right. In an age that places high value on public opinion surveys, we need to approach opinion polls critically.

Some faulty appeals are **appeals to status**. In this kind of faulty appeal, the one who makes the appeal abandons all logic and argues that something is true because someone has a certain status. Parents, teachers, and other authority figures are often guilty of faulty appeals to status. When a father, for instance, tells his child that smoking marijuana is wrong because the father says so, the father is appealing to his parental status, to his parental power. There may be valid reasons for saying that it is wrong to smoke marijuana, but parental status is not one of them. In education, the mathematical statement "2 + 2 = 4" is not true because the teacher says so. It's true because mathematics says so. The truth of the statement is independent of the teacher and the teacher's status.

## Faulty Sampling

When discussing ethical issues, people often make claims that are not supported by sound research. In a word, their claims are not backed up by facts. In order to understand the two forms of faulty research we are about to examine, imagine that a researcher wants to determine what Canadian college students think about capital punishment. Do Canadian college students support the death penalty or not? Faulty sampling is a type of faulty reasoning that can take either of two forms: insufficient sampling or unrepresentative sampling. Let's start with insufficient sampling.

When a person argues that something is true on the basis of a sample that is too small to support the conclusion, we have a case of **insufficient sampling.** If, for example, our researcher wishes to determine the views of Canadian college students regarding capital punishment but limits her survey to one or two colleges in Ontario, then her sample will be insufficient. It will not be big enough to support any conclusions that the researcher draws. A survey of one or two Ontario colleges does not entitle the researcher to make statements about all college students in Canada. A valid conclusion could only be drawn from a much larger sample of college students. Statements made on the basis of insufficient sampling are not trustworthy. We cannot rely on their accuracy and we must avoid them.

Insufficient sampling may be an important factor in stereotypical thinking, a subject that we will return to in Chapter 7. A **stereotype** is a false and misleading idea about a group and its members, and **stereotypical thinking** is uncritical thinking based on a stereotype. If an individual, on the basis of an insufficient sampling of a group, concludes that all of its members are lazy and dishonest, then the person will engage in stereotypical thinking about members of that group. If, for example, the first 20 people I meet from Boldova are rude to me, I am not entitled to conclude that all 10 million Boldovans are rude. My experience may not have been pleasant, but my sample is insufficient to support my conclusion.

A second form of faulty sampling is unrepresentative sampling. **Unrepresentative sampling** is sampling that does not include the characteristics of the larger population about which one will draw conclusions. To draw valid conclusions about the opinions of Canadian college students on capital punishment, for example, a researcher would have to use a representative sample of college students. The sample would, in all likelihood, be a random sample drawn from a wide variety of colleges across the country. If the researcher took her sample exclusively from Canadian police colleges, her sample would most likely be unrepresentative of college students in general. Such a sample would be unrepresentative and faulty. Its conclusions would be suspect and untrustworthy.

## Faulty Reasoning

We'll now take note of four forms of faulty reasoning: hasty generalization, circular argument, personal attack, and the "is-ought" mistake. Each one deserves careful attention.

When stereotypical thinking results in faulty conclusions, the kind we noted above in the discussion of faulty sampling, we describe the faulty conclusion as a **hasty generalization**. Inductive reasoning, done correctly, can produce valid conclusions. However, when people move too quickly from too little evidence to a faulty conclusion, then they are guilty of hasty generalization. Such generalizations must be avoided if we are to reason clearly.

Sometimes people are guilty of **circular argument.** Their argument goes around in a circle as they assume the truth of what they are supposed to prove. In the process, they are guilty of faulty reasoning. Certain religious arguments provide us with a good example of this kind of faulty reasoning. Consider, for example, Tom and Mary. Imagine that they have been discussing the Bahamian Vacation situation.

Tom, a devoutly religious person, begins by saying that swingers are adulterers and adultery is wrong. He says, further, that he knows this because the Bible condemns adultery and the Bible is God's word. Mary now asks Tom how he knows that the Bible is the word of God. If Tom replies that he knows this because the Bible says so, Tom is arguing in a circle. In turning to the Bible for proof that the Bible is God's word, Tom is assuming the truth of what he is supposed to prove. He is guilty of arguing in a circle.

When individuals respond to the argument of another person by attacking the other person's character, they are guilty of **attacking the person,** another form of faulty reasoning. This kind of faulty reasoning occurs in many areas of life, especially politics. If, for example, Bernard Landry, the Quebec separatist, argues that Quebec would be economically stronger if it separated from Canada, it is faulty reasoning to say that Mr. Landry is a liar who can't be trusted. Attacking his personal integrity does not address the economic argument that he has made. A proper and logical response to Mr. Landry would involve arguments about the economics of the proposed separation, not accusations about his character.

A third form of faulty reasoning, the **"is-ought" mistake,** involves an illegitimate move from the way things *are* in the world to the claim that things *ought to be* that way. It is not legitimate for me to argue, for example, that I ought to cheat on my income tax return because lots of others are cheating on theirs. The fact that people do cheat provides no logical support for the idea that people should cheat. The fact that the world is a certain way at the moment is not, in and of itself, sufficient reason to say that the world ought to be that way.

In policing, for example, the unethical conduct of some officers does not legitimize such conduct. Even if many officers engage in unethical practices, one cannot legitimately claim that this justifies others doing the same thing. The fact that things *are* a certain way in the world provides no logical basis for saying that things ought to be that way. There is, we might say, a logical gap between the way the world is and the way it ought to be. Another way of putting the point is to say that descriptive ethics and prescriptive ethics are logically distinct from one another.

## MODEL AND PROCESS

To help us do analytical ethics in a systematic way, the next two sections of this chapter offer a model and a process for us to use in our critical thinking about moral matters. Together they are valuable tools for thinking through ethical issues and making moral choices.

## The PRINCIPLES Model

Throughout this book we will repeatedly work with the five basic principles of ethical reasoning. These five principles are Goodness, Equality, Justice, Truth, and Freedom. Ethical choices are made when moral agents exercise their freedom to choose and act, after careful consideration of the impact that their actions will have on others. Careful consideration involves answering five questions, one for each of the five principles of ethical reasoning. The questions are

**Will my action harm others? (Goodness)**
The *principle of goodness* requires that we do good to others and not harm others.

**Will my action treat others equally? (Equality)**
The *principle of equality* requires that we treat all others as moral equals and that we not discriminate for or against them.

### Will my action be fair to others? (Justice)

The *principle of justice* requires that we be fair to others and that we don't treat them unjustly.

### Will my action be honest? (Truth)

The *principle of truth* requires that we be honest with others, and ourselves, and that we don't deceive others.

### Will my action limit the freedom of others? (Freedom)

The *principle of freedom* requires that we respect the freedom that others have to make their choices, and that we do not force them to do things our way.

People who observe the rules of critical thinking as they answer the five key questions above should be in a position to justify their actions as ethical ones. As you will see, however, each principle forces us to consider many important aspects of any particular issue. The remaining chapters of this book involve an examination of those important aspects and issues.

Each of us concerned about acting in an ethical manner in any particular situation must know and use the principles to answer the questions related to each principle. To assist you in remembering the **PRINCIPLES Model**, I offer the following picture.

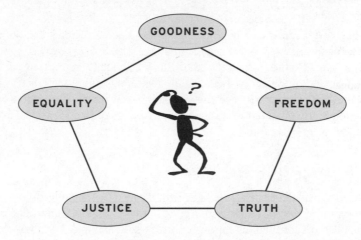

The PRINCIPLES Model

In the diagram, the moral agent stands at the centre considering what to do in a particular situation. Before deciding and acting, the moral agent will consider all of the five basic principles, answering the questions associated with each of the principles. The principles function like a checklist for the moral agent, ensuring that all ethically relevant aspects of a particular situation are considered carefully. One might also describe the model as a framework within which the moral agent makes moral choices. The moral agent is free to act, but will only act in an ethical manner if he or she considers all five of the principles. The principles provide a framework for the moral agent's freedom of choice. They set the moral or ethical limits on individual freedom.

## The DECIDE Process

Critical thinking is greatly assisted by having systematic ways of considering issues. The **DECIDE Process** provides a series of steps that can help us consider ethical issues in an orderly manner. The process is based on the standard problem-solving method of the sciences, and together with the PRINCIPLES Model, this process gives us a structured way in which to consider issues and make moral decisions. Hopefully, we will make good ones and act in ethically acceptable ways.

The DECIDE Process is offered below as a set of rules to follow in order to ensure that you engage in critical thinking in a systematic way. The DECIDE Process obviously gets its name from the first letter of the first word in each rule.

**D**efine the issue carefully.
**E**mploy the equality principle.
**C**onsider the consequences for all.
**I**nvolve all five principles.
**D**ecide with integrity.
**E**valuate your decisions.

The DECIDE Process can also be viewed as a set of critical questions that requires thoughtful answers. In question form, the DECIDE Process looks like this:

| | |
|---|---|
| What exactly is the issue? | (**D**efine) |
| Am I discriminating for or against anybody? | (**E**mploy) |
| Am I considering the impact on everyone? | (**C**onsider) |
| Have I considered all five principles carefully? | (**I**nvolve) |
| What is my decision and is it an honest one? | (**D**ecide) |
| Have I missed anything important? | (**E**valuate) |

To help you remember the steps of the DECIDE Process, I offer you the following picture.

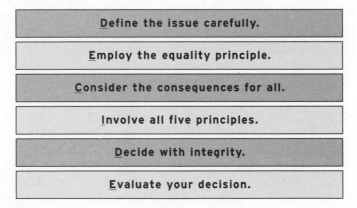

The DECIDE Process

## CHAPTER SUMMARY

We began this chapter by explaining that analytical ethics is the part of ethical inquiry that analyzes the language and logic of ethical discussion and debate. It is all about critical thinking in moral matters. We introduced the Bahamian Vacation situation to encourage critical thinking about a particular ethical issue.

We then examined the relationship between ethics and the law. We argued that ethics and the law are not necessarily the same. What is legal, for example, may not be moral. In addition, what is ethical may not be legal. Critical thinking shows that ethics and the law are not necessarily the same.

Next we reviewed the relationship between ethics and religion. Specifically, we examined the claim that people have to be religious in order to be moral. In response to the question, "Does a person have to be religious to be moral?" we said "No." We concluded that the original claim was false for several reasons.

We continued our look at analytical ethics with a discussion of ethical relativism. We noted that relativist thinking has been applied to both groups (cultural relativism) and individuals (subjectivism). In both cases relativism has fatal flaws in that it makes moral judgments inappropriate and meaningless. While ethical relativism promotes tolerance, it forbids moral judgments, an essential aspect of the moral life.

Next, we addressed another issue in analytical ethics, the question of free will. Hard determinists maintain that human beings have no freedom of choice. Soft determinists argue that humans have limited free will. The concepts of responsibility, accountability, praise, and blame are all essential to ethics, and they make sense only if humans have free will. The soft determinism view, we noted, is compatible with ethics and ethical choices. The assumption that humans are free to make choices is evident in certain key ethical terms. Those key ethical terms are *moral, immoral, amoral,* and *non-moral.* An analysis of the meaning of those terms revealed that their definition depends on the view that humans have freedom of choice.

We then reviewed some basic rules of critical thinking that must be applied when dealing with any ethical issue. We described deductive reasoning, reasoning that moves logically from general truths to particular ones. We also described inductive reasoning which, in contrast, moves logically from a series of particular truths to a general conclusion. Deductive reasoning that follows the rules of logic provides truths that we can know with certainty. Valid inductive reasoning yields probability, not certainty. Often, however, the probability is so great that we can act on it with great confidence, but not absolute certainty.

Next we examined three faulty appeals, each of which fails to meet the requirements of critical thinking. We reviewed faulty appeals to authority, public opinion, and status. A faulty appeal to authority is an appeal to someone who is not an expert on the matter in question or is biased with respect to the subject. A faulty appeal to public opinion is an appeal to the views of the public when those views are not clearly known or when those views are obviously incorrect. Lastly, a faulty appeal to status is an appeal in which the facts of a situation are ignored and the person making the appeal resorts to the personal power associated with his or her status.

Finally, we concluded our examination of analytical ethics by offering the PRINCIPLES Model and the DECIDE Process to assist readers as they consider the many ethical issues in the remainder of this book. The PRINCIPLES Model provides the ethical limits within which a moral agent makes choices. The principles of the model, when put into question form, provide a series of questions that a person should answer when making moral choices. The DECIDE Process provides a series of steps based on the standard problem-solving method. If the steps are followed, a person will be able to analyze a moral issue in a systematic fashion and arrive, hopefully, at an ethically defensible position or make an ethically defensible choice.

## MASTERING THE MATERIAL

Now that you have read this chapter, use the following guides to ensure that you have mastered the material.

## Analytical Ethics

1. Define the following: *analytical dimension, descriptive dimension, prescriptive dimension*
2. What is analysis?
3. Identify the two subjects of analytical ethics.

## Ethics and the Law

1. Define *law* and *ethical debate*.
2. Describe the relationship between ethics and the law.

## Ethics and Religion

1. Define the following: *religious duties, ritual duties, social duties*
2. Explain why the following are important in the discussion of ethics and religion:
   (a) moral atheists
   (b) God's existence
   (c) human authorities
   (d) contradictory claims
3. Summarize Plato's point about the commands of God.

## Ethics and Ethical Relativism

1. What two values does ethical relativism promote?
2. Identify two types of ethical relativism.
3. Describe cultural relativism and individual relativism.
4. What is another name for individual relativism?
5. Describe ethical universalism.

## Ethics and Determinism

1. Define *determinism*.
2. Describe hard determinism and soft determinism.
3. Which form of determinism allows us to make sense of ethics?

## Ethics and Key Ethical Terms

1. Define *moral agent* and identify the two essential characteristics of a moral agent.
2. Define the following: *moral, immoral, amoral, non-moral*

## Ethics, Logic, and Critical Thinking

1. Define *logic*.
2. Describe deductive reasoning and give an example of it.
3. Describe inductive reasoning and give an example of it.
4. Define *stereotype* and *stereotypical thinking*.

## Faulty Logic or Uncritical Thinking

1. Describe the following errors in reasoning, and give an example of each.
   (a) faulty appeal to authority
   (b) faulty appeal to public opinion
   (c) faulty appeal to status
   (d) insufficient sampling
   (e) unrepresentative sampling
   (f) hasty generalization
   (g) circular argument
   (h) attacking the person
   (i) the "is-ought" mistake

## Model and Process

1. Identify the five principles of the PRINCIPLES Model and explain its purpose.
2. Who stands at the centre of the PRINCIPLES Model?
3. Identify the six steps of the DECIDE Process and explain its purpose.
4. What scientific procedure forms the pattern for the DECIDE Process?

<table>
<tr><td>Media Watch:<br>Ethics in the News 2.1</td><td>Clarifying the terms of the abortion debate *by Dr. Henry Morgentaler*</td></tr>
</table>

In the ongoing debate on abortion it would be helpful to use terms which are fair and appropriate and based on current knowledge rather than obsolete unscientific notions.

Thus, while the term "fetus" is generally applied to the product of conception, in terms of actual embryological development we deal first with a zygote, one cell which results from the successful union of sperm and ovum and then multiplies. Following this we then have a morula, a blastula, a blastocyst and an embryo; the term fetus is applied from two months of gestation up to delivery.

It is therefore wrong to talk of "unborn" or "preborn" babies in the early stages of pregnancy; only about two to three months before delivery might these terms apply and nobody advocates that pregnancies be terminated at such a late stage of gestation except in extremely rare and life-threatening circumstances. The notion that there is a baby in the pregnant woman's uterus from the moment of conception is simply not true and has more to do with arbitrary religious dogma than our knowledge of embryological development.

Unfortunately, because of ignorance and the acceptance of dogma, anti-choice persons believe that abortion kills a baby. This is untrue and a monstrous lie. A woman who finds herself unwillingly pregnant and feels that she is not able to undertake the responsibility of mothering at the time may wish to terminate the development of an embryo or fetus before it becomes a baby. There is no baby there to be "killed" or "murdered" and it is arrogant and irresponsible to hurl these accusations.

A pregnant woman should not be called a "mother." She becomes a mother when she delivers a live baby. Similarly, a man responsible for impregnating a woman should not be called "father" until she delivers a live baby.

The term "abortionist" means anyone performing an abortion, whether a medical doctor or not. When it applies to doctors the proper term would be "medical abortionist" or, in my case, specialist in medical abortion.

"Pro-life" should definitely not be applied to anti-choice, anti-abortion people. The terms, "opponents of abortion (rights)," "anti-choice" or "anti-feminist" would be appropriate.

Pro-choice people care deeply about the quality of life and want women to become mothers when they choose to do so, because desired and wanted children have a better opportunity to receive love and affection crucial for their development into caring, responsible, emotionally healthy persons.

Thus, pro-choice is pro-life. The opposite of "pro-life" obviously is "pro-death" and this is what the anti-abortion people want to convey. It is utterly unfair and inappropriate and it is therefore wrong to describe the opponents of abortion as "pro-life."

I hope these remarks will help to bring about a more enlightened debate on abortion, devoid of insults and accusations. While I recognize that many persons opposing abortion are well-meaning and rightly concerned about the sanctity and meaning of human life, it would be a good thing for our democracy that they also respect the deeply-held convictions of those who favour abortion rights for women out of a concern for the protection of the life, health, fertility and dignity of women and for the well-being of children.

I hope that a debate and dialogue on these important issues may be possible in our country without invective and insults, in an atmosphere of mutual respect, recognizing the principle of freedom of conscience and religion in a pluralistic society.

Source: *Toronto Star*, November 30, 1989, A27.

---

## Media Watch: Ethics in the News 2.2

## Abortion argument is flawed
## *by Frank Jones*

Dr. Henry Morgentaler is up to his old tricks again. You'd think he'd know when to keep quiet.

His side in the abortion debate has won almost total victory under the terms of the bill now before a House of Commons committee. It allows women to get abortions in consultation with their doctors for almost any reason. Abortion is retained in the Criminal Code, but the chances of a woman or her doctor being prosecuted are nil.

Victory is not enough for Morgentaler.

According to my research, in an article in *The Star* last Thursday he used misleading scientific terms in support of what I'll call the "blob theory." You know the blob theory: It isn't a life we're aborting, dear, it's just a blob of tissue.

It isn't even right to describe the product of conception as a fetus, says Morgentaler. It begins as a zygote, and at different stages becomes a morula, a blastula, a blastocyst and an embryo.

As Dr. Paul Ranalli, a neurologist who is a member of Physicians for Life, said when I asked about the terms, "Who would want to cuddle up to a blastocyst?"

While Morgentaler is technically correct, there's a flaw in his argument. Women, according to Ranalli, do not receive abortions during any of the stages he describes because they occur before the woman knows she is pregnant.

### Seamless continuum

What Morgentaler and his supporters are trying to deny, said Ranalli, is that life is a seamless continuum that begins at conception and ends at death. Any divisions we impose, like viability or birth, are simply arbitrary.

"The genetic code is in place from the moment of conception," said Ranalli. As a neurologist he is able to read brain waves at six weeks. The heart beat begins after eight weeks. To pretend this is not human life is to deceive the lay public, he said.

But Morgentaler, in order to make abortion more acceptable, wants to rewrite the language of debate. He is even getting squeamish about being called an abortionist. In his case, he said, we should describe him as a "specialist in medical abortion."

Pregnancy is not a disease, and, says Ranalli, the conscientious doctor treating a pregnant woman knows he or she has two patients. Are the real needs of the one troubled patient being answered by a surgical procedure that ends the life of the other patient?

### Abortions of expediency

Ranalli is a Catholic, but comes to his convictions from a medical point of view. Differing from his church, he believes more effective contraception is one answer to unwanted births. He also believes that by giving women with unwanted pregnancies one solution— abortion—the government is shirking its responsibility to provide them with psychological and economic support.

Abortion may keep a woman on the production line or in the office today, but it may also deny her fulfillment and prevent her making her genetic contribution to Canada's future—both of which may be much more important.

And isn't it the ancient and honourable practice of medicine that is becoming a casualty in this affair? Do we want doctors who are healers or doctors who do whatever society wants them to, whether using liposuction on people with fat thighs or providing abortions of expediency?

What the patient demands today, the state may demand tomorrow, warns Ranalli.

And, of course, when politicians talk of it being "a matter between a woman and her doctor" they are ignoring reality. "The abortion clinic is not your neighbourhood GP," said Ranalli. The woman is not likely to meet the doctor until he begins the procedure, and it's all over in 15 minutes. And what does "choice" really mean when women are kept in ignorance about the development of the fetus, asks Ranalli.

He will be one of a group of pro-life doctors appearing before the Commons committee, although he has few illusions about their chances of changing anything. The new law, he said, "is next to nothing. But no law at all is a state of emergency." If the law is passed the debate won't end. Neither should it. Not while people like Morgentaler are trying to convince us this isn't an argument about human life.

Source: *Toronto Star*, December 4, 1989. C5.

# chapter three

# Prescriptive Ethics: Establishing Norms of Conduct in a Civil Society

## LEARNING OUTCOMES

After completing this chapter, you should be able to

- Distinguish between descriptive and prescriptive ethics
- Explain the role and importance of both descriptive and prescriptive ethics
- Discuss the difference between consequentialist and nonconsequentialist prescriptions
- Describe three consequentialist prescriptions for doing right
- Describe three nonconsequentialist prescriptions for doing right
- Identify consequentialist and nonconsequentialist influences on policing ethics

## INTRODUCTION

In Chapter 2 we studied analytical ethics, the part of ethics that analyzes the language and logic of ethical discussion and debate. Further, we noted a number of key issues that have been the subject of analysis. Keeping the importance of analytical ethics in mind, we now turn to two other aspects of ethics: the descriptive dimension and the prescriptive dimension. To fully understand what ethics is all about and to make informed ethical choices, an individual needs to understand and use all three areas of ethics.

In the sections that follow, we will first examine descriptive ethics, explaining what it is all about and providing the reader with some preliminary examples of this important aspect of ethical inquiry. We will follow that discussion with a careful look at prescriptive ethics, using two major ethical approaches as our guide. These approaches are found in the traditions called consequentialism and nonconsequentialism. While the names may appear intimidating, they need not be. We will proceed step by step, and the prescriptions associated with each of these traditions will become clear.

## DESCRIPTIVE ETHICS

The second important aspect of ethical inquiry is called descriptive ethics. This is the area of ethics in which one researches an issue in order to determine what the facts are with respect to that issue. For example, in the late 1940s an American researcher named Alfred Kinsey set about to find out the facts regarding sexual practices in the United States. He published his famous Kinsey Reports, one on men and the other on women, and shocked many who read his work. Actual sexual practices, he discovered, differed in many ways from the prescribed sexual norms of the day (Kinsey, 1948 and 1953).

The important point for us is to note that Kinsey tried to determine the actual practices of the American people. He was not trying to say what Americans should or should not do sexually. Had he done that, he would have been doing prescriptive ethics, the topic of our next section. **Descriptive ethics** describes the actual practices of people. Prescriptive ethics states what people should or shouldn't do.

When we study ethics, we need to do descriptive ethics in order to know the facts about an issue. If we study doctor-assisted suicide, for example, it would be helpful to know how many deaths occur in this way. In Canada, where the practice is illegal, it might be difficult to get the facts. Nevertheless, it would be helpful to know such facts if we are attempting to decide whether the practice should be legalized. Earlier in this century, when abortion was illegal, researchers tried to discover how many abortions were actually being performed on Canadian women. That research provides us with another example of descriptive ethics.

One more example may be useful. One of the arguments for capital punishment is called the *deterrence argument*. It says that we should have capital punishment because, if we do, it will deter people from murdering. This argument raises the question, "Is it true that capital punishment deters murderers?" To answer this question responsibly we would need to do some descriptive ethics. We would need, for example, to research jurisdictions that have capital punishment and compare murder rates in those jurisdictions to similar jurisdictions where there is no death penalty. We might also examine murder rates before and after the abolition or implementation of capital punishment in a particular place. Later, in Chapter 8, we'll revisit this subject.

The main point in this discussion is that we need to base our ethical arguments on the facts, and descriptive ethics is the part of ethical studies where we try to establish the facts. In the ethical issues that we explore later in this book we will attempt to describe the factual situation relevant to each issue. We'll get involved in descriptive ethics, for example, in our study of capital punishment. It will also play a key role in our examination of ethics in policing. In each instance, we will search for the facts in order to make the most informed arguments about an issue. Before we offer a prescription for moral action, we will want to do descriptive ethics.

In Chapter 2 we discussed a form of faulty reasoning called the "is-ought" mistake. We noted that one cannot logically draw the conclusion that the world ought to be a certain way (prescriptive ethics) on the grounds that it is that way in reality (descriptive ethics). The fact that large numbers of spouses do cheat on their partners, for example, is not a valid reason for taking the view that spouses *should* cheat on their partners. The fact that the average speed of vehicles on Ontario's Highway 401 is 120 kilometres per hour does not provide a logically valid reason for saying that we should travel at that speed on the 401. "I was just keeping up with the traffic, officer," is not a valid reason for speeding.

Descriptive ethics is important in that it requires us to investigate the facts of an issue. It is essential for our understanding of moral issues. We must not, however, commit the "is-ought" mistake in our reasoning about ethical issues. We must not confuse the way things "ought to be" with the way that they actually are.

Later in our studies we'll examine the subject of deviant subcultures within policing. The codes of ethics that we study spell out the ideal or expected behaviour of police officers. The ideals are, of course, statements of prescriptive ethics. In some instances, however, the actual practices of officers are inconsistent with law enforcement codes of ethics and, in some cases, the law. Putting it differently, the actual practices are deviant practices. Descriptive ethics is concerned with knowing what the actual practices of officers are.

We will examine, for example, some of the pressures that explain deviant behaviour—whether unethical, illegal, or both—but do not justify it. We will also explore the values and principles that justify the expected behaviours that are stipulated in the various codes that we will study. The disparity between actual and ideal practices, and the way one deals with those disparities, may well be the single most important aspect of our study of ethics, policing, and civil society. We'll want to ensure, among other things, that we do not make the "is-ought" mistake

## PRESCRIPTIVE ETHICS

In our review of descriptive ethics above, we made a number of references to prescriptive ethics. We noted that descriptive ethics describes how the world actually is while prescriptive ethics states how the world should be. **Prescriptive ethics** is about ideals, standards, and rules of conduct. It is about norms, the written and unwritten rules of a group. Because it is concerned with establishing the norms for ethical conduct, prescriptive ethics is also called **normative ethics**. Prescriptive ethics is the important part of ethics in which people say what one should or shouldn't do, what one ought to or ought not do, what one must or must not do.

Consider for a moment what a doctor's prescription is. It's a doctor's formula, based on her knowledge and experience, for making the patient well. It's a formula that the patient *should* follow. In life or death situations the patient *must* follow the prescription. If the prescription is followed, the patient should recover from whatever illness he's suffering. In prescriptive ethics, people prescribe actions that will bring about good or prevent or reduce harm. They are offering formulas for doing right and avoiding wrong.

We will be examining some general prescriptions for doing right in this chapter, and we will also study some very specific prescriptions later. For example, in our study of utilitarianism later in this chapter, we will note the utilitarian formula or prescription for doing right. One can describe it as a general prescription to be used in many specific situations. In contrast, when we look at the use of defensive force in Chapter 6, we will examine a much more specific prescription for defensive actions that are ethically justifiable. In both cases we will be doing prescriptive ethics, attempting to determine what the ideal or expected behaviour is.

Two general prescriptions will be of special interest to us as they have been extremely influential in the field of ethics. One of them, namely utilitarianism, I referred to in the last paragraph. The other prescription that also requires our attention is that of duty ethics. Both of these general prescriptions will occupy our attention before we turn to specific moral issues such as capital punishment.

Make careful note of the fact that the two prescriptions mentioned here and discussed below each contribute an important element to the PRINCIPLES Model and the DECIDE Process introduced in Chapter 2. The utilitarian concern for creating good consequences for everyone is an expression of the goodness principle of the PRINCIPLES Model, and the same concern for doing good underlies the third step of the DECIDE Process, "Consider the consequences for all." Of fundamental concern to duty ethics is the Principle of Equality. The duty ethics' insistence upon the moral equality of all human beings is captured in the equality principle of the PRINCIPLES Model. The concern for equality also underlies the second step of the DECIDE Process, "Employ the Equality Principle."

Before examining these two approaches, let's take a look at the two broad traditions of which utilitarianism and duty ethics are a part. We'll also examine some other approaches within each of these traditions that have not had the same level of impact on moral decision making as these two have had. What do we mean by the consequentialist and the nonconsequentialist traditions in ethics?

## CONSEQUENTIALISM AND NONCONSEQUENTIALISM

We all know that a **consequence** is the result or effect of an action. If I throw a rock at a picture window, the consequence will be, in all likelihood, a broken window. The smashed glass is the consequence, effect, or result of my throwing the rock. In other words, it is the outcome of my action. Persons who take the consequentialist approach to ethical matters always look at the consequences of an action to determine whether the action was right or wrong, good or bad.

I believe that most people are consequentialists in their moral life, at least much of the time. We often judge that an action was a good action if it had good results. Rescuing the drowning child from the river was a good thing to do, we say, because it had good results. A child's life was saved and a family was joyful as a consequence. The action had good outcomes so it was a good action, the right thing to do.

In contrast, the individual who drives drunk and kills an innocent bystander is judged to have done wrong. The outcome of the drunken driving was the death of an innocent person. Actions such as drunk driving are described, of course, as wrong or bad actions. The results of the action were harmful or hurtful, and it is these harmful outcomes that, in the view of many, make the action of drunk driving so reprehensible.

## The Consequentialist Prescription

**Consequentialism** is the name we give to the tradition that offers the following prescription for ethical behaviour: The right thing to do is the action that brings good consequences to persons affected by the action. An action is wrong, of course, if it brings about hurtful results. One challenge to the consequentialist approach to ethics is that people may disagree as to what constitutes a good result or a bad result. This particular challenge we will discuss later in our work.

## The Nonconsequentialist Prescription

Nonconsequentialists take a very different view of right and wrong, good and bad. They believe that something other than the consequences of an action make that action right or wrong. In other words, **nonconsequentialism** adopts the view that right and wrong are determined by something other than the outcomes of an action. In fact, the most radical of nonconsequentialists will argue that the consequences of an action must not be considered when deciding right and wrong. They look to standards other than consequences for determining whether actions are right or wrong.

What could these other standards possibly be? We'll examine some of them shortly, but let's first try to capture, in its most general form, the nonconsequentialist prescription for doing right and avoiding wrong. Nonconsequentialism offers the following prescription for the moral life: The right thing to do is the action determined by one's duty to persons affected by the action, irrespective of the consequences. For many readers this prescription may seem bizarre and extreme. Perhaps an example or two will help us to see what the nonconsequentialist intends.

Consider nurses working in a busy hospital. They often face repulsive tasks. Soiled bed linens and foul odours are most unpleasant. They can make a person sick, if one is not used to dealing with such situations. Consider now, the actions of nurses in these difficult circumstances. If they consider the consequences of changing the bed sheets and cleaning up the soiled mattresses, they might conclude that they would be so personally repulsed and upset that it is wrong for them to do these things. The nonconsequentialist, however, will argue that the right and wrong in this case is determined not by the consequences of the action, but by one's duty to do the action.

One can easily imagine other circumstances in which the right thing to do is determined by one's duty, not the outcomes of the action. Many of us might avoid paying taxes because of the harmful effects on our bank accounts. Police officers might avoid many different kinds of dangerous situations. Firefighters might stand back and watch the flames instead of entering the burning building to search for occupants. The nonconsequentialist believes that right and wrong, in these and other cases, are to be found in doing one's duty, not in the outcomes of the action.

Nonconsequentialism is often seen as an extreme approach to ethics and morality. When one sees it in the light of the examples above, however, many people see the point. How much of ethics, we might ask, can be handled on a purely consequentialist basis? Don't ethics and morality require something other than consequences? Isn't duty, of one kind or another, essential to the moral life? Could people live in community without the moral requirements of duty? Every important role in a civil society has its attendant duties. Perhaps it is this aspect of the ethical and moral life that the nonconsequentialists have placed the emphasis on.

Before examining consequentialist and nonconsequentialist prescriptions, let's consider another situation. Reflection on this case will help us to understand the various positions that we will discuss in the next section of this chapter. The situation is based on a true story from World War II (Fletcher, 1966, p.164). As in the case of the swingers on vacation from Chapter 2, questions about adultery arise in this situation.

| SITUATION 3.1 | Sacrificial Adultery |
|---|---|

Mrs. Braun is a German citizen who is being held prisoner in a Russian prison camp, thousands of kilometres from her home in Germany. Her husband and three young children are together in the family home. They are safe at the moment but always at risk as the war rages on. They have attempted several times to find out where Mrs. Braun is, but each time they have been unsuccessful. Mrs. Braun does not know what has become of her family because she has had no contact with them and no information about them since the time of her capture several months ago.

Meanwhile, in prison, Mrs. Braun learns that there are only three circumstances that will result in her release. First, she will get out of prison if the war comes to an end. Unfortunately, neither Mrs. Braun nor anyone else knows when that will occur. Second, if Mrs. Braun experiences a severe illness that the prison cannot treat, she will be sent to a remote prison hospital. The hospital is in eastern Russia, much farther from her home than the prison she is currently in. Third, she will be released and sent back to Germany if she becomes pregnant. Her captors will not bear the cost of keeping her or any other pregnant woman in prison. Pregnant women are sent back to their home countries because they are a liability.

A prison guard has made sexual advances toward Mrs. Braun on a number of previous occasions. Now he is making advances again. Should Mrs. Braun ask and allow the guard to impregnate her? Why or why not? You may want to write down your thoughts before we proceed to the next section. Be as clear and concise about your position as you possibly can.

Keeping the case of sacrificial adultery in mind, let's look at three versions of consequentialism before we turn, in a later section, to three versions of nonconsequentialism.

## CONSEQUENTIALIST PRESCRIPTIONS

We described the consequentialist approach above. Now we need to look at three different versions of consequentialism. What makes them all consequentialist approaches is the fact that they all look to the outcomes of an action—the consequences—to try to determine whether the action is right or wrong. They differ, however, with respect to whose consequences should be considered. Two versions of consequentialism, altruism and egoism, seem to be extreme forms. Utilitarianism, the third version, has been described as a middle-of-the-road approach. We'll examine each in turn, giving less time to the extreme versions and devoting more time to utilitarianism.

### The Altruistic Prescription

The Latin word *alter* means "other." **Altruism** is the form of consequentialism that takes the view that the right thing to do is what brings the best consequences for others only. As such, this extreme form of consequentialism has a noble but impractical ring to it. It says that we must always consider only the results or effects that our actions have on other people, never the effects that our actions have on ourselves.

Some would argue that this is the heart of ethics, to live for the good of others. Isn't this what Jesus and other great spiritual leaders were trying to tell the world? The right thing to do is whatever brings good consequences for others. This is, of course, the route of extreme self-denial. This approach argues, among other things, that one ought to "turn the other cheek" when one is assaulted on the cheek.

If Mrs. Braun were an altruist, she would consider the consequences of her action on everyone except herself. She would consider the possible outcomes for her children, husband, and anyone else affected by her proposed action. Presumably, she would even include the consequences for the guard. Calculating exactly what the outcomes would be is, of course, an extremely difficult matter. We will say more about that when we look at some criticisms of the consequentialist approach to right and wrong.

While the approach may sound noble and has inspired many to live for others, it has also been criticized by many as being naïve and ultimately hurtful to the altruist whose needs seem left out entirely. If they're not left out entirely, they are certainly left to the good will of others. This, the critics say, is a serious weakness of altruism.

## The Egoistic Prescription

The Latin word *ego* means "self." **Egoism** is the form of consequentialism that takes the view that the right thing to do is what brings the best consequences for oneself only. On this view one would, for example, do good to others only in so far as doing so would bring the best consequences to oneself. Egoism says that the right thing to do is always determined by the ultimate effects on oneself.

Critics of egoism have argued that this is not what ethics is all about. Some would argue that this is the very antithesis of ethics, selfishness disguised as a moral philosophy. Defenders of egoism counter that this is not selfishness, but the spirit of enlightened self-interest. If everyone, they argue, had this enlightened interest in themselves, the world would be an ideal moral place. You would look after yourself and I would look after myself. In addition, we would both have some concern for one another in the event that some day we should need each other.

If Mrs. Braun were an egoist, she would consider the consequences of her proposed action—sex with the guard—for herself only. As an egoist, she would consider the welfare of others only to the degree that their welfare benefits her. An egoist doesn't scratch your back because you are itchy. She does it because tomorrow her back may itch and she may need you to scratch hers. Mrs. Braun, as an egoist, would look at her choices solely in terms of her own self-interest.

Many have defended egoism as the best ethical approach for individuals to take in life. Also, the defenders argue, if adopted by political parties and governments, the best possible social order will result. Critics, as noted above, see egoism very differently. Individual human beings, they say, are self-centred enough as it is. Self-interest comes naturally to us and egoism does nothing to counter this self-serving tendency. Like altruism, the critics argue, it is an extreme approach that misses the point of ethical concern.

## The Utilitarian Prescription

The most popular of the consequentialist approaches to ethical decision making is the utilitarian approach. Because they believe that consequences determine the rightness or wrongness of an act, utilitarians are clearly consequentialists. Where they differ from the altruists and the egoists, however, is in their belief that everyone affected by an act has to be taken into account. Unlike the altruist who argues for others only, and the egoist who argues for self only, the utilitarian argues for a consideration of both self and others.

Compared to the other two versions of consequentialism, utilitarianism immediately seems to be more balanced. Perhaps that has been a major factor in its wide appeal. **Utilitarianism**, then, says that the right thing to do is what brings the best consequences for both self and others. The fathers of utilitarianism are Jeremy Bentham (1748–1832) and John Stuart Mill (1806–1873). You're most likely to hear the utilitarian prescription expressed something like this: "The right thing to do is whatever brings the greatest happiness to the greatest number of people" (Mill, 1967, p.398). You may also hear the prescription in the following form: "The right thing to do is whatever brings the greatest good to the greatest number of people."

The utilitarians get their somewhat odd name from the concept of **utility**. Anything that is useful has utility. Sport utility vehicles (SUVs), for example, get their name from their sportiness and their usefulness. In our cities, to cite another example, we have public utilities. These are useful things like electricity, water, and garbage disposal. They are useful in our daily lives. The name *utilitarian* is applied to these consequentialists because they believe that the right thing to do in any circumstance is the action that is most useful in bringing about the greatest amount of good for everyone concerned.

If Mrs. Braun were a utilitarian, she would consider the results of her proposed liaison with the guard from the standpoint of its impact on both herself and others. She would try to calculate the utility of the liaison in bringing about good for everyone concerned. If she believes that more good than harm will come from having sex with the guard, then she will invite him in because it will be the right thing to do. If more harm will come than good, then she must not invite him in. That would be the wrong thing to do.

The utilitarian approach to ethics has been extremely influential in the lives of both individuals and groups in society. In other words, utilitarianism has been the preferred approach to ethics of many people at the personal level, but it has also influenced political parties, governments, and other groups within society. For this reason, we need to note some points in its favour and some points that weigh against it. Let's look at some arguments for and against utilitarianism.

## Arguments for Utilitarianism

Three things need to be said in favour of the utilitarian approach.

First, it is a consequentialist approach and therefore it requires the consideration of outcomes when making moral decisions. How our actions affect others is very much what ethics is all about. Utilitarianism recognizes that a consideration of consequences is essential to the moral life. We'll refer to this argument in support of utilitarianism as the *consequences argument*. You can't do ethics or be ethical, say the utilitarians, without considering the impact of your actions on other people. The concern for creating good consequences and avoiding actions that produce bad consequences is a most commendable feature of utilitarianism.

A second point must be made in favour of utilitarianism. While all ethical approaches talk about the fundamental principle of the moral life, the principle of goodness, the utilitarians make goodness central in their approach to ethics. The goodness principle, we will note repeatedly throughout our study of ethics, is the principle that says we ought to do good to others and not harm them. Utilitarianism is all about bringing good consequences to others and to ourselves. That, they remind us, is what ethics is all about. We'll call this the *goodness argument* in support of utilitarianism.

A third argument in favour of utilitarianism is the *balanced approach argument.* Utilitarianism takes a balanced approach to consequences, giving consideration to both self and others. In this regard, it seems to avoid the extremes of the other two consequentialist approaches. Utilitarianism, then, urges us to consider all the stakeholders who may be affected by an action, including ourselves. There seems to be an immediate sense of fairness in this balanced approach, a fairness that has been recognized and valued by many.

## Arguments against Utilitarianism

The first argument against utilitarianism is an argument that can be mounted against all forms of consequentialism. Since consequences are only future events at the time when we are considering what action to take, it is impossible to know whether the consequences we intend to bring about will in fact occur. This first challenge focuses on the difficulty or impossibility of calculating the consequences of one's proposed actions. We'll refer to this argument against utilitarianism as the *calculation argument.* How, for example, can the imprisoned Mrs. Braun be sure that she will get pregnant by the guard? How does she know that she won't get a disease instead of a baby, or that she won't get a diseased baby? She doesn't know because she can't know the future. She may live in hope, but she can't live with certainty regarding future outcomes of her actions.

I may firmly believe that my intended action will bring the greatest good for the greatest number, but I may be wrong in my belief. Perhaps more harm than good will result. Calculating the consequences of an action with any degree of precision or certainty is difficult, if not impossible. Remember, too, that the utilitarians have argued that outcomes, not intentions, determine right and wrong. They can't take comfort in good intentions. The point of this first criticism is that the utilitarian approach to ethics lacks certainty. People, the critics argue, will never know for sure that they are going to do the right thing.

A second argument questions the fairness and balance that utilitarianism seems to have. Critics claim that the utilitarian approach can easily lead to a **tyranny of the majority**. **Tyranny** means "dictatorship that is extremely oppressive." We'll call this the *tyranny of the majority argument.* If the right thing to do is what brings the greatest good to the greatest number of people (the majority), it may well be that some people (the minority) will be treated hurtfully in the process. Critics argue that utilitarianism can be used to justify the mistreatment of a minority in the cause of "the greatest good for the greatest number."

Let's take an example to illustrate the point of the criticism. The majority of people in a country might justify slavery on utilitarian grounds. If the cheap labour provided by a relatively few slaves resulted in the economic success of the great majority of citizens in the country, then slavery is the right thing to practise. The goal (end) of economic prosperity for the majority, has, in this example, been achieved by evil means, the enslavement of the minority. The end, in this case, does not justify the means. As we proceed in our studies, we'll pay special attention to the "means-ends" issue. It is frequently a point of contention in ethics. Does the end, in any particular case, justify the means in that case?

In the Police Fundraiser situation in Chapter 1, for instance, many would argue that the end (restoring capital punishment, for example) does not ethically justify the means (identifying supporters by window stickers). In the Sacrificial Adultery case, many would maintain that the end (Mrs. Braun's reunion with her family) does not justify the means (committing adultery). Later, in Chapter 9, we'll examine the use of deception in policing. There we'll consider undercover operations, for example, where lies may be told in an attempt to achieve the conviction of a criminal. Does the end (conviction) justify the means (lying)? The "means-ends" issue, we'll see, surfaces frequently in ethical reasoning.

A third argument against utilitarianism, the *promise-breaking argument*, maintains that the utilitarian approach to ethics threatens a fundamental practice of ethics and morality, namely, truth telling and promise keeping. Utilitarianism, critics argue, legitimizes the breaking of promises. A married person, for example, might justify sexual infidelity on the utilitarian grounds that an undetected love affair would bring about a greater overall amount of happiness to the world. The lovers are happier than they were before the affair, and the unknowing spouses are no less happy than before. Overall, in the universe of the lovers and the unknowing spouses, there is more happiness than there was before the affair. According to utilitarianism, then, having the affair is the right thing to do. But that conclusion runs counter to one of our most prized moral practices, the making and keeping of promises. This, of course, is a very serious concern. Once again, many people would argue that the end (happiness) does not justify the means (sexual infidelity).

Having examined the consequentialist approach, noting particularly some of the pros and cons of utilitarianism, we now need to explore the nonconsequentialist approach.

## NONCONSEQUENTIALIST PRESCRIPTIONS

Earlier in this chapter we noted that nonconsequentialism takes a very different approach to moral matters than does consequentialism. Nonconsequentialism, you will recall, takes the position that something other than consequences determines right and wrong. For example, the right thing to do is what your duty requires you to do, regardless of the consequences. In this example, doing your duty is the right thing to do. In other cases, nonconsequentialists argue that the right thing to do is what God commands or what your feelings prompt you to do.

As we did with consequentialism, so we will do with nonconsequentialism. We will take a brief look at two versions that have had a limited popularity and a somewhat limited influence. More time will be reserved for a third approach, one that has had a major influence on the field of ethics. The first two approaches are the *command of God* approach and *emotivism*. The third approach is called *duty ethics*.

### The Command of God Prescription

The title of this nonconsequentialist approach suggests that it is a religious approach. While that is clearly true, we need to note that it is not the approach of all religions, only some. Many religions take a consequentialist approach to moral matters. The approach that we are considering here, however, does not. It is an approach that cuts across major world religions and, therefore, manifests itself within many different religious traditions. This approach is typical, however, of the most conservative of religious persons and institutions.

These conservative religious persons believe that their holy books are the word of God and that God's commands and wishes are clearly written out for all to see. The Ten Commandments of the Jewish, Christian, and Islamic traditions, for example, would be prominent in the command of God approach within those religious traditions. For the conservative Jew, Christian, or Muslim, God has spoken in the sacred writings. The Ten Commandments tell humans what is acceptable and what is not acceptable to God. The prescription for living an ethical life, the righteous life, is to be found in the holy book.

According to the **command of God prescription**, the right thing to do is what God has commanded humans to do.

A couple of examples may be helpful here. If God has forbidden adultery, then adultery is wrong because God has forbidden it. If God has forbidden stealing, then stealing is wrong because God has forbidden it. On this view, it is God's command that makes things right or wrong. Adultery is wrong because God forbids it, and that is the end of the matter. Arguing that one might increase the world's happiness by having an adulterous affair simply has no place in the command of God view. Consequences do not make actions right or wrong; only the command of God makes right and wrong.

In the case of Mrs. Braun, if she were a religious person such as we are considering here, her moral dilemma would not be much of a dilemma at all. If God has said, "You must not commit adultery," then the matter is settled. She must not have sex with the guard. The worthy goals of reunion with her family and her personal freedom are irrelevant. They cannot justify committing adultery because God's command, not consequences, determines what is right and what is wrong. The right thing to do is to obey the command of God.

While many of the world's religious people may take this approach to ethics, it is quite clear that it is an approach limited to those who have a very particular set of religious beliefs. It is not an approach to ethics that has wide appeal. As noted in Chapter 2, it relies, first of all, on the unproved belief that God exists. It is also problematic in that different religions have different commands from their God. While some commands are the same from one religion to another, others are not. For example, in most, if not all religions, God forbids murder. In contrast, in some religions God forbids the drinking of alcohol while in others God does not. Has God forbidden, critics ask, the consumption of alcohol or not?

A second nonconsequentialist approach says that right and wrong are determined by one's feelings, not the commands of God. Let's now explore emotivism, a nonconsequentialist approach that says that the question of right and wrong is solely a matter of feelings or intuitions.

## The Emotivist Prescription

In Chapter 1, as we reviewed some basic features of our human nature, we noted that humans are feeling, thinking, and acting beings. We said that human beings have affective, cognitive, and behavioural dimensions. The emotivist takes the view that right and wrong are determined by what we feel. On the **emotivist prescription**, the right thing to do is what you feel is right. In other words, this nonconsequentialist approach does not look to the outcomes of actions but, rather, to the feelings of the moral agent (actor). This approach is sometimes called **intuitionism** because it argues that our intuitions (special feelings) determine what is right and what is wrong in human relationships.

The command of God prescription that we described in the previous section took the view that God's commands determined what is right and what is wrong. Emotivism takes the view that each individual's personal feelings determine what is right and what is wrong. We often hear people say, for example, "If it feels right for you, then it is right for you." A popular expression from the 1960s and 70s was, "If it feels good, do it!" The same view is sometimes expressed using the cognitive term *think*. For example, you may have heard someone say, "If you think it's right, then it is right for you."

This approach to ethics strikes many people as being very tolerant. "I wouldn't do it myself, but if it feels right for you, then it must be right for you." We examined this point of view in Chapter 2 when we reviewed ethical relativism. There we noted a position called

**individual relativism**, a position that says that right and wrong are relative to each and every individual. Emotivism is, in fact, individual relativism because it states that right and wrong are determined by the feelings of each person. We also called it **subjectivism** because it reduces right and wrong to individual feelings. In other words, it makes ethics totally subjective.

To return to Mrs. Braun once again, the emotivist maintains that the right thing for Mrs. Braun to do is whatever she feels is right. If she feels that sex with the guard is the right thing to do, then it is. If, in contrast, she feels that sex with the guard is the wrong thing to do, then it is wrong. Mrs. Braun just has to go with her feelings of the moment. She has to act solely on her intuition of the moment. Notice that the consequences of her action are not to be considered. According to emotivism, her feelings, not the outcomes of her action, will determine right and wrong.

We noted in Chapter 1 that feelings are an important part of our human experience. From our feelings come our values, what we feel most strongly about. Ethics is based, in part, on feelings, and many ethical issues evoke our strongest emotions. Take, for example, the passion that often accompanies debates on abortion or capital punishment. While feelings are an essential part of the moral life, they cannot be the sole basis for determining right and wrong as emotivism advocates.

A simple illustration will suffice to show that emotivism is an untenable position. If, for example, I convince myself that I must steal some money to pay my bills by month's end, I might begin to feel that it is the right thing for me to do. On the emotivist view, if I feel that it's right for me to take your money without your consent, then it is right for me to do so. Emotivism says that my feelings about my actions make my actions right or wrong. This, however, makes ethics completely subjective and purely a matter of individual feeling. Surely my feeling that it's okay to take your money can't make it right to do so. If a police officer feels like beating up on a prisoner, would the officer's feelings make it right? If an officer feels like taking a bribe, would the officer's feelings make it right to take the bribe?

The examples above reveal another flaw in the emotivist approach. If I feel that taking your money is right and you feel that it is wrong, then my taking your money is both right and wrong. Ethics seems reduced to matters of taste. You feel it's wrong so it's wrong. I feel it's right so it's right. How can this be? What would we say about sexual assault, a beating, or adultery? Emotivism reduces all ethical conflict to mere differences in feelings. Surely ethics involves more than this.

The emotivist (intuitionist) approach to ethics is a nonconsequentialist approach with serious flaws. The subjectivity of this position has led many to reject it in favour of an ethics that is more objective. In the next section we will examine one such approach that has had a great influence on our understanding of ethics. Let's take a look at duty ethics.

## The Duty Ethics Prescription

Duty ethics is the last nonconsequentialist position we will examine. It is also the most complicated of the nonconsequentialist positions. One of the most influential accounts of this approach to ethics is that of Immanuel Kant (1724–1804). Kant was a brilliant but complex thinker who tried to establish a nonconsequentialist ethics based on clear thinking. In other words, he looked to human reason as the determiner of right and wrong.

He was very much aware of those who took the command of God approach and the emotivist approach to ethics. Additionally, he knew the utilitarian approach to right and wrong.

Each of these positions, he believed, was seriously flawed in one way or another. Kant, therefore, set about to demonstrate that ethics was independent of religious belief, was not merely a matter of feelings, and that it required more than a utilitarian calculation of consequences. To put the same point differently, he tried to avoid and overcome the weaknesses of the command of God approach, the emotivist approach, and the utilitarian approach.

According to duty ethics, three things together determine right and wrong. First, an action is right only if it is a clear command of reason. Second, an action is right only if it treats other human beings as ends in themselves. This second point is a way of saying that all human beings are moral equals, each person deserving of respect. Third, an action is right only if it is motivated by duty. Combining these three elements into one statement, **duty ethics** says that the right thing to do is the action that is commanded by reason, respectful of the dignity of others, and motivated by duty. Let's consider each point in turn.

## "Commanded by Reason"

What did Immanuel Kant mean by a command of reason? To answer this question we need to note the other sources of ethical prescriptions for which others have argued. The command of God approach makes God the source of right and wrong. This approach requires religious faith, something that some people don't have, and something that differs from one person to another. Emotivism makes individual feelings the source of right and wrong. This approach makes ethics totally subjective, a matter of personal taste. Kant saw that neither of these sources could provide a clear and certain set of moral rules acceptable to all.

Turning to the field of mathematics, a field known for its clarity and certainty, Kant saw a model for ethics. Mathematical statements have two qualities that struck Kant as critically important. First, a statement in mathematics must be non-contradictory. If, for example, I ask you to draw a "circular triangle," you will rightly accuse me of talking nonsense. A triangle is a closed, three-sided figure whose interior angles total 180 degrees, and the concept of a triangle is logically incompatible with that of a circle. In my request to draw a "circular triangle," the concept of circle contradicts the concept of triangle. The definition of a triangle provided above, however, is not self-contradictory. Moral rules, Kant argued, are like mathematical statements. They cannot be self-contradictory. Putting the same point differently, a valid ethical command of reason must be non-contradictory.

In addition, a second quality of mathematical statements also impressed Kant. Mathematical statements are universalizable. Consider once again the definition of a triangle. Not only is the definition of a triangle non-contradictory, but it is also universalizable. In simple terms, *all* triangles are closed, three-sided figures. All individual triangles, regardless of when or where they exist, are closed, three-sided figures. The statement is universally true. Notice further that a statement that is self-contradictory (e.g., "This circle is a triangle.") is nonsensical, and, if you try to universalize nonsense, you end up with nonsense (e.g., "All circles are squares."). That is exactly what happens in Kant's famous example that follows next, the example of the proposed false promise (Kant, 1967, p.340).

For a prescription to be a moral command of reason, said Kant, it must be both non-contradictory and universalizable. Imagine that you are thinking of making a false promise. You will borrow some money from a friend, promise to return it, but you will not keep your promise. To test whether this proposed action is ethical or not, Kant says that we must put it into the form of a moral prescription or **maxim**, as he called it. If the proposed action is an ethical action, the maxim (1) must not be self-contradictory, and (2) must be universalizable. Your maxim would be: "I promise to return the money, but I don't intend to do so." Will this maxim pass Kant's tests for a moral rule, an ethical command of reason?

No. First of all, the maxim is self-contradictory. The first part ("I promise to return the money") is contradicted by the second part ("I don't intend to do so.") Your maxim is as self-contradictory as my earlier notion of circular triangles. Consequently, your maxim doesn't meet the first requirement for a moral rule or command of reason. It is nonsensical. What about the second criterion, universalizability? As noted above, if you try to universalize nonsense, you still end up with nonsense. Your maxim, consequently, fails to meet the second requirement of a moral rule or command of reason. A true command of reason, according to Immanuel Kant, is universalizable. To say that everyone should promise but nobody should keep their promises is illogical and nonsensical. Your maxim fails the test. Therefore, it cannot be a moral rule.

These two qualities of mathematical statements—their non-contradictory quality and their universalizable quality—argued Kant, are also necessary qualities of ethical prescriptions. In what has come to be called the **categorical imperative**, Kant said that an action is immoral if the rule authorizing the action cannot be made into a rule for all human beings to follow. "Act only according to that maxim by which you can at the same time will that it should become a universal law" (Kant, 1967, p.339).

In our example of the false promise, the proposed rule fails both the non-contradictory test and the universalizability test. The proposed false promise is self-contradictory and it is not universalizable. It fails to meet the rational requirements of the categorical imperative. Consequently, it cannot be a moral rule. It would be ethically wrong to act on such a rule.

Applying his test to existing moral rules, Kant believed that the basic rules of ethics were commands of reason. Don't murder, don't lie, don't steal, don't break your promises, and other fundamental norms of the moral life met the test in Kant's view. Human reason, not faith and not feeling, provides the rules of human ethical conduct. He believed that he had shown that the prescriptions for moral conduct are established by human reason and are, therefore, clear and certain. They are objective, not subjective. They are available to all humans, not just those who have religious faith.

Unfortunately, Kant's moral rules were, like mathematical rules, absolute rules. **Absolute rules** are rules that have no exceptions to them. Also, Kant failed to prioritize the various absolute commands that he identified. Because of these problems, Mrs. Braun, on the view of duty ethics, would have, for example, an absolute duty to care for her children. She would also have an absolute duty to be sexually faithful to her husband. The first of these duties might justify having sex with the guard. The second of the duties forbids having sex with the guard. Kant offered no way out of conflicts between duties that are both absolute. It is difficult to see how duty ethics could provide Mrs. Braun with any practical guidance for her situation.

## "Respectful of the Dignity of Others"

Kant was also convinced that the "end-justifies-the-means" approach of utilitarianism was seriously flawed. He could see, moreover, how utilitarianism could lead to a tyranny of the majority. Human reason, however, provides the antidote to these potential abuses of utilitarianism. A simple, fundamental principle of all ethical conduct is clear. It is the principle of equality, the principle that maintains that all human beings are born equal in dignity and worth.

Kant knew that there were murderers, liars, and thieves. He wasn't so naïve as to think that in actual practice everyone led a morally upright life. His point was, once again, a point of logic. The conceptual world of ethics requires an equality principle for ethics to make any sense. In making moral choices, for example, ethics requires me to abandon my personal biases and prejudices. I should not, for example, treat others differently because they are of a different race than I am. That action would be discriminatory. Reason says that racial, ethnic, gender, and other characteristics are irrelevant to doing what is ethical. When it comes to ethical decisions and actions, reason is blind to all characteristics but one, our humanity.

The principle of moral equality underlies Kant's **practical imperative**. It is also at the heart of the religious concept of the golden rule, which says, "Do unto others as you would have them do unto you." This religious "rule of thumb" for moral conduct is an expression of the rational principle of equality. It is the rational "rule of thumb" for doing what is right and avoiding what is wrong. Kant expressed the practical imperative like this: "Act so that you treat humanity, whether in your own person or that of another, always as an end and never as a means only" (Kant, 1967, p.345).

He was saying that we should never treat another human being as a means to an end. Each human being is a unique end in himself or herself. The practical imperative, if observed, guarantees that our conduct will always be respectful of the dignity of others. The equality principle, if observed in moral matters, will protect against the abuses of any approach that suggests that the end justifies the means. Discrimination against the few in the best interests of the many is a violation of the practical imperative and, therefore, wrong.

## "Motivated by Duty"

Kant's great concern for the subjectivity associated with feelings caused him to examine the issue of motivation and ethical behaviour. We all know how emotion can override reason in the experiences of life. The passion of sexual pleasure, for example, has resulted in many people abandoning reason for the feelings of the moment. In another example, many a person has regretted lashing out at another person in the emotional heat of the moment. Often, in these kinds of situations, lives have been ruined because people acted on their feelings rather than their reason.

In moral matters, emotion can easily lead to self-serving behaviour, and it often does. A person knows, for example, that unwanted sexual touching is a form of assault, but passion runs so high at times that the rules of proper conduct are ignored and an assault occurs. Immanuel Kant believed that all our human feelings, not just lust or anger, could corrupt our moral actions. In Kant's view, ethical conduct is a matter of doing one's duty. For this reason he saw duty as the only morally acceptable motive for action.

Kant's concern for doing one's duty can be illustrated with the following example. In Chapter 7 we'll explore the point in greater depth. For the moment, however, consider briefly the case of a police officer pulling a driver over for speeding and running a stop. Upon reaching the car, the officer discovers that the driver is a close friend. How will the officer deal with this situation? Acting on his feelings for his friend, the officer might let his friend off, something the officer would not be likely to do for a stranger. Kant would argue that this is morally wrong. The ethically correct thing to do is to act on one's duty, not one's personal feelings. The officer has a moral duty to protect the public, and the officer's personal feelings do not justify giving a dangerous driver, friend or not, a break.

The importance of doing one's duty in ethical matters needs to be underscored. Kant, however, went too far in the view of some critics. Is it not possible for people do their duty with feeling? Can police officers carry out their duty to help a citizen in distress and also have good feelings about helping the person in trouble? Can nurses look after patients and have caring feelings toward them as well? The answer to all three questions is yes. There are times when feeling prompts exactly what duty requires. Kant was concerned, however, for the many occasions when acting on one's feelings would lead to unethical action. For this reason, he argued that duty was the only morally acceptable motive for action.

Reason, he believed, establishes the moral rules, and reason also recognizes the principle of the moral equality of all human beings. Lastly, reason understands that acts performed out of duty are acts in which self-service has been set aside for the sake of some greater service. The nurses and police officers mentioned earlier do their duty in the face of repulsive or dangerous circumstances. They do their duty even when their personal feelings of revulsion or fear would direct a different course of action.

The duty ethics approach to ethics has much to be said for it. It is a serious and well considered attempt to eliminate the problems associated with the other approaches to ethics that we have reviewed. It is not free of its own problems, problems that we have not explored in this account. Despite its imperfections, it is difficult to imagine a workable ethical approach that would not include the practical imperative, the principle of basic moral equality. Moreover, the emphasis on duty can act as an antidote to the excesses of personal feeling, especially in societies that place high value on individual rights.

## PRESCRIPTIVE ETHICS AND POLICING

Throughout this chapter I have attempted to point out certain connections between utilitarianism, duty ethics, and policing ethics. In later chapters, we will return to examine several issues in greater detail. For the moment, however, let's note three of them that are particularly important.

First, the utilitarian emphasis on doing good and preventing harm is central to policing. The fundamental duty of an officer, for example, is to "serve the community; to safeguard lives and property; and to protect the innocent ..." (The Law Enforcement Code of Ethics, 1991, par.1). In other words, the primary obligation is to do good and prevent harm. Also, the "end-means" concern that arises out of utilitarian thinking will occupy our attention on a number of occasions in our examination of ethical reasoning in policing. When, in policing, does the end justify the means, and when does it not?

Second, the Law Enforcement Code of Ethics begins with an immediate reference to a police officer's duty. Doing one's duty, we saw in our recent review of duty ethics, is essential to the moral life, including ethical conduct in policing. Among the emphases made by the duty ethics tradition is that of treating all people as moral equals. Treating people equally, as we will see, is what professional policing codes of conduct require. We'll return to the important subject of impartiality in the performance of duty later in our study, especially in Chapter 7.

Third, the various codes of ethics that we'll examine in the next chapter and throughout our study are all prescriptions for doing the ethically correct thing and avoiding those actions that are considered to be wrong. This chapter has introduced you to both the descriptive and prescriptive dimensions of ethics. It has focused, however, on prescriptive ethics. In particular, it has focused on the utilitarian and duty ethics contributions to our understanding of what ethical conduct is all about. In Chapter 4, we will look at a number of specific codes of conduct. Remember that each of them is a prescription for ethical conduct.

## CHAPTER SUMMARY

In this chapter we have extended our study of ethics to include the important areas of descriptive and prescriptive ethics. When doing descriptive ethics we examine the way things actually are in the world. We do this in order to do a better job in the area of prescriptive ethics, the part of ethics where we state how things ought to be. The former deals with the actual, and the latter with the ideal.

Next we distinguished between consequentialist and nonconsequentialist approaches to ethics. Consequentialists always look to the outcomes (consequences) of a proposed action in order to decide whether that action is right or wrong. In contrast, nonconsequentialists always look to something other than the consequences of a proposed action to determine whether that action is right or wrong.

We then described and commented on three consequentialist prescriptions: altruism, egoism, and utilitarianism. Altruism considers the consequences for others only, egoism considers the consequences for oneself only, and utilitarianism considers the consequences for self and others. Because of its greater influence, we examined utilitarianism in more detail than the others. We noted that that the utilitarian emphasis on consequences, goodness, and balance were positive elements in its favour. Problems related to calculating consequences, "end-means" thinking, and promise breaking, however, were all negative aspects of the utilitarian prescription.

Next, we studied three nonconsequentialist prescriptions: the command of God, the emotivist, and the duty ethics approaches. The command of God approach maintains that the will of God determines right and wrong, and emotivism maintains that one's feelings determine right and wrong. Duty ethics maintains that human reason determines right and wrong. It maintains, further, that ethical conduct requires impartial and respectful treatment of others, done for the sake of duty. We devoted more time to duty ethics because of its greater influence on the field of ethics.

We concluded our look at prescriptive ethics by emphasising the influence of the utilitarian tradition on policing ethics as well as influences from the duty ethics approach. In this chapter we were somewhat general in our presentation of these connections. In future chapters, we pointed out, we will return to these influences and examine them in much greater detail.

## MASTERING THE MATERIAL

Now that you have read this chapter, use the following guides to ensure that you have mastered the material.

## Introduction

1. What do the following dimensions of ethics deal with?
   (a) the analytical dimension
   (b) the descriptive dimension
   (c) the prescriptive dimension

## Descriptive Ethics

1.  Define *descriptive ethics.*
2.  What role does descriptive ethics play in the issue of doctor-assisted suicide?
3.  What role does descriptive ethics play with respect to the *deterrence argument* in the capital punishment debate?
4.  What is the "is-ought" mistake?
5.  Using deviance within policing as an example, explain the difference between prescriptive and descriptive ethics.

## Consequentialism and Nonconsequentialism

1.  Define *consequence.*
2.  Describe the consequentialist and nonconsequentialist approaches to ethics.

## Consequentialist Prescriptions

1.  Identify three different consequentialist prescriptions.
2.  Describe the following: altruism, egoism, and utilitarianism
3.  How did John Stuart Mill express the utilitarian prescription?
4.  Identify and explain three arguments for utilitarianism.
5.  Identify and explain three arguments against utilitarianism.

## Nonconsequentialist Prescriptions

1.  Explain the command of God approach to ethics.
2.  Explain the emotivist approach to ethics and give two other names for emotivism.
3.  Give the duty ethics prescription for ethical behaviour.
4.  State the categorical imperative of duty ethics.
5.  According to duty ethics, what are two essential qualities of a moral rule?
6.  State the practical imperative of duty ethics.
7.  State the golden rule.
8.  According to duty ethics, what is the only acceptable motive for moral actions?
9.  Which one of the five basic principles is the equivalent of the practical imperative?

## Prescriptive Ethics and Policing

1.  How is the utilitarian influence reflected in the fundamental duty of police officers?
2.  How is the duty ethics influence reflected in a police officer's professionalism?

## CRITICAL THINKING IN POLICING: THE PRINCIPLES MODEL

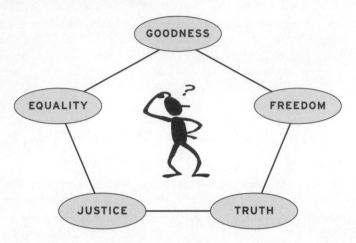

The five basic principles of the PRINCIPLES Model underlie all ethical prescriptions, regardless of whether the prescriptions are consequentialist or nonconsequentialist in origin or orientation.

## CRITICAL THINKING IN POLICING: THE DECIDE PROCESS

**D**efine the issue carefully.

**E**mploy the equality principle.

**C**onsider the consequences for all.

**I**nvolve all five principles.

**D**ecide with integrity.

**E**valuate your decision.

The DECIDE Process consists of a series of six steps based on the problem solving method of the sciences. It's designed to guide your thinking through a series of considerations that will result in ethical choices and actions.

| Media Watch: Ethics in the News 3.1 | The moral case for employment equity |
|---|---|

Ontario's new employment equity law, the first in Canada, will nudge public and private employers to live up to principles of equality most of them pay only lip service to. The law is needed to remove the barriers women, natives, the disabled and non-whites continue to face in finding jobs and getting promotions.

Statistics Canada data are irrefutable: These groups do *not* get a fair break. They are neither hired nor promoted in proportion to the *qualified talent* among them. Despite higher levels of education and labour participation rates, visible minorities remain under-employed. Natives and the disabled remain on the margins. Women among them do even worse, as do women of colour.

In tackling such systemic discrimination, the NDP government's new law, proclaimed Thursday, is eminently reasonable.

It does *not* set hiring quotas. It lets employers define goals and timetables. It gives them lots of time, not so much to hire from the designated groups as to lay down a plan to do so. It exempts companies with less than 50 workers. If anything, it is not bold enough.

It has no teeth to get at recalcitrant employers, while it imposes bureaucracy on the good ones. It does *not* cover the construction industry where unions, not employers, assign journeymen to job sites. It bows to another union sacred cow, seniority, which gets in the way of promoting new talent. It lets self-regulating professions—doctors, engineers, etc.—continue denying access to many, by arbitrarily refusing to recognize foreign degrees, training and experience.

But the NDP has chosen to move gingerly in the face of much grumbling, of the same sort that greeted federal moves in the 1970s to bring francophones into the civil service, and the bid in the 1980s to hire women. There are now, as then, many misconceptions:

- **That the law will discriminate against white males.**

Actually, the system has discriminated *in favour* of white males, as managers have followed the natural tendency to hire their likes. A white male usually hires another because that's what he feels most comfortable with. Employment equity simply seeks to end this discrimination and put everyone on a level playing field. How can anyone object to that?

- **That the law may lead to hiring of unqualified people.**

Employers don't go hunting for dunderheads, but inadvertently end up with some, including white males. As Judge Rosalie Abella, inventor of equity plans, said: "Why shouldn't women and visible minorities be entitled to their share of dummies?" Better still, why must we presume that women and non-whites are second-raters?

It is, however, possible that lazy employers will hire unqualified people just to get the government off their backs. They'll have themselves to blame because the law obliges them only to recruit in proportion to the *available talent* in designated groups, as listed by StatsCan for every profession in every region. If a Sudbury legal firm cannot find trained native lawyers, it need not let overzealous bureaucrats push it into hiring one. Nor should employers succumb to reverse discrimination and exclude white males from jobs. Job equity should stand for fairness, not retribution.

- **In slotting people by gender and colour, the law pushes us into an apartheid-like system which South Africa has just axed.**

This offensive distortion is a new twist on the old line that we're sacrificing individual rights at the altar of collectivities.

Unlike the U.S., Canada always has recognized group rights—natives, for a series of special treatments; Catholics and Protestants, for separate schools; anglophones and francophones, for linguistic guarantees; Quebecers, for the Civil Code. Why is identifying people by gender or colour or disability any more repugnant?

Fair-minded people who believe in true equality and justice for all would support the job equity law with the same moral vigour as they do the laws for a minimum wage or safe working conditions.

Source: *Toronto Star*, September 3, 1994, B2.

---

## Media Watch: Ethics in the News 3.2

## Courts should not reinstate a bad law

Like dinosaurs that escaped extinction and now emerge from a jungle swamp, some outdated ideologues have appeared in court to terrify Ontario. The Alliance for Employment Equity would drag us where we would not willingly go, down a dark, dead-end path of paranoia, by forcing the return of an unfair law that ordered reverse discrimination.

Scary. Most Ontarians will pray the alliance fails. And if the courts work as they should, a parade of appeals will end in the group's defeat.

Voters already passed judgment on the Employment Equity Act of the former NDP government. In the 1995 election, an overwhelming majority rejected it, choosing the Tories who pledged to scrap it, or the Liberals who promised to radically change it. One of Mike Harris's first and most popular acts was to axe this detested, detestable bit of legislation.

It isn't that Ontarians favour workplace discrimination. Overwhelmingly, they don't. What they couldn't stomach was a law that ordered every employer with 50 or more workers to label staff according to race, sex, or whether they were disabled or Aboriginal. Then the employer had to make every job category reflect the makeup of the community. "Quotas" weren't admitted. But numbers were the heart of the law. Employers had to put in place "targets" for hiring and promotion. For a stick, the law wielded $50 000 fines.

The act was contrived, illogical, punitive and offended public ideals of justice. In the worthy cause of fighting discrimination, the NDP institutionalized its own brand of prejudice and drove a wedge into the fissures of race and gender running through the province.

The law would have punished individuals innocent of any wrongdoing while compensating others who had never been wronged. Even before it passed, people in Waterloo Region saw the injustice of affirmative action when the Kitchener fire department rejected a white male applicant in favour of women and visible minorities he outscored on tests.

No court will order the reintroduction of the NDP legislation. Judges know their job is to enforce existing laws, not write new ones. The people fighting this case are right when they say the Charter of Rights forbids discrimination based on race, sex or disability. But they are wrong to believe that the Charter forces governments to pass specific laws, in particular the excessive law brought in by the NDP.

There is still work to be done fighting discrimination in Ontario. But Bob Rae's Employment Equity Act is dead and buried. Exhuming it now would be truly terrifying.

Source: *Kitchener-Waterloo Record*, November 1996, A10.

## chapter four

# Codes of Conduct: Examining the Ethical Standards of a Civil Society

## LEARNING OUTCOMES

After completing this chapter, you should be able to

- Distinguish among values, principles, and norms
- Describe two ways of satisfying human needs
- Define *ethical code* (*moral code* or *social code*)
- State prescriptions for moral conduct from Hindu and Buddhist religious traditions
- Identify four community values within the Ten Commandments of the Jewish, Christian, and Muslim religious traditions
- Summarize the rights and freedoms of the Universal Declaration of Human Rights
- Summarize the rights and freedoms of the Canadian Charter of Rights and Freedoms
- Identify six forms of misconduct specified by the Code of Conduct of the Ontario Police Services Act
- Identify the fundamental duty of a police officer from the Law Enforcement Code of Ethics
- Describe eight qualities of an ideal police officer as presented in the Law Enforcement Code of Ethics

# INTRODUCTION

In Chapter 1 we described the basic human needs that contribute to individual and group value systems. **Values**, you will recall, refer to all the things that are important to an individual or a group. Since food, water, and shelter are necessary for survival, human beings place high value on them. In addition, the satisfaction of social needs such as affiliation, achievement, and power are important. All the things associated with the satisfaction of these various needs are valuable to humans.

Nature, we noted, doesn't always provide enough food and water for everyone. At times, human beings in conflict add to the problem. Shortages occur because of circumstances created by human beings as well as by Mother Nature. In addition, human greed causes some to satisfy their needs and wants without concern for the welfare of others. Consequently, life often becomes a struggle between and among humans, who are all determined to survive. In situations like these, and even in times of plenty, the human effort to satisfy needs and wants can move in either of two directions.

On the one hand, people can enter into a "state of war," exercising stealth and power for the betterment of themselves and the members of their group. Naturally, this is a great risk because others will do the same thing. Life then becomes an uncivilized jungle in which "might makes right." That is, life becomes a matter of survival of the fittest. We should note, also, that even within civilized communities, some individuals and some groups behave as outlaws. They attempt to satisfy their own needs and wants by unlawful means, at the expense of others. This approach is what we have called an uncivilized approach, in which life is very likely to be nasty, short, and brutish.

In contrast, people can co-operate with one another, using principles of ethical or moral reasoning. **Principles**, you will recall, are the basic ideas upon which other ideas are built. Compromise, for example, can be a practical way of trying to satisfy one's basic needs while allowing others to do the same. Fair distribution of whatever supplies are available can replace vicious and selfish actions. This approach is the approach of ethics and the law in a civil society. This is the approach of those who are civilized.

When people take the civilized approach, they establish **norms**, or rules of conduct, that everyone in the group is to follow. Communities are created and members strive to satisfy their needs co-operatively, according to the rules. In this chapter, we will focus on a number of codes of ethics, identifying the basic values and principles that are the foundation of these codes. It is the application of these values and principles to the specific problems of human life and relationships that allows for a civilized solution to human problems. This is the way of ethical reasoning, the way of civilized communities.

# ETHICAL OR MORAL CODES

I indicated in Chapter 1 that I will use the terms *moral* and *ethical* interchangeably. Our subject in this section is what we sometimes call moral codes and at other times call ethical codes. What is a moral or ethical code? The answer is very simple. A **code**, first of all, is a set of norms, rules or expectations. An **ethical code**, then, is a set of rules that prescribes moral conduct within a community. It specifies what a community will or will not accept in the relationships between and among its members.

If codes are intended for entire societies, we refer to them as **societal codes**. If they are intended for groups of professionals within a society, we call them **professional codes**. Below, we will study both societal and professional codes, providing specific examples of both kinds. The Canadian Charter of Rights and Freedoms, for example, is a societal code. In contrast, the Law Enforcement Code of Ethics is a professional code.

Later in this chapter we will also note that the entire human race can be viewed as a single community for which there are basic ethical principles derived from universal human needs and values. Often, in a world of exceptional ethnic and racial diversity, we tend to see ethics as the relativist does. It's hard to see the shared values and principles in such a diverse world. Underlying the surface differences, however, there are human beings struggling in their own ways to survive and thrive. There are, we will see, basic moral principles that are essential to civilized life. We refer to these principles as **universal principles** because no group can live as a community without employing these principles in its codes of conduct. Before we look at some modern codes based on universal principles, let's first take a brief look at some ancient ones.

## CODES FROM RELIGIOUS TRADITIONS

Some of the world's oldest codes of conduct are found within religious communities. In addition to religious duties and ritual duties, the world's religions have prescribed moral conduct or **social duties**. We mentioned these duties in our review of ethics and religion in Chapter 2. Social duties, you will recall, are codes of conduct. Hinduism, for example, requires practitioners of Raja Yoga to refrain from causing harm to others, lying, stealing, engaging in sexual misconduct, and being greedy. In addition, Hindus who practice Raja Yoga must keep themselves clean, develop contentment, practise self-control, cultivate meditation, and devote themselves to contemplation (Smith, 1958, p.48).

Another religious tradition, Buddhism, recommends the Eightfold Path to spiritual peace. Among the eight steps that lead to spiritual bliss are steps that constitute an ethical code of conduct. Faithful Buddhists must not kill, steal, engage in sexual misconduct, tell lies, or drink intoxicants. The moral code also forbids earning one's living from occupations such as slave owning, drug dealing, and prostitution (Smith, 1958, p.106). Such occupations are outlawed by the code because of the harm they bring to members of the community.

Jews, Christians, and Muslims share the Ten Commandments, a code of conduct that dates back thousands of years to the time of Moses. Also known as the Mosaic Code, this social code has been extremely influential in shaping conduct in the Western world. What values and principles of the ancient Jewish community underlie the ethical requirements of their code? Reflection on this community and its rules can give us a clearer picture of the relationship of values and principles to the norms or rules of the group. Let's look briefly at this community and its code of conduct.

## THE TEN COMMANDMENTS

Centuries ago, according to Jewish belief, God gave Moses a set of commandments that Moses then passed on to the Jewish people, the Children of Israel. These commandments have become, over centuries, the basic moral code of Jews, Christians, and Muslims. The code provides us with an interesting set of religious obligations and moral rules. The fact that the code comes from a religious tradition is not our concern. We simply want, at this point, to note some features of this well-known code.

The Ten Commandments, in a modern translation, follow:

1. Worship no god but me.
2. Do not use my name for evil purposes.
3. Worship and rest on the holy day.
4. Respect your father and mother.
5. Do not murder.
6. Do not commit adultery.
7. Do not steal.
8. Do not accuse anyone falsely.
9. Do not desire another person's spouse.
10. Do not desire another person's property.

## Underlying Values

We will limit ourselves to an examination of commandments four through eight because they provide a good example of a moral code, a code that states a person's obligation to one's fellow human beings. Let's look in greater detail, now, at those commandments that form an ethical code of conduct within the Ten Commandments. Remember that we are focusing on this code in order to identify its underlying values. Later, we will do the same kind of thing with respect to other codes, particularly law enforcement codes of conduct.

Within the Jewish community, the fourth commandment requires respect for one's parents, the fifth forbids murder, the sixth forbids adultery, the seventh forbids theft, and the eighth forbids lying. All of these rules stipulate what is expected in the individual's relationships with other members of the community. What values of this ancient community underlie these rules of the code? What things of importance were protected by the rules of the community?

First, the community clearly valued the family unit. In virtually all societies, the family is seen as the key building block of the community, and it must have been so for this ancient Jewish community. Family, their code says, is important. The fourth commandment requires children to respect their parents, and the sixth requires spouses to respect one another by not cheating sexually. Both of these commandments are designed to protect the family, a critically important part of the Jewish value system.

Second, they valued human life. Modern translations of the ancient texts capture the true meaning of the fifth commandment. It prohibits murder, the wilful and unlawful killing of another human being. The fifth commandment shows that the Jewish people valued the lives of the members of their community. No civilized community can, of course, condone the wanton killing of its own members. Every civilized community must forbid such behaviour. Failure to do so would result in anarchy.

Third, the Jewish community valued truth telling and honesty. The eighth commandment forbids members making false accusations against others. "Don't accuse anyone falsely" is another way of saying "Don't tell lies about others." Obviously, truthfulness and integrity are essential within a group if members are to build and maintain trusting relationships. The co-operation necessary for the development of community is based on truthfulness and trust. In order for families and communities to develop as strong units, the people involved must value the truth and they must act with integrity.

Finally, this ancient Jewish community valued personal property. The seventh rule forbids taking what doesn't belong to you. It recognizes that personal property is important to people whether they have acquired it by inheriting it, receiving it as a gift, or working to get it. The rule forbidding theft respects legitimate ownership of personal property, something important to all members of the community.

Whatever groups feel strongly about, they will protect by establishing rules for all members to follow. Those things of greatest value to the community will be reflected in its moral code, its statement of the basic rules for conduct within the community. Having looked at the ethical code of this ancient and relatively small community, let's turn now to the largest community we know of, the human community. An examination of the United Nations Universal Declaration of Human Rights is most interesting in that it addresses all members of the family of nations.

## THE UNIVERSAL DECLARATION OF HUMAN RIGHTS

The Mosaic Code that we just examined is an ancient code that dates back thousands of years. We turn our attention now to a code that was written at the end of World War II. After the devastation of the second great global conflict of the twentieth century, the nations of the world, through the United Nations, wrote the Universal Declaration of Human Rights (the Declaration). Written and published in 1948, the Declaration states the rights of each individual human being within the global community of nations. The Declaration continues to set forth the ideal of a civil society into the twenty-first century.

Civil societies, you will recall from Chapter 1, have three defining characteristics. First, they are free or democratic. That is, the members of civil societies participate in the election of their governmental leaders. Second, civil societies are pluralistic. They are made up of a variety of different groups, none of which has absolute power. Power is balanced among the various constituents of the society. Third, no one is above the law. Civil societies are marked by the rule of law. The Declaration provides the human community with a template or pattern, as it were, for civilized life.

One of the interesting things about this modern code is that it is in many ways similar to the ancient code of Moses. While interesting, this point is not really that surprising. When any group of people establishes norms of conduct for its members, certain basic principles will be essential to the building and maintaining of a community. These principles were essential within the ancient Jewish community, and they are essential to building a community of nations in modern times. Underlying any attempt to create a community of individuals that can work in a co-operative fashion are certain basic moral or ethical principles. Before identifying these principles, let's take a look at the Universal Declaration.

The Universal Declaration is composed of two parts, the Preamble and the Articles. The **Preamble**, or introduction, states in seven short paragraphs why the Declaration is necessary. Having provided the reasons, the document presents the 30 **articles** that comprise the substance of the Declaration. At this point, I'll paraphrase the statements of the

Preamble and then summarize the Articles. The full text of the Declaration can be found in the Appendices.

## Paraphrasing the Preamble

Whereas recognition of human dignity and human rights is essential for freedom, justice, and peace in the world,

Whereas past disregard for human rights has resulted in barbarous acts, and a new and free world has become the highest goal of the human family,

Whereas human rights must be protected by the rule of law if rebellion against tyranny and oppression is to be avoided,

Whereas the United Nations have reaffirmed their faith in human rights, human dignity, and human equality, and have determined to promote social progress and better standards of life in a freer world,

Whereas member nations have pledged to promote universal respect for and observance of human rights and freedoms,

Whereas a common understanding of these rights and freedoms is essential to the keeping of this pledge,

Now, therefore,

The General Assembly,

"Proclaims this Universal Declaration of Human Rights as a common standard of achievement for all peoples and all nations, to the end that every individual and every organ of society, keeping this Declaration constantly in mind, shall strive by teaching and education to promote respect for these rights and freedoms and by progressive measures, national and international, to secure their universal and effective recognition and observance, both among the peoples of Member States themselves and among the peoples of territories under their jurisdiction."

## Examining the Preamble

Noteworthy, at the beginning of and throughout the Preamble, is the emphasis on the dignity and equality of each individual human being. This emphasis, you will recall, is the same one that Immanuel Kant made with the practical imperative in duty ethics. He recognized that a rationally based ethics requires the concept of the equal dignity of each individual. If individuals have equal dignity, then it follows that they have equal rights.

Article 1 of the Universal Declaration describes this moral dignity and the equality of rights of the individual in the following words: "All human beings are born free and equal in dignity and rights. They are endowed with reason and conscience and should act toward one another in a spirit of brotherhood."

Neither the United Nations nor Immanuel Kant was so naïve as to think that this equality is actually practised in the world. The Preamble, for example, mentions "barbarous acts that have outraged the conscience of mankind." Both could see injustice on all sides. Both recognized, however, that an ethical community that wished to achieve co-operation among its individual members had to begin with the basic principle of equality. Both recognized, further, that the rule of law requires this same principle.

The Preamble says that if rebellion is to be avoided, individual human rights must be protected by the rule of law. In Chapter 1 we noted this point, arguing that any government that regularly disregards individual rights invites rebellion from the citizenry. We see, in this part of the Preamble, the close connection between ethics and the law. That relationship we examined in a preliminary fashion earlier in the text. We will continue to note and study the relationship between ethics and the law as we proceed.

Before summarizing the individual articles of the Declaration, we need to make careful note of the purpose of the Preamble's emphasis on individual rights. The opening paragraph says that the "recognition of the inherent dignity and of the equal and inalienable rights of all members of the human family is the foundation of freedom, justice, and peace in the world." In other words, respect for individual rights is the rational foundation for establishing a community that can enjoy freedom, justice, and peace. That, of course, is the essence of civilized life and the goal of all civil societies.

## Summarizing the Articles

### Equality Rights and Freedoms (Articles 1–5)

The Declaration first underscores the equality of all human individuals. It then guarantees the rights and the freedoms of the Declaration to everyone without discrimination on the basis of race, colour, sex or other superficial characteristics. The right to life, liberty, and security of person is affirmed. Next, the Declaration guarantees freedom from slavery and inhumane treatment of any kind that is inconsistent with the rights noted above.

### Legal Rights and Freedoms (Articles 6–12)

Next, the legal rights and freedoms of members of the human family are addressed in several articles. Recognition before the law and protection of the law are mentioned first. Freedom from arbitrary arrest, presumption of innocence, and the right to fair and impartial trial follow. In addition, freedom from arbitrary interference with one's privacy, family, home, and correspondence are guaranteed, as is protection of one's reputation.

### Mobility Rights and Freedoms (Articles 13–15)

Three articles address mobility rights and nationality rights. First, mobility rights are guaranteed to all. Each person has the right to move about freely within his or her homeland, to leave and return to one's country, and to seek asylum outside one's country should that become necessary. Next, the right to nationality, to belong to a country, is also guaranteed.

### Family Rights and Freedoms (Articles 16–17)

First, marriage and family rights and freedoms are articulated. These include the right to marry and found a family with spouses being free to enter into their marriage arrangements. Next, the right to own property alone or in association with others is affirmed.

## Expression Rights and Freedoms (Articles 18–20)

Three articles speak to freedom of thought, conscience, and religion. The right to express one's thoughts, beliefs, and opinions is also affirmed, as is the right of peaceful assembly.

## Political Rights and Freedoms (Articles 21–22)

Political rights, the right to elect governments, to participate in them, and to receive services from them are all emphasized in Article 21. Social and cultural rights that are necessary for social security and the development of both personality and dignity are affirmed in Article 22.

## Employment Rights and Freedoms (Articles 23–25)

Next, rights to work and leisure are affirmed. The right to a decent standard of living and security are guaranteed. Also guaranteed is protection against the loss of these rights due to unemployment or sickness. So, too, are the special needs of mothers and children.

## Educational Rights and Freedoms (Articles 26–27)

The right to an education that fosters personal development, the promotion of peaceful relationships, and participation in the arts and sciences is guaranteed.

## Rights and Duties (Articles 29–30)

The second-last article underscores the duty of individuals to their communities. It also stipulates that the rights and freedoms of each individual are limited by an equal consideration of the rights and freedoms of others. The last article states that no person or group has the right to destroy any of the Declaration's rights and freedoms.

## THE CANADIAN CHARTER OF RIGHTS AND FREEDOMS

Readers who are familiar with the Canadian Charter of Rights and Freedoms (the Charter), the Ontario Human Rights Code, and similar codes from other jurisdictions will immediately recognize the similarities between these codes and the Universal Declaration of Human Rights. These other codes are patterned after the Declaration, and the important thing for us to note is the fact that all these codes are based on the same fundamental ethical principles, principles such as equality, justice, and freedom.

We should also emphasize the fact that the Canadian Charter of Rights and Freedoms is the document used to determine the legitimacy of all Canadian laws. As such, it is Canada's most important legal document. In later chapters we will make a number of references to the Charter as we examine particular ethical issues. For the moment, we are simply making note of the important connection between the Universal Declaration, the Charter, and Canadian law.

As I did with the Declaration, I will now do with the Charter. I will provide a brief paraphrase and summary of the document. The full text of the Charter can be found in the Appendices.

## Summarizing the Charter

The introduction to the Charter is straightforward, stating that Canada is founded upon principles that recognize the supremacy of God and the rule of law.

### Guarantee of Rights and Freedoms (Section 1)

The Charter indicates immediately that the rights and freedoms that it guarantees are not absolute. They are limited, but only by reasonable legal limits that can be justified in a free society.

### Fundamental Freedoms (Section 2)

The fundamental freedoms guaranteed to everyone are the following: freedom of conscience and religion; freedom of thought, belief, opinion, and expression; freedom of peaceful assembly; and freedom of association.

### Democratic Rights (Sections 3–5)

Every citizen of Canada has the right to vote in elections. The maximum term of office of a government is set at five years, with an extension being allowed in time of war. Elected members must sit at least once per year.

### Mobility Rights (Section 6)

This section guarantees citizens freedom of movement within Canada and the freedom to leave and return to Canada. Citizens can move in order to reside in another province and to seek employment in that province.

### Legal Rights (Sections 7–14)

First, the Charter guarantees the right to life, liberty, and security of person. Then it protects citizens against unreasonable search, seizure, detention, and imprisonment. If citizens are arrested or detained, they must be informed promptly of the reason. Moreover, they have the right to counsel and the right to have the validity of their detention determined.

If citizens are charged with an offence, they have the right to be informed promptly of the reason, to be tried within a reasonable time, and to be presumed innocent until proven guilty. Innocence or guilt is to be determined in a fair and public hearing by an independent and impartial tribunal. Furthermore, every citizen has the right to trial by jury for serious offences. If acquitted of an offence, citizens cannot be tried for that offence again. So, too, if they have been convicted and have served their sentence.

Protection against cruel and unusual punishment is guaranteed. In addition, witnesses providing evidence are protected against self-incrimination, except where perjury is committed.

### Equality Rights (Section 15)

Protection from discrimination based on race, national or ethnic origin, colour, religion, sex, age, or disability is guaranteed in this section. Everyone is equal before and under the law, and everyone has equal protection and benefit of the law. Provision is made for laws and programs whose purpose is the betterment of disadvantaged individuals or groups.

## Language and Other Rights (Sections 16–34)

Guarantees regarding the right to use the official languages of Canada are provided. Provincial language rights in New Brunswick are made clear. In addition, the right to minority language education is affirmed.

The enforcement of the Charter is addressed, Aboriginal rights and freedoms are guaranteed, and the application of the Charter is made clear.

## PROFESSIONAL CODES

The Declaration and the Charter can be described as societal codes in that they spell out the expectations for the conduct of all members of a civil society. Professional codes of ethics, we saw earlier, differ from these societal codes in that the professional codes are prescriptions for the conduct of members of particular groups within the larger society. Consequently, professional codes are much more specific in their focus. We'll see, however, that they employ the same basic ethical principles that societal codes do.

Members of a profession form a subgroup within the broader society. They are, in effect, subcultures that establish sets of rules for their members, specifying how their members are to relate to one another and the rest of society. An important part of any subculture is the values and principles that shape the subgroup's code of conduct. A group of professionals within a community, for example, will establish a code of ethics to govern the relationships between its members and the people the profession serves. Such codes state the expectations of the profession for its members. Doctors, nurses, teachers, police, and many other professional groups have such codes.

If we consider the function of professional codes in terms of the public served by the profession, not the profession itself, at least three purposes can be identified. First, the code can function to assure the public that they will receive a certain kind of service from members of the profession. Second, the code can serve to improve public relations, allowing, for instance, the public to understand the profession's standards and practices. Codes can also function as a kind of liability protection against frivolous attempts to criticize the profession should such attempts arise (Kleinig and Zhang, 1993, p.9).

Within the profession itself, a code of conduct can serve a number of different purposes. First, it can provide individual members with personal standards of professional practice. Second, the profession may use its code as a focal point for establishing an organizational ethos or sense of identity. Third, codes can be used as benchmarks for measuring member performance and improving it. Last, professional codes are often used as teaching devices, orienting new members to the profession's standards of practice (Kleinig and Zhang, 1993, p.13).

It will be useful for us to examine certain aspects of professional codes for two reasons. First, we can gain a better understanding of what ethics is all about. Second, and more specifically, we can identify the basic principles that are at the heart of such codes. We also need to underscore the important point that a profession's code must not contradict the broader moral code of society. Professional codes, we'll see, must and do complement the basic moral and legal position of the larger community.

Before we examine some specific codes of conduct from the field of law enforcement, let's consider the following situation. You may want to write down your responses to the questions at the end. Hopefully, you will also have an opportunity to discuss the case with others. After you've considered the situation carefully, look for any statements from the codes below that speak to the situation. Some statements will be obviously relevant. Others may not be so obvious.

| SITUATION 4.1 | Lunch at Al's Diner |
| --- | --- |

It's your fifth week on the job as a newly hired police officer. Your shift partner, a senior constable with 15 years experience, stops at Al's Diner, a popular family restaurant where the two of you take your lunch break together. The diner is almost full, but your server quickly finds you a table and takes your order. You both order a hamburger deluxe, coffee, and pie. At the end of the meal, as you get some money out to pay for your lunch, the senior officer tells

you that there's no need to pay. He tells you that lunch is always "on the house" at Al's. Turning to Al, who is across the room, your partner smiles, waves, and heads out to the cruiser without paying. Al waves back, smiles, and says, "See you again soon!"

What would you do in this situation? Explain your reasoning. We'll return to Al's Diner later. Before we do, we need to examine some law enforcement codes of conduct.

## LAW ENFORCEMENT CODES

We'll now take a look at some specific codes of conduct from the field of law enforcement. Following are the Code of Conduct from the Ontario Police Services Act (OPSA) and the Law Enforcement Code of Ethics (1991) of the International Association of Chiefs of Police (IACP).

## The Code of Conduct (Ontario Police Services Act)

### CODE OF CONDUCT

1.   In this code of conduct,

"record" means any record of information, however recorded, whether in printed form, on film, by electronic means or otherwise, and includes correspondence, a memorandum, a book, a plan, a map, a drawing, a diagram, a pictorial or graphic work, a photograph, a film, a microfilm, a sound recording, a videotape, a machine readable record, any other documentary material, regardless of physical form or characteristics, and any copy thereof.

2.   (1) Any chief of police or other police officer commits misconduct if he or she engages in,

(a)   DISCREDITABLE CONDUCT, in that he or she,

   (i)   fails to treat or protect a person equally without discrimination with respect to police services because of that person's race, ancestry, place of origin, colour, ethnic origin, citizenship, creed, sex, sexual orientation, age, marital status, family status or handicap,

    (ii)  uses profane, abusive or insulting language that relates to a person's race, ancestry, place of origin, colour, ethnic origin, citizenship, creed, sex, sexual orientation, age, marital status, family status or handicap,

   (iii)  is guilty of oppressive or tyrannical conduct towards an inferior in rank,

   (iv)  uses profane, abusive or insulting language to any other member of a police force,

    (v)  uses profane, abusive or insulting language or is otherwise uncivil to a member of the public,

   (vi)  wilfully or negligently makes any false complaint or statement against any member of a police force,

  (vii)  assaults any other member of a police force,

 (viii)  withholds or suppresses a complaint or report against a member of a police force or about the policies of or services provided by the police force,

   (ix)  is guilty of an indictable criminal offence or a criminal offence punishable upon summary conviction,

    (x)  contravenes any provision of the Act or the regulations, or

   (xi)  acts in a disorderly manner or in a manner prejudicial to discipline or likely to bring discredit upon the reputation of the police force;

(b)  INSUBORDINATION, in that he or she,

    (i)  is insubordinate by word, act or demeanour, or

   (ii)  without lawful excuse, disobeys, omits or neglects to carry out any lawful order;

(c)  NEGLECT OF DUTY, in that he or she,

    (i)  without lawful excuse, neglects or omits promptly and diligently to perform a duty as a member of the police force,

   (ii)  fails to work in accordance with orders, or leaves an area, detachment, detail or other place of duty, without due permission or sufficient cause,

   (iii)  by carelessness or neglect permits a prisoner to escape,

   (iv)  fails, when knowing where an offender is to be found, to report him or her or to make due exertions for bringing the offender to justice,

    (v)  fails to report a matter that is his or her duty to report,

   (vi)  fails to report anything that he or she knows concerning a criminal or other charge, or fails to disclose any evidence that he or she, or any person within his or her knowledge, can give for or against any prisoner or defendant,

  (vii)  omits to make any necessary entry in a record,

 (viii)  feigns or exaggerates sickness or injury to evade duty,

   (ix)  is absent without leave from or late for any duty, without reasonable excuse, or

    (x)  is improperly dressed, dirty, or untidy in person, clothing or equipment while on duty;

(d)  DECEIT, in that he or she,

    (i)  knowingly makes or signs a false statement in a record,

      (ii)  wilfully or negligently makes a false, misleading or inaccurate statement pertaining to official duties, or

     (iii)  without lawful excuse, destroys or mutilates a record or alters or erases an entry therein;

(e)  BREACH OF CONFIDENCE, in that he or she,

      (i)  divulges any matter which it is his or her duty to keep secret,

     (ii)  gives notice, directly or indirectly, to any person against whom any warrant or summons has been or is about to be issued, except in the lawful execution of the warrant or service of the summons,

    (iii)  without proper authority, communicates to the media or to any unauthorized person any matter connected with the police force,

    (iv)  without proper authority, shows to any person not a member of the police force or to any unauthorized member of the force any record that is the property of the police force;

(f)  CORRUPT PRACTICE, in that he or she,

      (i)  offers or takes a bribe,

     (ii)  fails to account for or to make a prompt, true return of money or property received in an official capacity,

    (iii)  directly or indirectly solicits or receives a gratuity or present without the consent of the chief of police,

    (iv)  places himself or herself under a pecuniary or other obligation to a licensee concerning the granting or refusing of whose licence a member of the police force may have to report or give evidence, or

     (v)  improperly uses his or her character and position as a member of the police force for private advantage;

(g)  UNLAWFUL OR UNNECESSARY EXERCISE OF AUTHORITY, in that he or she,

      (i)  without good and sufficient cause makes an unlawful or unnecessary arrest, or

     (ii)  uses any unnecessary force against a prisoner or other person contacted in the execution of duty;

(h)  DAMAGE TO CLOTHING OR EQUIPMENT, in that he or she,

      (i)  wilfully or carelessly causes loss or damage to any article of clothing or equipment, or to any record or other property of the police force, or

     (ii)  fails to report loss or damage, however caused, as soon as practicable; or

(i)  CONSUMING DRUGS OR ALCOHOL IN A MANNER PREJUDICIAL TO DUTY, in that he or she,

      (i)  is unfit for duty, while on duty, through consumption of drugs or alcohol,

     (ii)  is unfit for duty when he or she reports for duty, through consumption of drugs or alcohol,

    (iii)  except with the consent of a superior officer or in the discharge of duty, consumes or receives alcohol from any other person while on duty, or

    (iv)  except in the discharge of duty, demands, persuades or attempts to persuade another person to give or purchase or obtain for a member of the police force any alcohol or illegal drugs while on duty.

(2) A police officer does not commit misconduct under subclause (1)(e)(iii) if he or she engages in the described activity in his or her capacity as an authorized representative of an association, as defined in section 2 of the Act.

(3) A police officer does not commit misconduct under subclause (1) (f)(iii) if he or she engages in the described activity in his or her capacity as an authorized representative of an association, as defined in section 2 of the Act, or of a work-related professional organization.

3. Any chief of police or other police officer also commits misconduct if he or she conspires, abets or is knowingly an accessory to any misconduct described in section 2.

This particular code of conduct enjoys an interesting status among professional codes. It is obviously a professional code of conduct, but it is one whose significance is so great that it has been written into law. In other words it is both an ethical code and a legally enforceable one. Not all professional codes of conduct, however, are enshrined in law.

In the next section we will examine another professional code of ethics. Our examination of professional codes has the same purpose as our studies of the Ten Commandments and the modern Universal Declaration of Human Rights. That purpose is to identify the ethical values and principles that form the basis for the rules of any civilized group. When we look at professional codes, we are obviously looking at codes of conduct that exist within the framework of a larger community. As we pointed out earlier, professional codes must be consistent with the codes of the broader society of which the profession is a part.

Before turning to the next code, what statement or statements from the OPSA Code of Conduct relate directly to the situation you faced at Al's Diner? Why do you think those statements are included in the Code? To put the last question differently, what is so important to the persons who wrote the code that they would include those particular norms? What values and principles, in other words, underlie these particular parts of the Code?

## The Law Enforcement Code of Ethics

In 1957 the International Association of Chiefs of Police developed The Law Enforcement Code of Ethics (IACP Ethics, 1957), a code of ethics for police officers. It was accompanied by another document called the Canons of Police Ethics (IACP Canons) at the time of its release. Together, they functioned as the standard code of ethics for police services in Canada, the United States, and other countries for some 30 years. In 1991, the IACP produced an updated version of the Code of Ethics (IACP Ethics, 1991) that differed only in the language that it used. The substance of the Code remained unchanged. Once again, when issued in 1991, the Code was accompanied by the Canons.

Two years earlier, in 1989, another code was developed that adopted a new form and, to some degree, new content. This document was called the Law Enforcement Code of Conduct (IACP Conduct, 1989). Despite some initial controversy over the Code of Conduct, it has taken its place alongside the two versions of the Code of Ethics and the Canons as the IACP's official codes of conduct. Together, they serve as codes of conduct for professional police officers in many countries.

As you read the Code of Ethics below, keep the following questions in mind: What values does the Code support? What principles underlie the Code? What behaviours are prohibited or required? Also, identify specific statements in the Code that relate to the situation at Al's Diner. Remember that values are things of the heart, things that are most important to the group. Principles are the basic ideas of the Code and they relate directly to the stated or implied values. Behaviours are, of course, the actions that are being encouraged or discouraged by the Code. Finally, before examining this code, note that it takes the form of a solemn pledge rather than a set of rules.

## Law Enforcement Code of Ethics (1991)

As a law enforcement officer, my fundamental duty is to serve the community; to safeguard lives and property; to protect the innocent against deception, the weak against oppression or intimidation and the peaceful against violence or disorder; and to respect the constitutional rights of all to liberty, equality and justice.

I will keep my private life unsullied as an example to all and will behave in a manner that does not bring discredit to me or to my agency. I will maintain courageous calm in the face of danger, scorn or ridicule; develop self-restraint; and be constantly mindful of the welfare of others. Honest in thought and deed both in my personal and official life, I will be exemplary in obeying the law and the regulations of my department. Whatever I see or hear of a confidential nature or that is confided to me in my official capacity will be kept ever secret unless revelation is necessary in the performance of my duty.

I will never act officiously or permit personal feelings, prejudices, political beliefs, aspirations, animosities, or friendships to influence my decisions. With no compromise for crime and with relentless prosecution of criminals, I will enforce the law courteously and appropriately without fear or favour, malice or ill will, never employing unnecessary force or violence and never accepting gratuities.

I recognize the badge of my office as a symbol of public faith, and I accept it as a public trust to be held so long as I am true to the ethics of police service. I will never engage in acts of corruption or bribery, nor will I condone such acts by other police officers. I will co-operate with all legally authorized agencies and their representatives in the pursuit of justice.

I know that I alone am responsible for my own standard of professional performance and will take every reasonable opportunity to enhance and improve my level of knowledge and competence.

I will constantly strive to achieve these objectives and ideals, dedicating myself before God to my chosen profession ... law enforcement.

What statement or statements of this code relate to the situation at Al's Diner? Once again we need to ask questions. Why do the authors include them in the Code? What is so important to them that they make them a part of the officer's pledge? What values have prompted them to include the relevant statements?

Let's now examine this code as we did the Ten Commandments. Remember that we are looking for answers to questions like the ones we noted earlier: What values does the Code support? What principles underlie the Code? What behaviours are prohibited or required? Before you continue with the next paragraph, you may want to write down what you think are the basic values and principles that underlie the Law Enforcement Code of Ethics.

## The Fundamental Duty

The Code begins with the "fundamental duty" which states clearly that police officers are to "serve the community." Service to the community, in other words, is the basic obligation of the law enforcement officer. The word *service* is critically important because it implies that police officers are not above the communities in which they work. They serve the community in a variety of ways that the Code goes on to stipulate.

More specifically, officers serve in three ways. They serve the community by safeguarding lives and property, protecting citizens, and respecting the constitutional rights of citizens. What values underlie the various statements of this code? What is important to police services in a civil society? Obviously, what is important to policing and society is a certain kind of police officer, an officer who displays the qualities that the Code emphasizes. Officers who possess these qualities will do their jobs well within a policing agency. They will also function as role models within the society that they serve.

## ROLE MODELS

The second paragraph of the Code makes an interesting and most important point. The Code requires the law enforcement officer to be exemplary in both her private and professional life. The pledge is to "keep my private life unsullied" and "behave in a manner that does not bring discredit to me or my agency." This is, in effect, a requirement to be a model at all times, on duty or off.

It's also important to note that the ethical standards set by the Code are demanding. Police officers occupy a special place in the life of a civil society. They are guardians of societies that are built on individual freedom and the rule of law. As such, officers are to be models for all members of society, models of the highest standards of ethical conduct.

Let's now note some of the specific characteristics of a police officer that are valued by both policing agencies and society. Eight characteristics are evident within the various statements of the Code: courage, self-restraint, altruism (concern for others), honesty, obedience (to the law and departmental rules), trustworthiness (keeping information confidential), impartiality, and professionalism. There are a number of important points to be made with regard to each of these qualities. Also, remember that we are focusing on only one code at the moment and that the list of eight qualities is not exhaustive.

The qualities described below express the values of the IACP. They express the qualities of character that are most important in a police officer in a civil society. Values, as we have noted, give rise to principles that, in turn, give rise to norms of conduct. In this code the norms are stated as a series of promises rather than a set of rules. Here are the qualities of the ideal officer, a model for all members of a civil society.

## Courageous

Policing can be a risky business, one that requires courage. **Courage**, of course, is bravery in the face of danger. Officers may face danger in many ways as they carry out their duties. The Code captures the range of possible dangers in a brief but important statement: "I will maintain courageous calm in the face of danger, scorn or ridicule." Danger includes both physical and psychological threats. We are well aware of the many physical perils that officers may face. In addition to those, the Code mentions "ridicule" and "scorn," dangers that might be called psychological. Later, the officer promises to enforce the law courteously, appropriately, and "without fear." Threats, for example, will not prevent officers from carrying out their duties.

When a community is threatened in any way, it is critically important that citizens see their protectors as courageous persons. The confidence of the community is at stake. If members of the community perceive their guardians as being fearful, then fear strikes the entire community, and the consequent upset can easily lead to disregard for the law. Fear and lack of confidence in one's designated protectors may, for example, lead to vigilante justice. In such cases, fear results in a form of lawless conduct that is incompatible with life in a civil society. Civil societies need courageous protectors in order that citizens will remain calm in the face of danger.

## Self-Restrained

As was noted above, the constitutional rights of all citizens are of utmost importance. When officers pursue lawbreakers they often do so under very stressful circumstances. In attempting to calm an unruly crowd, for instance, they may face "danger, scorn, and ridicule." Under such stressful conditions the temptation to react in anger is great. But uncontrolled anger is not a civilized response; it is a part of life in the "jungle"; it is gut reaction, not reasoned response. How extremely important it is, then, that law enforcement officers practise **self-restraint**, self-control of one's emotions or impulses.

If a suspect has insulted an officer, put the officer at great risk, and then spit in the officer's face, personal feelings urge the officer to administer immediate retribution in order to "teach this guy a lesson he'll never forget." That, however, is not the professional approach, the one that requires officers to exercise self-restraint and to act in accord with the highest legal and ethical standards.

To keep one's emotions under control in a tense situation and to function on the basis of reason and the law is a most demanding quality, and a most admirable one. The Code clearly recognizes the importance of an officer's capacity to exercise self-restraint. This, however, is but one example of the importance of this quality. Officers frequently have easy access to the possessions of others and the opportunity for quick but illegal profit. Officers who lack self-restraint and indulge themselves, at the expense of the community, harm individuals and bring their profession into disrepute.

## Altruistic

Another important quality expected of the law enforcement officer is **altruism**, concern for the welfare of others. Our culture tends to encourage the opposite, self-interest and self-indulgence. Think, for example, of the following expressions that are less than altruistic: "Always look out for number one," "Nice guys finish last," "If it feels good, do it," and "Do your own thing." Each of these expressions promotes self-indulgence rather than concern for others. Civil societies, societies that value individual rights, must always balance self-interest with the interests of others. This code recognizes that fact and recognizes, further, that police officers are models of altruism.

The Code requires that officers be "constantly mindful of the welfare of others." It is important that officers have concern for others, just as they have a concern for themselves. In order to be altruistic, we noted in Chapter 1, a person needs to have empathy for others. You will recall that **empathy** is the ability to feel what someone else is feeling. The Code clearly expects officers to be empathetic and altruistic in a world that often promotes only self-interest. Once again, we see the importance placed on service to others, and, once again, we see the high moral standards established by the Code.

## Honest

Next, the Law Enforcement Code expects **honesty** or truthfulness from officers. Honesty and integrity are critically important for any relationship. It's honesty and integrity that allow us to trust one another. If police are to be trusted by the people they serve, then officers need to be honest. Think for a moment of a situation in which someone has lied to you about some important matter and you have found out. Your relationship to that person is immediately affected in an important and negative way.

It's no different for police officers in their relationships with the members of the community in which they serve. If our protectors lie to us, then whom can we trust? Truth and honesty are critically important in all human relationships, and this code clearly recognizes that fact. The reputation of both the individual officer and the profession are at stake. One quick way for officers to bring discredit both to their agency and to themselves is to be dishonest in words or actions.

## Trustworthy

If people are **trustworthy**, you can put your confidence in them. They are reliable and worthy of one's trust. One thing that fosters trust between people is the keeping of confidences. Officers routinely see and hear things that are the private and personal business of members of the community. Should officers inappropriately communicate this information to others, citizens might be humiliated or otherwise harmed. Confidentiality is valued by all. Breaching confidentiality destroys trust, keeping confidences builds it.

Confidentiality is, of course, related closely to the honesty that we examined briefly above. In the case of honesty, the point is that the officer must not willingly distort truths that he has come to know. In the case of confidentiality, it is a matter of not communicating, inappropriately, certain information that the officer has come to know. In each case, a breach of the principle—confidentiality or honesty—can easily lead to mistrust of both the officer and the agency. A community's guardians must be trustworthy in the eyes of the community members.

## Obedient

The Code also requires obedience of officers. To be **obedient** is to comply with the law or the orders of superiors. In the oath, the officer swears "obedience to the law and the regulations of my department." Obedience is often seen in a negative light in societies that value individual freedom. Conformity and obedience are very similar concepts, and they often limit individual self-expression. A moment's reflection, however, will make clear that no community can function effectively without thoughtful and reasonable obedience, both to leaders within the community and to the rules of the community. Societal and organizational inefficiency would be the minimal result, and chaos would be the worst-case scenario.

## Impartial

Serving the community in a highly professional manner requires officers to rise above their own personal "feelings, prejudices, political beliefs, aspirations, or friendships" to serve in accordance with the ethical standards of the agency and the legal standards of society. Officers are to serve and protect with impartiality. To be **impartial** is to be fair-minded, objective, and unbiased. It is easy and quite natural for us to favour our friends in any given situation. It is easy to do something that agrees with our political beliefs. It is easy to act from personal prejudice. The difficult challenge to law enforcement officers is to follow duty and the standards of their profession when personal inclinations lead them in other directions.

One critically important aspect of professionalism is the capacity to act with impartiality. To be impartial, as we noted above, means to be objective. It means that the professional rises above stereotypical thinking, with its attendant prejudices and discrimination, and deals with people and situations in an unbiased and rational manner. The professional police officer, for example, does not play favourites. He discriminates neither for nor against others. He carries out his duties "without fear or favour, malice or ill will."

In Chapter 7 we will explore this extremely important matter of professional impartiality in greater detail. For the moment, however, let's note two things that will be a part of that discussion. We'll return to Al's Diner to make the points.

First, in accepting a gratuity from Al, the officers may be compromising their impartiality. In other words, they may not be able to deal objectively with Al if, for example, they pull him over for reckless driving the next day. They may see him as a friend rather than a dangerous driver and treat him differently from other dangerous drivers. They may play favourites when duty requires them to be objective for the good of the public.

Second, the other customers in the diner may get the impression that the police have their favourites, people like Al, and that the police can be bought. In a civil society, police officers are expected to be impartial, and the perception of that impartiality is critically important for the delivery of police services. Both impartiality and the perception of impartiality are critically important for police services within a civil society. We'll return to this subject later.

## Professional

All professions expect their members to continually improve their levels of theoretical knowledge and practical skills. Policing is no exception. To be **professional** is to function at the highest level of knowledge and skill. In the Code, officers assume personal responsibility for their professional development and commit to it. While the statement within this code is very brief, statements from other codes make the specifics clear. Among other things, officers are to know the limits of their authority, be familiar with the law, relate effectively to members of the public, co-operate with other officers and agencies, and understand the justice system.

The Canons that accompany the IACP Code of Ethics emphasize the importance of diligent study and self-improvement. In order to carry out the important responsibilities entrusted to them, officers must apply the sciences to their work, establish and maintain effective human relationships, and provide educational leadership with respect to public safety. By constant learning and self-improvement, officers "hold police work to be an honourable profession rendering valuable service" to community and country.

## CHAPTER SUMMARY

In this chapter we first described the relationship of values and principles to norms, pointing out that the values and principles of a group generate the rules of conduct of the group. Next we reviewed two ways by which people can attempt to satisfy their needs, one an uncivilized way and the other a civilized one.

After defining the expressions *ethical code, moral code, societal code,* and *professional code,* we noted ethical codes of conduct within the religious traditions of Hinduism and Buddhism. We then examined the Ten Commandments, an important code for Jews, Christians, and Muslims. We focused our attention on commandments four through eight, describing them as a moral code. We identified the values that the ancient Jewish community protected with these commandments. Among the many things that they valued were family, life, truth, and property.

Next, we turned to important societal codes. The Universal Declaration of Human Rights is the United Nation's statement on the rights of individuals within the family of nations. The intention is that the code be applied within the social life of all member nations. We paraphrased the Preamble, examined its statements, and then summarized the Articles of the Declaration. We also noted its relationship to the Canadian Charter of Rights and Freedoms and went on to summarize the articles of Canada's most important legal document.

Turning our attention to the nature of professional codes, we identified several purposes served by such codes. They can be used to assure the public, contribute to the improvement of public relations, and provide insurance against challenges to the profession. Inside the profession, they can function as personal standards of performance, contribute to a sense of professional identity, and serve as teaching tools.

Next we examined the Code of Conduct of the Ontario Police Services Act, noting the six forms of misconduct identified by the Code. These included discreditable conduct, insubordination, deceit, corrupt practice, unlawful or unnecessary exercise of authority, and damage to police property.

An examination of the Law Enforcement Code of Ethics of the International Association of Chiefs of Police followed next. We saw that the Code, expressed as an oath, identifies the fundamental duty of an officer as the duty to serve the community. Such service includes the safeguarding of lives and property, the protection of citizens, and respect for the right of all citizens to life, liberty, and justice. The Code further requires police officers to be models of courage, self-restraint, altruism, honesty, obedience, trustworthiness, impartiality, and professionalism.

## MASTERING THE MATERIAL

Now that you have read this chapter, use the following guides to ensure that you have mastered the material.

## Introduction

1. Define the following: *values, principles, norms*

## Ethical or Moral Codes

1. Define the following: *code, ethical code, moral code, societal code, professional code*

## Codes from Religious Traditions and the Ten Commandments

1. State 10 norms of conduct from Hinduism's Raja Yoga.
2. State six norms of conduct from Buddhism's Eightfold Path.
3. Which commandments among the Ten Commandments form a moral code?
4. What four values underlie the moral code of the Ten Commandments?

## The Universal Declaration of Human Rights

1. What is the Universal Declaration of Human Rights?
2. State six reasons for the Declaration from its Preamble.
3. Identify eight categories of rights and freedoms from the Articles.
4. State the duty required of every individual.

## The Canadian Charter of Rights and Freedoms

1. What document was a model for the Canadian Charter of Rights and Freedoms?
2. What role does the Charter play with respect to Canadian law?
3. Identify six categories of rights and freedoms from the Charter.

## Professional Codes and Law Enforcement Codes

1. State three external functions and three internal functions of professional codes of ethics.
2. Identify six forms of misconduct from the Code of Conduct of the OPSA.
3. Identify the fundamental duty of an officer from the Law Enforcement Code of Ethics.
4. What are the three ways in which the fundamental duty is carried out?
5. What are the eight characteristics of an ideal police officer?
6. Which ethical principle underlies the non-discrimination rule in the Code of Conduct of the Ontario Police Services Act?
7. What group developed the Law Enforcement Code of Ethics and Code of Conduct?

## CRITICAL THINKING IN POLICING:
## THE PRINCIPLES MODEL

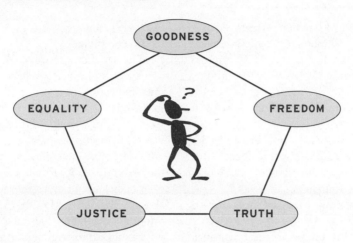

The figure in the centre of the PRINCIPLES model is you, the moral agent. Your personal freedom to make an ethical choice is limited by considerations that must include all five of the principles of ethical reasoning.

## CRITICAL THINKING IN POLICING:

**D**efine the issue carefully.

**E**mploy the equality principle.

**C**onsider the consequences for all.

**I**nvolve all five principles.

**D**ecide with integrity.

**E**valuate your decision.

## THE DECIDE PROCESS

The DECIDE Process guides your reasoning through steps that will maximize your understanding of moral issues and allow you to make personal choices that are ethically defensible.

## Media Watch: Ethics in the News 4.1

## 5 Cambridge police officers awarded for excellence

Five Cambridge police officers received awards at Cambridge Council Monday for their excellence in fighting crime.

Cambridge MPP Gerry Martiniuk, a member of the Ontario Crime Control Commission, presented the awards to the officers.

They included Sgt. Frank Sinko, Const. Pat Lilley, Const. Eugene Silva, Const. Tony Christiansen and Const. Elefterios Liargovas.

The men were praised for their work on two cases.

One was related to the break-in at MicroAge Computers on Bishop Street in April 1999.

A police investigation began after a fire was set at the computer warehouse to cover up the break-in and theft of 138 laptop computers.

The second case involved catching a suspect as he was robbing a restaurant, the fourth in a string of robberies in the city.

Sgt. Wally Hogg said the officers were able to stop the man and arrest him without firing their guns, even though the man refused to drop his handgun.

"They showed great communication skills." The John Howard Society of Waterloo-Wellington was also presented with an award for fighting crime.

Source: *Kitchener-Waterloo Record*, July 11, 2000, B3.

## Media Watch: Ethics in the News 4.2

## Beyond the call of duty

Like many professionals, police may find a certain routine in their work. There isn't much glory in picking up residents who are inebriated or in holding a radar gun on a busy street.

But police work does have an element of drama. Police officers never know when they will risk their lives to help people in distress. Whether their split-second decisions succeed or fail, they deserve recognition.

The medallions that the Waterloo regional police department awarded last week to several officers are an attempt to provide that recognition. The officers indeed deserve commendation: Curtis Rutt, for his efforts at the Parkhill Dam in Cambridge, Dave Shaw and Kevin McCarthy for rescuing a boy in a fire, and Paul Wilkie for trying to save two children in a fire. Frank Monteiro also received a citation for an investigation.

When interviewed about awards, police officers often seem slightly embarrassed to be called heroes. They say they were just doing their job. This reluctance, to seek public praise is no reason why it shouldn't be given.

Source: *Kitchener-Waterloo Record*, October 14, 2000, A18.

## chapter five

# Principles: Identifying the Basic Ethical Concepts of a Civil Society

## LEARNING OUTCOMES

After completing this chapter, you should be able to

- Identify the five basic principles of ethical reasoning
- Describe certain relationships among the principles
- Explain the relationship of the basic principles to the law
- Describe the role of ethical debate in establishing or changing the law
- Provide examples of each principle from two societal codes of conduct
- Provide examples of each principle from two professional codes of conduct

## INTRODUCTION

We began our study of ethics in Chapter 1 by exploring the role of ethics in a civil society. Human beings, we noted, possess both reasoning powers and emotion. In taking action to satisfy their basic needs and their wants, members of human groups can co-operate according to certain rational principles, or they can do battle with one another for any available resources. Humans, we said, can attempt to satisfy their needs in a civilized or an uncivilized manner. The members of a civil society are committed to the way of ethics and the law, the way of the civilized. So, too, are society's guardians, the police.

At the end of the last chapter, we noted a number of characteristics typical of the ideal police officer. Among those traits were self-restraint and impartiality. These traits illustrate particularly well how the role of the police officer is based upon the values of a civil society. Officers are called, for example, to exercise self-control in circumstances that provoke a person to respond in anger. A courageous, self-controlled reaction to such situations is desirable. It is likely to cool things down. Angry outrage stemming from personal feelings is not. Such reaction will tend to inflame the situation.

Officer impartiality in the exercise of duty further illustrates the point. Impartial treatment of citizens, based on the principle that all citizens are of equal worth, is the way of the civilized. In contrast, policing motivated by preference or prejudice is the way of tribalism, the way of the uncivilized. When officers favour certain people and discriminate against others, they display behaviour associated with uncivilized and unethical conduct. In Chapter 7, where we explore the principle of equality, we'll examine the subject of impartiality in greater detail.

Members of a civil society must see beyond the sphere of their own personal needs satisfaction to the needs of other members of the group. They have to have a certain degree of empathy and be sufficiently altruistic to commit to rules that permit all members of the group to have a fair chance to survive and thrive. Police officers who live by the ethical standards of their professional codes serve and protect all citizens equally and, in the process, model the ideals of civil society in their conduct.

In a civil society, the establishing of new rules or the changing of existing rules is also conducted on the basis of rational considerations. When members of a civil society set about to establish a new law, a public debate is conducted. In Canada, for example, at the federal level, the debate occurs in the House of Commons and the Senate. The debate takes place between parties that share common ethical principles, the ones we explore in this chapter. The parties differ, however, in the value they place on one principle over another in a specific situation. The abortion debate provides a good example.

Both extremes in the abortion debate value the principles of life and freedom. They also share other ethical principles such as equality, justice, and truth. Given a different moral issue, like pornography, opponents in the abortion debate might well agree with each other. In the matter of abortion, however, one side places greater value on a woman's freedom to choose while the other side places greater value on the life of the unborn. What is most important to the two parties, what they value, in this particular situation is obviously different.

When the government of a civil society enacts a law on any important issue, the enactment does not usually end the debate. This is understandable because the opponents prior to enactment will, in all likelihood, hold the same values after the law has been established. Opponents will use the same common principles to continue the debate that arises out of differing values. The common principles, as noted above, are the subject of this chapter. We will describe each of them in detail below.

In Chapter 2 we saw that rational consideration of a community's norms involves defining terms so that everyone has a common understanding of the issue in question. We saw, furthermore, that logic must be applied in the debate that takes place regarding the law. Such debate, if it is to meet the rational standards of a civil society, must obey the rules of logic and be based on the facts of the situation in question. Our study of **analytical ethics** was intended to clarify the aspect of ethics and the law associated with language and logic. We also pointed out that the determination of the facts of any given case is the domain of **descriptive ethics**. In this chapter and throughout the remaining chapters we will continue to apply the insights of both analytical ethics and descriptive ethics to our subject.

The attempt to say what is right conduct and what is wrong conduct falls to **prescriptive ethics**. In Chapter 3 we looked at two influential traditions within the realm of prescriptive ethics, namely, the consequentialist and nonconsequentialist traditions. Of particular interest to us were the utilitarian prescription and the duty ethics prescription. More recently we examined five specific prescriptions or codes of conduct: the Ten Commandments; the Universal Declaration of Human Rights; the Canadian Charter of Rights and Freedoms; the Ontario Police Services Act, Code of Conduct; and the Law Enforcement Code of Ethics.

The basic principles of ethical reasoning that we will describe in the next sections are the essential principles of a civil society. These principles are at the heart of ethical discussion and debate, and these same principles are at the heart of the laws of a civil society. They are the principles that police officers of a civil society are sworn to uphold. No group can function co-operatively as a community if these principles are not adhered to by most of its members. Let's identify these basic principles and comment on various aspects of their significance.

## THE PRINCIPLES OF ETHICAL REASONING

Five basic principles are essential to life in a moral community or civil society. These principles are absolutely necessary if any group is to live with a degree of harmony and co-operation among its members. What are the five principles of ethical reasoning? They are the goodness principle, the equality principle, the justice principle, the truth principle, and the freedom principle. In simpler terms, they are goodness, equality, justice, truth, and freedom. These are, of course, the five principles of the PRINCIPLES Model that are incorporated in the six steps of the DECIDE Process. We'll now examine each principle in turn.

## THE GOODNESS PRINCIPLE

The fundamental concept of ethics is that human beings ought to do good and not harm one another. To do the ethical thing is to do what is right, what brings good to members of the community. People may not agree, in a specific situation, as to what the right thing to do is, but no one will argue that the right thing to do is to hurt or harm other members of the community. To do what is moral or ethical is to do what brings good consequences to members of the group.

Expressed as a positive duty, the goodness principle says: "Do good." To do good for others is, of course, to act in ways that make their lives better or prevent their lives from becoming worse. If a person is starving to death, then providing her with food is a good thing. It is the right thing to do. If a person is freezing in the cold, then providing him with a warm place to stay is a good thing to do. It is the right thing to do.

The goodness principle can also be expressed as a negative duty: "Don't harm." Human beings can harm or hurt one another in many ways. Harm may be physical as in death or injury. It may be psychological as in the case of threats and terror. Harm may be economic as in theft or fraud. Much of ethical discussion is devoted to identifying the many harms that humans ought not to do. Codes, like the Criminal Code of Canada, spell out the most important of these harmful actions and indicate the punishments that will result if members of the community harm others in these ways. All of the codes of conduct that we have examined thus far include, directly or by implication, the principle of goodness.

The fundamental duty of a police officer, you will recall from Chapter 4, is to serve the community through safeguarding lives and property, protecting members of the community, and respecting the rights of all citizens. The fundamental duty is to do good, to prevent harm and to refrain from doing harm.

Consider the following situation based on a real-life report (Canadian Press, 2000).

---

**SITUATION 5.1**    **Unruly Prisoner**

You have been recently hired as a constable and are serving in a small detachment in a rural community. Your partner has been on the force for six years. One night the two of you are alone at the local jail where one person is in custody. The prisoner is a middle-aged female known for her heavy drinking and bad temper. She's in jail as the result of a drinking spree. Since her lockup, a couple of hours ago, she has been ranting, raving, and spewing obscenities at you and your partner. Your repeated efforts to calm her have been fruitless.

Your partner approaches the video surveillance equipment, says that he's making an adjustment, and then proceeds to the cell door where the prisoner continues to rant. He unlocks the door and opens it. The prisoner lunges at him but falls to the floor in the process. He grabs her by the hair, drags her on her knees from the cell, and hits her on the side of the head with his fist. He then drags her back into the cell, closes the door, and locks it. The prisoner settles to the floor, quietens down, and falls to sleep. "She'll be fine in the morning," your partner says. "The sleep will do her good." He once again approaches the surveillance equipment. You notice that the record light comes on.

What would you do in this situation? What would you say? What action would you take? If you have the opportunity, discuss your views with others. In what way or ways does the principle of goodness apply to this situation? Identify sections of the codes below that would apply to this case.

---

## Goodness in the Universal Declaration of Human Rights

According to the Universal Declaration of Human Rights, members of the human community are to act in ways that ensure that others will not suffer harm. It requires individuals to do what is good or right, and not to harm others. One can easily see this in the statements guaranteeing the right to life and security of person. The Declaration also protects members from enslavement, torture, and cruel punishment. Furthermore, the goodness principle underlies the statements that protect family, work, and property. Indeed, one can see the entire document as an attempt to ensure the welfare of all citizens. The various rights and freedoms cited in the Declaration are a means to the goal of providing goodness for all members of society.

## Goodness in the Canadian Charter of Rights and Freedoms

The Canadian Charter of Rights and Freedoms has as its fundamental goal the welfare of all Canadian citizens. The fundamental freedoms guaranteed in Part I, section 2, are the following: freedom of conscience and religion; freedom of thought, belief, opinion and expression, including freedom of the press and other media of communication; freedom of peaceful assembly; and freedom of association. These basic freedoms plus the right to "life, liberty, and security of the person" (Part I, section 7) clearly identify the goal of Canadian society as the welfare of its people. The Charter is designed to give all Canadians a fair opportunity to have a good life in a good society. In a word, the Good Society is the ultimate end. The Good Society is, of course, further defined in terms of all five of the basic principles, because goodness cannot be achieved without equality, justice, truth, and freedom.

## Goodness in the Ontario Police Services Act, Code of Conduct

The principle of goodness underlies a number of stipulations in the Code of Conduct of the Ontario Police Services Act. Officers are guilty of discreditable conduct, for example, if they "use profane, abusive, or insulting language relating to a person's race, ancestry, place of origin, colour, ethnic origin, citizenship, creed, sex, sexual orientation, age, marital status, family status or handicap" (2.(1)(a)(ii)). The use of abusive and insulting language is a form of psychological harm that one person can inflict upon another. The Code clearly forbids such abuse. The same point is made with respect to fellow officers (2.(1)(a)(iv)) and members of the public (2.(1)(a)(v)).

Inflicting physical harm is also forbidden by the Code. Officers are guilty of offences if they assault another officer (2.(1)(a)(vii)) or use any unnecessary force against a prisoner or other person contacted in the execution of duty (2.(1)(g)(ii)). Causing economic harm to the police service is also forbidden. Officers are guilty of an offence under the Code if they "wilfully or negligently cause loss or damage to any article of clothing or equipment" (2.(1)(h)(i)). The rules of conduct noted here and others that have not been mentioned are all rules generated by the goodness principle, the principle that requires us to do good and not harm.

## Goodness in the Law Enforcement Code of Ethics

Since the primary purpose of policing is to protect the lives and property of members of the community, it is not surprising to find the goodness principle within the Law Enforcement Code of Ethics. The Code begins, for example, by identifying the fundamental duty of a police officer. That duty, as we saw above, is to safeguard the lives and property of community members, especially the innocent, the weak, and the peaceful. Members of the community, the Code continues, are to be protected from violence and disorder, two grievous harms. As the guardians of society, police officers are to do good and not harm. Officers promise, in paragraph 2 for example, "to be constantly mindful of the welfare of others."

All codes of conduct, ethical and legal, will include norms that promote goodness and prohibit harm. As noted above, doing good and refraining from harm is the ultimate goal of both legal codes and professional codes of conduct. These codes encourage the actions that will most likely result in good consequences for the community or prohibit those actions that will bring bad consequences. One can easily see how the utilitarian approach to ethics that we examined in Chapter 3, with its emphasis on the "greatest good for the greatest number," is firmly rooted in the principle of goodness. So, too, are the codes that we have just reviewed.

## THE EQUALITY PRINCIPLE

While utilitarianism focuses on doing good, we saw earlier that the utilitarian approach can lead to abuses. In Chapter 3 we discussed the problem of the tyranny of the majority. The good that one group enjoys, for instance, may be accomplished at the expense of another group. We also noted in Chapter 3 that duty ethics offered an antidote or protection against these potential abuses. Immanuel Kant spoke of the practical imperative, the rational principle of moral equality. One person should never use another person, he said, as a means to an end. In simple terms, one person should never use another person.

Kant was not objecting to using the services of another person, as we do when we go to a dentist. We use that person to have our teeth examined, but the dentist willingly provides this service for a fee. Kant had in mind the many cases in human experience where one human being treats another human as if the other person were a thing, not a human being. He recognized that human reason and human choice were the elements that made human beings noble beings who ought to be treated with dignity. These human qualities, he argued, made all human beings equal in moral value.

Without an equality principle, one individual might seek his own good at the expense of another. The individual thief, for example, tries to increase his own good by stealing the possessions of another person. The same applies at the level of groups. Without the protection of the equality principle one group might seek its own good without any great concern for the welfare of members of another group. Human history is full of examples of such abuses. The practice of slavery and the Holocaust are but two dramatic ones.

The equality principle, like all the basic principles, can be expressed either as a positive duty or a negative duty. As a positive duty, it might be expressed as follows: "Treat others as equals." Expressed as a negative duty: "Don't discriminate against others." Along with the goodness principle, the equality principle acts as the bulwark of ethics and the law in a civil society. It is, as Kant saw clearly, essential for ethical conduct.

---

| SITUATION 5.2 | **Shift Partner** |
|---|---|

You have been assigned a new shift partner who has repeatedly made derogatory racist and ethnic comments and jokes about the people that you see as you patrol the streets of a major city. She doesn't do this outside the cruiser, so nobody else hears her remarks. Although you haven't worked with her very long, you are scheduled to work with her for some time to come.

What, if anything, would you do in this situation? Explain your reasoning. If her remarks are always made within the car, is any harm being done? As you read the codes below, look for any statements that might apply to this case.

---

## Equality in the Universal Declaration of Human Rights

The equality principle is also central to the Universal Declaration of Human Rights that we studied in Chapter 4, and to human rights statements in general. The first line of the

Preamble to the Universal Declaration of Human Rights, for example, refers to the "equal and inalienable rights of all members of the human family." Later in the Preamble there is reference to the "equal rights of men and women," the two broad classes into which human beings are often divided.

The first two articles of the Declaration make the matter of moral equality even clearer. Article 1 states that "all human beings are born free and equal in dignity and rights." Every individual human being, the Declaration continues in the second Article, is "entitled to all the rights and freedoms set forth in this Declaration, without distinction of any kind, such as race, colour, sex, language, religion, political or other opinion, national or social origin, property, birth, or other status."

## Equality in the Canadian Charter of Rights and Freedoms

The Canadian Charter of Rights and Freedoms, in Section 15, puts the matter of equality in the following way. "Every individual is equal before and under the law and has the right to equal protection and equal benefit of the law without discrimination and, in particular, without discrimination based on race, national or ethnic origin, colour, religion, sex, age or mental or physical disability." It is interesting to note, and we will return to the point later, that the Charter does not preclude laws, programs, or activities designed to lessen the condition of disadvantaged groups within Canadian society. In Chapter 7 we will discuss employment equity programs and the charge that they are a form of reverse discrimination.

## Equality in the Ontario Police Services Act, Code of Conduct

The Equality Principle is prominent in the Code of Conduct of the Ontario Police Services Act, informing two sections of the Code. Those sections stipulate that discrimination by officers on the basis of race, ancestry, sex, and a number of other characteristics constitutes discreditable conduct. The Code states that any officer, "commits misconduct if he or she engages in, (a) DISCREDITABLE CONDUCT, in that he or she, (i) fails to treat or protect a person equally without discrimination with respect to police services because of that person's race, ancestry, place of origin, colour, ethnic origin, citizenship, creed, sex, sexual orientation, age, marital status, family status or handicap" (Section 2.(1)). In the treatment and protection of the public, the Code clearly expects the professional impartiality that we noted in Chapter 4 when we highlighted the police officer as a role model within a civil society. Once again, the Code, in its emphasis on the principle of equality, is in harmony with the Universal Declaration and the Canadian Charter of Rights and Freedoms.

## Equality in the Law Enforcement Code of Ethics

The fourth code examined earlier, the Law Enforcement Code of Ethics, also includes the principle of equality. Prominent at the end of the first paragraph of the Code is the officer's promise to "respect the constitutional rights of all to liberty, equality, and justice." In these words the Code makes it clear from the start that equality is a constitutional right that must be respected. Note further that this statement includes the word *all*. The right to equal treatment is a right that all members of a civil society have. No distinctions are to be made on the basis of creed, race, or other factors that, from an ethical point of view, are irrelevant.

In the third paragraph of the Law Enforcement Code, the officer promises the following: "I will never act officiously or permit personal feelings, political beliefs, aspirations, animosities or friendships to influence my decisions." If a person allows personal feelings, political beliefs or aspirations to colour his or her judgment, then that individual is likely to discriminate either for or against others. In either case, the officer's impartiality will be lost. If an officer shares the same political beliefs as a citizen, for example, then that citizen may "get a break" from the officer. If the citizen holds differing views, then the officer might "get tough" with that person. Animosities and friendships, too, may lead to a loss of impartiality, as may the acceptance of gratuities. As the Canons of Police Ethics put it, officers are to carry out their sworn duties without "preference or prejudice" (Article 6, Conduct Toward the Public).

Police officers hold a public trust that involves, among other things, the public's belief that society's guardians will act impartially and not discriminate against a citizen because of race, origin, colour, religion, sex, age, or disability. In holding this public trust, police officers exhibit one of the noblest of qualities in a civil society, impartiality with respect to the enforcement of the law. A police officer's non-discriminatory treatment of members of the community fosters trust in society's protectors and contributes to the peace and security of society.

## THE JUSTICE PRINCIPLE

The principle of justice is closely linked to both the goodness principle and the equality principle. Justice, we should note immediately, is another word for fairness. The justice principle is, in fact, often called the fairness principle. To treat someone fairly, for example, is to act justly toward that person. The justice principle, expressed as a negative duty, says, "Don't be unfair to others." As a positive duty, it says, "Treat others fairly." Notice the close connection that exists among the three principles above. A simple example will illustrate the connection. If a teacher discriminates against a student because of her race (equality), the teacher is unfair to the student (justice), judging her on the basis of skin colour rather than performance. Such discrimination causes harm to the student (goodness), who may, for example, fail the course because of the teacher's prejudice.

### Distributive Justice

Careful analysis of the concept of justice reveals that justice has to do with distributing the good things of society in a fair way to society's members. It also has to do with distributing punishments to errant members of the community. For this reason, we often use the expression "**distributive justice**" to capture the nature of this principle. Whether distributing rewards or punishments to its members, every civil society must have a concern for justice.

### Three Approaches to Distributive Justice

There are three basic ways in which we can try to be fair to others in our dealings with them. First, to be fair to someone often means to give her what she has earned, to give him what he deserves. This is the principle upon which paycheques and school marks are normally distributed. If a worker does the job, he earns a paycheque. If a student works hard, she deserves the good grade. We refer to this way of being fair to others as the **merit approach** to distributive justice. We give people what they deserve, earn, or merit.

There is, however, a second way of being fair to others. There are circumstances, for example, where fairness means giving people equal shares of the good that is available for distribution. Family life provides us with a good example of this second approach. In the distribution of an estate upon the death of the parents, it is common practice to give each surviving child an equal share of the estate. This practice illustrates the **equity approach** to distributive justice.

We can imagine, too, circumstances in the workplace and in school settings where the equity approach might be the fairest way to act. Members of teams in the workplace or school, for instance, might receive the same group bonus or be given the same team grade for a group project. The equity or equal shares approach is a common way to be fair to others in many different settings.

A third approach to being fair is the special **needs approach**. In our society, we have recognized that physical disabilities, for example, have denied some members of our communities opportunities that others have enjoyed. Consequently, we have built wheelchair ramps, installed elevators, and redesigned roadway curbs in an effort to provide those with physical challenges the same opportunities that others have. It is only fair, we have argued, to do these things for the physically challenged.

The same arguments have been made with respect to the mentally challenged. School budgets, for instance, routinely include costs for students with special cognitive needs. Once again we have argued that it's only fair to budget for these students with special needs. A far more controversial application of the special needs approach has occurred in the area of employment and educational equity. Affirmative action plans are based on the concept of socially created disabilities. Various minority groups within society, it has been argued, have been socially disabled by the discriminatory practices of the majority.

While our society has readily sought justice for the physically challenged and the mentally challenged, it has not so readily embraced the cause of the socially challenged. Indeed, some say there is no comparison. Reverse discrimination arguments quickly come to the fore as males, for example, see females challenging their employment preserves. The same reverse discrimination arguments are often made, of course, against the affirmative action efforts of other minority groups, such as racial and ethnic minorities.

This situation presents us with a most interesting example of ethical debate in society. Those arguing for affirmative action say that they have been unfairly treated. They want justice. Those making the reverse discrimination argument say the same thing. Affirmative action is not fair, they insist. We should not have to pay for the sins of previous generations. They, like their adversaries, want justice. They want to be treated fairly in competitions in education, the workplace, and other forums in society.

We need to be familiar with each of the three approaches to distributive justice: the merit, equity, and needs approaches. Furthermore we need to remember that justice is closely linked to equality and goodness. Discussion of any one of these basic principles usually leads quickly to considerations associated with the others. This will also be true of the principles of truth and freedom.

Before proceeding to those principles, however, consider the following case. The situation on which it is based will be discussed in Chapter 7.

| | |
|---|---|
| SITUATION<br>5.3 | **Fire the Firefighter?** |

A female firefighter has been employed with a fire department for two years. During that time she has done her job well, receiving good evaluations of her performance. She has not, however, passed a fitness test that is required of all firefighters in the department. In fact, she has failed the fitness test four times. The test requires firefighters to run 2.5 kilometres in 11 minutes or less. She is the only member of the department who has failed the test. As fitness is extremely important in firefighting, her repeated failure to pass the test has raised the issue of her dismissal from the department. You are a member of a committee established to review the case. The committee is to recommend a course of action to the chief, regarding the future of the firefighter.

Will you recommend dismissal or not? What are your reasons? What questions would you ask at your committee sessions? What further information would you want or need in order to make a recommendation that is fair? How do statements from the following codes relate to this situation?

## Justice in the Universal Declaration of Human Rights

The justice principle informs three important parts of the Universal Declaration of Human Rights. First, in cases where a person's basic rights have been violated, the individual has the right, according to Article 8, to an "effective remedy" by a competent tribunal. The right to such a remedy exists, for example, in the province of Ontario. In Ontario, a citizen whose human rights have been violated can take his case to the Ontario Human Rights Commission where he can seek an effective remedy, that is, a fair hearing and commission action to stop the violations. Such remedies are matters of justice.

A second application of the justice principle occurs in Articles 10 and 11, where the matter of criminal charges against an individual are addressed. The Declaration states that everyone is entitled "to a fair and public hearing by an independent and impartial tribunal in the determination of his rights and obligations and of any criminal charge against him." The words *fair, independent,* and *impartial* all underscore the right to a fair trial, the right to justice. All civil societies apply this principle in their codes in order to ensure that the society is a just society.

The Universal Declaration also applies the justice principle to the education and work of members of the human family. Article 26 identifies the right to education. After stating that elementary education shall be free and compulsory, it goes on to say that professional and higher education "shall be equally accessible to all on the basis of merit." In these words the Declaration asserts the equal right of all to educational opportunities, with ability (merit) being the deciding factor. Here the Declaration employs the justice principle, adopting the merit approach with respect to fairness.

Addressing the right to work, Article 23 first prescribes "just and favourable conditions of work" for members of the human community. Then it proceeds to use the equity approach to justice by prescribing the right to "equal pay for equal work." Remuneration for work, it continues, must be "just and favourable." We see in this part of the article the application of both the equity and merit approaches to justice. "Equal pay for equal work" requires non-discriminatory treatment of workers (the equity approach), and "just and favourable remuneration" requires a fair wage for service provided (the merit approach).

## Justice in the Charter of Rights and Freedoms

Let's take a look now at the justice principle as it is applied in one section of the Canadian Charter of Rights and Freedoms. The Charter is the constitutional foundation for the rights of all Canadians, the document that prescribes the fundamental principles of Canada as a civil society. All laws in Canada must be consistent with these principles. These principles are, we have argued, the basic ethical principles that are necessary for the functioning of a civilized community, a civil society.

The Legal Rights section of the Charter illustrates the application of the justice principle to the lives of Canadians. Every Canadian, the Charter says, has the right to life, liberty, and security of person and the right not to be deprived of these except in accordance with the "principles of fundamental justice." Everyone, moreover, is protected against unreasonable search, seizure, detention, and imprisonment.

Persons charged with an offence have the right to all of the following: prompt explanation of the charge, trial within a reasonable time, protection from self-incrimination, and the presumption of innocence. Persons convicted of an offence also have rights. Specifically, they have the right not to be subjected to cruel or unusual punishment. Even punishment, says the Charter, is to be fair. It is to be just. In the Legal Rights section, then, the Charter ensures that citizens will be treated fairly with respect to the law and legal proceedings.

In the various paragraphs of the Legal Rights section of the Canadian Charter of Rights and Freedoms we have an excellent example of a civil society protecting its citizens by requiring that the legal process be just (fair). Someone charged with an offence is considered innocent until proven guilty, and the Charter requires due process in the determination of innocence or guilt. A brief look at history and contemporary dictatorships will quickly convince us of the importance of the justice principle in a free and civil society. The rule of law, based on fundamental ethical principles, demands impartial legal proceedings for every citizen. We will examine procedural justice later, in Chapter 8.

## Justice in the Ontario Police Services Act, Code of Conduct

As with the previous principles, the principle of justice underlies certain parts of the Code of Conduct of the Ontario Police Services Act. An officer, for example, is guilty of Neglect of Duty if he or she "feigns or exaggerates sickness or injury to avoid duty" (2.(1)(c)(viii)) or "is absent without leave from or late for any duty, without reasonable excuse" (2.(1)(c)(ix). Officers who violate these sections of the Code are being unfair to the police service, their employer. The employer is entitled to fair a day's work for a day's pay. One might also argue that the absent officers are not carrying their fair share of the load compared to their fellow officers. Additionally, one can make a reasonable argument that such conduct is unfair to the public that pays taxes for police services.

Also forbidden in the Code is unlawful or unnecessary arrest. An officer commits misconduct if he or she "without good and sufficient cause makes an unlawful or unnecessary arrest" (2.(1)(g)(i). The injustice done here, of course, is an injustice to a member of the public who has been detained. Simply put, it is unfair to arrest someone without a very good reason. Notice that in such cases the injustice occurs because the individual hasn't done anything to deserve (merit) arrest. Moreover, persons unlawfully or unnecessarily arrested have been deprived of their freedom, a serious harm in a free society. Three ethical principles are violated in cases of unnecessary arrest. The arrest is unfair because there is no valid reason for it (justice). The arrest denies innocent persons their liberty (freedom). The unlawful or unnecessary arrest of a citizen in a civil society harms that person (goodness).

## Justice in the Law Enforcement Code of Ethics

Prominent in the first paragraph of the Law Enforcement Code of Ethics is the principle of justice. After identifying an officer's fundamental duty as service to the community (goodness) and underscoring respect for the constitutional rights of all citizens (equality), the Code identifies the specific rights of liberty, equality, and justice. Here in a single paragraph, the Code ties together the four basic principles of goodness, freedom, equality, and justice.

Later, in paragraph 3, the police officer swears "to enforce the law courteously and appropriately without fear or favour, malice or ill will, never employing unnecessary force or violence and never accepting gratuities." To enforce the law "without fear" means that officers will not be intimidated in their duties. Yielding to intimidation would result in an unfair application of the law. People who intimidate officers would get preferential treatment compared to those who don't intimidate officers. Justice would be compromised. This point applies equally, of course, to officers who would intimidate other officers.

The officer also promises to enforce the law "without favour." Favouring a friend who has been pulled over for speeding is not fair or just. Strangers would receive different treatment under the same law for the same infraction. Furthermore, the officer promises to enforce the law while "never accepting gratuities." The acceptance of gratuities is forbidden as it too might lead to an unjust enforcement of the law. People who give gifts might be favoured over others as an officer's impartiality is compromised. Accepting gratuities can lead to favouring the donor. Moreover, it can foster the perception in the minds of the public that police officers can be bought. Recall Situation 4.1, Lunch at Al's Diner.

## THE TRUTH PRINCIPLE

The fourth of the basic ethical principles is the principle of truth. Truth telling or honesty is a prerequisite for any healthy relationship between or among individuals or groups, and no group of people can create a civil society without insisting upon truth telling. It is not surprising, then, to find that, wherever individuals have formed groups to ensure their common welfare, they have expected group members to tell the truth to one another.

Honesty is expected, of course, not only in words but also in deeds. Honest actions are as important to the group as honest words. The word *integrity,* when applied to an individual, conveys the idea that the person is trustworthy in both word and deed. We say, for example, that John has integrity, meaning that he is truthful in speech as well as behaviour. Because the principle of truth applies to both words and deeds, it underlies many of the rules of conduct within a civil society.

We also need to note that people can deceive others through acts of commission and acts of omission. If I deliberately lie to you, then I engage in an **act of commission**. I distort the truth. This kind of lying involves **deception by distortion**. I might also deceive you, however, by failing to tell you everything that you are entitled to know about a situation. In this latter case, I omit certain things from my story in order to mislead you. Misleading you by deliberately omitting to tell you important information is an **act of omission**, a form of deception. Such lying involves **deception by omission**. If you knew the whole story, you would have a very different understanding of events. That, no doubt, is why the traditional courtroom oath requires a witness "to tell the truth, the *whole truth*, and nothing but the truth."

Also noteworthy at this point is the close relationship between the principle of truth and the principle of freedom. In Chapter 3 we examined the key words *moral* and *immoral.* We observed that these words include the idea of knowing right and wrong and choosing either to do what is right or to do what is wrong. In order to make a truly free choice, one has to have knowledge of one's options. This is the idea behind the concept of **informed consent**. If, then, I distort the truth about a situation by lying to you, I deprive you of the opportunity to make an informed decision. In brief, my deception affects your freedom.

The truth principle might be expressed as a positive duty in forms such as the following: "Tell the truth" or "Be honest." As a negative duty, it might appear in forms like this: "Don't lie" or "Don't deceive." Before we proceed to a review of the truth principle in the various codes that we are examining, let's consider another situation.

| SITUATION 5.4 | The Whole Truth |
|---|---|

You are in your eighth month of service as a new constable. You have been assigned to exercise a search warrant along with two other officers. One has three years service and the other has nine. You are looking for marijuana, marijuana-growing equipment, and any other evidence pertinent to an arrest and conviction. The three of you catch the lone occupant of the house by surprise and soon have gained entry to the house. The occupant offers no resistance. You and the nine-year veteran watch the occupant in the living room as the other officer enters another room to begin the search. He closes the door as he enters but it swings silently and partially open behind him. You see him take cash from a table and place it inside his jacket. Neither the other officer nor the occupant sees what you see because they are facing away from the door. When the officer returns to the living room, he says, "We've got all we need. Let's take him in." Turning to the occupant, the other officer says, "Keep co-operating as you have and things will go easier for you." The occupant is put under arrest.

What will you say or do about the events you have witnessed? What will you write in your notebook? Explain your reasoning. What do the codes that follow have to say about this situation? What about the principles we have already examined? How do they fit?

## Truth in the Universal Declaration of Human Rights

In Article 10, the Universal Declaration cites the right of every individual "to a fair and public hearing by an independent and impartial tribunal" in any accusation of criminal conduct brought against the individual. Clearly, a trial cannot be fair and impartial if truth telling and honesty are not required of all who participate. Laws against perjury are intended to prevent dishonest testimony. The courtroom is a place for the facts to become clear and the truth to be told.

The right to an education, expressed in Article 26, is also an important part of the Universal Declaration. Education, of course, requires a free pursuit of the truth. Education is not the same as indoctrination. Indoctrination has the purpose of getting people to follow the thinking of a particular group. Education is all about acquiring facts and information, learning the truth about important areas of human experience. The right to an education is, in short, the right to the truth.

## Truth in the Canadian Charter of Rights and Freedoms

In the section of the Charter quoted earlier, the legal rights of Canadian citizens were spelled out. Among these rights is the right, upon arrest, detention, or indictment, to be informed promptly of the reasons for these actions. The right to information is the right to the truth about one's circumstances. In countries where brute power rules, persons are routinely arrested without the benefit of knowing why. In civil societies such as ours, however, citizens have the right to be informed. Citizens have, in a word, the right to the truth.

In section 23 of the Charter, the minority language rights of Canadians are addressed. Here, as in the Universal Declaration, the right to an education is clearly a right to discovering the truth for oneself. While the specific concern in section 23 is educational rights as they relate to different language groups in Canada, the underlying subject is the right to an education. The remarks made above in connection with the Universal Declaration obviously apply here as well.

## Truth in the Ontario Police Services Act, Code of Conduct

Truth telling and honesty are vitally important for any professional group, police professionals being no exception. As noted earlier in our study, honesty and integrity are essential for the development and maintenance of healthy relationships, whether personal or professional. The Code of Conduct of the Ontario Police Services Act recognizes the importance of the Truth Principle. Following are four sections of the Code that are based on the principle of truth.

An officer is guilty of misconduct, specifically deceit, if he or she "knowingly makes or signs a false statement in a record," (2.(1)(d)(i)) Officers are also guilty of deceit if they "wilfully or negligently make a false, misleading, or inaccurate statement pertaining to official duties" (2.(1)(d)(ii)). Again, an officer is guilty of deceit if he or she "without lawful excuse, destroys or mutilates a record or alters or erases an entry therein" (2.(1)(d)(iii)). Lastly, an officer is guilty of discreditable conduct if he or she "wilfully or negligently makes any false complaint or statement against any member of a police force" (2.(1)(a)(vi)).

## Truth in the Law Enforcement Code of Ethics

The fundamental duty of the officer, according to the Law Enforcement Code, is to serve the community. Among the specific acts of service identified in the first paragraph is "to protect the innocent against deception." Unfortunately, even in a civil society, some members prey upon others attempting to profit personally by deceiving them. All forms of fraud, of course, provide examples of this kind of deception. The officer promises to serve by protecting innocent members of society from those who would profit from deception.

In the second paragraph, the officer swears to be "honest in thought and deed" both in personal and professional life. Here the officer promises to conduct himself with the kind of integrity that we noted as we began this section on truth. In so doing, the police officer is an example of the kind of behaviour that is expected in a civil society. Those who are honest in thought, word, and deed are trustworthy persons. They earn the respect of honest members of society, contributing enormously to life in a civil society. In Chapter 4, you will recall, we saw that honesty and trustworthiness were key qualities of the ideal officer.

One other aspect of the truth principle, as it appears in the Law Enforcement Code, needs to be highlighted. Specifically, it is the matter of maintaining appropriate confidentiality with respect to the private lives of citizens. Police officers routinely learn all kinds of private information about members of the community. By pledging to keep these things confidential and maintaining confidentiality, an officer earns the respect of members of the community. The truth about our private lives is very important to us, and the Law Enforcement Code clearly recognizes that fact.

One further point from the Code needs to be noted. Paragraph 4 makes reference to the badge of office, referring to it as a "symbol of public trust." The words *trust* and *truth* are closely related. As mentioned at the very beginning of this section, one cannot have any kind of healthy relationship with another person if there is not truthfulness between the parties. The trust we place in others is essentially based on their truthfulness toward us. If they lie to us and we learn of it, trust will be broken. The Code acknowledges this important point as the officer accepts the badge as "a public trust" to be held so long as the officer "remains true to the ethics of police service."

We now turn to the last of the five basic principles of ethical reasoning, the freedom principle.

## THE FREEDOM PRINCIPLE

We made one of our first references to freedom in Chapter 2 where we briefly discussed the issue of **freedom** and **determinism**. There we pointed out that ethics makes no sense unless people have freedom of choice. The concept of free choice, to put it differently, is logically necessary if ethics is to be meaningful. If there is no freedom, we argued, then it makes no sense to praise or blame people for their actions. The concepts of responsibility and accountability only make sense if moral agents choose freely.

One approach to ethics, that of libertarians, sees the freedom principle as the most important of all the ethical principles. All of the other principles that we have examined, say the libertarians, can be put into their proper place by observing one basic ethical principle. **Libertarians** argue that individuals should have maximum freedom to do what they choose, subject only to others having the same degree of liberty. Many view this libertarian position as an extreme that is too simplistic. They argue that a civil society requires additional principles, in particular, the ones that we have been examining. Obviously, I have taken this latter approach to our study of ethics in this book.

The point of the first paragraph in this section is that moral agents are agents who freely choose their courses of action, are responsible for them, and accountable to the community in which these actions take place. A further important point about the freedom principle has to do with one individual depriving others of their freedom to make choices. This, needless to say, is one of the great harms that we can inflict on others. If my choices deprive you of your freedom, then I have harmed you. In a free and civil society, actions that deprive others of their personal right to choose are serious offences indeed.

Think for a moment of the thief's actions. If your car is stolen, for example, the thief has taken your property. He has also taken away your freedom to use your property. If you owned a hundred vehicles that were all available for your use, perhaps the loss of one would not be such a great harm. It would be an offence, of course, but your freedom to get about in a car is not impacted nearly as much as if the thief takes your only car. The point we are making here is simply that many actions, like theft, are assaults on our freedom as well as the illegitimate removal of our property.

The freedom principle, like the other four principles, can be expressed as a positive duty or a negative duty. "Don't force or coerce others" is an example of the latter. "Respect the freedom of others" is an example of the former. It has been said that the highest respect one person can show toward others is to let them make their own choices. In a civil society based on ethical principles and the rule of law, freedom is an essential value. Consider now the following situation.

---

| SITUATION 5.5 | **Neighbourhood Pornography** |
|---|---|

You're sitting at home one evening when the doorbell rings. You answer the door and are greeted politely by a woman and a man who appear to be in their late thirties. They introduce themselves and begin to express their concern about the pornography being sold at the variety store at the end of your street. They mention both magazines and videos that are available in the store. Despite the fact that the owner of the store keeps the magazines on a top shelf behind a partial screen, they argue that naked bodies and pornographic titles are readily visible. So, too, they continue, is the pornography on the covers of adult videos. They ask you to sign the following petition that they are circulating throughout your neighbourhood:

> We the members of the Fleetwood Subdivision petition the mayor and the city Council to take all appropriate steps to remove the pornographic materials (e.g., *Playboy*, *Penthouse*, all similar magazines, and adult videos) from Bonus Variety Store at the corner of Maple and Oak Streets in our neighbourhood. These obscene materials are incompatible with the family values that our neighbourhood believes in. Children, adults, and families are being harmed by the presence of this obscene material in our family community. This material is an affront to us and it is an extremely bad

influence in our midst. We urge you to act quickly on this important matter.

You note that some 20 neighbours have already signed the petition. What would you do in this situation? Will you sign the petition? Why or why not?

Explain your reasons. If you have the opportunity, discuss the situation with others. How do the statements from the following codes relate to the situation above? What about earlier statements based on other principles?

## Freedom in the Universal Declaration of Human Rights

As we've done with the other principles, we will now examine some of the codes that we have been working with in order to see what role the freedom principle plays in them.

The Universal Declaration, it can be argued, is all about freedom. In the brief Preamble alone the word *freedom* occurs seven times. Furthermore, in the Articles that follow the Preamble, the theme of freedom is ongoing. The importance of individual freedom is acknowledged repeatedly as the Declaration identifies specific freedoms such as freedom of movement, residence, thought, conscience, religion, belief, opinion, and expression.

## Freedom in the Canadian Charter of Rights and Freedoms

What has just been said about the Universal Declaration can now be said for the Canadian Charter of Rights and Freedoms. This should not be a surprise as the United Nations document is the model for much of what appears in the Charter. Canada, following in the tradition of free and civil societies, has ensured its citizens of fundamental rights and freedoms in this constitutional document.

Section 2 is entitled Fundamental Freedoms and it lists the following: conscience, religion, thought, belief, opinion, expression, peaceful assembly, and association. Furthermore, when one considers carefully the idea of "rights," it is easy to see that a right is really the freedom to do something without interference from others. If I have the legal right to a piece of property, for example, that means that I have the freedom to use that property, subject only to limitations of the law. You and others do not have the freedom to use that piece of property though you may well have the freedom to use other properties.

## Freedom in the Ontario Police Services Act, Code of Conduct

A **tyrant** is a despot or evil dictator who exercises absolute power over others. When one human being treats another in an oppressive manner, we refer to the oppressor's actions as **tyrannical behaviour**. The Code notes that superior rank in the police service is not a licence for tyrannical behaviour. Junior officers may be under the command of seniors, but commanding officers must not be oppressive. They must not go beyond what is reasonable to ensure compliance with commands.

An officer is guilty of discreditable conduct, according to the *Code*, if he or she "is guilty of oppressive or tyrannical conduct toward an inferior in rank" (2.(1)(a)(iii)). Junior officers must be respected for the duties that they fulfil in the service. Abusive behaviour infringes on the freedom that is necessary to carry out one's duties in a professional manner. Tyrannical behaviour on the part of a superior interferes with or denies the freedom that officers of lower rank need in order to do their work as professionals. Moreover, it is an affront to their personal dignity.

One further point needs to be made. Here we will mention it in passing. Later, in Chapter 7, we will return to it for a closer look. The Code forbids an officer from "directly or indirectly" soliciting or receiving "a gratuity or present without the consent of the chief of police" (2.(1)(f)(iii)). The primary concern, no doubt, is that an officer's impartiality may be compromised. Officers, for instance, may play favourites as the result of receiving gratuities. Gratuities, then, may restrict an officer's freedom to act impartially. In other words, the officer owes something to the donor and, therefore, is not entirely free to do his duty objectively. This is a subtle point, but an extremely important one.

## Freedom in the Law Enforcement Code of Ethics

The Law Enforcement Code of Ethics underscores the importance of the Freedom Principle in its first paragraph. Part of the officer's fundamental duty is to respect the "constitutional rights of all to liberty, equality, and justice." Liberty, of course, is freedom. The Code, then, requires officers to respect and protect the freedom of all citizens.

Though the principle is not mentioned directly, it is certainly an important part of the promises to enforce the law "without fear or favour" and to refuse to engage in "acts of corruption or bribery." Earlier in our look at the principles of equality and justice, we noted that fear, favour, corruption, and bribery destroy an officer's sworn duty to enforce the law impartially.

If we consider these forbidden practices from the point of view of the freedom principle, we can see that they restrict an officer's freedom to choose. In effect, they prevent an officer from doing her duty. Fear, favour, corruption, and bribery can interfere with the freedom an officer needs in order to act impartially on behalf of all members of the community. Officer discretion also requires the freedom to make a reasonable judgment about a particular offence. The right to exercise discretion freely must not be compromised by either favouritism or animosity. We'll return to the relationship between impartiality and discretion in Chapter 7. For the moment, let's note that police officers freely choose their profession, and they need to be free to do their jobs.

## CHAPTER SUMMARY

We began this chapter by reviewing the importance of satisfying human wants and needs, a subject that we first looked at in Chapter 1. We then noted that people can try to satisfy their needs and wants in co-operative, civilized ways or in competitive, uncivilized ways. The first way is the way of ethical conduct and the rule of law. The second way is the way of unethical conduct and disregard for the law.

We then returned briefly to the characteristics of an ideal police officer, showing how the qualities of self-restraint and impartiality were consistent with the values and principles of a civil society. Officers are exemplars of desirable conduct in a civil society. All members of a civil community, both civilians and officers, must have a degree of altruism and empathy for others if the society is going to function in a civil manner.

We reviewed the analytical and descriptive dimensions of ethics, the parts of ethics that deal with language, logic, and the facts of a moral issue. Then we reviewed the prescriptive aspect of ethics, that part of ethics in which people state what is acceptable or unacceptable behaviour within a group. This prepared us for the examination of the various prescriptions of the codes that form the subject of study in this chapter.

Underlying the various prescriptions are the fundamental principles of ethical reasoning, the principles we first noted in Chapter 2. These are the principles of goodness, equality, justice, truth, and freedom. We then explained some important aspects of each principle, stated each principle both as a positive duty and as a negative duty, and proceeded to illustrate the application of each principle within the codes selected for study in this chapter.

More specifically, we first focused our attention on two societal codes, the Universal Declaration of Human Rights and the Canadian Charter of Rights and Freedoms. We pointed out how each of the five basic principles has generated specific statements within each code. Societal codes are codes of conduct designed for use within very large groups of people, entire societies, for example, such as Canada.

Next, for each principle, we examined two professional codes from the field of law enforcement. We noted how the five basic principles of ethical reasoning underlie the various statements from the Ontario Police Services Act, and the Law Enforcement Code of Ethics. Professional codes are codes of conduct that state the expectations regarding the behaviour of their members who practise within a society.

Through our study of both societal and professional codes, we saw that the basic principles of ethical reasoning provide the conceptual foundation for codes of conduct within a civil society.

## MASTERING THE MATERIAL

Now that you have read this chapter, use the following guides to ensure that you have mastered the material.

### Introduction

1. Explain civilized and uncivilized means of satisfying needs.
2. Identify two qualities of an ideal police officer that illustrate basic values of a civil society.
3. Explain the role of empathy and altruism in the life of a civil society.
4. Describe the role of ethics in establishing and changing the laws of society.
5. Distinguish among analytical, descriptive, and prescriptive ethics.

### The Principles of Ethical Reasoning

1. Identify the five basic principles of ethical reasoning.

## The Goodness Principle

1. State the goodness principle in the form of both a positive and a negative duty.
2. Cite sections from two societal codes that are derived from the goodness principle.
3. Cite sections from two professional codes that are derived from the goodness principle.

## The Equality Principle

1. State the equality principle in the form of both a positive and a negative duty.
2. Cite sections from two societal codes that are derived from the equality principle.
3. Cite sections from two professional codes that are derived from the equality principle.

## The Justice Principle

1. What is another name for the justice principle?
2. Identify and explain three different approaches to distributive justice.
3. State the justice principle in the form of both a positive and a negative duty.
4. Cite sections from two societal codes that are derived from the justice principle.
5. Cite sections from two professional codes that are derived from the justice principle.

## The Truth Principle

1. Define *integrity*.
2. What is lying by commission, and what is lying by omission?
3. Explain the importance of truth for informed consent.
4. State the truth principle in the form of both a positive and a negative duty.
5. Cite sections from two societal codes that are derived from the truth principle.
6. Cite sections from two professional codes that are derived from the truth principle.

## The Freedom Principle

1. How do libertarians view the freedom principle?
2. State the freedom principle in the form of both a positive and a negative duty.
3. Cite sections from two societal codes that are derived from the freedom principle.
4. Cite sections from two professional codes that are derived from the freedom principle.

## CRITICAL THINKING IN POLICING: THE PRINCIPLES MODEL

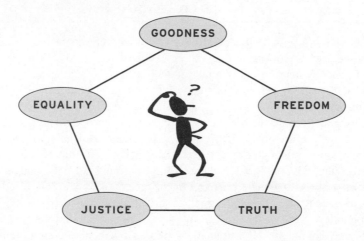

Moral agents know the five principles of ethical reasoning and their attendant duties, and they choose freely to act in accord with those duties in the best interests of all concerned.

## CRITICAL THINKING IN POLICING: THE DECIDE PROCESS

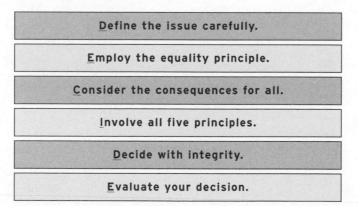

**Step #1: Define the issue carefully**. This step reminds you to be crystal clear about the meaning of the words and expressions that you use, whether the subject is adultery, euthanasia, abortion, pornography, or any other.

| Media Watch:<br>Ethics in the News 5.1 | Officer dragged and hit<br>female prisoner,<br>colleague testifies |
|---|---|

CALGARY – A police officer testified that he saw a colleague drag a female prisoner by her hair out of a jail cell and hit her across her face as she was on her knees.

Calgary police Const. Jim McManus told the Law Enforcement Review Board Thursday he was with Const. Bill McLean on Jan. 31, 1998, when they checked on prisoner Donna Christian, who was in custody on a charge of being drunk in public.

McLean admitted he hit Christian but said it was only because she lunged at him, yelling and punching.

"As she hit me, I hit her with my right hand to the side of her head," McLean said. "I think I hit her very hard."

McManus also testified that he believes McLean tampered with video surveillance equipment.

"I just got a funny feeling about it," McManus said of watching McLean insert a videotape into the machine.

"It was the way he looked around. It was very cautiously. I had an uneasy feeling."

Almost three hours of tape, which should have been operating during the incident, recorded nothing.

McLean said he retrieved the tape later because he noticed the recording light was not on. He insisted he took out the tape, looked at it, reinserted it and it started recording.

Christian handed the review board photos taken about eight hours after her arrest, which showed her with a black eye and bruising on her wrists and legs.

The board has the power to impose a range of penalties, from a reprimand to a dismissal.

Source: *Kitchener-Waterloo Record*, January 29, 2000, D20.

| Media Watch: Ethics in the News 5.2 | Knock down unfair workplace hurdles |

A critical victory was won last week when a British Columbia woman was given back her job as a firefighter even though she failed a fitness test.

Advocates of sexual equality will cheer the Supreme Court of Canada's ruling that made this possible. But anyone who values plain old common sense will do the same.

The top court was right to knock down a hurdle that the B.C. Forest Service could not justify. In so doing, the court telegraphed a vital message to all employers: Job standards can discriminate—even against a specific group, such as women. But to be permissible, the discriminatory standard has to be directly relevant to the job in question.

In this case, the fact that Tawney Meiorin could not run 2.5 kilometres in 11 minutes simply had no demonstrable bearing on her ability to fight fires. She had done the job for two years and earned good evaluations. But she failed a running test four times. So she was fired.

In turfing her, the B.C. Forest Service was stupid, not malicious. It was trying to do the right thing after a firefighter died in the line of duty and a coroner's inquest called for tougher fitness standards to prevent other tragedies.

But there were two problems with the running test. It was harder for women to pass than men. And there was no proof it was relevant to the job. This was the clincher.

If firefighters need to be able to haul a heavy hose, those too weak to do it can be barred from the job. Women could argue that such a strength requirement discriminates against them because women on average lack a man's muscular power. But if this strength is needed for the job, the discriminatory standard would be legally acceptable.

But Meiorin's case was different. Her inability to run fast did not impair her proven ability to battle blazes in the woods—or make her a danger to herself or her colleagues. The top court's decision does not in any way put the nation's forests at risk. But it does put at risk unfair and irrelevant hiring standards and Canadian employers should know that they have been warned.

Source: *Kitchener-Waterloo Record*, September 14, 1999, A6.

## chapter six

# Goodness: Preventing Harm and Doing Good in a Civil Society

## LEARNING OUTCOMES

After completing this chapter, you should be able to

- Describe, in general terms, the good that is the goal of a civil society
- Express the goodness principle both as a positive duty and a negative duty
- Summarize arguments for and against the use of lethal force as a defence
- Summarize arguments for and against euthanasia in each of its three forms
- Summarize arguments for and against abortion
- Describe the legal status of each of the issues in the chapter
- Explain the key terms associated with each of the chapter topics

## INTRODUCTION

The ultimate goal of a civil society is the good of its members, citizens who have the right, for example, to "life, liberty, and security." Each member of society has needs that must be satisfied and desires for a happy life. A civil society establishes laws designed to permit its members to satisfy their basic needs and wants in a way that affords all others the same opportunity. As a member of a civil society, you are free to seek your own personal happiness, but you are obligated to leave others free to do the same. In no case is anyone's freedom unlimited. The ultimate goal is the welfare of all.

**Goodness** refers to the experience of things that are beneficial to one's health and welfare. In attempting to reach the goal of goodness for all, a civil society establishes rules of conduct derived from the ethical **principle of goodness**. Citizens have, first of all, a **negative duty**. They are not to hurt or harm other members of society. Furthermore, they have, generally speaking, a **positive duty** to do good for others and to prevent harm to them. Laws within civil societies are established in accordance with these duties, duties that are derived from the **goodness principle**.

As specific laws are developed, they will limit individual freedom to one degree or another. In more restrictive societies the lawmakers will establish stricter rules that limit the freedom of individuals to a greater degree than the rules of less restrictive societies. In either type of society, however, some citizens will agree with certain laws and some will not. Despite disagreement, civil societies always require compliance with existing laws.

In the three topics that follow, the goodness principle is central to the ethical debate. As is always the case, however, the other four principles of ethical reasoning also come into play. As the ethical debate about the goodness or rightness of assisted suicide, for example, is carried on, questions of equality, justice, truth, and freedom will inevitably arise. Often differences of view will hinge on the value placed on one principle over another. In the capital punishment debate, for instance, some people place greater importance on punishment than on rehabilitation of the offender. Others place the value on rehabilitation.

Taking all five of the principles of ethical reasoning into account, but focusing especially on the principle of goodness, we'll examine ethical questions associated with the issues of self-defence, euthanasia, and abortion. Because each of these topics raises questions about the taking of human life, the goodness principle will be central to the discussion. Many would argue, for example, that the greatest harm we can do to other humans is to take their lives. Can killing in self-defence be morally justified? Can killing be morally justified with respect to euthanasia? Can it be justified in the case of abortion?

## USING DEFENSIVE FORCE

The safety and security of its members is one of the most important aims of a civil society. To this end, societies have always established armed services to protect and defend their members from attack by outsiders. Moreover, they have always created police services to protect and defend their members from those within the society that would do others harm. Furthermore, civil societies have always permitted individual members to defend themselves or others when police officers are not present to provide necessary protection.

In our look at the use of defensive force, we will focus primarily on the matter of individual citizens defending themselves or others against attack. We will see, in the process, that the same ethical principles that apply to citizens defending the innocent apply to the police. This should not be surprising in that the actions of the police are deemed legitimate only if their actions comply with the law and the ethical principles upon which the law is established.

In the case below and the summary of arguments that follow, we will discuss the most extreme form of defensive force, killing in self-defence. The criteria for a justifiable self-defence also apply to defensive actions short of killing. That is, they apply equally to both killing in self-defence and inflicting serious injury in self-defence.

| SITUATION 6.1 | Self-Defence? |
| --- | --- |

On a cold January day, a mother attempts to strangle her 16-year-old son to death. This is her last abusive act toward him, though it certainly was not her first. The boy had been raised by his grandparents until he was eight years old. From then on, he lived with his mother and suffered physical and emotional abuse at her hands, abuse that included daily beatings and constant belittling. The day after she tried to strangle him, the slight teenager stabbed her to death. Using two different kitchen knives, he stabbed her 10 times, putting an end to her abusive ways.

What punishment, if any, do you think the boy deserves? Is this a case of self-defence? Why or why not? If you have an opportunity, discuss this case with others before continuing your reading.

It was a cold January day in 1997 when the mother attempted to strangle her 16-year-old son to death. She was unsuccessful in her attempt. The next day her son stabbed her to death. In court, the young man's lawyers argued that his mother had repeatedly abused him for a period of eight years. The defence of child abuse was the first of its kind in Canada and proved partially successful, the boy being convicted of manslaughter. (Canadian Press, 1998). The defence of *child abuse* parallels the *battered woman* defence that has proved successful in both Canada and the United States in recent years. Are these cases of self-defence?

Clearly not, wrote George Jonas in his article "Ruling Tells Women It's OK to Kill": "…the law of self-defence has never justified acts of violence committed in fury, frustration, or revenge. If someone beat you to a pulp on Monday, you couldn't stab him on Tuesday, and plead 'self-defence'—not even if you thought he might do it to you again on Wednesday" (Jonas, 1997). Jonas is concerned that successful legal defences based on prior abuse will legitimize pre-emptive strikes, including lethal ones, upon abusers. He is also concerned with private citizens meting out vigilante justice.

Jonas seems correct in his analysis. Traditionally, self-defence has been limited to defending oneself or others during an attack, not retaliating after an attack. In recent years, however, Canadian courts have determined that killing an abusive partner or abusive parent as an act of self-defence is justifiable. In light of this relatively new development in Canadian law, we need to review the criteria traditionally associated with the use of lethal force in defending oneself. Before we do so, let's first examine some of the key arguments against and in support of killing in self-defence.

In the following discussion, for ease of presentation, I will use the expression "self-defence," but it should be noted that the arguments and underlying principles regarding self-defence also apply to use of force in the defence of someone other than oneself.

# Arguments against Killing in Self-Defence

The *religious argument* against killing in self-defence says that only God has the right to take a human life and therefore it is wrong for one human to kill another. Human beings, it is often said, must not "play God." Since this particular argument surfaces in different moral issues, a number of points need to be made with reference to the soundness of this argument.

Because it is a religious argument, it is subject to all the counter-arguments that we noted in Chapter 2. First, the *religious argument* relies on the unproved assumption that there is a God who gives and takes human lives. Second, assuming that God does exist, this argument claims to know the will of God in these matters, a further claim that cannot be substantiated. Third, assuming, for the sake of argument, that there is a God and that the deity does not want humans to play God, logic tells us that we ought not, then, to save life or in any way alter God's world. To do so, according to the argument, would be to play God. This point, of course, reduces the original argument to absurdity.

The *pacifist argument* is a second argument against killing in self-defence or the defence of others. A **pacifist** is a person who believes that humans must not deliberately harm or kill other humans under any circumstance. The pacifist takes an **absolutist** position, allowing for no exceptions to the rule against harming and killing. From the pacifist point of view, there is never any justification for killing another human being.

A careful analysis of pacifism suggests that its ultimate goal is the welfare of all members of society or the entire human family, a very worthy goal that is based on the principle of goodness. If that is the goal, then it would seem that pacifism, in certain instances, inevitably ends up in a self-contradictory position. For example, even when the only way to end a mass killer's killing spree is to shoot him to death, the pacifist must not pull the trigger. It is difficult, if not impossible, to see how the pacifist's non-action in this situation furthers the pacifist goal.

By refusing to kill the assailant, the pacifist permits further killing, something the pacifist is opposed to. By killing the assailant, the pacifist deliberately ends a human life, something that the pacifist must never do. Indeed, by refusing to shoot the killer, the pacifist spares the life of a vicious person while contributing by inaction to the deaths of innocent persons. This dilemma seems to raise serious questions about pacifism in general and, in particular, about the pacifist view of killing in defence of the innocent. As a strategy of civil disobedience practised by Mahatma Ghandi and Martin Luther King Jr., pacifism seems morally defensible. In the difficult case above, it seems not.

The *domino argument* is a third argument against killing in defence of the innocent. It says that killing in defence of the innocent is morally wrong because condoning such killing will devalue human life and lead to more killing in other situations. In other words, if we knock the first domino over, then other dominoes will topple. Approving of killing in self-defence, it might be argued, will lessen the value of human life and lead to the approval of killing in other situations such as mercy killing.

The *domino argument* appears frequently in ethical debates. It is also known as the *slippery slope argument*. Imagine, for a moment, a steep clay slope that is very wet. Take one small step at the top of that slippery slope and you'll slide down to the bottom. The images—dominoes and slopes—that underlie the labels for this argument differ, but the argument is the same under either label. When a person argues that we must not approve of one action because it will lead to some other harmful action, then the person is making a *domino* or *slippery slope argument*.

## Arguments for Killing in Self-Defence

Can killing in self-defence be morally justified? The primary argument for killing in defence of the innocent is the *necessary evil argument*. This argument says that killing in defence of the innocent is a necessary evil that can be morally justified under certain specific circumstances. Note first that the argument recognizes killing another human as an *evil*. Supporters of this argument do not see killing as a good thing. Given certain circumstances, however, they argue that such killing can be justified as a necessary action. It is the lesser of two evils.

According to the *necessary evil argument,* in order for killing in defence of the innocent to be ethically defensible, three conditions must prevail. The first condition is that the victim must have a reasonable belief that the aggressor's actions constitute a real danger to his life or physical well-being. In legal terms, there must be a "reasonable apprehension of death or grievous bodily harm." Name calling, for example, doesn't constitute a serious danger. Firing a gun, thrusting a knife, and similar forms of violent assault do.

The second condition is that the aggressor's assault must be an unprovoked attack. The defender is the victim of an "unlawful assault." It doesn't mean that the victim is generally innocent. An unscrupulous car salesman, for example, is not innocent with respect to his sales practices. If he's attacked by a thug without provocation, however, he is considered innocent with respect to that attack. The defender, to put it differently, did not initiate the confrontation.

The third condition is that the defender must use the minimal force necessary to stop the attacker. If an attack on an innocent victim can be repelled by any means short of killing, then the defence must take that line. Killing must be a defence of last resort. Expressed in legal terms, the victim must believe, "on reasonable grounds, that he cannot otherwise preserve himself from death or grievous bodily harm." Repelling the attacker with threats, fists, or other non-lethal means is morally preferable according to the *necessary evil argument*.

## Proportional and Minimal Force

How much force is ethically acceptable in self-defence? First, defensive force must be proportional to the force used by the attacker. **Proportional force** is force that is roughly equivalent to the force employed by the assailant. Second, what is ethically required is proportional force that is the **minimal force** necessary to subdue the attacker. Proportional force that is the minimal necessary is considered reasonable force. Addressing this point, the Law Enforcement Code of Conduct puts it this way: "A police officer will never employ unnecessary force and will use only such force in the discharge of duty as is reasonable in all circumstances."

Consequently, killing is ethically defensible only if it is a necessary last resort. Even then, as we have noted, it is viewed as an evil. This very real evil is, however, the lesser of two evils, one being the death of an innocent person (the victim) and the other being the death of a vicious person (the assailant).

We should note three additional points before we leave the subject of the defensive use of force.

## The Police and the Military

One is the difference between police officers carrying out their protective roles in society and the military defending a country. The ethical criteria that we have just reviewed are binding on police officers as they carry out their responsibilities with respect to protecting and defending the members of a civil society. The police, for example, are morally justified in killing only if killing is a last resort and all the other conditions apply. In contrast, soldiers in battle have a duty to kill enemy soldiers, last resort or not. Having said this, we need to note that even war must be conducted according to certain rules. The deliberate killing of non-combatants, for example, is forbidden.

## The Just War

The second point for us to note is that the criteria that form the basis of the *necessary evil argument* in self-defence also form the basis for the *just war argument*. Many reasons have been given for going to war, and often the reasons do not justify the massive harm that war inflicts upon people. One argument that seems morally defensible, however, is the *just war argument*. If an aggressor state wages war (real danger) against another country that has done nothing to deserve the attack (unprovoked attack), then the innocent country has the moral right to wage a defensive war (minimal force) if that war is necessary to repel the enemy. The just war, then, can be described as a form of group self-defence.

## Defence and Other Issues

The third point is that the notion of group self-defence can be applied to the issues of capital punishment and euthanasia. One argument in support of capital punishment, for example, takes the view that capital punishment is a legitimate form of group self-defence, at least under certain circumstances. It is also possible to view the ancient Eskimo practice of abandoning the elderly, allowing them to die, as a form of group self-defence. An aging member whose disabilities hindered the tribe's ability to move on to a new food supply may well have been seen as a threat to the group's survival. Better that one die alone than that many perish together.

Having completed our review of self-defence, let's proceed now to a look at the controversial topic of euthanasia, another topic in which the taking of human life and the goodness principle are a central issue. We put our pets to death to end their suffering. Is it morally justifiable to do the same to human beings?

## EUTHANASIA

A large majority of Canadians, when asked about doctor-assisted suicide, believe that taking the life of a terminally ill person who experiences great suffering is not morally wrong if the person wishes to die. In fact, they take the position that it is the right thing to do. But isn't killing another human being a great harm, a fundamental breach of the principle of goodness? Doesn't that principle forbid us to hurt or harm others? Aren't we to do good, and not harm? Isn't one of the basic rules of all civil societies the rule that says: "Thou shalt not kill?"

The question to which Canadians responded was a fairly detailed question. It read: "When a person has an incurable disease that is immediately life-threatening and causes that person to experience great suffering, do you, or do you not think that competent doctors should be allowed by law to end the patient's life through mercy killing, if the patient has made a formal request in writing?" Seventy-seven percent of those who were polled took the position that such killing was morally acceptable. When the incurable disease is "not immediately life threatening," the percentage drops to 57 (Edwards and Mazzuca, 1999).

Because euthanasia is a complex issue, we need to proceed with caution, identifying three different forms of euthanasia and examining each in turn. Once again, it is essential that we do some analytical ethics, defining our terms clearly.

## Three Forms of Euthanasia

The word *euthanasia* comes from the Greek language and literally means "good death" or "happy death." Today many people would say that the word *euthanasia* means "doctor-assisted suicide" or "mercy killing." While those are legitimate interpretations of the word, we need to be more precise in our definitions. Consequently, we'll look at three different forms of euthanasia: (1) natural death, (2) assisted suicide, and (3) mercy killing.

The single word *euthanasia* can be used to describe three different situations in which the life of another human being ends, directly or indirectly. The first form, natural death, is often called **passive** or **indirect euthanasia** because no direct action is taken to kill the person. In contrast, both of the other forms, assisted suicide and mercy killing, are called **active** or **direct euthanasia** precisely because a direct or active step is taken to kill the person.

If we proceed to describe and define each of these three situations clearly, we will be in a better position to understand the euthanasia issue. We will then be able to consider the soundness of the various arguments that are put forward with respect to this important issue. First, however, give thought to the following situation.

---

| SITUATION 6.2 | Maintenance Operation |
| --- | --- |

A baby boy is born and suffers severe brain damage shortly after birth. An operation is performed immediately to place a shunt to drain fluid from the child's brain. The boy lives for seven years in what one doctor calls a "semi-vegetative state," attending a special institutional school for the severely mentally challenged. At age seven, the shunt fails. A neurosurgeon can replace the shunt in a routine operation. Upon examining the child, however, he advises the parents that their son will die painlessly if the operation is not performed. Hearing this, the parents ask the doctor to put their child to sleep.

Should the doctor perform the operation or not? Should the child be put to sleep or not? Explain your reasoning. As you read further, try to determine the form of euthanasia the doctor has suggested. What form have the parents suggested?

---

## (1) Natural Death

Often, when someone is terminally ill and suffering, people will say that the right thing to do is to keep the person comfortable and to let nature take its course. **Natural death** is a form of euthanasia in which a terminally ill person is allowed to die naturally. In other words, nature is allowed to take its course and no steps are taken to hasten nature's process. The individual's wishes may or may not be known. Natural death is also called passive or indirect euthanasia because no active or direct steps are taken to kill the person. If we know that the person wants to die, then we refer to **passive, voluntary euthanasia.** If we don't know the person's wishes, then we refer to **passive, non-voluntary** (not involuntary!) **euthanasia**, or natural death.

In Canadian hospitals today, **Do-Not-Resuscitate (DNR) orders** are common for desperately ill patients. The DNR code on a patient's chart tells caregivers to let the person die if, for example, the person should have a heart attack. No heroic measures are to be taken. The person is to be kept comfortable and nature is to be allowed to take its course. The individual is not killed; rather, the person experiences a natural death.

The current practice has evolved over many years as society has gradually taken the position that keeping a terminally ill person alive at all costs is unethical. Resuscitating an elderly patient with terminal cancer, for example, and keeping her alive on life support equipment is generally considered to be wrong. In this kind of situation, **heroic** or **extraordinary measures** seem inappropriate and an affront to the dignity of the patient.

Take note, however, that precisely the same treatment, considered heroic or extraordinary in the circumstances of our example, may not be heroic or extraordinary in different circumstances—if they are used, for instance, to revive a twenty-five-year-old person severely injured in an automobile accident. The *situation* determines whether actions are heroic or not. The particular equipment or treatment does not.

Canadian doctors, bound by a legal duty to care for their patients, long feared that charges of abandoning the patient might be brought against them. This fear prompted many doctors in the past to use all the latest equipment to keep their patients alive at all costs. In 1992, doctors attending Nancy Bolduc sought the Quebec Superior Court's approval before disconnecting her life-support equipment (Wood, 1994). She was not allowed to die until the court sanctioned the action, providing doctors and others protection against charges of abandoning the patient. Nancy Bolduc was fully aware of her situation and requested that she be removed from life support. When the courts finally approved, her life support systems were removed. Her ensuing death was natural and a death that she wanted. It was a voluntary natural death.

In the ongoing ethical debate about euthanasia, the consent of the person whose life is in question is critically important. Today, persons with life-threatening illnesses who are mentally competent are routinely asked, upon entering hospital, to read and sign an **advanced directive form**, a form that directs caregivers to provide care according to the wishes of the patient. Persons entering nursing homes are asked to do the same. If they are not mentally competent, close family members are asked to sign on their behalf. Today, some people express their wishes long before they find themselves in difficult circumstances. They make living wills.

In the Maintenance Operation case above (Situation 6.2), the doctor is suggesting that the child be denied the operation. It is difficult to understand why the doctor advised that course of action. In effect, the doctor appears to have been willing to abandon his patient to a natural death. Note, however, that the child is neither suffering from an incurable disease, nor is he experiencing great suffering. Moreover, the wishes of the child are not known and there is nothing "extraordinary" or "heroic" about the operation. The parents, if their words are taken literally, are requesting mercy killing, an even more drastic action than that proposed by the doctor.

In 1983, Stephen Dawson, the boy in the story upon which this situation is based, became a ward of the state after social workers at his hospital intervened, fearing that

Stephen would be left to die (Ross, 1983, p.27). Further court proceedings granted custody to the parents and it appeared that Stephen would be denied his operation. The British Columbia Supreme Court, however, reversed the decision of the lower court and ordered the operation. "The court's presumption," it said, "must be in favour of life." Stephen received his belated operation and returned to his hospital school.

## Living Wills

An *advanced directive form*, when completed by the person whose life is at risk, is a type of living will. **Living wills** are documents that are written by mentally competent persons that express their wishes with respect to a possible time in the future when they are no longer mentally competent. Should they end up in circumstances where they are rendered mentally incompetent, then the living will conveys their wishes. Such wills exist because civil societies value an individual's right to choose. They value the freedom principle. When we examine the two forms of active euthanasia, assisted suicide and mercy killing, we will note that knowing the wishes of the individual whose life is at stake is the ethically significant difference between the two.

## Arguments for and against Natural Death

The least controversial form of euthanasia, natural death, is still opposed by many. Three arguments are often made against it. The *abandonment argument* says that failing to start treatment or stopping treatment constitutes abandonment of the individual and is therefore wrong. Closely related to this argument is the *possible cures argument* that says that a medical cure may be discovered or a miracle cure may occur. Allowing someone to die a natural death eliminates these possibilities and, therefore, it is wrong. Often, a *domino argument* is also made. The approval of passive euthanasia, the argument says, will lead to the approval of active or direct euthanasia. Society will slide down a slippery slope.

In contrast, three arguments are often made in favour of allowing someone to die. The first, the *right to choose argument*, is based firmly on the freedom principle. It says that humans have a fundamental right to decide whether they want to live or die. To keep a person alive against his will, according to this argument, denies the person this basic right and is, therefore, wrong. It should be noted that this argument assumes that we know the will of the person. Sometimes we do, but at other times we don't.

The *mercy argument* says that keeping a suffering person alive by heroic means—keeping him, for example, on life support equipment or doing CPR—extends the period of suffering and is therefore unethical. The right thing to do is to be merciful by keeping the person comfortable until nature takes its course and the person dies a natural death. Closely related to this argument is the *death with dignity argument*. It says that keeping a person alive through extraordinary or heroic measures fails to respect the dignity of the person. That, the argument maintains, is morally wrong.

## (2) Assisted Suicide

A second and more controversial form of euthanasia is assisted suicide. **Assisted suicide** is a form of euthanasia in which a direct action is taken to end the life of a terminally ill person who has asked to be killed. Because a direct or active step is taken to terminate the life of another, this form of euthanasia is also called active or direct euthanasia. Moreover, because the person to be killed has asked to be killed, assisted suicide is also called **active, voluntary** or **direct, voluntary euthanasia**.

Unlike Nancy Bolduc who simply wanted to die a natural death, Sue Rodriguez wanted to be killed. Suffering from Amyotrophic Lateral Sclerosis (ALS) or Lou Gehrig's disease, she wanted to end her life but could not do so herself. Consequently, she sought help, arguing all the way to the Supreme Court of Canada for the right to doctor-assisted suicide (Wood, 1994). In Canada, committing suicide is not a crime; assisting others to end their lives, however, is a crime and it carries a maximum penalty of 14 years imprisonment. The Court denied Sue Rodriguez' request, citing society's concern for "the young, the innocent, the mentally incompetent, and the depressed."

It should be noted that I have called this form of euthanasia "assisted suicide," not "doctor-assisted suicide." I have chosen the broader label because there are cases in which persons assisting others to commit suicide are not doctors. Such cases arise in wartime on the battlefield, for example, when one soldier may kill another because the other is suffering and asks to be killed. In peacetime, too, persons assisting in a suicide are not always medical doctors. The case of Mary Jane Fogarty cited below is a case in point. When people debate the assisted suicide issue, they often assume that the discussion is about doctor-assisted suicide. In any such discussion or debate we do well to state our assumptions clearly.

## Similarities and Differences

One thing is the same in both the Bolduc and Rodriguez cases and one thing is different. From a moral point of view, both the similarity and the difference are important. The thing that is the same is the fact that both women wanted to die. Both were of sound mind and both decided that they preferred death to life. They were both moral agents who understood their circumstances and chose to die. Both of their cases are cases of voluntary euthanasia. Neither, however, could die on her own, and that leads us to the difference between the cases.

The thing that is different in the two cases is that Nancy Bolduc simply wanted to die. She didn't ask anyone to kill her. She only wanted to let nature takes its course, to die a natural death. In contrast, Sue Rodriguez wanted someone to do what she herself could not do. She wanted someone to kill her. Bolduc's situation is one of passive or indirect euthanasia (natural death) while Rodriguez' is one of active or direct euthanasia (assisted suicide).

## Arguments against Assisted Suicide

In previous sections of this chapter we reviewed a number of arguments against killing in self-defence and against natural death. A number of these arguments are also employed against assisted suicide. The *religious argument*, the *pacifist argument*, the *domino argument,* and the *possible cures argument,* for example, have all been used as arguments against assisted suicide. Having examined them earlier, we will not repeat them now. Instead, let's look at three other arguments against assisted suicide.

The *justice argument* says that it is unfair for people to ask others to kill them. As we noted earlier, the justice principle is also called the fairness principle. In discussions of the morality of suicide, one argument that is often made is that suicide is morally wrong because it is unfair to the survivors. The argument under consideration here takes a similar approach but focuses on the individual who is asked to end the life of another. It is unfair and, therefore, ethically wrong, the argument says, for one person to ask another to do such a serious thing, namely, to kill another human being.

A second argument, the *hospice alternative argument*, takes the position that we can keep terminally ill persons comfortable, through hospice care, until nature takes its course and death occurs naturally. This argument is, of course, an argument that advocates a less extreme action than killing. There is a parallel here to one of the conditions for justifiable self-defence. Specifically, it is the point that the minimum necessary force to subdue the attacker is morally preferable to killing the attacker. If a course of action less extreme than killing is possible, many argue that that is the morally preferable thing to do.

Hospice care is an approach to caring for the terminally ill that was initiated by Dr. Cisely Saunders of London, England in the late 1960s (Hurst, 1996). She believed that hospitals were poorly equipped to deal with the terminally ill as they were established primarily to cure people of their illnesses. Many people died in sterile hospital rooms, not in the comfort of their homes. She believed that a new form of care, **hospice care**, was necessary, one in which persons could be kept comfortable in home-like surroundings until they died a natural death. In a hospice, the staff is geared to caring for patients because curing them is not possible. Today many hospitals provide hospice care. In hospitals, this care is usually called **palliative care**; a palliative being anything that soothes or comforts.

Hospices or palliative care units focus on care, not cure. They specialize in the relief of physical pain and offer various forms of emotional support. A very personalized approach to caring for the dying allows the patient to have personal belongings, such as quilts and pictures, in their rooms. Even supervised pet visits may be permitted. Doctors and nurses provide the physical necessities while counsellors and clergy offer psychological and spiritual support in a team effort to allow for a natural death with dignity. For many, hospice care is a morally preferable alternative to assisted suicide.

A third argument against assisted suicide is called the *possible abuses argument*. This argument says that approving of assisted suicide will give persons the opportunity to kill others for selfish reasons while claiming to be merciful. Family members, for example, may pressure an ailing grandparent into assisted suicide, not because they want the grandparent to have death with dignity but because they want the inheritance.

In a 1995 Nova Scotia case, Mary Jane Fogarty was convicted of aiding and abetting a suicide. She assisted her friend Brenda Barnes to commit suicide, becoming the first person in Canada to be convicted for that crime. In addition to helping Barnes end her life, Fogarty apparently wrote Barnes' suicide note for her, a note that made Fogarty the recipient of all of Barnes' possessions, including a $100 000 life insurance policy (Canadian Press, 1995). A case like this one illustrates clearly the concern expressed in the *possible abuses argument*.

## Arguments for Assisted Suicide

Supporters of assisted suicide make a counter-argument to this last argument. The *legal protections argument* says that protection against potential abuses can be written into any law that would legalize assisted suicide. Advocates often cite the legislation and regulations that have been established in jurisdictions where assisted suicide is permitted. The Northern Territory, an Australian state, and the state of Oregon in the United States are examples. The Netherlands, too, is often cited as a model. There, the lower chamber of parliament recently passed a law permitting doctor-assisted suicide. The upper chamber is expected to ratify the bill in 2001 (Canadian Press, 2000).

As we noted earlier, the primary argument for passive euthanasia, the *right to choose argument,* is based on the principle of freedom. An individual's right to decide whether to live or die, the argument urges, is the most important ethical consideration. Competent individuals should have the right to decide whether theirs is a quality life that is worth living or not. This *right to choose argument* is also the fundamental argument in support of assisted suicide.

The *mercy argument,* also discussed above under natural death, is another key argument in support of assisted suicide. If individuals are mentally competent, believe that their lives are of poor quality, and want to die but can't kill themselves, then they should be helped to die for mercy's sake. When our pets suffer and there is no hope of cure, the argument goes, we put them to death to be merciful to them. Why would we not do the same for a fellow human being? Isn't a human being of greater value than a pet? The ethical thing to do is to be mercifully kind to suffering humans, isn't it? Supporters of the mercy argument say "yes" to these questions.

Before examining mercy killing, let's consider another case. This situation is based on events that occurred in 1982, about a year before the Stephen Dawson case that we looked at above.

| SITUATION 6.3 | **Pain Relief** |
| --- | --- |

An infant girl is born severely disabled and is immediately put on life support systems. Her condition is so severe that she will die without these mechanical aids. Her parents, suspecting that their child is brain dead, tearfully agree with the attending physician who advises them to take the child off life support. The child is removed from the equipment. A nurse, concerned that the child is in pain, asks a second doctor to help her relieve the infant's pain. Without consulting the parents or anyone else, the doctor writes an order for 15 milligrams of morphine—50 times the normal dose—and gives it to the nurse to administer to the baby. The dose will not only relieve any pain, it will also kill the baby.

What, in your opinion, should the nurse do? Consider as many courses of action as you can. What would be the best thing to do? Give your reasons. Also, make note of any circumstances in the situation that you think are odd.

## (3) Mercy Killing

In the view of many, mercy killing is the most extreme form of euthanasia. **Mercy killing** is a form of euthanasia in which a direct action is taken to kill a terminally ill person without knowing that person's wishes. Mercy killing is direct, non-voluntary euthanasia. Unlike assisted suicide, in mercy killing the wishes of the person whose life is in question are not known. Under Canadian law, the premeditated killing of another person is murder, and the penalty for murder is life imprisonment. Murder, of course, is what a Saskatchewan court found Robert Latimer guilty of in the death of his 12-year-old daughter Tracy.

Tracy Latimer suffered from cerebral palsy, and her father, Robert, believed that his daughter was in constant pain. He couldn't stand the thought of Tracy undergoing another operation. On a Sunday morning when the rest of the family was in church, he placed his daughter in the family pickup truck and pumped carbon monoxide gas from the running engine into the cab, killing Tracy (Jenish, 1994).

Robert Latimer was eventually convicted of second-degree murder, a crime that carries a penalty of life in prison with no eligibility for parole for 10 years. The jury recommended a one-year sentence. The judge, however, sentenced him to two years, a lighter than usual sentence that is permissible under a special constitutional exemption clause. Supporters of Robert Latimer were dismayed that he had to serve time at all. In contrast, many advocates of the rights of the disabled could not believe that one could kill a disabled person and receive so light a sentence.

In 1998, after a long series of legal encounters, the Saskatchewan Court of Appeal affirmed that Latimer is guilty of murder in the second degree, and it overturned the earlier sentence, imposing a life sentence with no possibility of parole for 10 years. In January 2001, the Supreme Court of Canada rejected Robert Latimer's appeal, upholding the Saskatchewan high court sentence.

## Arguments against Mercy Killing

One of the arguments that is frequently brought forward in opposition to mercy killing is a special version of the *possible abuses argument.* We noted that argument previously in our discussion of assisted suicide. There, the potential abuse was that a person might kill for selfish reasons, not merciful ones. That concern is also part of the argument here, but there is an added dimension of concern with respect to mercy killing.

The added concern has to do with the question, "Who determines the quality of a person's life?" Advocates of the rights of the disabled, for example, argue that it is too easy for an able-bodied person to make the judgment that a disabled person's life is of poor quality. There is a fear that some people will take it upon themselves to judge that the lives of other persons are of such poor quality that death is preferable to life. This is exactly the judgment, it is argued, that Robert Latimer made with respect to his daughter Tracy.

Andrew Coyne, writing in *The Globe and Mail* following the deaths of Sue Rodriguez and Tracy Latimer, makes an additional argument that is often linked to the *possible abuses argument* that we have just reviewed (Coyne, 1994). The *sanctity of life argument* says that all human life is sacred or precious in itself, regardless of its quality. **Sanctity of life,** then, refers to life's sacredness or holiness. The word *sanctity* means sacred or holy. Our society, Coyne argues, is sliding down a slippery slope that leads to death because it has lost its reverence for all human life. In the process, more and more humans are taking the view that they can determine whether another person's life is worth living or not. People, it is argued, will make more and more negative judgments about the quality of the lives of others because society has lost sight of the fact that all human life is sacred.

A third argument, the *hospice alternative argument,* is often added to the two previous arguments against mercy killing. We noted this argument earlier during our examination of assisted suicide. If it is judged by society that a human life is one of suffering and poor quality, then society can provide hospice care for that individual. Such care, it is argued, can relieve the suffering of the individual and provide death with dignity in a supportive, caring setting. Killing is not necessary.

## Arguments for Mercy Killing

Advocates of mercy killing make a number of arguments in support of terminating the lives of others. The *quality of life argument* says that killing someone whose life is one of suffering and poor quality is morally preferable to keeping the individual alive through heroic measures or hospice care. *Quality*, of course, refers to the degree of excellence that something possesses. To keep someone alive when that person will never return to a meaningful and productive life is cruel and immoral. Life is not sacred in and of itself, the argument continues. It is the quality of a human life that is important, and that is the ethically significant point.

A second argument in favour of mercy killing is the *burdens argument*. When an individual's life is of poor quality and there is no hope of recovery, then both family and society carry an unnecessary burden. It is morally wrong, the argument continues, to keep a person alive under these circumstances. Families are placed in the position of having to watch, sometimes for very long periods of time, the futile life and slow death of a loved one.

This emotional burden at the personal level may also include a financial burden in jurisdictions where society doesn't bear the cost of care. And, where society does bear the burden of cost, it is wrong, the argument continues, because there is no reasonable hope of the individual returning to a productive life. Merciful killing of the individual, it is argued, is in the best interests of all, the individual, family, and society.

The concern for persons abusing mercy killing can be dealt with as it was in the case of assisted suicide. If mercy killing were condoned, potential abuses could be protected against. The *legal protections argument* says that society could endorse mercy killing under legally restricted conditions in order to prevent abuses. Only a doctor with family approval and medical-team certification, for example, could legally end the life of a person. Other important conditions might also be included. The law can be written, it is argued, to protect against possible abuses.

Situation 6.3 is based on the very short life of Candace Taschuk (Ross, 1983, p.24). The events took place in an Edmonton hospital. The second doctor, the one who ordered the lethal dose, was the first doctor in Canada to be charged with murder in a case of euthanasia. Dr. Nachum Gal, a visiting resident physician, returned to his native Israel where he escaped prosecution by Canadian authorities. At the time, there was no extradition agreement between Canada and Israel (Ross and Elliott, 1983). The nurse was never charged.

Euthanasia is a contentious issue in society, but even more contentious, it seems, is the matter of abortion. Let's turn our attention to that issue now, remembering that we are examining a number of moral concerns that fall under the principle of goodness, the principle that says we are to do good and not harm others in society.

## ABORTION

An **abortion** is an expulsion of a fetus from its womb before the fetus is viable. When the expulsion occurs as an accident of nature, it is called a **spontaneous abortion** or miscarriage. When an expulsion is the result of human intervention, it is called an **induced abortion**. Spontaneous abortions, while often traumatic, have not been the subject of moral debate. Ethical questions and concerns abound, however, with respect to induced abortions.

The issue of abortion may well be the most contentious moral issue in our society today. The debate between those who take the pro-life position and those who take the pro-choice position, as the extremes in the debate have come to be known, has filled the media on a regular basis. No other issue has led to violence in the streets to the degree that this issue has. Violent confrontations outside abortion clinics and sniper shootings of abortion providers are examples.

In Canada three doctors have been the victims of sniper shootings. Doctor Garson Romalis of Vancouver, Dr. Hugh Short of Ancaster, and Dr. Jack Fairman of Winnipeg were all injured by snipers who were intent upon doing them harm. Many, including the police, believe that these shootings are related to the fact that these doctors provided abortion services, services that were legal in Canada at the time of the shootings. Each of these doctors escaped death but not injury. Dr. Barnett Slapien of Buffalo, New York, was not as fortunate. He was killed. Police in both Canada and the United States continue to search for his killer.

## The Legal Status

Abortion is currently legal in Canada, but that has not always been the case. Prior to 1969 all abortions were illegal, and the maximum penalty for performing an abortion was life in prison. From 1969 to 1988, therapeutic abortions were legal in Canada provided that four conditions were met. The abortion had to be approved by a hospital committee, performed in a hospital, performed by a doctor, and performed to protect the life or health of the pregnant woman. In 1988 the Supreme Court of Canada struck down the therapeutic abortion law on the grounds that it was unconstitutional.

During the 1970s and 1980s, Dr. Henry Morgentaler led the fight for abortion rights in Canada. He was convicted a number of times for providing abortions outside the parameters of the law, and he spent time in jail (Riley, 1983). Eventually juries in Quebec refused to convict him. He then took his case to the rest of Canada, opening up abortion clinics in Manitoba, Ontario, and Nova Scotia. Again he faced charges in court. Eventually the Supreme Court was required to pass final judgment on his actions.

Morgentaler always believed that abortion was a matter between a woman and her doctor, a matter of one's right to make a choice, free from the interference of others. The court battles were eventually won by convincing the justices that the therapeutic abortion law was unfair to Canadian women. Women in communities with liberal-minded abortion committees, for example, had abortion virtually upon request, while women in communities with conservative committees were denied access to safe abortions. In 1988 the Supreme Court declared the law unconstitutional and no new abortion law has replaced it.

## Legal Rights of the Fetus

As with many issues in life, the differing views on abortion fall into extreme conservative, extreme liberal, and moderate points of view. We will examine the extreme positions first and then turn to a moderate view of the issue. Before doing so, however, we'll first review a Canadian case that has contributed to the ongoing public debate on fetal rights.

In 1996 an emotionally distraught woman, Brenda Drummond, placed a loaded gun into her vagina and fired a pellet into the brain of her near-term fetus. Two days later, she delivered her son, Jonathan. She didn't tell anyone of his injury and didn't seek medical help for him. Eventually, doctors discovered the injury and removed the pellet. Jonathan survived (Stern, 1997).

A charge of attempted murder was laid against the mother. The charge was soon withdrawn, however, as a fetus has no legal rights under Canadian law. In effect, there was no person to murder or attempt to murder. Eventually, the mother was convicted of child neglect, failing to provide the necessities of life. Once she delivered, there was, legally speaking, a person to neglect.

This particular case highlights the moral and legal dilemma of abortion. How can it be, many ask, that two days prior to birth—or even two minutes prior, for that matter—fetal life can be destroyed with impunity? Isn't such life entitled to the protection of the law? Many disagree with the law, but the law is clear. There is no legally recognized person prior to birth.

## The Extreme Pro-Choice Approach

Various arguments are made in support of the extreme pro-choice position.

The *right to choose argument* is not so much an argument, perhaps, as it is an assertion. Essentially, it says that during the time of her pregnancy a woman has an absolute right to decide what will happen to her body. This argument is one in which its advocates place high value on the principle of freedom. A woman's right to make her own choices is the focal point of this approach to the issue of abortion.

The *developmental argument* says that a human person is not present at conception but is in development throughout pregnancy, becoming a reality only at or near birth. To terminate a pregnancy is not to kill a person. The argument takes the line that the fetus is only a *potential* person. It becomes an actual person, on this view, only at birth. That, of course, is the position taken by Canadian law on this issue.

A third argument is the *quality of life argument*. It says that a woman alone has the right to decide when her life or the life of her fetus is a quality life. An unwanted pregnancy, for example, can be terminated in order to ensure the her life is of sufficient quality and that she, with the help of her doctor, is the sole judge of what constitutes a quality life. Economic matters are valid considerations as is the rare, but most horrific, experience of becoming pregnant due to rape.

## The Extreme Pro-Life Approach

Those who take the extreme pro-life position make a number of arguments in support of their position. Here are two of the central points.

The *sanctity of life argument* says that all human life is sacred, including human life in the womb. Following the principle of goodness, advocates of this approach insist that we must not wilfully harm others. To intentionally kill an innocent person is an especially grievous harm. There is an absolute moral requirement, it is maintained, to refrain from intentionally ending the life of an innocent person.

Advocates of the extreme pro-life position make a further argument that is intimately linked to the sanctity of life argument. The *conception argument* says that a human being exists from the moment of conception. Human parents contribute egg and sperm that unite to form a new human being, a new person. On this approach, an actual human being comes into existence at conception. This new person, as noted above, is seen to be innocent and must, therefore, be protected from harm.

Pro-life advocates also make the *adoption argument*. Adoption, they maintain, is a morally required alternative to abortion. If a woman believes that her life and the life of her unborn child will be of poor quality, then she should carry her baby to term and give her child up for adoption. Adoption is considered a morally required option in that the alternative, aborting the child, is seen as murdering an innocent human being. On this view, the "adoption option" is an ethical solution to concerns about the quality of life of both mother and child.

Extreme pro-life advocates also argue that conception through rape does not justify the termination of a pregnancy. The horror of rape is acknowledged, but the product of conception is seen as an innocent victim, an innocent human being created through terrible circumstances. To kill an innocent human being, as noted previously, is morally unacceptable on this view.

## The Moral Standing of the Fetus

When one focuses on the earliest moments after conception—the biological stages of the zygote, morula, blastula, and blastocyst, for example—it is not difficult to understand why many people do not see these cell clusters as a person. It is equally easy to understand why people who take that view place greater value on the mother than on the embryonic or fetal life within the mother. (Reread Media Watch items 2.1 and 2.2 at the end of Chapter 2.)

In contrast, when one focuses on the time just prior to birth—the stage of the near-term fetus—it is not difficult to understand why many argue that such a fetus deserves protection of the law and that it is entitled to rights not unlike those the mother has. It's hard to imagine that this fully developed fetus is not a human being with moral standing. The fetus, in the time immediately prior to birth, many argue, is entitled to the full protection of the law.

When, in the progression from conception to birth, does a human person begin to exist? When, in other words, does the fetus have moral standing? At conception, argues one extreme. At birth, argues the other. What both points of view have in common is that they are both extreme views and absolutist views.

An **absolute**, you will recall, is a principle or rule that has no exceptions. One can never justify going against the rule because it has been determined, in advance, that there is no exception to the rule. On the one hand, a woman's right to choose is seen as inviolable. On the other, the fetus's right to life is inviolable.

## A Moderate Approach

Many who have thought about the issue of abortion believe that a third point of view is morally defensible. The moderate position on abortion is not simply a cynical, middle-of-the-road political position. It is an honest attempt to deal with a very challenging and emotionally charged moral dilemma. On the moderate view, life in the womb is valued but so is a woman's right to choose. Throughout the gestation period, the rights of both fetus and mother are taken into consideration.

During the first **trimester**, or one-third of a normal 39-week pregnancy, the fetus is accorded minimal rights while the mother is accorded maximal rights. This amounts to abortion upon request in the first 13 weeks of a pregnancy. As the fetus develops in the second trimester, the moderate view accords it more rights but does not ignore the mother's rights. A pregnancy can be justifiably terminated during this period if the fetus is determined to have a serious defect or if the mother's life is at risk. In the third trimester, the fetus is accorded rights almost equal to those of its mother. On the moderate view, only a risk to the mother's life would justify an abortion this late in a pregnancy.

Most abortions are performed very early in a pregnancy. Almost 90 percent occur in the first trimester, with an additional nine percent occurring before the mid-point of a normal pregnancy, at roughly 20 weeks. R. David Andrew of Queen's University School of Medicine in Kingston makes the point that the human neocortex does not even exist prior to the 20th week of gestation (Andrew, 1991). The **neocortex** is that part of our anatomy that is responsible for our distinctly human traits, traits such as complex language, precision movements of eyes and hands, incredible memory storage, and the power of forethought. It is responsible for both consciousness and voluntary control of bodily movements.

In our time, *death* is defined as "death of the brain." More specifically, when the neocortex fails to generate electrical impulses, a person is considered clinically dead. On the basis of this commonly accepted definition, we say that a person ceases to exist when the neocortex ceases to function. Could Andrew be suggesting that a human person begins to exist when the neocortex begins to function? I think so, and his argument is compelling for many. If we determine human death by the cessation of neocortical waves, why wouldn't we determine human birth by the commencement of such waves? A person begins to exist when the neocortex begins to function. On this view, "birth" occurs in the womb about five months along in the pregnancy.

It is information such as Andrew provides that lends support to the moderate position on abortion. It is this kind of information that ensures that a reasoned moderate position, as described above, is not just a cynical sitting on the political fence in the abortion debate, a debate that continues to challenge the minds and hearts of people on all sides.

## CHAPTER SUMMARY

We began this chapter with a brief look at the principle of goodness, noting that it is a fundamental principle within any civil society, the principle that insists that we do good to others and not harm them. Under this principle, we examined three important ethical issues: self-defence, euthanasia, and abortion.

With respect to self-defence, we first looked at a recent case in which the courts accepted sustained child abuse as justification for killing an abusive parent. We noted the similarity to cases in which abused women have defended themselves by killing their abusive partners. Next we reviewed arguments for and against killing in self-defence. In the review, we highlighted the traditional criteria for justifiable self-defence as expressed in the *necessary evil argument*. We concluded our study of this issue by examining the concepts of proportional force and minimal force, the use of force by police and the military, and the *just war argument*.

Next we turned to the topic of euthanasia, noting that there are three forms of euthanasia: natural death, assisted suicide, and mercy killing. We defined natural death and discussed key concepts such as DNR orders, heroic measures, and living wills. Arguments for and against natural death were then reviewed.

We proceeded to define assisted suicide, discussed the Bolduc and Rodriguez cases, and examined arguments both for and against assisted suicide. We also included a description of hospice care, an alternative to assisted suicide. We noted further that assisted suicide is illegal in Canada, carrying a maximum penalty of 14 years.

Mercy killing, the third form of euthanasia, was then defined. We discussed the Latimer case and then looked at arguments for and against mercy killing. The question of what constitutes quality of life was addressed, as was the question of who decides what constitutes a quality life. We noted that Canadian law makes mercy killing a crime, the crime of murder, punishable by life imprisonment.

Last of all, we turned to a review of the abortion issue. We defined abortion, distinguishing between spontaneous and induced abortions. Next, we summarized the legal history of abortion in Canada. We then turned to the question of fetal rights and used the Drummond case to highlight the moral difficulty of determining the moral standing of the unborn.

We reviewed the extreme pro-life position and the extreme pro-choice position, noting the key arguments that surface in the debate between these extreme views. We then concluded with a description of a moderate approach to the abortion question.

## MASTERING THE MATERIAL

Now that you have read this chapter, use the following guides to ensure that you have mastered the material.

## Introduction

1. What is the ultimate goal of a civil society?
2. State the goodness principle as both a positive and a negative duty.

## Using Defensive Force

1. How do civil societies protect against external and internal threats?
2. What concerns George Jonas regarding successful defences based on prior abuse?
3. Identify and explain three arguments against killing in self-defence.
4. What is a pacifist?
5. What is an absolute position?
6. Explain the self-contradiction in the pacifist position regarding self-defence.
7. What is a *slippery slope argument*?
8. State the *necessary evil argument* in support of killing in self-defence.
9. Identify the three criteria traditionally used to justify killing in self-defence.
10. Explain the concepts of proportional and minimal force.
11. How do military and police roles differ with respect to the use of lethal force?
12. State the *just war argument* including its three criteria.

## Euthanasia

1. What is the literal meaning of *euthanasia*?
2. Identify three forms of euthanasia.

## Natural Death

3.  Define *natural death* and give two other names for this form of euthanasia.
4.  What is a Do-Not-Resuscitate order?
5.  What are heroic measures and what makes them heroic?
6.  Explain the significance of the Nancy Bolduc case.
7.  What is a living will?
8.  Identify and explain three arguments against natural death and three arguments in defence of it.

## Assisted Suicide

9.  Define *assisted suicide*.
10. Explain the significance of the Sue Rodriguez case.
11. Describe how the Bolduc and Rodriguez cases are similar and how they are different.
12. Identify and explain three arguments against assisted suicide and three arguments in defence of it.
13. Define and describe *hospice care* and give another name for it.
14. Explain the significance of the Mary Jane Fogarty case.

## Mercy Killing

15. Define *mercy killing*.
16. What is the significance of the Tracy Latimer case?
17. Identify and explain three arguments against mercy killing and three arguments in defence of it.
18. State the legal protections argument for mercy killing.

# Abortion

1.  Define *abortion* and describe two types of abortion.
2.  Identify the four criteria of a legal abortion under Canada's old abortion law.
3.  What is the significance of the Brenda Drummond case?
4.  State three arguments for abortion offered by extreme pro-choice advocates.
5.  State three arguments against abortion offered by extreme pro-life advocates.
6.  Summarize the moderate view of rights in each of the trimesters of a pregnancy.

## CRITICAL THINKING IN POLICING: THE PRINCIPLES MODEL

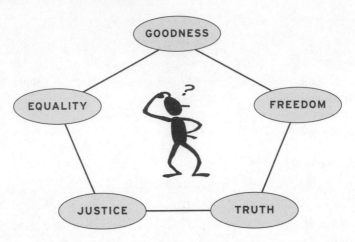

Moral agents act ethically when they choose to act in ways that will produce good for themselves and others and when they choose to avoid causing harm to themselves or others.

## CRITICAL THINKING IN POLICING: THE DECIDE PROCESS

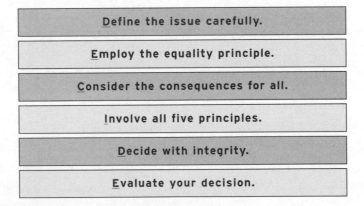

**D**efine the issue carefully.

**E**mploy the equality principle.

**C**onsider the consequences for all.

**I**nvolve all five principles.

**D**ecide with integrity.

**E**valuate your decision.

**Step #2: Employ the equality principle.** This step reminds you that everyone is of equal moral value and that you need to think objectively and act impartially, showing neither preference nor prejudice.

| Media Watch: Ethics in the News 6.1 | Abused youth killed mom, sentenced to six months |

TORONTO—A youth who stabbed his abusive mother to death was sentenced Tuesday to six months in closed custody in one of the first cases in which child abuse was raised as a defence.

The teen, who was 16 at the time, stabbed her 10 times with two different kitchen knives a day after she tried to strangle him in January 1997, court heard.

Neither the teen, who had pleaded guilty to manslaughter, nor his mother can be named under provisions of the Young Offenders Act.

The diminutive youth, who was raised by his grandparents and had no memory of his mother before he was eight, suffered years of physical and emotional abuse at her hands, including being beaten almost daily, court heard.

There was also testimony that she frequently belittled him and that she had planned to leave her family for a job in California the day after the stabbing.

Dr. Charles Ewing, an American forensic psychologist, testified that there are direct parallels between battered women who kill their abuser and children who kill abusive parents.

Raising child abuse as a defence is new in this country.

"This is certainly the first case in Canada of this type that has come before the courts, though there is a history of it in the United States," defence lawyer Steve Skurka told reporters.

The youth must spend a further four months in open custody followed by 12 months probation.

Source: *Kitchener-Waterloo Record*, October 21, 1999, A4.

| Media Watch: Ethics in the News 6.2 | Give terminally ill the right to die |
| --- | --- |

In the end, Sue Rodriguez had it her way. She died Saturday at home, never succumbing completely to the paralyzing effects of Lou Gehrig's disease. Only the federal government's persistent refusal to recognize the rights of the terminally ill marred her peaceful passage.

Equally unfortunate is the need for the investigation begun after MP Svend Robinson called the RCMP to her home in Victoria, B.C. He was with her at the time of her doctor-assisted suicide.

Although it is legal to commit suicide, it is a crime to counsel, aid or abet someone else. That means anyone too ill or disabled to perform the act has fewer rights than an able-bodied person.

It was this discrimination that Rodriguez devoted the last few years of her life to fighting. Her case—the first to challenge the issue of assisted suicide—simply divided the Supreme Court of Canada. The court decided against her on the grounds that the law was needed to retain respect for life, to prevent Canada from sliding down a slippery slope to involuntary euthanasia, and to protect the vulnerable from abuse.

However, a new study from Simon Fraser University suggests that assisted suicide takes place anyway. Rather than prevent it, the absence of guidelines actually appears to have contributed to greater suffering at the hands of individuals who lack sufficient medical experience. A similar problem arose when women were forced to get illegal "back-alley" abortions.

Appropriate safeguards could easily be introduced. In a strong dissent in the Rodriguez case, Supreme Court Chief Justice Antonio Lamer outlined possible guidelines for legal assisted suicide, opening the door wide for Parliament to act.

To soften the federal law, B.C. recently passed new provincial guidelines giving the Crown the discretion to decide whether to lay charges in individual cases. But Rodriguez would never have been satisfied with such hit-and-miss justice, and neither should Canadians. Everyone—regardless of their physical ability—should have the right to die with dignity.

As Sue Rodriguez wrote to federal Justice Minister Alan Rock from her death bed: "I hope that my efforts will not have been in vain."

Source: *Toronto Star*, February 15, 1994, A16.

## chapter seven

# Equality: Treating Others Impartially in a Civil Society

## LEARNING OUTCOMES

After completing this chapter, you should be able to

- Define *equality*
- State the equality principle as both a positive duty and a negative duty
- Identify the equality principle within the Universal Declaration of Human Rights
- Identify the equality principle within the Charter of Rights and Freedoms
- Identify the equality principle within the Code of Conduct of the Ontario Police Services Act
- Identify the equality principle within the Law Enforcement Code of Ethics
- Describe and discuss certain equality issues associated with racism and sexism
- Describe and discuss equality with respect to patriotism and family favouritism
- Describe and discuss equality issues associated with professional conduct

## INTRODUCTION

In Chapter 5 we identified the five basic principles upon which a civil society is established. One of those principles is the principle of equality. **Equality**, of course, means having the same rights and responsibilities as others. In our study in that chapter we noted references to the **principle of equality** in the Universal Declaration of Human Rights, the Canadian Charter of Rights and Freedoms, the Code of Conduct of the Ontario Police Services Act, and the Law Enforcement Code of Ethics. It is not surprising that the **equality principle** appears repeatedly in these documents as this principle is one of the fundamental ethical principles of any civil society. Stated as a **positive duty**, the equality principle says, "Treat others as moral equals." Stated as a **negative duty**, it says, "Don't discriminate against others."

Also, in our earlier studies of prescriptive ethics in Chapter 3, we noted the importance of the practical imperative in our study of duty ethics. You will recall that duty ethics, among other things, saw clearly how conduct as prescribed by utilitarianism could end up being discriminatory. When utilitarians pursue the greatest good for the greatest number, for example, a minority of people may suffer great harm in the process. The practice of slavery was cited as an example of how the good of the majority can be established at the expense of the minority. The end does not necessarily justify the means.

To counter the weaknesses in the utilitarian prescription, Immanuel Kant recognized that the principle of equality is an essential principle of any ethical system. This principle, you will recall, is the principle that requires us to treat each and every person as a human being, not a thing. Never use another human being solely as a means to your end, he argued; always treat others with the respect that human beings deserve. The human capacity to reason and to make choices, he believed, are the two characteristics that distinguish humans from all other beings. They are the qualities that require humans, morally speaking, to respect one another.

Applying the equality principle, the Universal Declaration of Human Rights states that it is wrong to discriminate for or against another person solely on the basis of "race, national or ethnic origin, colour, sex, language, religion, political or other opinion, national or social origin, property, birth, or other status." To discriminate against another person because of skin colour, for example, is to discriminate on the basis of superficial qualities of the individual. A person's nobility resides in her humanity, her capacity to reason and make choices, not in her skin colour. We have also seen that the Canadian Charter of Rights and Freedoms is consistent with the Declaration on this matter.

As we saw in both Chapters 4 and 5, the Code of Conduct of the Ontario Police Services Act, in harmony with the Declaration and the Canadian Charter of Rights and Freedoms, forbids discrimination by police officers. An officer is guilty of discreditable conduct if he or she "fails to treat or protect a person equally without discrimination with respect to police services because of that person's race, ancestry, place of origin, colour, ethnic origin, citizenship, creed, sex, sexual orientation, age, marital status, family status or handicap."

We need to note clearly, however, that individuals can lose their right to equal treatment by conducting themselves in morally unacceptable ways. The thief, when apprehended and convicted, loses his right to equal treatment. His right to freedom, for example, is taken away as punishment for his offence. We will return to this point in the chapter on justice, where we will examine the subject of punishment. There we will note a number of important connections between the equality principle and the justice principle.

## THE GOOD SOCIETY AND THE GOOD PERSON

### The Good Society

Ancient philosophers, like Plato, often discussed the qualities that defined, in their view, the "Good Society." In our time, many would argue that the Good Society is the society that lives by the principle of equality, treating all its members with equal respect, according them equal rights and freedoms under the law. That, no doubt, is what the United

Nations had in mind when it proclaimed the Universal Declaration of Human Rights to be "a common standard of achievement for all peoples and all nations." The Declaration's purpose is to ensure "that every individual and every organ of society ... shall strive by teaching and education to promote respect for these rights and freedoms and by progressive measures, national and international, to secure their universal and effective recognition and observance." The Declaration, centred on the equal dignity of all members of the human family, prescribes the qualities of the ideal civil society, the Good Society of modern times.

## The Good Person

The philosophers of the past also occupied themselves with the qualities of the "Good Person." What characteristics, they asked, are associated with being a virtuous human being? An essential quality of the Good Person in our time, it would seem, is the ability and the willingness to treat all other members of the human family equally, respecting the inherent dignity of all. Respect for the dignity of the individual human being may well be the key to conducting oneself in an ethical manner. If one fails to see others as moral equals, then all kinds of unethical practices are likely to follow with respect to those other persons. Racism reveals this fact clearly, and it continues to survive only because of the ignorance and malice of those who prefer to live by their prejudices rather than the facts.

As a nation, Canada values the equality principle. That is not to say that Canada hasn't favoured or doesn't favour certain racial groups over others. Many Aboriginal persons and persons of colour, for example, will argue that racism is alive and well in Canada. Even a cursory review of the history of the nation will reveal both individual and institutional practices that have discriminated against minority groups.

Having acknowledged racist elements within Canadian society, it is important to underscore that Canada is a civil society founded on basic human rights and freedoms that are protected by law. The Canadian Charter of Rights and Freedoms guarantees equality of all citizens under the law. Section 15, entitled Equality Rights, forbids discrimination based on race, national origin, ethnic origin, colour, religion, sex, age, or mental or physical disability. Throughout, the Charter places high value on the equality of all members of the Canadian family. Canada, as a civil society, endorses the ideal set forth in the United Nations Declaration and pursues that ideal through the rule of law.

In Chapter 4 we presented eight characteristics of the ideal police officer. The eight traits expected of an officer are qualities that are desirable in all citizens. We underscored the fact that police officers are role models for members of a civil society. What makes a good police officer makes a good person. The qualities of the good officer, you will recall, are the following: courage, self-restraint, concern for others, honesty, obedience, trustworthiness, impartiality, and professionalism. The last two traits, impartiality and professionalism, are particularly relevant to the issues in this chapter.

## STEREOTYPES AND DISCRIMINATION

A **stereotype** is a false and misleading idea about a particular group and its members. Often the stereotypes of other races, for example, include the notion that these others are morally weaker than and intellectually inferior to members of one's own group. Consequently, such ideas foster fears of those who, according to the stereotype, can't be trusted. In addition, the ideas foster the feeling that one's own group is superior to the other group and entitled to dominate its members.

Thinking that employs stereotypes is called **stereotypical thinking**. Since it is based on false and misleading ideas, this kind of thinking inevitably results in faulty reasoning. Stereotypes are not based, for example, on valid inductive reasoning, but on flawed and lazy thinking. People who use stereotypical thinking on a regular basis, and many people do, are guilty of faulty reasoning. Faulty reasoning is a subject that we first examined in Chapter 2.

Stereotypical thinking is at the heart of prejudice. A **prejudice** is a pre-judgment. To be prejudiced is to pre-judge people and events. We judge that a person of a particular group has certain traits, for instance, before we even meet the person. Individuals are pre-judged on the basis of flawed ideas. Stereotypical thinking and prejudice exist in our heads. They are part of our **cognitive dimension,** our rational side. As is always the case, what is in our heads affects what is in our hearts.

The **affective dimension** of our humanity, you will recall, refers to our emotional or feeling side. Stereotypes influence our emotions. More specifically, they obviously discourage **empathy**, the moral feeling. People who cannot identify emotionally with the circumstances and feelings of other persons are much more likely to discriminate against those others and treat them unjustly. Psychopaths are seriously disturbed persons who have no empathy whatsoever for others. Consequently, they can do the most heinous things to others and have no feelings of guilt. The more people use stereotypical thinking, the more they resemble psychopaths. Consider, for a moment, how racists treat their victims.

What is in our heads and what is in our hearts inevitably determines our behaviour. Our thoughts and feelings motivate our actions. It is no surprise, then, that stereotypical thinking and a lack of empathy leads to discriminatory behaviour. Prejudice is a flawed way of thinking, and discrimination is prejudice put into action. **Discrimination**, we have noted several times, refers to the unequal treatment of others based on ethically irrelevant criteria. Discrimination is a part of the **behavioural dimension**, the actions of human beings. It is discrimination that codes of conduct forbid, and they do so because discrimination violates the equality principle. Notice further that discrimination is unfair treatment, a violation of the justice principle.

When stereotypical ideas and prejudices become the dominant ideas of an institution of society, we refer to the resulting discrimination as **systemic discrimination**. Entire social systems become racist or sexist, for example, and these systems discriminate against one group or another. To put the point differently, stereotypical thinking pervades the institution in its policies and practices. Systemic discrimination can occur with respect to race, ethnicity, gender, religion, and any number of other factors.

## RACISM

**Racism** is discrimination based on a person's racial characteristics. The history of the human species is, to a large degree, a history of racism. For all our intelligence, we seem to have failed miserably on many occasions with regard to the equal treatment of differing racial groups. Apartheid in South Africa, slavery in the United States, and the treatment of Aboriginal Peoples in Canada are good examples of this sad practice. These practices have occurred, in large part, because of racist beliefs within the human family. Stereotypical thinking has resulted in prejudice and discrimination with respect to many different racial groups.

| SITUATION 7.1 | Important Lessons |
|---|---|

You're approaching the end of your first month as a constable in a small city. It's a bitterly cold winter night and you are patrolling a rough part of town with your partner, a 15-year veteran of the force. He spots a local man staggering along the sidewalk and tells you to pull the cruiser to the curb. Before you know it, your partner has put the man into the back seat of the car. He slams the door shut, climbs back into the car, and tells you to drive toward the outskirts of town. "I'm going to teach you and him an important lesson tonight. You're going to learn how to deal with Indians and he's going to learn how to sober up."

You stop at a deserted spot outside of town. Your partner pulls the man from the cruiser, pushes him to the ground, and strips him of his jacket, shoes, and socks. Back in the car, your partner tells you to head back. "He'll learn his lesson," he says, "and now for yours. Keep your mouth shut about this. His kind don't learn any other way and a lot of people in town just don't understand that. Our report will say that we had a quiet night."

What would you say or do? Be specific and explain your reasoning. If possible, discuss this situation with others and get their views. How is this situation similar to Situation 5.2: Shift Partner in Chapter 5? How is it different?

## Racial Stereotypes

Racial stereotypes and prejudices, like all stereotypes and prejudices, are difficult to eradicate within a society. Children of racist parents acquire their parents' biases very early, and others who share similar views reinforce those prejudices. Very early in life, many children begin to relate to individuals of a different race on the basis of flawed, stereotypical ideas. They prejudge these individuals, believing that their ideas about members of the other race are accurate. Prejudice, flawed ideas in the mind, then leads to discrimination, unfair treatment of the individual.

Is it possible that this kind of stereotypical thinking was at work in a recent incident in Saskatchewan? Two police officers in Saskatoon, it is alleged, took an unruly native outside of town, stripped him of his clothes, and left him to freeze in the sub-zero temperatures. According to Aboriginal leaders, such practices are not new. Is this the most recent racist act in a long series of such acts? Native leaders think so (Canadian Press, 2000).

The officers, who were suspended pending further investigation, may have taken it upon themselves to go beyond their lawful responsibilities to act as vigilante judges, juries, and executioners. They may have acted on the basis of racist beliefs. If this was the case, then both the individual and society suffered an injustice as a result. When such actions occur, then the proper functioning of a civil society is put at risk. Racism is a threat to individuals, groups, and civil society as a whole.

## SEXISM

Many of the points that have been made regarding racism can be repeated with respect to sexism. **Sexism** is discrimination based on gender. Indeed, sexism is just another form of prejudice and discrimination that is based on stereotypical thinking. In this case, of course, the faulty ideas are not associated with skin colour but, as the definition suggests, gender. The male sexist believes that women are genetically suited to do certain tasks, usually those associated with raising children and maintaining a household. Female sexists also employ stereotypical thinking with respect to males. Such thinking often results in discrimination against men.

Sexist ideas and stereotypes have been passed from one generation to the next for centuries. Since our history has been one of male dominance over females, the sexism that usually demands our attention involves males discriminating against females. While feminist reactions to the paternalistic views and practices of male sexists can be found throughout history, only recently have women's struggles for equality had a major impact on the democratic, civil societies of the late twentieth century. Despite greater equality for women in some societies, many others continue to operate within the thought world of sexist ideologies. Sexism, like racism, is alive and well.

---

**SITUATION 7.2**    **The Balcony Rapist**

You are a member of an elite investigating team that is tracking a serial rapist in a large city. The rapist is called "The Balcony Rapist" because, in each of four attacks, he has entered the victim's bedroom from the balcony of her apartment. In each case, the victim was a single woman between the ages of 28 and 40 years who lived alone. Your team has identified a six-square-block area in which the rapist operates. You have also identified 13 women in that area who fit the victim profile. While you have not identified a specific suspect, your team is extremely confident that it will have the rapist in custody soon. His *modus operandi* has given you all you need to capture him the next time he strikes. Any warnings to potential victims or the public, however, are very likely to tip him off and send him underground.

You understand the importance of the secrecy of your operation, but you also wonder about the safety of the potential victims. Your team's task, of course, is to apprehend the rapist. Do you think you should make victim safety an issue with the team? Should the potential victims be warned or not? Explain your thinking. If possible, discuss this situation with others and get their views. We'll return to the Balcony Rapist later.

---

## Sexism in the Workplace

Recent debates about **employment equity**, equality of opportunity and remuneration in the workplace, reveal something of the conscious or unconscious sexism that has been, and no doubt continues to be, a part of our society. In addition, these debates provide us with an excellent example of the important role that ethical debate plays in a civil society. In the past, many Canadian women also fought for **educational equity**, equality of opportunity in schooling, a parallel cause that has proved largely successful. The same sexist views that kept women in inferior positions in the workplace kept them at a disadvantage in the world of higher education. In this review of sexism in Canada, however, we'll restrict ourselves to the employment equity issue.

In the twentieth century in Canada and many other Western societies, it became very clear that women were underpaid compared with their male counterparts. On average, a woman's annual income was about a third less than that of a man. Part of the explanation for the difference, but only a small part, was the predominance of males in supervisory positions that generally paid higher wages. This point, however, simply served to highlight another aspect of the problem faced by women in the workplace. In a man's world, women found it difficult or impossible to rise to positions of leadership. Another aspect of the inequity was the male preservation of certain kinds of jobs for males. In simple terms, many males believed that men were better suited to jobs like firefighting and policing than were women.

## Systemic Sexism

When the analysis was complete with respect to the wage disparity and the disproportionate numbers of women in management positions and certain professions, one conclusion was overriding. Both the sexist attitudes of individuals and organizations contributed to the disparities. **Systemic sexism** refers to social systems that have consciously or unconsciously embraced sexist ideas in the development and implementation of their policies.

Entire institutions, for example, can consciously or unconsciously adopt sexist ways of thinking and acting. Systemic sexism has led to discrimination against women and has kept women at a disadvantage in the Canadian workplace. Once the source of the employment inequity was made clear, the goal of improving the status of women in the workplace became a political objective for many Canadians. But, how does a society change a system that has for so long been the standard way of doing business?

The Canadian Charter of Rights and Freedoms does not guarantee **equality of outcome** or **equality of results** to Canadian citizens. That is, the Charter doesn't say that at the end of the workday both men and women must get the same amount of pay. It does, however, guarantee **equality of opportunity**, an equal chance for men and women to compete for available jobs. Furthermore, its principles require that persons doing work of equal value be paid an equal wage. An employer can't discriminate on the basis of gender in such matters. Moreover, as we saw in Chapter 4, the Charter statement on Equality Rights "does not preclude any law, program, or activity that has as its object the amelioration of conditions of disadvantaged individuals or groups."

## Equity in the Workplace

In order to eliminate inequities in the workplace, governments have established **affirmative action** or **employment equity programs**. These are programs that require employers to hire and promote members of historically disadvantaged groups and to pay them equitably. Affirmative action can be administered in any one of three ways. All three ways, however, are subject to the criticism that they are morally wrong because they are forms of reverse discrimination. We'll return to the *reverse discrimination argument* in a moment.

Before we do, however, let's examine the *special needs argument* that is used to justify affirmative action laws and programs. In a civil society like Canada, the argument begins, we have long maintained the view that persons with physical or developmental disabilities deserve special assistance. For example, we spend tax dollars to make schools accessible to those with physical challenges. Likewise, we spend tax dollars on special programs for the developmentally challenged. Many Canadians readily support these actions that benefit their fellow citizens with special needs. They are convinced that it is only fair to provide special help for these special needs.

Women in the workplace, the reasoning continues, have also had a disability. They have been unable to get work or a promotion because they are women. They have a **social disability**, it is argued, a disadvantage created by social circumstances. Prejudices, discrimination, and stereotypical thinking have disadvantaged women in the work world. No less than a physical or mental disability, a social disability puts a person at a disadvantage. Women need special help to overcome that disadvantage. Affirmative action is the special help.

## Administering Equity Programs

Earlier, we said that there were three methods of administering affirmative action in the workplace. Let's return to those three methods now. One is the *tie-breaking approach*. If two candidates are equally qualified for a job, then the tie is broken in favour of the female. A second method is the *extra-points approach*. Throughout the job interview, female applicants are given extra points because they are from a disadvantaged group. Consequently, a woman could be hired ahead of a man with superior qualifications. The third method is the *quota system approach*. On this approach, an employer must hire a predetermined number of women, and men cannot compete for those positions (Hurka, 1999, p.189).

## The Charge of Reverse Discrimination

In response to these attempts to right an historical wrong, to level the playing field, many argue that these approaches are simply discrimination in reverse. The *reverse discrimination argument* says that jobs should be given on the basis of merit. Available jobs should go to those with the best qualifications as determined in a fair competition. The affirmative action approaches described above, it is argued, all share a common flaw. They all discriminate against males. They are unjust.

In 1994, in the province of Ontario, the New Democratic Party (NDP) government enacted the Employment Equity Act, an act based on the *special needs argument*. The law was short-lived as a newly elected Progressive Conservative (PC) government repealed the act. The editor of *The Kitchener-Waterloo Record*, writing in support of the PC government's action, employed the *reverse discrimination argument,* calling the Employment Equity Act "unfair and illogical." "Even before it passed," wrote the editor, "people in Waterloo Region saw the injustice of affirmative action when the Kitchener fire department rejected a white male applicant in favour of women and visible minorities he outscored on tests" (Editorial, *K-W Record, 1996*).

A more recent editorial in the same newspaper, however, makes it clear that reverse discrimination is not necessarily an easy thing to detect. Citing a 1999 Supreme Court of Canada decision, the editor writes, "A critical victory was won last week when a British

Columbia woman was given back her job as a firefighter even though she failed a fitness test" (Editorial, *K-W Record,* 1999). Earlier, in Chapter 5, we considered a situation based on this case, Situation 5.3, Fire the Firefighter?

After failing a running test four times, Tawney Meiorin was fired by the B.C. Forest Service. The Supreme Court determined that her firing was indefensible as she had done her job successfully for two years. The Court found that the failed running test that led to her dismissal was not relevant to her job as a firefighter. The editorial concludes, "The top court's decision does not in any way put the nation's forests at risk. But it does put at risk unfair and irrelevant hiring standards and Canadian employers should know that they have been warned" (Editorial, *K-W Record,* 1999).

The editor believes that the B.C. Forest Service was not malicious in its firing of the woman. Assuming that the writer is correct on this point, what we may have here is an example of an employment standard produced by unconscious, systemic sexism. The editor says, "But there are two problems with the running test. It was harder for women to pass than men. And there was no proof it was relevant to the job. This was the clincher" (Editorial, *K-W Record,* 1999). One has to wonder at this point whether the tests on which the male firefighter from Kitchener outscored his female competitors were fair tests. If they were, then the *reverse discrimination argument* has some force to it in that case. If they weren't, then it doesn't.

## Sexism in Policing

There is no question that, historically, policing has been one of those professions in our society that was by and large a male preserve. Major changes have occurred and continue to occur, however, as more women enter the police service. According to Statistics Canada, there were 7149 female police officers and 48 151 male police officers in Canada in 1999. One out of eight officers, or 13 percent, were female officers. Moreover, the number of female officers is on the increase, growing by seven percent over the previous year (Canadian Press, 1999). Employment equity programs have had an effect in policing as they have in other areas of Canadian life.

In this regard, it should be noted that in 1998 only three women had risen to the rank of chief of police in Canada: Christine Silverberg in Calgary, Lenna Bradburn in Guelph, and Gwen Boniface of the Ontario Provincial Police. Since then, Silverberg and Bradburn have left their positions. In the case of Lenna Bradburn, 94 percent of Guelph's police association voted non-confidence in their chief in late 1999. Members of the association focused on changes to the service introduced by Bradburn, changes that officers clearly opposed. Outsiders, like Christian Aagaard, felt that sexism played a part in the affair. "Bradburn's leadership," he writes, "never emerged from a bleak mid-winter of backstabbing, and one suspects the knives were often sharpened on the whetstone of sexism" (Aagaard, 2000).

In a 1998 Ontario decision, Justice Jean MacFarland identified systemic sexism as the cause of a Toronto police failure to warn women that a serial rapist was at large in their community. A woman, known only as Jane Doe, sued the Toronto Police Service for failing to protect her from the "balcony rapist" (Gombu, 1999). She was used as bait, she argued. She won her case, and that led to a $220 000 damage payment, a public apology from then chief David Boothby, and a major overhaul of Toronto's sexual assault unit (Editorial, *Toronto Star*, 1999). The Balcony Rapist situation above, Situation 7.2, is based on the Jane Doe case.

## The Role of Values in Ethical Debate

The debate over employment equity that we have been reviewing clearly illustrates an important point about the role of ethical values in the debates of a civil society. The point was first made in Chapter 1 and repeated briefly above in the present chapter. Ethical debate is debate about the standards of conduct in a civil society. It is debate that employs the principles of ethical reasoning—equality and justice, in the discussion of firefighters above—but also involves different values. Some people will place more value on a given principle while others will place less.

In the wake of the Jane Doe decision, we saw ethical values moving some people to praise the judge's decision. They saw it as a victory against a longstanding foe, sexism. Irene Smith, director of the Avalon Sexual Assault Centre in Halifax, said the following: "Sexual stereotypes die hard. They've got 99 lives." She added, "I think the Jane Doe decision ... will make the police start to perhaps take a different approach and be less stereotypical in their response to sexual assault" (Covert, 1998). In contrast, putting the emphasis elsewhere, George Jonas maintains that the ruling went too far. He calls the judge's accusations of sexism "pure balderdash." Jonas alleges that feminist ideology has "infiltrated the media as well as the judicial system." He quotes University of Western Ontario law professor Rob Martin approvingly. Martin wrote that it was "utterly unacceptable that judges make judgments which are entirely statements of ideology and have nothing to do with the facts and have nothing to do with the law" (Jonas, 1998). The culprit, for Jonas and Martin, isn't sexism but feminism.

We made the point about the role of values differences when we looked at the extreme positions in the abortion debate. Here we have a different debate, the employment equity debate, but we have the same kind of values difference leading to different positions. To remain civil, a society must allow for rational debate on important issues, but it must also insist on compliance with any existing law. Regardless of the law in effect, disagreement over the law is very likely to occur. As long as the disagreement is and remains a battle of ideas and the existing law is observed, a society will remain civil. Essential, then, to harmony within any society is a rational process for introducing and changing the laws of that society.

# FAMILY FAVOURITISM AND PATRIOTISM

To *discriminate* literally means to "differentiate or distinguish" between or among people or things. If you know the difference between a Ford and a Chevrolet, for example, you can discriminate between the two cars. You can differentiate between them. In our discussion of racism and sexism, however, we went beyond the basic meaning of the word *discriminate* to the ethically significant use of the word.

**Discrimination**, in the ethically significant sense of the word, is to favour one group over another solely because of ethically superficial qualities such as skin colour or gender. **Favouritism** is discrimination that is partial to a particular group. The opposite of favouritism is impartiality. **Impartiality** is objectivity. To be **impartial** is to be unbiased, objective, and without prejudice. Impartiality, then, involves treating all groups equally, without discrimination.

If I give preferential treatment to white people, for example, then I discriminate in their favour. I'm partial to them. In contrast, if I'm prejudiced against members of another group, then I discriminate against them. I am not impartial or unbiased with respect to my treatment of the members of that group. With respect to that particular group, I lack objectivity.

## Impartiality in the Treatment of Others

Our discussion of racism and sexism has taken the view that the discrimination that follows from racist and sexist beliefs is wrong. Ethics requires us to be impartial in our treatment of others. A teacher who favoured black students in her class, for example, would be considered to be acting unethically. She would not be treating non-black students as equals, and she would, therefore, be unfair to the non-black students in her class. Success in school is supposed to be a matter of achievement, not favouritism.

It is the moral concern for maintaining impartiality in the grading of students, for example, that produces rules of student conduct that forbid bribery. Codes of student conduct routinely forbid the offering of bribes because such practices can, obviously, compromise a teacher's impartiality. Society needs graduates who have passed fair tests fairly, graduates who have the requisite knowledge and skills to do their jobs properly. To graduate because of favouritism would be morally wrong. It is unfair to other students, future employers, and society in general.

We have noted a similar concern for maintaining impartiality in policing. The Canons of Police Ethics, for example, state that officers shall "guard against placing themselves in a position in which any person can expect special consideration or in which the public can reasonably assume that special consideration is being given. Thus, they should be firm in refusing gifts, favours, or gratuities, large or small, which can, in the public mind, be interpreted as capable of influencing judgment in the discharge of duties." Note that two key concerns are identified. First, there is the concern that the donor will expect, and worse yet, will get "special consideration." Second, there is the concern that the acceptance of a gratuity may lead to a public perception that special consideration will be given to the donor.

## Can Partiality Ever Be Justified?

Is favouritism always wrong? Can it ever be justified? If it can be justified in certain circumstances, what are the conditions associated with its justification? Consider two types of favouritism that seem to be morally acceptable in our society. Consider patriotism and family favouritism. In a thought-provoking article entitled "Patriotism: Like Family Love or Racism?" Thomas Hurka addresses this question (Hurka, 1999, p.33). If racism is morally wrong, Hurka asks, why isn't patriotism, love of one's country, equally wrong? And how can we morally justify the partiality we show to members of our own families? Why isn't family favouritism wrong?

Many argue that patriotism *is* like racism and that it *is* morally wrong. Patriotism, they contend, is showing favouritism to people who are citizens of one's own country. Since citizenship is a superficial feature, ethically speaking, partiality to one's own kind cannot be morally justified. Hurka argues that the issue is not quite that simple. He says that often, but not always, patriotism is more like family love than racism. When it is like family love, it can be justified on the same grounds that are used to justify family favouritism.

## Justifying Family Favouritism

What is it that provides moral justification for the favouritism that we show toward the members of our own families? We are partial to them and treat them in many ways that discriminate in their favour. Hurka says that there are two aspects of family life that can justify the mutual favouritism that family members show toward one another. The first is the close, personal interaction that is typical of families, and the second is the good that such close interaction produces (Hurka, 1999, p.35).

Although he doesn't say, we can assume that Hurka means that the good produced is good not only for the family but also for society. The family that loves, nurtures, and protects its children, for example, produces good for its children and good within the family. In the process, the family produces good for society because society benefits when these children become productive citizens, capable of empathy and caring concern for their fellow citizens. Family favouritism, it is argued, produces good children and good citizens.

## Justifying Patriotism

Can patriotism be morally justified on the same grounds as family favouritism? With respect to the two elements noted above, patriotism is like family favouritism in one respect but not the other. In an important sense, one works with the other citizens of one's country to produce good. Economic success is an example of such good. Hopefully this good benefits members of one's own country but also other members of the human family in other countries. It is this good that Hurka believes is the primary justification for certain forms of patriotism.

Patriotism obviously does not involve close, personal interaction with all the other members of one's societal family. In this regard, patriotism is unlike family life. Nevertheless, in a civil society, members do elect their leaders and work together in various ways for the success of the country. Citizens of a country like Canada work together mainly through the institutions of society, not close personal interaction. Because patriotism resembles a family only loosely, it is justified primarily in terms of the good that it produces. If patriotism produces evil, as it did in the Holocaust, then it is morally wrong. If it produces good, as in cases of international peacekeeping, then it is morally defensible.

Racism and sexism are different from both family favouritism and patriotism. Neither racism nor sexism, as we described them earlier, involves close personal interaction with all members of one's own group. Furthermore, neither of them involves even institutional connections with all members of their respective groups. While it can be argued that racism and sexism produce good for the members of their respective groups, both are considered morally wrong because they produce harm for those who are not members of the group.

It seems impossible to justify racism or sexism in that they, by their very nature, are based on falsehoods (the stereotypes), discriminate unfairly against others, and inflict great harm on others. These forms of favouritism appear to be beyond moral justification. Can other forms of favouritism be ethically justified, perhaps along the lines that family favouritism was?

## PERSONAL AND PROFESSIONAL FAVOURITISM

Doctors, nurses, lawyers, teachers, police officers, and members of other professions have special responsibilities to provide their services within the law and in an ethical manner. The law states the fundamental responsibilities of each profession, and professional codes of conduct detail the ethical requirements for carrying out those legal responsibilities. Professionals have obligations with respect to the public they serve, their professional colleagues, and their own families. In a word, their legal and moral obligations are complex.

Consider a doctor working in a small town. She is at the local hospital preparing to operate on a patient who lives in the town and has been waiting for surgery for a couple of months. Just prior to beginning surgery, two teenagers are rushed into emergency, having been seriously injured in a car accident. One teen is her son and the other is her son's girl-friend. The girlfriend is the daughter of the doctor's colleague who is also at the hospital preparing to operate on a patient of his that has, like the first doctor's patient, been on a waiting list for months. These are the only two doctors on duty and available at the time.

Without exploring all the legal and ethical questions that might arise out of this situa-tion, let's note the responsibilities of the first doctor. She has responsibilities to her surgery patient who is a member of the public. Because of the emergency situation resulting from the car accident, she has responsibilities to two other patients who are also members of the public. In the latter case, however, one patient is also a family member, her son, while the other is a family friend, her son's girlfriend. The situation is further complicated by the fact that this doctor is a personal friend of the second doctor.

## The Complexity of Professional Responsibilities

I've asked you to consider this imaginary situation because it highlights, in a dramatic way, the complexity of the obligations that fall to the first doctor at the time of the incident. Most professionals with families find themselves in situations similar to these at one time or another in their professional careers. The circumstance may not be as dramatic as those described above, but the questions of legal and moral obligation will be similar.

Given a complex set of moral obligations, how does one decide which obligation has first priority? Does every situation require, ethically speaking, the strict impartiality that we described in our examination of racism and sexism, or is there room for a certain degree of partiality as we described in our review of patriotism and family favouritism? If there is room for partiality, under what conditions is it ethically justifiable?

If the doctor in our scenario above leaves her first patient to treat her son, is such action morally defensible? Is it simply a matter of unacceptable favouritism? If she acts out of motherly concern, is she breaching her professional and ethical obligation? What if her action is motivated, not by motherly concern, but by the fact that her son is, from a med-ical point of view, the one most in need of immediate attention? What arguments could the doctor make at an inquiry to defend herself against a charge of abandoning the first patient and favouring her son?

## Professional Discretion

All professions require their members to act within the law and the ethical code of the pro-fession. But those ethical codes often allow for discretionary action on the part of the profes-sional. **Discretionary action** is any action taken on the basis of one's professional discretion. What that means is that individual professionals can make some reasonable choices in the exercise of their duties. **Professional discretion** is the authority or freedom to make reason-able decisions in carrying out one's professional responsibilities. Provided that the person can justify his actions as reasonable under the circumstances, the person is seen to be acting with-in the law and the ethical code of the profession.

Earlier in our studies, particularly in Chapter 4, we examined the Law Enforcement Code of Ethics, and we have made numerous references to that code throughout our study.

The International Association of Chiefs of Police (IACP) developed that code in 1957. More recently, in 1989, IACP published an updated code called the Law Enforcement Code of Conduct. While the two codes are essentially the same, the more recent one includes a section entitled "Discretion."

The Discretion section reads as follows:

> A police officer will use responsibly the discretion vested in his position and exercise it within the law. The principle of reasonableness will guide the officer's determinations, and the officer will consider all surrounding circumstances in determining whether any legal action shall be taken.

> Consistent and wise use of discretion, based on professional competence, will do much to preserve good relationships and retain the confidence of the public. There can be difficulty choosing between different courses of action. It is important to remember that a timely word of advice rather than arrest—which may be correct in appropriate circumstances—can be a more effective means of achieving a desired end.

Before we turn to professional impartiality, we need to make a critically important point that we will repeat later. The professional discretion of a police officer is discretion with respect to the seriousness of an *offence*. It does not include the freedom to discriminate either for or against the *offender*. In other words, discretion is not a licence to disregard one's sworn duty to treat all citizens equally without regard to their race, ethnicity, gender, or other characteristics.

## Professional Impartiality

**Professional impartiality** is the professional duty to treat people equally without discrimination. It is the duty to act neither from preference nor prejudice in carrying out one's responsibilities. Before turning to some examples and raising some questions about professional and personal favouritism in policing, let's note one other section of the Law Enforcement Code of Conduct that is relevant to our inquiry because it parallels closely the principles that we underscored in our look at racism and sexism.

In the section Performance of the Duties of a Police Officer, the Code states:

> A police officer shall perform all duties impartially, without favour or affection or ill will and without regard to status, sex, race, religion, political belief or aspiration. All citizens will be treated equally with courtesy, consideration and dignity.

> Officers will never allow personal feelings, animosities, or friendships to influence official conduct. Laws will be enforced appropriately and courteously and, in carrying out their responsibilities, officers will strive to obtain maximum co-operation from the public. They will conduct themselves in appearance and deportment in such a manner as to inspire confidence and respect for the position of public trust they hold.

The basic moral principle that we have been studying in this chapter is the principle of equality. This principle is the one that requires individuals to treat others as moral equals and to act impartially with respect to people of different races, ethnic groups, and genders. It is the principle that forbids favouritism. The ethical requirements derived from the equality principle are clearly illustrated in the two paragraphs from the Law Enforcement Code of Conduct cited above. These ethical requirements are, of course, exactly the same requirements that we saw in the United Nations Universal Declaration of Human Rights, the Canadian Charter of Rights and Freedoms, and the Code of Conduct of the Ontario Police Services Act.

We need to remember, at this point, that the equality principle is only one of the five principles of ethical reasoning. All five must be taken into consideration whenever one makes moral choices. We have already seen the close connection between equality and justice in cases of discrimination. The other principles are those of goodness, truth, and freedom. Goodness was the subject of Chapter 6, and Chapters 8, 9, and 10 will be devoted to justice, truth, and freedom respectively. As we consider the situations that follow, we will want to keep all five principles in mind.

| SITUATION 7.3 | Drunk Driver |
|---|---|

You are alone in your cruiser at 1:30 a.m. From your location in a mall parking lot, you observe a car pulling out from the parking lot of a bar across the road. The car goes over the curb as it leaves the lot. It begins to weave erratically across the centre line of the road as it accelerates toward the outskirts of the city. An oncoming car is forced off the road and into a shallow ditch, but it returns safely to the roadway. You take up pursuit with your cruiser lights flashing. You pull the car over without further incident just inside the city limits.

As you confront the driver you see that his eyes are red and that he is having difficulty focusing. The smell of alcohol is strong and the driver's speech is slurred. On the floor of the car you notice a smouldering cigarette and immediately recognize it by its sweet smell. It's marijuana.

What would you do in this situation? What charges, if any, would you lay? Explain your reasoning. Remember that you are sworn to uphold the law but that the ethical code of your profession authorizes the use of discretion as you deal with the situation.

Would your actions change given the different scenarios that follow below? If they would change, how would you justify the different approaches? If they wouldn't change, on what grounds would you justify your approach? You may want to write down your thoughts as you consider each of the following scenarios. There are eight of them.

In scenario #1, the driver is an ordinary citizen that you have never met before. In scenario #2, the driver is a well-known member of a racial minority in your community. You and the driver are not of the same race. In scenario #3, the driver is an outspoken feminist from your community. She regularly writes letters to the editor of the local newspaper, pushing her cause. In scenario #4, the driver is the son of the mayor. In scenario #5, the driver is the daughter of your constable coach. You are a rookie on the force. In scenario #6, the driver is a fellow police officer who is off duty. In scenario #7, the driver is your brother. In scenario #8, the driver is your son who is in the second year of a police foundations program. In each scenario, we are looking at a first-offence situation.

It is difficult to imagine taking different, yet ethically defensible, courses of action in each or some of these different scenarios. Different courses of action would require moral justification, and none of the differing circumstances seem to be significantly different from an ethical point of view. Treating the driver differently in each or some of the different scenarios would seem to be a clear breach of the equality principle. In each scenario, the offence is the same. In each scenario, the driver has posed exactly the same danger to the public.

The fact that the drivers are colleagues or family members, for example, does not provide an ethically defensible reason for treating them differently. In this case, personal or professional favouritism is unethical and indefensible. Favouring family members in the home is one thing; favouring them when carrying out one's professional duty is quite another. If readers, at this point, are saying to themselves that they would never arrest and charge a family member or a fellow officer, then they are simply saying that they would not act ethically in such a case. They are also saying, whether they know it or not, that they are prepared to act illegally for family or colleagues.

If, moreover, readers appeal to the right of discretion, then that right has been misunderstood. Discretion, in this situation, cannot be a cover for family or professional favouritism. Discretion refers to the matter of charging or not, and, given the nature and number of offences committed in this case, it seems unreasonable to do anything but lay charges. Discretion does not mean that one is free to charge strangers but let one's family members go free when both have committed the same offence. Discretion, we have noted repeatedly, applies to the offence committed, not one's relationship to or personal opinion of the offender.

The inappropriateness of partiality or favouritism becomes abundantly clear when we take a more serious case than the one above.

| SITUATION 7.4 | Shopping Mall Killer |
|---|---|

You have been called to the scene of an ongoing incident at a local shopping mall. Someone is shooting at people in the parking lot. From a raised and secluded spot beside the mall, the shooter is firing at persons in the lot. Several are wounded and at least three are dead. Despite lengthy and continuing attempts to talk the shooter into surrendering, the sniper continues to fire. Killing the sniper is the only way to stop the carnage that is going on. You have manoeuvred into a position where you have a clear shot at the sniper. He continues firing into the lot.

What would you do? Explain your reasoning.

Most readers, I believe, will say that they would shoot to kill. The rampage must be stopped, and, if killing the sniper is the only way to do so, then there is a duty to kill the shooter. Now, from a moral point of view, does it matter that the shooter is a member of a racial minority, a male or a female, the mayor's child, a fellow officer, or a member of your family? The murderer must be stopped. If you were a police officer in a position to shoot and kill the killer, would you be able to justify not shooting on the grounds that the killer is your colleague or a member of your family? Surely, not.

It might be emotionally easier to shoot a stranger, but the moral requirement is to end the bloodshed. The fact of the matter is that your child or colleague is wantonly killing the children and colleagues of other people. How, ethically speaking, could one reasonably claim that one's own child or colleague is worth more than the ones being killed? One can't. As noted above, discretion involves a professional judgment about the offence, not one's relationship to the offender.

Consider one more case. This time, imagine a far less extreme situation than that of the shopping mall killer.

---

**SITUATION 7.5** — **Repentant Speeder**

You are alone in your cruiser on a Sunday morning shift in late July. There is virtually no one on the road as the sun rises into a clear blue sky. A vehicle approaches you from the north travelling at a high rate of speed, 110 kilometres per hour in a 60 kilometre-per-hour zone. You turn on your flashers and take up pursuit. To your surprise, the speeding car slows, pulls to the roadside, and stops. Upon approaching the vehicle, you find a 20-year-old male behind the wheel. Tears well up in his eyes, he apologizes, and pleads not to be charged. He appears genuinely repentant. A careful examination of the vehicle shows that it is clean. There is absolutely no evidence of alcohol or drugs. Both driver and car are clean and a check reveals that the driver has no record of any kind.

What would you do in this situation? What charges, if any, would you lay? Would you lay the maximum charge possible? Would you let the driver off with a warning? Explain your reasoning. Remember that you are sworn to uphold the law but that the ethical code of your profession authorizes the use of discretion as you deal with the situation.

---

Now, imagine as we did before that there are eight different scenarios attached to this case. In the eight different scenarios, the only thing that changes is the description of the driver. In scenarios #1 through #8, respectively, the driver is a citizen, a minority group member, a feminist, a mayor's son, the daughter of a fellow officer, a fellow officer, a brother, and a son. Could you justify, on moral grounds, treating these different drivers in different ways? To repeat what was said in the first case above, discretion refers to the officer's decision to charge or not charge. It refers, if a charge is to be laid, to what that charge will be. Discretion is a judgment about the seriousness of the offence, not the status of the offender. Here, given the facts of the case, a warning might be in order, although laying a charge might also be appropriate. We note again, the status of the offender is irrelevant.

## Professional Discretion, Impartiality, and Consistency

The consistency demanded by logic leads us to the same conclusion regarding the question of treating the different drivers differently. Ethical reasoning would view any differing actions, for example, charging the minority person but letting your son off with a warning, as discriminatory. To favour family in the enforcement of the law is an ethically unacceptable form of discrimination. The same is true in the case of colleagues, even though colleagues sometimes seem like family.

Treating people equally is not an easy task. In fact, it is often very demanding. But the ethical life is demanding. It requires us to sacrifice our personal prejudices and preferences for the good of all members of society. In an age and society that places such high value on the individual, ethical conduct seems much more challenging than ever. In this regard, it has been said that the principle of equality is the critical principle in an individual's or a society's pursuit of goodness.

To do good for all, regardless of gender, race, colour, or creed, is the goal of the Good Person and the Good Society. There is a nobility of character in those good men and women who rise above their personal prejudices and preferences to conduct themselves in an ethical manner on an ongoing basis. When individuals carry out their professional duties in such a manner, they demonstrate the highest of human qualities. All civil societies require such professionals because their ethical conduct is consistent with the moral principles upon which civil societies are established. They are models for all to imitate.

## CHAPTER SUMMARY

After defining equality, we stated the principle of equality as both a positive and a negative duty.

We then went on to point out that the equality principle is central to the modern ideal of the Good Society. We also pointed out that concerns for equality are essential to the ideal of the Good Person in today's civil society. Returning to the qualities of an ideal police officer as presented in the Law Enforcement Code of Ethics, we noted that the principle of equality is the ethical foundation for an officer's impartiality and professionalism. We reviewed the other qualities as well: courage, self-restraint, altruism, honesty, obedience, and trustworthiness.

Next, we discussed stereotypes and stereotypical thinking. We underscored the fact that such thinking is flawed thinking that leads to faulty judgments, in particular, prejudice. These errors in the cognitive realm lead to diminished empathy in a person's affective dimension. Consequently, discriminatory actions (behavioural dimension) are much more likely to occur. We also noted the phenomenon of institutional or systemic discrimination.

We proceeded then to discuss racism and sexism, forms of discrimination arising from stereotypical thinking regarding racial groups and women. We discussed sexism in the workplace and societal attempts to bring equity to the workplace. Employment equity, or affirmative action, was defined and three methods of administering equity programs were reviewed. The charge of reverse discrimination was also discussed. A discussion of sexism in policing concluded our review.

If the equality principle demands equal treatment of others, how can we justify the favouritism associated with family and patriotism? The answer to that question was our next subject. After commenting on the role of values in ethical debate, we discussed family favouritism and patriotism, forms of discrimination that appear to be morally defensible. We noted that they are ethically defensible only if they bring good both to family and those outside the family; namely, the members of one's society and other nations.

Finally, we examined the subject of personal and professional favouritism. We noted first that professional relationships can be very complex. Given this fact, we proceeded to examine a police officer's right of discretion, the authority to make reasonable judgments about the offences that people commit in society. Next, we reviewed the police officer's duty to be impartial, to treat offenders equally without discrimination in the exercise of professional responsibilities. Through a series of situations and scenarios, we highlighted the distinction between professional discretion and professional impartiality. We concluded the chapter with comments regarding the role of the Good Person in a Good Society, and pointed to police officers as role models for a civil society.

## MASTERING THE MATERIAL

Now that you have read this chapter, use the following guides to ensure that you have mastered the material.

### Introduction

1. Define *equality*.
2. State the equality principle as both a positive and a negative duty.

### The Good Society and the Good Person

1. What principle is fundamental to a Good Society in our time?
2. What is essential to the character of the Good Person in modern time?
3. Identify eight characteristics of the ideal police officer.

### Stereotypes and Discrimination

1. Define the following: *stereotype, stereotypical thinking, prejudice, empathy, discrimination, systemic discrimination*
2. Why is empathy called the "moral feeling"?

### Racism

1. Define *racism*.
2. How are racial stereotypes perpetuated?
3. Summarize the "Saskatoon incident."

### Sexism

1. Define the following: *sexism, educational equity, employment equity*
2. What are affirmative action or employment equity laws?
3. State the *special needs argument* for employment equity.
4. Identify and explain three methods of administering employment equity programs.
5. State the *reverse discrimination argument* against employment equity.
6. What percentage of police officers are women?

7. How does the Jane Doe case illustrate sexism in policing?

8. How do different reactions to the Jane Doe case illustrate the role of values in ethical debate?

## Family Favouritism and Patriotism

1. What is the literal meaning of *discriminate?*

2. Define *discrimination* as used in ethics.

3. Define *favouritism* and *impartiality.*

4. What is wrong with bribery?

5. What is wrong with accepting gratuities?

6. What criteria are used to justify family favouritism and patriotism?

## Personal and Professional Favouritism

1. Describe the complexity of professional relationships.

2. Define *professional discretion.* To what, specifically, does officer discretion apply?

3. How does the Law Enforcement Code of Conduct describe discretion?

4. Define *professional impartiality.* To what, specifically, does officer impartiality apply?

5. How does the Law Enforcement Code of Conduct describe impartiality?

6. What does it mean for a person to have "nobility of character"?

---

## CRITICAL THINKING IN POLICING: THE PRINCIPLES MODEL

Moral agents act ethically when they treat all others equally, discriminating neither in favour of others nor against others.

## CRITICAL THINKING IN POLICING: THE DECIDE PROCESS

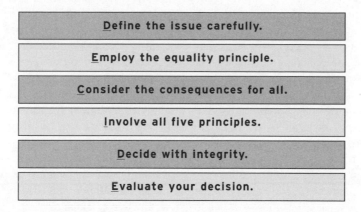

**D**efine the issue carefully.

**E**mploy the equality principle.

**C**onsider the consequences for all.

**I**nvolve all five principles.

**D**ecide with integrity.

**E**valuate your decision.

**Step #3: Consider the consequences for all.** This step reminds you to consider the beneficial and harmful effects of a proposed action on all who will be affected by your action.

---

Media Watch:
Ethics in the News 7.1

## Police sensitivity to rape victims still a problem
*by Kim Covert*

A judge's stinging indictment of the way Toronto officers bungled a 1986 rape investigation has people who work with victims across the country reporting that police response to complaints is still very much hit and miss.

"Sexist stereotypes die hard," says Irene Smith, executive director of the Avalon Sexual Assault Centre in Halifax. "They've got 99 lives."

Justice Jean MacFarland condemned the systemic sexism that led Toronto police not to warn women that a serial rapist was at work in their area. She awarded more than $220 000 in damages to the woman known as Jane Doe, one of the man's victims.

An assessment done by the Halifax centre this year suggests some police officers could learn a thing or two.

"It came out loud and clear that there was a need for police officers to receive sensitivity training," Smith says.

Many clients complain police decide too often that there isn't enough evidence to lay charges—and too quickly. In one case, the decision was made even before forensic information had come back from the lab, Smith says.

"I think the Jane Doe decision … will make the police start to perhaps take a different approach and be less stereotypical in their response to sexual assault."

Following MacFarland's July 3 ruling, Toronto police released a list of 20 improvements they say they've made to their procedures following several high-profile cases, including those of Doe and sex-killer Paul Bernardo.

The force has set up a sexual assault squad, enhanced training on rape trauma for uniform officers, and surveys victims to rate the force's handling of their cases.

Sometimes it takes a Bernardo or a Doe to be a catalyst for change. Sometimes all it takes is a change in staff.

Karen Smith, executive director of Edmonton's sexual assault centre, says the retirement of several officers three years ago opened the door to a whole new philosophy in the sex-crimes unit.

Smith says while the officers who replaced them aren't all younger, their approach is more modern.

Smith's group has helped train recruits and has developed a real working relationship with the squad. Some members of the police service even volunteer at the centre.

"I can't say enough positive about the sex crimes unit in Edmonton right now," says Smith.

That's music to the ears of Det. Rick Wilks, one of the unit's seven officers, all of whom have at least 15 years experience.

Wilks says the force takes a "global" approach that doesn't stop once the investigation is over. Police are involved with sexual assault centres, the parole board, halfway houses and relapse programs.

Unit officers also take courses in dealing with victims and give lectures to new recruits.

At the Saskatoon Sexual Assault Centre, executive director for Kalhi Cridland says some officers are beginning to show a "human touch."

Police are tapping crisis centres in many communities for training on how to deal with victims. But Cridland says there's still a long way to go.

"We'd like actually to have whoever's working with the victim to somehow exude the attitude that they believe the victim," says Cridland.

Bernice Connell, who heads up the Rape Crisis Centre in the northwestern Ontario town of Kenora, says she's less likely to hear victims complain about police than 10 years ago. In fact, in recent cases, victims have commented on how supportive police were.

Police seem willing to train to do the job better, she says, but often the money for training isn't there.

Still, old attitudes persist.

"The question is still not to the perpetrator, 'Why did you assault this person?' The question is still, 'Why were you out at 11 o'clock?' or 'Why did you have a drink? You should know better,'" Connell says.

Source: *Kitchener-Waterloo Record*, July 13, 1999, A3.

| Media Watch: Ethics in the News 7.2 | RCMP investigates police link to freezing deaths of two men |
|---|---|

SASKATOON—The Mounties are taking over a probe into allegations Saskatoon police officers may have been involved in the deaths of two aboriginal men found frozen on the outskirts of the city.

John White, Saskatchewan's deputy justice minister, said the RCMP were called in by Saskatoon police Chief Dave Scott on Wednesday.

"We have asked the RCMP ... to conduct the investigation into those deaths," White said "We will proceed with the normal criminal investigation and, if required, prosecutorial decision."

Investigators are probing the deaths of Lawrence Wegner, 30, and Rodney Naistus, 25. Wegner's body was found Feb. 3 in a field near a power plant—five days after Naistus's corpse was spotted in the same area.

Saskatoon police began investigating the matter Feb. 4 after a third native man complained two uniformed officers in a marked cruiser drove him to the same area where the dead men were found.

Darrell Night said officers stripped him of his jacket before they threw him out of their cruiser and told him to walk back to the city in sub-zero temperatures in the first week of February.

Don Worme, Night's lawyer, said the police repeatedly directed racial slurs at his client. He has advised Night not to talk to the media.

"He was traumatized by the whole ordeal. It has caused him to reconsider his confidence in the public system," Worme said.

Two unnamed senior constables were suspended with pay last week in relation to the incident, but Scott said there is no evidence linking them to the deaths of the other two men.

"I suspended these members simply because I want to maintain public trust and the trust of our aboriginal community," he said.

He refused to release their names or disclose what they had told him.

Some natives suggested the men may have been dropped off in frigid temperatures by police as a punishment and criticized Scott for not firing the two officers.

"If an ordinary person did this, dropped off even a dog on the outskirts of the city in cold weather, somebody would have to face the consequences," said Lawrence Joseph, vice-chief of the Federation of Saskatchewan Indian Nations.

Joseph said reports of police harassing aboriginals and dropping them off on the outskirts of Saskatoon are nothing new. "It's not an isolated incident. The problem is widespread," he said "We get reports of these incidents and they go undetected, unresponded to by police authorities."

Wegner, a 30-year-old student at Saskatchewan Indian Federated College, was last seen alive Jan. 30. A friend said he had injected drugs earlier in the evening.

Naistus was celebrating a reunion with his brother and cousin after a stint in jail earlier in the day, relatives said.

It's not clear when he disappeared.

Source: *Kitchener-Waterloo Record*, February 17, 2000, A3.

## chapter eight

# Justice: Treating Others Fairly in a Civil Society

## LEARNING OUTCOMES

After completing this chapter, you should be able to

- Define *justice*
- Explain the symbolism in the classic statue of Justice
- Through an example, show the connection between equality, justice, and goodness
- State the justice principle as both a positive duty and a negative duty
- Explain the merit, the equity, and the special needs approaches to justice
- Define *social justice* and give three examples of social justice movements
- Define *distributive justice* and describe three approaches to it
- Define *criminal justice, enforcement justice, legal justice, penal justice,* and *procedural justice*
- Describe three approaches to penal justice
- Identify, analyze, and criticize four arguments for capital punishment
- Identify, analyze, and criticize three arguments against capital punishment
- Give two examples of enforcement justice issues

# INTRODUCTION

**Justice**, simply put, is fairness. This chapter on justice, then, looks at fairness in human relationships. We can all react strongly when others treat us unfairly, and our individual sense of injustice seems to go back to early childhood. As very young children, for instance, we were upset when a sibling, without our consent, took what belonged to us. It might have been a toy or a favourite blanket that, when taken away, triggered an expression of anger, our first cries of injustice. Even before we could speak, we seemed to have a sense of what was fair and what wasn't.

We noted previously that the **principle of justice**, the subject of the present chapter, and the principle of equality, the subject of the last chapter, are closely related as basic principles of a civil society. One of the important things that we need to do in the present chapter is to clarify further the relationship between these two principles. As we proceed, a number of connections will be noted. Before we go further, however, let's note one important connection between the two principles as it reveals itself in the traditional symbol of justice.

That symbol, a blindfolded woman holding a measuring scale in one hand and a sword in the other, is instructive. She is blindfolded so that she will treat all individuals *equally*, regardless of their skin colour, gender, or other irrelevant features. In other words, her blindfold ensures the impartiality associated with the equality principle. That impartiality was the key theme of Chapter 7.

She also has a scale in her hand to balance the degree of punishment given to an offender with the seriousness of the offence committed. Her scale ensures that any punishment handed out is fair and just. It ensures that the punishment fits the crime and that offenders get their just deserts. The concern for balancing the degree of punishment with the degree of harm done is a concern of justice, a concern for fairness. The **justice principle** with its emphasis on fairness is, as noted above, the subject of this chapter. It is not surprising that the principle of justice is also called the principle of fairness.

In the following example, notice how these two principles, equality and justice, are related to a third principle, the principle of goodness. A teacher who treats his students unequally (equality principle)—favours students of his own race, for example, and discriminates against students of another race—necessarily treats his students unfairly (justice principle). Such discrimination is unfair and it causes harm (goodness principle) to the students that he discriminates against. They are disadvantaged by the teacher's attitude. Classroom success no longer depends on merit. It now depends on an arbitrary factor, teacher preference.

## The Duties of Justice

Having defined justice as fairness, we can now state the justice principle in terms of both a positive duty and a negative duty. Translated into a rule of conduct, a **positive duty**, the principle becomes: "Be fair to others." Expressed as a **negative duty**, the principle says: "Don't treat others unjustly." Once again, the duties are quite simple to state. The challenges and complexities surface, however, when one is faced with doing one's duty in specific situations. Parents and teachers know well, for example, how challenging it can be to treat one's children or one's students fairly. Both parents and teachers hear the charge "But that's not fair!" on a somewhat regular basis.

## Approaches to Justice

To be just means to be fair. Although this definition is very straightforward and simple, concerns for justice can get somewhat complicated. For example, there are at least three basic ways in which we can try to be fair to one another. Sometimes, the fair thing to do is to give others what they deserve. At other times, the fair thing to do is to give equal shares to others. At still other times, the fair thing to do is to meet the special needs of others. We presented these approaches to justice briefly in Chapter 5. We need to review them now.

One of the most common approaches to justice is to try to give people what they deserve. If, for example, a student attends classes, studies hard for tests, and performs well on the tests, then the student deserves a good mark. She earns, for example, an "A" in the course. She deserves the high mark because she has worked hard and achieved a high standard. It's only fair to give her what she deserves. Because this approach attempts to balance rewards with achievement, giving people what they have earned, it is called the **merit approach** to fairness. It is also called the *deserts approach* to fairness. *Deserts,* of course, comes from the word *deserve.*

A second approach to justice is called the **equity approach**. Often in life, the fairest thing to do is to give equal shares of something to others. Many parents, when they write their wills, use the equity approach in establishing the terms of their will. Each child, on this approach, receives an equal share of the parents' estate. The assumption is that all children were loved equally by the parents and that the equity approach recognizes and expresses this. The parents are being fair to their children by giving equal shares to them.

The word *equity* comes from the Latin *aequitas* and means equality. I have chosen to use *equity*, instead of *equality*, in this discussion of the ways in which we can be fair to others. I will use the word *equality* to refer to the basic moral equality of all human beings, the equality expressed in the principle of equality. I will use the word *equity* to refer to the equal-shares approach to being fair, the approach associated with the principle of justice.

One can imagine situations in which parents would not give equal shares to their children. If, for example, one child is born with a severe disability and the government provides only a small disability pension for that child, then the parents might recognize the special needs of the disabled child by leaving a larger portion of their estate to that child. It would, we say, only be fair to the child with special needs. If the other children in the family are doing well financially and are able to look after themselves, then the **needs approach** seems to be the fairest approach in such circumstances. The special needs approach, then, is a third way by which we can try to be fair to others.

---

| SITUATION 8.1 | **Justice in the Park?** |
|---|---|

A woman walking her dog on a trail through a heavily wooded public park one afternoon notices two adult males engaging in mutual masturbation beside a car. The car is parked at the end of a roadway that provides access to park trails. Upon returning home, the woman calls a city councillor to complain. The councillor, in turn, calls the police. Responding to the complaint, several undercover police officers are dispatched to the park to investigate.

One of the undercover officers, walking a trail in a remote part of the park, observes a lone adult male close by on an adjacent trail. The man greets the officer, points to a secluded area a few metres away, and says: "It's cooler in there. Want to join me?" The officer quips, "Is that your office?" and proceeds to follow the man along the trail into the bush. "Are you a cop?" the man asks. "No, I'm not," responds the officer, "I'm unemployed at the moment." The man turns around, moves toward the officer, and touches the officer's groin. The officer immediately responds, "You're under arrest!" He takes the man into custody, charging him with sexual assault.

The next day a local newspaper carries a story of the arrest and identifies the man as a prominent businessman and a member of his town council. The man, a closet homosexual until the news story breaks, resigns his job as the news spreads swiftly through the community. When he later appears in court to face the charge of sexual assault, the charge is dropped when the arresting officer fails to appear.

Still later, the man files a suit against the police, alleging that his constitutional rights have been violated and that he was the victim of police entrapment. The police, he maintains, have treated him unjustly.

Has an injustice been done in this situation? Do you think the man has a valid case or not? Do you think the police officer was within his rights to arrest the man? What is your view of the role the media played in revealing the man's identity? In what other ways might the police have responded to the original complaint? What other information, if any, would you like to have before forming your final opinion?

## SOCIAL JUSTICE

**Social justice** refers to the fair treatment of all members of a given society. It is also about the equal treatment of members of society because, as we noted above, justice and equality are closely related. The last half of the twentieth century saw several interesting struggles for social justice in many countries of the Western world. Groups that felt that they had been treated unfairly for a long time began to fight to obtain the same rights enjoyed by others.

Blacks in the United States, for example, participated in a prolonged civil rights movement aimed at achieving justice through equality with other members of society. Women in many countries, unhappy with the injustices that they experienced in the workplace and in society generally, undertook a lengthy battle for equal and fair consideration within a male-dominated society. Homosexuals, too, fought for equal rights and fair treatment under the banner of gay rights.

In each of these movements for social change, we can see the connection between equality, justice, and goodness that we noted above in the introduction. Discrimination resulted in injustices that harmed individuals of the disadvantaged groups. While the subject of social justice is a most interesting one, we will reserve more time in this chapter for the subjects of criminal justice, procedural justice, and distributive justice.

Before we examine the subject of distributive justice, consider the following situation.

---

| SITUATION 8.2 | Election Campaign |
|---|---|

You're attending a federal election campaign debate in your local community centre. Two candidates with very different views have squared off on the subject of taxes.

Candidate Will B. Wright promises to cut spending on various social programs that he argues are a waste of taxpayer money. Spending on welfare has to be trimmed, he says, because of all the welfare fraud that wastes tax dollars. Spending on prisons needs to be reduced because prisons have become country clubs for criminals. Spending on early childhood education also needs to be trimmed, says Wright, because there is no proof that it benefits children or society. He says that it's just a very expensive form of babysitting that taxpayers pay for. Spending cuts in these three areas alone, he says, will result in a major tax reduction for all Canadians. The money saved will end up in your pocket. You worked hard to earn it, says Wright, and you are the one who deserves to keep it.

Candidate I.M. Loeft promises to spend your tax dollars very carefully but makes no promise to reduce your taxes. Instead, he asks you to consider the importance of early childhood education for the children involved and for the future of society. He also asks you to reflect on the importance of helping those who are unable to help themselves. He's committed to eliminating welfare fraud, but he says that there is really very little fraud in the system. Most recipients, he says, genuinely need society's help. As for spending on prisons, Loeft says that the money has been well spent. If convicted persons can receive an education, and job and life skills training, then they can contribute to society when they are released from prison after serving their time. Your hard-earned tax dollars, argues Loeft, will be well spent.

Which of the candidates are you inclined to vote for? Why? What values do you have that you share with the candidate that you'll support? Briefly describe the value system of the candidate that you will not support. If possible, discuss this situation with persons who take a different approach from your own.

---

## DISTRIBUTIVE JUSTICE

**Distributive Justice** refers to fairness in a society's distribution of its benefits and burdens to its members. When people consider life within a civil society, questions arise as to how society should distribute the benefits and burdens of society in a fair manner to its members. Different people argue for different approaches, each seeing one approach to justice as superior to another. Since groups of people who share similar ideas often join forces to promote their views, it is quite natural for political parties to form. Those parties then take different approaches to answering the question of how to distribute a society's benefits and burdens fairly.

What are these benefits and burdens? Individuals within a society, especially a prosperous society, benefit from the combined efforts of members of that society. In Canada, for example, we tend to have more employment opportunities than many other nations. Further, we benefit from excellent health care services and educational opportunities. As members of our society, however, we also carry burdens. We must, for example, give a portion of our earnings away in taxes. In a time of war, we might have to bear the burden of the soldier, risking our lives in the defence of our country.

What is the fairest way for a society to distribute its benefits and burdens? Political parties answer this question differently, adopting different approaches to taxation and the redistribution of wealth in Canada. What is the fairest system of taxation? In answer to this question, some will emphasize the principle of merit, arguing that people who work hard and generate wealth deserve to keep as much of their wealth as possible. At the candidate's meeting (Situation 8.2), candidate Will B. Wright seems to espouse this point of view.

Others, emphasizing the special needs of certain members of society, will place the emphasis on the needs approach. They value community and compassion more than the accumulation of individual wealth. They seem to want to be their brother's keeper to some degree. Candidate I.M. Loeft seems to take this approach to the distribution of society's wealth. Still others try to take a middle-of-the-road approach between Wright and Loeft, emphasizing equity, need, merit, and moderation.

What we see in the matter of distributive justice is something we have noted before. When we examined the abortion issue, we saw that equally reasonable people could end up at opposite ends of the spectrum of debate. The reason for this, we said, lay in the relative value placed upon fetal life and adult choice. Some value a woman's right to choose more than the right of the unborn to life. Others value the life of the unborn more than a woman's freedom to choose. What the two parties value, what is most important to them, shapes their view and the arguments that they use to justify their positions.

In matters of distributive justice something similar occurs. Equally reasonable people may value very different things. The conservative, for example, values individual achievement, while the liberal values compassion for the needy. The moderate values balance, a little bit of both. Values, whatever people feel strongly about, direct their rational arguments one way or another.

In Chapter 1, we said that humans are both cognitive and affective beings, and that both dimensions are important for ethics. Different members of a civil society will feel differently with respect to the basic principles on which their society is founded. They will place more value on one principle than another, in any given situation. This is true for questions of distributive justice and criminal justice. It is also true for specific issues such as capital punishment, a subject that we will examine later in this chapter.

## CRIMINAL JUSTICE

A civil society, you will recall, is a society in which people elect their leaders, establish rules of conduct through rational processes, and live by the rule of law. Everyone gives up a certain amount of personal freedom but receives a certain amount of security in return. Citizens can concentrate on work and family because they do not live in an environment where there is constant warfare and constant fear. Generally speaking, reason and the rule of law produce a stable form of community life, a civil society.

The principles on which civil societies are founded also inform the society's approach to punishing its errant members. In a civil society, punishment is not a matter of personal vengeance, vigilante justice, or cruel and unusual treatment. The same principles that determine the nature of the society itself also direct the thinking of society when it comes to the subject of punishment. As we'll see, however, that doesn't mean that everyone agrees on how to deal with offenders. Despite differences of view, in a civil society there is a rational process for dealing with those who break the laws of society.

That process includes, as we noted in Chapter 1, people who fulfill various roles that society establishes for the good of its members. There are elected persons who make the laws (legislators), a society-sanctioned group to enforce the laws (police), impartial individuals or groups that make judgments regarding guilt or innocence (juries and judges), and a society-sanctioned group that ensures that the sentences imposed by the courts are carried out (correctional officers).

In a very important sense, all four of these areas of societal life are involved in the subject of criminal justice. Legislators define the offences that are criminal. Police enforce the laws and charge suspected criminals. Courts determine the guilt or innocence of alleged criminals. Finally, correctional officers administer penalties to those who have been determined to be criminals. We'll focus primarily on policing, court proceedings, and corrections in our look at criminal justice, devoting most of our time to the treatment of convicted offenders.

Before we turn to the specific issue of capital punishment, we need to explore the more general topic of criminal justice. **Criminal justice** refers to fairness in apprehending and charging suspected criminals, fairness in the trials of persons charged with criminal offences, and fairness in the treatment of those convicted. The first aspect in this definition, I will call **enforcement justice**. We will return to this aspect of criminal justice later. The second aspect I will call **legal justice**. We'll also return to legal justice later in this chapter. Our immediate subject will be the third aspect of criminal justice, fairness in the treatment of those convicted. I will refer to this aspect as **penal justice**.

In the situation below, a number of questions of fairness arise. Take time to consider the various persons in the case and give thought to whether they are treating others fairly, given the situation.

| SITUATION 8.3 | Shopping Mall Sex |
| --- | --- |

A city shopping mall has become a meeting place for some of the community's male homosexuals. They have casual sexual encounters in the cubicles of the men's washroom. After several customer complaints, the mall manager calls in the police, who install hidden cameras and videotape the activities of the men. After several days of surveillance, the police lay charges against 30 men. The local media are called to a police press conference where the chief of police identifies all those charged. One of the accused, a member of a local church and a Sunday school teacher, drives out into the country where he douses himself and his car with gasoline. He ignites the gasoline and dies in the ensuing fire.

What do you think, ethically speaking, of the actions of the various persons in this story? More specifically, what's fair or unfair in the actions of (1) the men? (2) the mall manager? (3) the police? (4) the media? and (5) the man who commits suicide? Discuss the situation with others, if you have the chance. There are some obvious similarities to Situation 8.1, above, Justice in the Park. Are there any significant differences? In your view, was justice served in these two cases?

We have seen a number of instances of gay men seeking sex in public places. We noted earlier that sex in a public place, be it gay sex or straight sex, is an offence. Why people have sex in public places is an interesting question, one best answered, perhaps, by psychologists. In the two cases included in this chapter, we have been concerned with questions of justice, not psychology.

Our question in ethics is not "Why do they do that?" but "Are the offenders being fair to society and is society treating them fairly, given their actions?" In the real world events upon which Situation 8.1 is based, an Anglican priest was "outed" as a consequence of the incident that occurred in Kitchener's Homer Watson Park. Situation 8.3 is based on events that occurred in a mall in the Niagara region. Those events resulted in the public outing of several gay men.

## PENAL JUSTICE

Much of the discussion throughout the rest of this chapter will be about the third aspect of criminal justice, the fair treatment of offenders. The adjective *penal* comes from the noun *penalty* and the verb *to penalize*. Our subject, then, is fairness in society's criminal penalties.

When someone has been convicted of a criminal offence, what constitutes fair treatment of that person? Differing values, we will see, lead to two different answers to that question. Societal debates about the appropriateness of a particular punishment, for example, frequently hinge on whether a person feels that the punishment was too light or too harsh, a "slap on the wrist" or "cruel and unusual."

Some people believe that justice is a matter of **retribution**, paying offenders back for what they have done. "An eye for an eye," as the ancient saying goes. Others feel that justice is a matter of **rehabilitation**, correcting the deviant's errant behaviour. Before exploring the details of these two differing approaches to penal justice, let's note two things that they have in common. Sometimes this common ground goes unnoticed because of the sharp differences that we'll soon describe.

### The Common Ground: Protection and Deterrence

People on both sides of the debate about penal justice agree on two important points. The first point is that society must be protected from offenders that would further harm society. The penalty, among other things, provides protection for society. In a given case, however, there may be disagreement as to whether society has been sufficiently protected. The second point of agreement is that the treatment of the offender must deter others from committing the offender's crime. What constitutes deterrence in any given situation, you might have guessed, is open for debate. The deterrent effect of punishment, we need to note, is an ongoing and challenging issue for everyone concerned with penal justice.

### The Differences: Retribution versus Rehabilitation

The view that sees penal justice as primarily a matter of punishment is called either the **punitive justice approach** or the **retributive justice approach**. The adjective *punitive* comes from the root *to punish*. Justice, from this perspective, is served when retribution occurs. *Retribution* is another word for *punishment*. The opposing view that sees penal justice as a matter of rehabilitation is called **rehabilitative justice** or **corrective justice**. Justice, from this perspective, is served when the rehabilitation of the convicted person occurs. When errant behaviour has been corrected, then justice has been served.

We'll now examine these two approaches in some detail. It should be no surprise that the ideas associated with fairness in general, and distributive justice in particular, will be keys to understanding societal differences toward the treatment of its errant members. In this regard, you'll want to remember the three approaches to distributive justice that we noted earlier in this chapter: merit, equity, and need. The third approach to penal justice, the **compensation approach**, is compatible with both of the other two approaches. We will come back to the compensation approach later.

## The Retribution Approach to Penal Justice

Imagine for a moment the kind of scale that people formerly used to weigh things, the kind of scale that blindfolded Justice holds in her hand. The scale consisted of two pans linked by a chain that was suspended at its mid-point from a balance beam. At the granary, for example, the merchant would place a standard two-kilogram weight on one pan of the scale. On the other, he would place an empty bag. As he filled it with grain, the pan on which the bag sat would gradually begin to lower under the weight of the grain. Eventually the two pans would be in balance, the point at which an equal amount of weight sat on each pan. The merchant had weighed out two kilograms of grain.

It is precisely this image of the weigh scale that the retributionist has in mind when considering a crime and an appropriate punishment for that crime. Another word for punishment, we noted above, is retribution, the word from which retributionists obviously derive their name. They see the crime on one pan of the imaginary scale and the punishment for that crime on the other. Punishment is fair, on their view, when it balances or fits the crime. The key point is that the degree of punishment must balance the amount of harm that has been done. The punishment, as we say, must fit the crime. Note also that this approach is grounded in the **merit** or **deserts approach** to being fair. Offenders deserve punishment because of the harm they have done.

One can readily see how people in ancient times perceived that justice was done only when the scale of justice was balanced. If someone poked out the eye of another, then the scale would balance at the point when the offender's eye was poked out. If a tooth were knocked out, then the scale would balance when the offender's tooth was knocked out. If a hand were cut off, the scale balanced with the removal of the offender's hand. "An eye for an eye, a tooth for a tooth, and a hand for a hand" became the retributionist rule for just punishment, fair retribution.

Obviously, the concept of balance is central to the retributionist image of justice. We need to note clearly a point that we made earlier. That point is that the purpose of punishment is to balance the suffering of the victim with an equal amount of suffering for the offender. In other words, punishment is administered for punishment's sake. The intention, on this view, is not to teach a lesson for rehabilitative purposes, but solely to inflict an equal amount of pain on the offender as was inflicted by the offender upon the victim. Strict justice, on this view, would exclude the possibility of reducing a sentence for mercy's sake. A merciful reduction would pervert justice by creating an imbalance between the crime and the punishment for that crime.

The retribution approach to punishment is still, of course, a very popular approach in our time. In the capital punishment debate, for instance, the retributionists will argue that only "a life for a life" will be just punishment for the crime of murder. Regardless of one's stand on the death penalty, many people will agree that punishment should fit the crime, that there should be a balancing of crime and punishment. What constitutes a balance or fit in a particular instance, however, is often a matter of controversy.

While the image of the scale of justice is a simple one that is easy to picture, the application of the underlying concept of just punishment to particular offences is not always easy. The Biblical expression "life for life, eye for eye, tooth for tooth, hand for hand, foot for foot, burn for burn, wound for wound, bruise for bruise" (Exodus 21:23-25) is easy enough to remember and recite. Consider the difficulty, however, of applying the principle to certain crimes. What would we do, for example, with the rapist? Would we rape him, "a rape for a rape?" And what would we do with a shoplifter who has no shop? Do we steal from the thief?

We need to think about these kinds of questions because they highlight the fact that achieving justice in a civil society is not a simple matter. In times past, the eye-for-an-eye approach may have been fair punishment for those who employed it. Today, in a civil society like Canada, justice is somewhat more complicated. The very purpose of punishment as retribution is seen by many as a primitive form of societal vengeance. The Charter of Rights and Freedoms suggests as much when it forbids cruel and unusual punishment. While many Canadians want tougher penalties, perhaps even a life for a life, others see punishment differently.

Before turning to an alternative approach to punishment, one derived from utilitarian thinking, let's make one further point about the attempt to balance punishment and crime. It is very difficult for a society to arrive at agreement on what constitutes a balance between a particular crime and the punishment for that crime. Is armed robbery, for instance, balanced by 5, 10, or 15 years in prison? How much time in prison for any particular crime achieves a balance between that offence and the punishment? Different people will answer the questions differently. One can easily see how difficult it must be for legislators to establish fair punishment for any particular crime.

The retribution approach attempts to balance crime and punishment, and punishment, on this view, we have said, is administered for punishment's sake. That is its purpose. Indeed, as we have pointed out, this approach seems to exclude consideration of the merciful reduction of a particular sentence because such a reduction would dilute justice and create a new imbalance in society. We have also said that many Canadians support this approach to punishment and use it to argue for the restoration of capital punishment. Others disagree on the capital punishment issue, but also more generally. Let's now consider a popular alternative to the retribution approach.

## The Rehabilitation Approach to Penal Justice

In Chapter 3, we looked at a number of different ways by which people have tried to establish norms for ethical conduct within a civil society. We noted that prescriptions for ethical conduct tend to take either a consequentialist or a nonconsequentialist approach to establishing rules of conduct. You will recall that consequentialists always decide what is right or wrong by considering the results of a proposed action. The most popular of the consequentialist positions is utilitarianism.

Utilitarianism is the view that says that the right thing to do in any circumstance is the action that brings the greatest amount of good over bad for everyone concerned. John

Stuart Mill expressed the approach in terms of "the greatest good for the greatest number" of people in a society. When utilitarians discuss justice and punishment issues, they take exactly the same approach to this subject as they do to any other. What I have called the rehabilitation approach to punishment is the utilitarian approach to penal justice. Because rehabilitation programs are designed to correct deviant behaviour, this approach is often called the "corrections approach." This approach seems to parallel the special needs approach discussed earlier: society needs protection, and the offender needs punishment, rehabilitation, and, eventually, reintegration into society.

The corrections approach has been described as a future-oriented approach to punishment. The retribution approach is past-oriented in that it always sees punishment as a reaction to an event that is in the past. For retributionists, punishment is given today because of an offence that occurred yesterday. In contrast, the rehabilitation approach sees punishment as a determinant of future events. Society punishes in order that greater good will come in the future. The offence punished is, of course, always in the past. On the rehabilitation approach, however, punishment always looks to the future.

To be more specific, punishment is administered in order that offenders will not repeat their offences in the future. To that end, one can see why the corrections approach is supportive of rehabilitation or correctional programs in prisons. The right thing to do when punishing an offender is whatever brings the greatest good to the greatest number in society in the future. Rehabilitation programs are programs designed to correct the offender's errant behaviour. A released offender who does not re-offend but returns to society as a productive citizen is the goal of punishment.

Critics, however, sometimes make the *luxury schools argument* against certain rehabilitation programs. Prisons are transformed, the critics say, from places of punishment into luxury schools for the deviant. In order to accomplish the reform of the offender, it is argued, society makes the mistake of making prisons pleasant places to be, with health, education, and employment services paid for by the citizens who have suffered at the hands of the offender. This, critics maintain, rewards wrongdoers for their offences. At great expense to taxpayers, they continue, offenders get to go to luxury schools where they learn how to be better criminals by associating with their schoolmates, other convicted offenders.

Defenders of the rehabilitation approach argue that the *luxury schools argument* is an exaggeration and a misunderstanding. Rehabilitation programs are not rewards for bad behaviour. They are educational and training programs to assist offenders to change their ways during their time of punishment. This is punishment, of course, as the offenders have lost their right to participate freely in society. Will primitive and dismal conditions in prison in any way correct errant behaviours? Will tough justice that emphasizes harsh treatment produce more considerate and productive citizens upon release? No, say those who take the corrections approach.

Isolating individual offenders and subjecting them to severe punishment will not produce the "greatest good for the greatest number." Such an approach produces only despair and hostility. In no way, they argue, does it teach offenders appropriate ways to live with others in a civilized manner.

Punishment, the rehabilitationist says, consists of the loss of one's freedom, a severe punishment for any member of a civil society. The time of punishment, however, must be devoted to rehabilitating the offender. Such rehabilitation, it is argued, benefits both the offender and society. Corrective justice is, on the rehabilitation approach, one of the marks of a truly civil society. Penal justice, on this view, is not about vengeance. It is all about fairness, civility, and the future of society.

## The Compensation Approach to Penal Justice

We now need to note a third approach to punishment, one that can complement either the retribution approach or the rehabilitation approach. In other words, it doesn't compete with either of them but supplements them. The **compensation approach** to punishment is a very old approach, one that sees repaying the victim as an essential purpose of punishment. In ancient times, if one person stole another person's ox, then just punishment was, or included, the return of the ox to its rightful owner. Today, many people argue that in matters of crime and punishment the victim is often forgotten.

In recent years, for example, we have seen the growth of victims' rights groups, the development of victims' bills of rights, and the introduction of victim-impact statements in court proceedings. If the concept of victim compensation is an ancient one, why are we only now seeing victim compensation initiatives in our society?

The answer is fairly simple. In ancient times, crime was viewed as an offence against the *individual*. Today, crime is viewed as an offence against *society*. In the murder of Smith, for example, the case is one of the "Crown versus Jones," the accused murderer, not one of "Smith (or his family) versus Jones." The "Crown" refers to the monarchy but is symbolic of the people. The offence is deemed to be an offence against all members of society, not just the unfortunate individual who was murdered. There are at least two reasons for this historical shift of emphasis.

One reason is that when the state (the Crown) is party to a dispute and the courts decide, then there is an end to the matter. Appeals are allowed, of course, but eventually the matter is decided. In ancient times, and still in some places today, the matter doesn't end. Individual against individual, family against family, the *vendetta* goes on in some cases for generations. A **vendetta** is a blood feud that is carried on between families to avenge the murders of their respective members.

Another reason for the historical shift was to introduce a greater degree of objectivity or impartiality into the settling of a dispute. When two individuals quarrel, it is often impossible for them to determine the facts of the dispute. Personal biases dominate and the impartial assessment of events is difficult, if not impossible, to achieve. When the state is party to a dispute, there is a much greater likelihood of an impartial hearing. In a civil society committed to democracy and the rule of law, some of the most important rules are those that govern the procedures for resolving disputes. We mentioned these procedural norms earlier in this chapter. It is time to say more about them now.

## PROCEDURAL JUSTICE

A very frustrating experience for many is that of seeing the case of an obviously guilty person thrown out of court on a technicality. Our frustration should not blind us to the significance of such events. When a case is dismissed on a technicality, it is being thrown out due to some breach of procedural rules. The significance of such events lies in the fact that the rules of justice in a civil society are valued more highly, in any particular instance, than the innocence or guilt of the individual whose case is dismissed.

**Procedural justice**, as we are concerned with it here, refers to fairness in the rules that govern the enforcement of law, the trials of alleged offenders, and the punishment of those convicted. Civil societies are societies in which no one is above the law. Citizens, police, lawyers, judges, and others must conduct their affairs within the rules of the game, the procedural norms. A guilty person must be found guilty and punished in accordance with the rules governing arrest, trial, and punishment. The reason is clear. It is the procedural rules of a civil society that protect the innocent and guarantee a fair trial for all.

When police officers break the law in pursuit of offenders, lawyers withhold evidence at trial, justices discriminate in their judgments, and correctional officers administer their own personal punishments, then the system is at risk. When these things occur, the system goes on trial and the ignoring of these breaches of procedure renders the system guilty. Civil societies must ensure that nobody is above the law. It is the rule of law that guarantees peace and security for all members of society, and all members of society must conduct themselves in accordance with the law.

Now it is clear that societies are not perfect. People break the laws on a regular basis. Sometimes they are caught and sometimes not. So, too, procedural justice fails all too often and this sometimes goes undetected. Despite the imperfections of daily life in society, the members of a civil society work toward the ideal as it is spelled out in constitutions and the law. Not to strive for the ideal is to revert to the law of the jungle. The Good Person works to build a Good Society. A large part of that important work is to live by the rules, the rules that promote and sustain civilized life.

Later, in our review of certain aspects of the capital punishment debate, we'll return to the matter of procedural justice. There, we will take note of wrongful convictions in Canada that have prompted widespread concern. For the moment, however, consider the following situation.

| SITUATION 8.4 | Critical Vote |
| --- | --- |

You are a rookie constable with a large regional police service, and you are attending the annual meeting of the police association. Senior officers, including your coach, have urged you to be present to support a motion to petition the government to restore capital punishment. The executive of the association has prepared the motion, and they unanimously urge its adoption. The motion reads:

> Whereas our duty is to serve and protect the community, and
>
> Whereas we risk our lives in the exercise of our duty, and
>
> Whereas serious crimes like murder are on the rise, and
>
> Whereas, society is best protected from convicted murderers by the ending of their lives, and
>
> Whereas, the death penalty serves as an effective deterrent to would-be murderers, and
>
> Whereas the cost of keeping convicted murderers alive is excessive given what they've done, and
>
> Whereas, justice demands a life for a life,
>
> We, therefore, petition the Minister of Justice to take immediate steps to restore capital punishment to Canadian society at the earliest possible date.

Will you vote for or against the motion? Explain your reasons in either case. If you have the opportunity, discuss the situation with others.

# CAPITAL PUNISHMENT

The imperfection of justice systems that we discussed in the section on procedural justice above has become one of the main points of discussion in the capital punishment debate. In Canada, for example, the justice system failed Donald Marshall Jr., Guy Paul Morin, David Milgaard, and Thomas Sophonow. They are alive today, not guilty of the offences for which they were convicted. If Canada had not abolished the death penalty, in all likelihood these innocent persons would have been put to death. We will examine the *execution of innocents argument* below, along with other arguments for and against the death penalty, but first we need to make some general observations about the issue of capital punishment.

One point to be noted immediately is that the death penalty has not been limited to the crime of murder. Often in debates today, the assumption made is that the debate is solely about punishment for murder. Earlier in this chapter, we cited the "eye-for-an-eye" quotation from the Biblical book of Exodus. In Exodus, Chapter 21, it says that death is the penalty to be imposed for murder, the deliberate and unjust killing of another (21:14). However, it also states that death is the appropriate penalty for hitting one's parents (21:15), cursing one's parents (21:17), or kidnapping a slave (21:16).

In Canada, prior to the abolition of capital punishment, death was a legally sanctioned penalty for murder, rape, and treason. During the period 1962 to 1967, on a trial basis, Canada abolished capital punishment for all crimes except the murder of police officers and prison guards. The trial period was extended until 1976 when the death penalty was abolished for all crimes. In some other countries today, in addition to murder, the death penalty exists for such offences as adultery and drug dealing. Most societies in the Western world, however, have gradually abolished capital punishment for all crimes. A notable exception to this trend is the United States of America.

## Arguments for Capital Punishment

Let's begin with two points. First, for ease and clarity of presentation, we will examine arguments pro and con on the assumption that the debate is about capital punishment for first-degree murder, not any other offence. While some, for example, would argue for the death penalty in cases of rape, child molesting, and other serious crimes, we'll limit ourselves to murder. Second, we should note as we begin that people on both sides of the issue agree that offenders have forfeited certain basic rights. Those favouring the death penalty argue, obviously, that murderers give up their right to life itself. Those against argue that certain rights have been forfeited, but not necessarily the right to life.

One of the most prominent, if not the most prominent argument, for capital punishment is the *retribution argument*. We noted the key ideas of the retribution approach to punishment in general in an earlier section of this chapter, and we needn't repeat them here. Applying those ideas to capital punishment in particular, retributionists argue that murderers violate all the rights of their victims and, consequently, the only just punishment is death. Only the death of the murderer, they maintain, can restore the balance of justice. In their view, justice requires a life for a life.

A second argument in favour of the death penalty is the *defence of society argument*. This argument says that society must defend itself from murderers who have proved that they are the most vicious members of society. The only effective, long-range, and certain protection of society is achieved through the death of the murderer. The executed murderer will never harm society again. Other punishments, like life in prison, it is argued, may see the release of the offender who is then free to kill again.

A third argument for capital punishment is the *deterrence argument*. This argument proceeds as follows. If murderers are put to death for their crimes, then others in society will take heed and refrain from murdering. In other words, the death of a murderer will deter others from committing this heinous crime. To be effective, it is argued, the death of the murderer must be publicized. Some advocates take the view that the best publicity is achieved through executions that take place in public, a practice that still exists in some countries today.

A final argument in support of capital punishment is the *economic argument*. The annual cost to the taxpayers of Canada for the safekeeping of one maximum-security inmate is approximately $65 000 (Canadian Press, 2000a). At that rate, if a convicted murderer remains in prison for a period of 20 years, the cost is $1.3 million. The *economic argument* says that the expense involved in keeping a murderer in prison is not justifiable. Why, it is said, should society keep murderers alive at great public expense when they have done such harm to others? It is cheaper for society to rid itself of one of its vicious members and that, it is argued, is the right thing to do.

## Arguments against Capital Punishment

The *devaluation of life argument* maintains that killing-as-retribution is a primitive practice that hardens a civil society, contributing to an increasing insensitivity to the value of life in that society. To respond to murder with another killing is regressive, the argument continues, and a denial of the value of life. Some would add that the death penalty is nothing more than state-sanctioned murder. In our time, when there appears to be a growing insensitivity to life's value, it is wrong for the state to add to this perception. The death penalty only hardens the members of society, diminishing the value of life and society itself.

Opponents of the death penalty provide arguments to counter the other pro-death-penalty arguments that we saw earlier. I will mention these very briefly before moving on to two other arguments that require our attention. First, society can protect itself from a murderer's potential harm by imprisonment and rehabilitation rather than putting the murderer to death. Second, studies repeatedly show that the death penalty does not deter others any more effectively than does life imprisonment. Third, the economic cost to taxpayers of court appeals in jurisdictions with the death penalty far exceeds the cost of incarceration in those that don't have the death penalty.

Earlier, we made reference to the *execution of innocents argument*. It has become an important argument as people continue to engage in ethical debate about the death penalty. The argument is simple and focuses on matters of procedural justice. In each of several Canadian cases, the argument proceeds, innocent persons were convicted of murder. In each case, these innocent persons became the victims of systemic failures to ensure a fair trial. Donald Marshall, Guy Paul Morin, David Milgaard, and others would have been put to death for crimes that they did not commit. The frequency of miscarriages of procedural justice provides sufficient rational grounds, this argument maintains, to abolish capital punishment or to prevent its restoration.

A final argument needs to be noted. In Chapter 7 we discussed racism, sexism, and other forms of stereotypical thinking that lead to prejudice and discrimination. The *inequality argument* maintains that capital punishment is wrong because minority group members are put to death in numbers disproportionate to their numbers in the population at large. Stereotypical views are pervasive and they are instrumental, it is argued, in the treatment of minorities. Minority groups and the poor frequently receive unequal treatment under the law. The discriminatory practices of majority groups are wrong at any time, opponents of the death penalty argue, but especially when they involve the taking of human life.

## The Protection of Society

At the beginning of this section on Penal Justice, we noted that both retributionists and rehabilitationists share a concern for the protection of society. The retribution approach argues that society is best protected from convicted murderers by putting them to death. Those executed will never kill again. Society can be certain of that fact.

The rehabilitation approach responds with two points. One point is that life in prison may not guarantee the protection of society with perfect certainty, but the probability that convicted murderers will kill again is very small. Between 1965 and 1988, for example, 650 lifers were paroled. Two killed again. That gives a rate for that time period of 0.3 percent or about 3 out of a thousand. (Canadian Press, 1995). It's absolutely tragic for their victims and families. Nevertheless, the **recidivism rate**, the rate of re-offending, is very low for the crime of murder.

In Canada, statistical research may provide a partial, but only partial, explanation for the low recidivism rate here. Statistics Canada, for 1999, reports that 84 percent of murder victims knew the person who murdered them. Family members account for 35 percent, and acquaintances make up the other 49 percent (Canadian Press, 2000b). Murders in Canada may largely be crimes of passion, offences associated with violence in the family and disputes among acquaintances. Most murderers may simply lack self-restraint, as opposed to being hardened criminals.

What isn't addressed in the preceding point about recidivism and murder is the extremely high recidivism rate among sexual offenders (Gillis, 1998). While data show only a six percent rate of recidivism for sex offenders within three years of release, the rate jumps to over 50 percent when a longer period of time, 10 years, is considered (Kaihla, 1995). The high rate of recidivism for sexual offences raises serious questions about penal justice for such offenders. Would capital punishment, for example, be a just penalty for repeat sexual offenders? We'll return to the subject of repeat sexual offenders in Chapter 10.

The second point that rehabilitationists make with respect to the protection of society is drawn from the criteria for the ethical defence of the use of lethal force. When we looked at self-defence in Chapter 6, we noted the principle of minimal force. That principle applied here in a case of societal self-defence would require minimal force in the defence. If society can protect itself without killing, then that is the morally preferable way to proceed. Rehabilitationists argue that the protection of society can be accomplished without resorting to the death penalty.

## The Matter of Deterrence

In addition to a common concern for the protection of society, we earlier made note of the fact that both the retributionist approach and the rehabilitation approach share a common concern for the matter of deterrence. The *deterrence argument*, we saw, was one of the arguments in the capital punishment debate.

The retributionist has traditionally argued that the death penalty has a greater deterrent effect than life imprisonment. The rehabilitationist has traditionally argued that the death penalty does not provide any greater deterrence than life in prison. Which side is correct is a question for descriptive ethics to decide. You will recall from Chapter 3 that descriptive ethics is the dimension of ethics that examines how things actually are in the world. It tries to establish the facts of a moral issue. Let's look at some facts.

In Canada, if the retributionists are correct, we should have seen the murder rate rise after capital punishment was abolished. Did that happen? The answer is "No." From a murder rate of 3.09 per 100 000 in 1975, the year prior to abolition, to a rate of 1.76 in 1999, the murder rate has declined more or less steadily (Canadian Press, 2000b).

A major U.S. study of the death penalty and deterrence, conducted in 2000, also concludes that the death penalty is no greater a deterrent than life in prison (Bonner and Fessenden, 2000). Ten out of 12 states without the death penalty, for example, have murder rates lower than the national average. Moreover, during the past 20 years, states with capital punishment have had murder rates anywhere from 48 percent to 101 percent higher than states without.

---

| SITUATION 8.5 | **Forensics Expert** |
|---|---|

You are a forensics expert at a forensic science laboratory that routinely provides evidence in criminal cases. For some time you have been concerned about the procedures in the lab. In your view, the labelling of evidence, its storage, and its investigation are done in a rather careless manner. You have reported your feelings to your supervisor on several occasions, but nothing has changed.

Currently you and two other experts, both of whom have several years more experience than you, are examining evidence—hairs and fibres—for testimony at a murder trial. A man acquitted in an earlier trial is on trial again because of new evidence in the form of hairs and fibres taken from the murder victim's clothes. Police believe that the evidence will link the accused to the victim and lead to a conviction. These are the hairs and fibres that your team is examining.

Twice now, you believe that your fellow scientists have contaminated the key evidence. They deny that the evidence has been contaminated, and they have prepared a report for testimony in court. The testimony will confirm police allegations, and the Crown attorneys will be pleased to have this damning evidence. The report is to be introduced as testimony in court tomorrow. Your colleagues have already sent copies to the judge, police investigators, and the prosecution. Your colleagues believe that the evidence is solid. You have your doubts.

What will you do? Will you yield to the majority, your two colleagues? Will you tell anyone about your reservations? If so, who? Explain your reasoning.

# Wrongful Convictions

I began the section on capital punishment by referring to the well-known cases of Marshall, Milgaard, and Morin. We need to return to those cases now, as we conclude our look at the death penalty debate. One of the strongest arguments against capital punishment is the *execution of innocents argument*. As strong as it is, however, we need to note that it carries no weight in cases where there is absolute certainty regarding the identity of the murderer. Sometimes we know, with perfect certainty, who the murderer is. In such situations, other arguments will be at the centre of the debate.

The *execution of innocents argument* is a stark reminder, however, of the failure of the criminal justice system in the cases mentioned. The exoneration of Donald Marshall, Jr. and Guy Paul Morin led to commissions of inquiry that attempted to determine why justice went wrong. Their wrongful convictions generated intense scrutiny of the criminal justice system and yielded many important recommendations.

The inquiry into the circumstances of Marshall's wrongful conviction revealed a variety of concerns. The actions of police, prosecution lawyers, and defence lawyers were all called into question. In particular, questions were raised regarding the competence of police investigators. In addition, the failure of Crown prosecutors to disclose evidence that could have led to Marshall's acquittal was a major concern. Unethical practices may well lie at the heart of that concern. Lastly, the efforts made by defence lawyers on behalf of their client also seemed questionable.

In addition, inquiry recommendations that racial minorities be given better protection in the legal system, that more visible minority judges be appointed, that a special native court system be established, and that a native justice institute be established all point to racism as a significant factor in the case. Our earlier comments, in Chapter 7, regarding the reality of racism in Canada seem to be borne out by these recommendations of the Marshall inquiry. The ethical requirement to treat others equally and impartially is, sadly, not met in all too many instances.

In the Morin inquiry, Judge Fred Kaufman criticized the actions of prosecutors, forensic scientists, government representatives, and police. The judge believed that no Crown prosecutor or police officer "ever intended to convict an innocent person" (Wickens, 1998). Many questionable actions were attributed, rather, to **tunnel vision**. Tunnel vision is a type of narrow mindset that results in a lack of objectivity and serious errors in judgment.

Zeroing in on Morin as the key suspect, investigators apparently developed tunnel vision. They focused on him and then sought evidence to convict, ignoring or missing evidence that might point in other directions. The tunnel that they chose to enter limited their vision to one suspect. In the process, objectivity was lost and serious errors in judgment were made.

Tunnel vision may also be responsible for the pressure that officers placed on Janet Jessop, the mother of the murder victim, Christine. Janet Jessop and her son Kenneth originally told police that they had arrived home at 4:10 p.m., but they testified in court that they arrived home at 4:35 (Fennell and Hawaleshka, 1997). The original time would have excluded Morin as a suspect, as he could not have made it home from his job in Toronto before 4:14. Why did the Jessops change their story? They trusted the police, Janet Jessop said, and the police thought it more likely that the Jessops had arrived home at 4:35. Morin, on that view, remained the prime suspect.

Scientists from the Centre of Forensic Sciences also received sharp criticism. The Crown used evidence provided by the Centre to link four hairs and 12 microscopic fibres found on the victim's clothes to Morin's car. The inquiry heard that personnel from the Centre hid the fact that they had contaminated this key evidence in the laboratory. An anonymous letter, written by a staff member from the Centre of Forensic Sciences to the inquiry, revealed the contamination. Defence lawyers knew nothing of this at either of Morin's two trials. Bruce Durno, president of the Criminal Lawyers' Association, demanded a separate investigation into the Centre. "It is absolutely clear that false evidence was presented," said Durno (Fennell and Hawaleshka, 1997).

Judge Kaufman did not assign moral blame to anyone involved in the Morin case. Instead, he attributed the miscarriage of justice to incompetence, much of it resulting from tunnel vision. The wrongful convictions of Marshall, Milgaard, Morin and others give us pause, however, to think of the potential for unethical conduct as well as incompetence. The Marshall inquiry, as noted above, indirectly pointed to unethical practices (racism) in its recommendations.

There is a lot of room in the criminal justice system, as there is in life generally, for individuals to profit through unethical conduct. Lawyers might advance their careers, for example, by withholding the evidence that, if not disclosed, will allow them to win and the other side to lose. Police officers, too, might put career advancement ahead of objectivity as they ensure that they "nail their man." In the next chapter we'll take a look at deception in policing and other areas of life as we explore the principle of truth. Wrongful conviction because of incompetence is a tragedy. If wrongful conviction occurs because of unethical conduct, it is an even greater one.

## The Ongoing Debate

We have noted some of the main arguments on both sides of the capital punishment debate. The various arguments do not end the debate regardless of whether a society has or does not have the death penalty. In this sense, the capital punishment debate is not unlike other ethical debates such as abortion. The law is one thing and ethical debate is another. Equally reasonable people, because they value one thing more than another, end up taking different positions. In the capital punishment debate, for example, some people emphasize punishment of the offender while others value the reform of the offender. Values, we have noted throughout our study of ethics, are things of the heart, things that people feel strongly about.

Civil societies are possible only because humans share many common values and principles. As noted in Chapter 1, every individual human has certain basic needs in common with every other human. Food, clothing, and shelter are examples. Such common needs generate common values. Food, clothing, and shelter are important to everyone. Furthermore, society itself can remain civil only if its members value the fundamental principles of goodness, equality, justice, truth, and freedom. These are the principles of ethical reasoning.

On any particular issue, different individuals will put the emphasis in one place or another. In the debate over the death penalty, as we have seen, some will see justice as a matter of retribution. Others will see it as a matter of correction. If people are reasonable on both sides, invalid arguments can be identified and discounted. The debate can then continue on other issues, as controversy is ongoing in a civil society. In the final analysis, the test of a civil society lies in the degree of compliance with any existing laws and the willingness to make any changes to the law through rational debate.

## ENFORCEMENT JUSTICE

Before leaving the principle of justice, let's return briefly to the case on which Situation 8.1 (Justice in the Park?) is based. It raises questions about enforcement justice, fair treatment in the apprehending and charging of suspected offenders. The priest (in the situation scenario it was a businessman) who was charged with sexually assaulting the undercover officer—those charges were dropped, you recall—argued unsuccessfully in court that he was the victim of police **entrapment**. His $4 million claim was denied as the judge supported the actions of the police. The man's lawyer believes that an appeal court, perhaps the Supreme Court, will eventually overturn the lower court decision. Only time will tell if that is the case. The appeal, if it occurs, will centre on matters of justice in the enforcement of the law.

The case also raises questions about possible **discrimination**. Would the police have responded to the complaint with several undercover officers if the complaint had been about heterosexual activity in the park? One doesn't know. Would the city councillor or the original complainant have acted on the basis of heterosexual activity in the park? Again, one doesn't know.

If any of the actions were based on the fact that the incident involved gay sex, then it reveals discrimination against gays. Sex in a public place, homosexual or heterosexual, is inappropriate. Given the fact that it is an offence, however, one wonders if gays and straights are treated equally in society's response to the offence. Is there fairness in the treatment of both gay and straight offenders? Is there equality in the treatment of both? Situation 8.3: Shopping Mall Sex, raises some of the same questions regarding discrimination.

## CHAPTER SUMMARY

We began this chapter by defining justice as fair treatment of others. After stating the principle of justice as both a positive and a negative duty, we distinguished the principle of justice from the principle of equality, noting that they are very closely related. We saw how the figure of "Blind Justice" illustrates this close connection. We also noted how breach of these two principles results in harm, a violation of the goodness principle.

Justice, we continued, can be achieved in some cases by giving people what they deserve or merit. In other cases, the fairest thing to do is to give individuals equal shares. In yet other cases, meeting someone's special need is the fair thing to do. These three approaches to justice, we pointed out, are used in various aspects of justice issues.

We commented briefly on three important social movements of the late twentieth century. The civil rights movement sought justice for blacks in the United States. The women's movement fought for justice for women, equality with their male counterparts in the workplace and society in general. Also mentioned was the gay rights movement that sought fair treatment of homosexuals. The close connection between equality, justice, and goodness was evident in all three social movements.

Next, we examined the concept of distributive justice, exploring three different approaches to distributing the benefits and burdens of society among the members of society. Again, we saw merit, equity, and need as approaches to fairness in the distribution of society's benefits and burdens.

Our consideration of distributive justice led to a discussion of criminal justice. We pointed out that criminal justice can be divided into three important areas. Enforcement justice has to do with fairness in the enforcement of the law. Legal justice relates to fairness in the judgment of persons charged with offences. Penal justice is about fairness in the treatment of offenders.

Next, we explored the subject of penal justice. We noted that the two competing views of penal justice share common concerns when it comes to the protection of society and the deterrence of would-be offenders. They differ significantly, however, in other ways. The retribution approach sees justice as a matter of punishment, balancing the scales of justice. The rehabilitation approach, guided by the utilitarian principle, sees justice as a matter of bringing the greatest good to the greatest number in the future. It therefore focuses on correctional programs, not retribution.

Procedural justice was our next consideration. It has to do with fairness in the rules and procedures associated with policing, the courts, and the correctional system. Violation of procedural rules in any area of a civil society's life, we noted, creates injustice. A civil society must have concern for procedural justice. It must protect the rules that permit justice to be done.

Next we reviewed some basic arguments for and against capital punishment. We identified four arguments commonly given in favour of the death penalty, and then noted three arguments against it. We returned to the subjects of the protection of society and the deterrence of would-be criminals, relating them to the capital punishment debate.

We then revisited the *execution of innocents argument* against capital punishment to make observations about the inquiries into the wrongful conviction of innocent persons.

In the Donald Marshall Jr. case, racism appears to have been a factor in his wrongful conviction. Other factors involved police and lawyer ineptitude, with ethical questions raised by the Crown's withholding of evidence. In the Morin case, no moral or legal blame was levelled. Concern was expressed for the apparent tunnel vision that resulted in a loss of objectivity and poor judgment. We pointed out the potential for ethical misconduct contributing to wrongful convictions.

Finally, after underscoring the fact that the capital punishment debate is an ongoing one, we made a few remarks about enforcement justice. Using Situation 8.1, we raised questions pertaining to fairness in the apprehending of offenders. We asked whether heterosexuals would have experienced the same undercover police response that the gay men did. We wondered whether the complainant and the city councillor would have acted in the same way if the sex in the park were of the heterosexual variety. Lastly, we also noted that the entrapment issue might not yet be over. Did the arresting officer's words and actions constitute an unfair entrapment of the gay man?

## MASTERING THE MATERIAL

Now that you have read this chapter, use the following guides to ensure that you have mastered the material.

# Introduction

1. Define *justice*.
2. Describe the traditional symbol of justice.
3. How are impartiality and fairness symbolized?
4. State the justice principle as both a positive and a negative duty.
5. Identify three ways of being fair to others.

# Social Justice

1. Give three examples of movements for social justice.
2. How are equality, justice, and goodness linked in matters of social justice?

# Distributive Justice

1. Define *distributive justice*.
2. Give examples of the benefits and burdens of society.
3. State the three ways of distributing society's benefits and burdens.

# Criminal Justice

1. Identify four key areas of life in a civil society.
2. Define the following terms: *criminal justice, enforcement justice, legal justice, penal justice*

# Penal Justice

1. What two concerns do retributionists and rehabilitationists have in common?
2. Describe the following approaches to penal justice:
   (a) the retribution approach
   (b) the rehabilitation approach
   (c) the compensation approach

# Procedural Justice

1. Define *procedural justice*.
2. To what four areas of life in a civil society does procedural justice apply?

# Capital Punishment

1. Identify, analyze, and criticize four arguments for capital punishment.
2. Identify, analyze, and criticize three arguments against capital punishment.

3. Define *recidivism rate*.

4. What is the recidivism rate for murder in Canada?

5. What other crime has a very high rate of recidivism?

6. What do Canadian statistics reveal about murder rates and capital punishment?

7. What does a 2000 U.S. study reveal about murder rates and capital punishment?

8. Summarize the results of the Marshall inquiry.

9. Summarize the results of the Morin inquiry.

10. Summarize the ongoing debate over capital punishment.

11. What role do values play in the ongoing debate?

## Enforcement Justice

1. In what way does the case of sex in the park highlight the issue of discrimination?

2. In what way does the case highlight the issue of entrapment?

---

## CRITICAL THINKING IN POLICING: THE PRINCIPLES MODEL

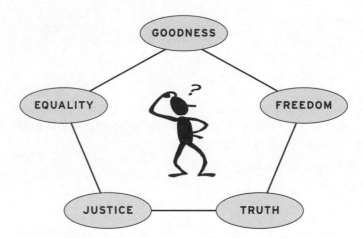

Moral agents act ethically when they treat others justly, being fair (1) on the basis of what others deserve (merit), (2) on the basis of giving equal shares to others (equity), or (3) on the basis of the special requirements of others (need).

## CRITICAL THINKING IN POLICING: THE DECIDE PROCESS

> **D**efine the issue carefully.

> **E**mploy the equality principle.

> **C**onsider the consequences for all.

> **I**nvolve all five principles.

> **D**ecide with integrity.

> **E**valuate your decision.

**Step #4: Involve all five principles**. This step reminds you to include all five principles —Goodness, Equality, Justice, Truth, and Freedom—in your thinking and actions.

---

### Media Watch: Ethics in the News 8.1

## Rape shield protections upheld by Supreme Court

*Canadian Press*—Laws restricting how defendants in sex assault cases can use an accuser's sexual past were judged fair and constitutional yesterday by Canada's top court.

As women's groups celebrated, a lawyer representing the man who challenged the so-called rape shield laws issued a warning.

"I firmly believe there are men doing very difficult time in prison having been wrongly convicted of sexual assault," said Lawrence Greenspon, lawyer for Andrew Scott Darrach.

"And I don't think this judgment is going to help that situation at all."

The legal pendulum has swung too far in favour of complainants to the detriment of those facing sexual assault charges, Greenspon said.

Laws limiting what evidence about sexual histories that defendants can introduce are "a prescription" for wrongful convictions "and I think it's a result of a political shift," he said.

Not so, said the Supreme Court of Canada, in a 9–0 judgment upholding Parliament's approach to a much-debated issue.

Criminal Code provisions amended in 1992 strike the right balance between a complainant's right to privacy and an accused's right to a full and fair defence, says the ruling written by Judge Charles Gonthier.

Source: *Kitchener-Waterloo Record*, October 13, 2000, A4.

## chapter nine

# Truth: Being Honest and Having Integrity in a Civil Society

## LEARNING OUTCOMES

After completing this chapter, you should be able to

- Define *truth,* and distinguish among truth, falsehood, mistakes, and lies
- State the truth principle as both a positive and a negative duty
- Distinguish between good lies and bad lies
- Distinguish between deception by distortion and deception by omission
- Describe the role of confidentiality in policing
- Discuss the role of honesty and integrity in schools
- Discuss the role of honesty and integrity in marriage
- Discuss the role of honesty and integrity in policing
- Explain the *utility of deception argument* for deliberate deception
- Distinguish between authorizing and justifying deception in policing
- Describe the legitimate and the illegitimate codes of silence in policing
- Distinguish between explaining silence and justifying it

# INTRODUCTION

The Law Enforcement Code of Ethics includes a number of statements derived from the **principle of truth**. The most obvious one is the officer's promise to be "honest in thought and deed" in both "personal and official life." Other references in the Code also emphasize the importance of both personal and professional integrity. For a civil society to function in a civil manner, the truth must be valued and practised. Moreover, for a police service to function effectively in a civil society, its members must be committed to telling the truth and acting with integrity. In this chapter we'll explore the importance of honesty and integrity in a civil society. Our subject is **truth** and the **truth principle**.

In his famous work, the *Republic*, Plato tells the story of a shepherd named Gyges who finds a magic ring. When he puts it on his finger, he becomes invisible. When he takes it off, he becomes visible once again. Gyges used the magic of the ring to commit adultery with the queen, kill the king, and take over the kingdom. If there were two such rings, says Plato, "no one would be so incorruptible that he would stay on the path of righteousness" (Plato, 1961, p.607, s360b). Without fear of punishment, Plato believes, everyone would be a thief, a liar, and a murderer.

Is there any reason, apart from fear of punishment, for humans to tell the truth to one another? Plato, in this selection, seems to think not. A closer look at honesty, however, reveals some very simple but extremely important things. Truth and trust, for example, are very closely related. None of us can maintain a healthy, trusting relationship with someone who lies to us. All healthy relationships in our personal, work, and social lives require truth telling and honesty in order to survive and thrive. Trust is based on truth.

If I lie to you and you find out, you will not be able to place your trust in my word. If I deliberately deceive you through my actions and you find out, you will not be able to trust me. I become untrustworthy and unreliable. When this happens, relationships fall apart, whether they are personal, social, or professional. Truth telling and honesty are absolutely essential for all healthy human relationships. Most of us treasure good relationships and tell the truth in order to maintain them. At least, most of the time we do.

This chapter is about the principle of truth. Because we value relationships in life, and because relationships depend on the truth, it is not surprising that the principle of truth is fundamental to the proper functioning of a civil society. The basic duties are the **positive duty** "Be truthful" and the **negative duty** "Don't lie or cheat." In this chapter we will examine many different aspects of truth telling and we will consider a number of all-too-common practices that are deliberately deceitful. As with the other principles studied so far, we'll begin with a definition.

# DEFINING TRUTH

A **truth** is a statement that accords or agrees with reality. To tell the truth, then, is to make statements about a state of affairs that matches the reality of that state of affairs. A parent, for example, asks her child, "Have you put your clothes away?" If the child has put his clothes away, and replies, "Yes, I have" then the child's statement is true. If, however, the child says, "Yes, I have" and he has not in reality put them away, then his statement is false. Being false, the statement could be either a simple mistake or a lie, depending on certain other factors. We'll explore those factors now, starting with lies.

What is a lie and what does it mean to tell a lie? A **lie** is a statement or action that is knowingly false and made with the intention of deceiving another person. We need to note three important ideas in this definition. First, a lie may take the form of a statement or an action. Second, a lie involves a falsehood that the liar knows to be false. Third, the lie is a deliberate attempt to deceive someone else. Careful analysis of this definition and a bit of reflection reveal that there are good lies and bad lies, ones that are morally acceptable and ones that are not.

Take the case of a surprise birthday party for a dear friend of yours. In order to pull it off, you and others will have to make statements and take actions that you know are false. You will have to tell your friend, for instance, that you are going to a concert when in fact you will be going to your friend's party. You will, perhaps, show your friend a concert ticket that you have borrowed from a classmate. In words and actions you will knowingly tell lies. All of this you will do deliberately to deceive your friend into thinking that you will be at a concert on your friend's birthday. Of course, you will tell many other lies along with others to pull off the surprise. And if you pull it off, you and your friends will be very proud of yourselves for having been such good liars.

## Good Lies

What makes this a **good lie,** of course, is the fact that all the deception is directed toward the achievement of a good end, the happy surprise for your friend. This common experience of life should help us make one important point about truth telling and honesty. That point is that the principle of truth is not an absolute principle. There are ethically defensible lies. In other words, there are morally acceptable exceptions to the rule, "Don't lie." Some of them involve circumstances much more serious than a surprise party. Would a lie told to get the conviction of a suspected thief, who has stolen on previous occasions, be a good lie or a bad lie? Would lies told to get a confession from a suspected rapist be good lies or bad?

## Bad Lies

When is a lie a bad lie? What makes deliberate deception wrong? The answer to these questions is somewhat complex, but we'll offer some preliminary thoughts. Later, as we consider various issues, we can add to what we say here. A lie is usually considered a **bad lie** when it is done for self-serving reasons. If, for example, I am trying to gain an advantage over others in a competitive situation, then my deception is wrong. If I take what does not belong to me by telling lies, then my lies are bad lies. We can immediately see a close connection between the truth principle and that of justice. In each of the above examples of lying, my lying and deception are unfair to others. Having introduced the idea of good lies and bad lies, we need to emphasize the fact that normally when we use the word "lie" we mean a bad lie.

## Making Mistakes

One further preliminary point needs to be made. Unlike a lie, a **mistake** is a simple error that involves no deliberate deception. A mistake does involve a false belief that the person making the mistake doesn't realize at the time of the mistake. Increasingly, people seem to confuse lying with making mistakes. The following story illustrates the point. Perhaps you have had a similar experience.

Recently, I visited a shoe store and asked the clerk for a size nine in a particular style. The clerk told me that she had that style in a nine at the back of the store. She proceeded to the back to look for them. When she returned, she said: "I *lied*. We don't have that in a nine. Sorry." The fact of the matter is that the clerk did not lie. She made a mistake. If she had lied, she would have told me that the store had size nines in the back when, in fact, there were none and she knew that there were none. What actually happened is that she thought that the store had nines, but she was mistaken. The store didn't have any size nines. Mistakes are not lies, and lies are not mistakes. We need to be clear on the difference between the two.

## Truth and Integrity

Remember our definition of *truth* above. To tell the truth, we said, is to make statements that are factual, statements that reflect reality. If I tell you truthfully that I am planning to go to a concert on your birthday, then it is the case that I intend to go to a concert on the day that you celebrate your birth. Truth telling and honesty always involve a match between our statements and the way the world actually is. Furthermore, if our actions are true, then they involve no deceit. Like our words, our actions are true when they reflect reality, when we don't give false impressions to others. When people act truthfully on a regular basis, we say that they have **integrity**. What we mean is that their words and deeds are in accord with reality.

## THE WHOLE TRUTH

The well-known courtroom question, "Do you swear to tell the truth, the whole truth, and nothing but the truth?" is a question that recognizes that there is more than one way to lie. Since courts must get at the facts of a case in order to judge matters fairly, truth telling is critical, and the telling of the whole truth is essential. What underlies the question is the fact that people can lie in either of two ways, by deliberately distorting the facts or by deliberately choosing to omit certain facts. Both are forms of lying. In both cases the truth suffers.

Professors of religion have for centuries referred to two kinds of sins, **sins of commission** and **sins of omission**. People can sin against their neighbours, for example, by deliberately injuring them or by failing to help them when they have been accidentally injured. In the first case, one is guilty of a sin of commission, and in the second, a sin of omission. Where the truth is concerned, as we noted above, people can deliberately distort the facts (**deception by distortion**) or they can omit relevant facts (**deception by omission**). Police officers, for example, who intentionally distort the facts when recording their notes record lies. Those who intentionally leave out relevant information do the same, by omission.

## TOO MUCH TRUTH

Sometimes people tell too much of the truth. That is, they share information that they have with people who should not receive the information. In many professions, including policing, confidentiality is vitally important. **Confidentiality**, of course, is secrecy. The Law Enforcement Code of Conduct states: "Whatever a police officer sees, hears or learns of that is of a confidential nature will be kept secret unless the performance of duty or legal provision requires otherwise." Why is confidentiality so important to the medical, nursing, legal, policing, and other professions?

None of these professions can fulfill their obligations to the public if they can't get accurate information from the people they serve. We all know how quickly we stop disclosing personal information to someone that we learn is a gossip. We don't want our private matters spread to people who have no right to them. If professionals break confidence with the people they serve, then their profession is likely to suffer from a lack of public confidence. Breach of confidence, we can see, is a breach of trust that can harm both the individual served and the profession. In some instances, too much truth may be as harmful as too little.

Later in this chapter, we will contrast this legitimate code of silence, professional confidentiality, with an illegitimate one, the so-called blue wall of silence.

## WHAT MAKES A LIE A BAD LIE?

Earlier we asked the question, "What makes a lie a bad lie?" The first answer that we gave was that lies told for self-serving purposes are bad lies. When people distort the truth (or omit to tell it) and they do so for their personal advantage or benefit, then we judge the lying to be morally wrong. This kind of deception, of course, occurs frequently. Examples include acts like showing false identification at a bar and cheating on a final exam. Both acts are self-serving and attempt to gain advantage for the individual who does them.

Are there other kinds of bad lies? Lies told to deliberately harm or hurt another person provide us with a second type of bad lie. Lies told to ruin a reputation, for instance, are examples of this type of bad lie. They are bad because they are deliberate attempts to harm others. They violate the goodness principle which says, "Don't harm!" Civil societies have always recognized that such lying is harmful by passing laws that forbid defamation, either written (libel) or spoken (slander).

In addition to the two factors above, there is a third. Sometimes people lie to others because they believe that others can't handle the truth. This provides us with an example of a third type of bad lie. People who feel superior to others are likely to tell this kind of lie. This lie is a bad lie because it is disrespectful of one's peers. It's often associated with an attitude called **paternalism**, an attitude in which one person treats an equal the way a father (the Latin for *father* is *"pater"*) might treat a young child.

Often in such cases, a person is trying to protect someone else from a truth that may hurt. With very young children, this may be the right thing to do. When it involves adults who are one's peers, it is not. In addition to distorting or withholding the truth, this type of lie is an affront to the dignity of the person lied to. The liar does not give the other person the opportunity to make an informed choice, that is, to decide freely after considering the facts. Lying in order to protect someone from truth that may hurt implies that the person cannot handle the truth.

At this juncture, we need to repeat a point that we made previously about the word *lie*. Normally, when we talk about lies, we are referring to bad lies, not good ones. We distinguished good lies from bad lies in order to highlight and clarify certain things about distortions or omissions of the truth. Having said that, it is important for us to remember that generally speaking lying is wrong. That, of course, is why it is one important topic among many in ethics.

---

| SITUATION 9.1 | Identical Twins |
| --- | --- |

You're a student in a community college that has a common first year for students interested in Law and Security Administration and Policing. The curriculum is that of the Police Foundations Program. From day one, your professors have underscored the importance of academic performance. In addition to being physically fit and scoring well on the G.A.T.B., you know that grades will really count in the competition for the limited seats in the Police Foundations stream. In the second semester, applications will be received from students wishing to pursue a career in policing. Knowing this, you have worked hard and are doing reasonably well, though you're not at the top of the class. You do know, however, that you definitely want to get into policing.

A classmate of yours, Ron Brown, is an identical twin. Ron has had grades about the same as yours throughout the semester. He, like you, intends to apply for the Police Foundations stream. You don't see Ron as a threat because your marks are a bit higher than his are. At a party one night, you meet Don, his twin brother, who is an A+ student at a local university. Ron and Don are identical in appearance and you can tell them apart only by the pierced ears that Don, the university student, has. Ron, your classmate, refuses to get his ears pierced. He is an adamant opponent of male ear piercing and has shared his feelings about the practice on several occasions.

During the final exam week you sit next to Ron in all your exams. On the last day of exams, you notice that your classmate has holes in both ears, but no rings. You immediately conclude that it is Don beside you, and you wonder if he has been writing Ron's exams all week. You haven't talked with Ron—or, is it Don?—throughout the week because he's always been the last to enter the exam room and the first to leave. One thing is absolutely certain. Ron has never followed that pattern as long as you've known him. You now wonder if Don has written all of Ron's exams and wonder, further, whether your classmate's final exam results will gain him entry into policing, ahead of you.

Assume that you are absolutely convinced that Don has written Ron's last exam. What will you do in this situation? Who, if anyone, will you speak to at the college? What will you say? Explain your reasoning.

## HONESTY IN SCHOOL

Cheating in school is a perennial concern for educators, students, and members of the public. A quick check of a college handbook will reveal a whole range of practices that violate the code of academic honesty. Using unauthorized notes, for example, or engaging in unauthorized collaboration during a test are forbidden practices. Other offences include plagiarism, falsification of records, and impersonation. The list is long, but underlying all the offences is one basic principle, namely, that students must do their own work. Simply put, students must earn their credentials.

The various forbidden practices all distort the truth in one way or another. If these practices go undetected, especially if engaged in by large numbers of students, a great deal of harm can be done. First, it is unfair to hardworking and honest students that dishonest students should gain advantage and receive credit when it is undeserved. Second, the school may suffer harm as an institution if unqualified graduates ruin the school's reputation. Third, employers and the public suffer harm when they receive less than they are entitled to from a graduate.

Academic dishonesty may well have been around as long as education itself. In competitive situations such as that of Situation 9.1, the pressure to come out on top can be very intense. Each year, as semesters end in colleges and universities, cheating tends to increase. The methods are varied and, in some cases, very creative. There are the age-old practices as well, practices such as cribbing, bringing unauthorized notes into a test. The plagiarism of essay content also has a long history.

Whether the method is new or old, the basic offence is the same. The cheater doesn't earn her credit, and that, as noted above, has a negative impact in a number of ways. Cheating offends against the merit approach to justice. It's only fair, society says, that students earn their grades. By the way, the impersonation that occurs in Situation 9.1 is not a simple matter of offending against a teacher or college. It's a criminal offence punishable on summary conviction (St. Clair College, 1997, p.13).

Throughout our study of ethics we have underscored the importance of the five basic principles upon which a civil society is established. So far we have discussed, in some detail, the importance of goodness, equality, and justice. The next chapter will examine individual freedom. As we explore truth telling and honesty in this chapter, we would do well to reflect on the importance of honesty in all areas of a civil society's life. Communities are built on mutual trust, and trust is only possible where people tell the truth to one another. This applies to all members of society in their roles as citizens. It also applies to all in their various roles as workers, neighbours, and family members.

| SITUATION 9.2 | Duty Calls |
|---|---|

Constable Tim Swift is the husband of Wanda and the father of Tom, Lois, and Pat. He spends time with his wife and children and they enjoy one another as a family. Tim has a good job as a police investigator, a job he enjoys very much. Because of his growing expertise, duty often calls Tim out of town to meet with teams of investigators from different parts of the province.

Two years ago, while on a week's trip to a northern community, Tim met a female investigator who was at the same conference. They struck up a friendship that resulted in them having sexual intercourse twice during their stay in the north. Neither was looking for any relationship apart from that of the moment. They practised safe sex and treated each other with warmth and respect. They agreed not to contact one another and have kept that agreement.

Upon returning home, Tim did not tell his wife about his experience. He feels that what she doesn't know won't hurt her. He's also sure that he loves his wife dearly. It was, he believes, a moment's pleasure that will in no way hurt his wife or family.

What, if anything, has Tim done wrong? Be specific and explain your reasoning.

## HONESTY IN MARRIAGE

One of the most important experiences of life is that of having a close, loving relationship with a spouse or partner. Such relationships are among the most intimate and meaningful of human experiences. The success of such relationships depends, of course, on truth and honesty between partners. We'll take time to consider honesty in marriage now, before we consider a number of truth-telling issues in policing. Specifically, at this point, let's look at adultery.

Since ancient times, codes of conduct have routinely forbidden adultery. Why is this the case? What is wrong with adultery? In order to answer those questions, we should first have a definition of the word. *Adultery* is usually defined as follows: "sexual intercourse between a married man and someone other than his wife, or sex between a married woman and someone other than her husband."

This definition specifies married partners, but many today would include common-law partners in the definition. Sexual unfaithfulness can occur in common-law arrangements just as easily as in marriages. Still others would also include homosexual partnerships in the definition, maintaining that sexual infidelity in those relationships is also adulterous. Combining these additional factors, the definition might be revised to read, simply, "Adultery refers to sex between a person and someone other than that person's life partner."

If we now ask our earlier question, "What's wrong with adultery?" a number of responses are predictable. To be sure, one answer will focus on the breaking of promises. Since most adulterers will not publicize their actions, it is very likely that lies have been told, or lies are being lived, or both. What's wrong, then, is that adulterers not only break their promises to their partners, but they also lie to them. If we ask further, "So what?" we are likely to hear that adultery is harmful to the non-adulterous partner, that it leads to the destruction of the relationship, and that it contributes to the demise of the family. These often are, in fact, the consequences of adulterous experiences.

However, what if the adulterous experience is a weekend fling, after which the non-adulterous spouse never finds out, the relationship remains intact, and the family does not break up? What, then, is wrong with adultery in such a case? One answer that goes beyond the promise-breaking and harmful-results responses is an answer that stresses a point that we made previously about human dignity.

We noted that our human dignity is rooted in our capacity to make informed choices. Even if the non-adulterous spouse never finds out and no grievous consequences occur, the adulterer has given the spouse neither the opportunity to consider the proposed adultery nor the opportunity to freely decide whether to approve of it or not. The cheating, then, seems to be wrong in that it is disrespectful of the dignity of the partner. This dignity is, of course, the dignity of a moral agent.

Consider now, the following bit of utilitarian calculus. In the universe of Constable Tim, his wife, and his lover, there is more happiness after Tim's sexual liaison than before. Tim's wife is neither more nor less happy than before the experience, because she knows nothing of it. His lover is happier than she was because the experience was so good. Tim's happiness quotient is also higher after the sexual encounter. The right thing to do, you will recall from utilitarianism, is whatever brings the greatest happiness to the greatest number. On this calculation, it seems that Tim did the right thing.

If you're inclined to reject this end-justifies-the-means argument out of hand, remember your reaction to this case later in this chapter. When we consider the *utility of deception argument*, will you reject it out of hand? It's the argument used to justify police deception in achieving their ends.

Above, we said that Tim's failure to inform his wife and get her approval for his sexual liaison was an affront to his wife's dignity. That, we said, was one thing that was morally wrong in the case. What will we say, though, if a person informs her partner that she wants to have sex with someone else and her partner says okay? Think back to Situation 2.1: Bahamian Vacation. You may want to reread that situation before proceeding.

## DO SWINGERS COMMIT ADULTERY?

Many readers will find this question to be an odd one, and many will say that the answer is obvious. But is the answer obvious? Consider first what we said above about adultery. What seems to make adultery wrong, we said, are the self-serving, harmful, and disrespectful aspects, not necessarily the sexual aspect. Consider further, the case of a husband and wife who agree to be swingers. Because they have agreed to swing, they aren't cheating on one another, they aren't disrespectful of one another, and, by our definition, they aren't acting in a self-serving manner. They are adults who consent to have sex with persons other than their partners.

Our original definition stipulated that adultery was sex with someone other than one's partner. On that definition, swingers would still appear to be committing adultery. The original definition, however, may have omitted the main objection to adultery, the reason that makes it wrong. The original definition makes no mention of cheating, breaking promises, harmful consequences, or self-serving actions. It may well be that people assume these things when they condemn adultery. Good definitions, however, should leave no essential element of the definition unstated. It seems that the original definition has done just that.

It would appear that the answer to our question is obvious, given the original definition of adultery. That answer is "Yes, swingers commit adultery." We are now left with a further question, however, and that question is: "Is the adultery committed by swingers wrong?" We'll leave the reader to ponder that question and turn our attention to important questions about honesty in policing. Let's begin with another situation.

| SITUATION 9.3 | True Confessions? |
| --- | --- |

Two investigating officers have been interrogating a suspect for seven hours. He's a suspect in a series of arsons in the community. He's in tears and very distraught. Despite repeated denials on his part, the officers continue to insist that the man is guilty and they keep pressing him for a confession.

During the course of their interview, the officers minimize the seriousness of the crimes, saying that the buildings torched were mostly "eyesores." In addition, they tell the suspect that the eight fires set could be "bundled together" into one charge if he confesses, implying that the courts will then go easier on him. The man's fiancée's car was destroyed in one of the fires, and the officers tell him that she won't be charged with insurance fraud if he confesses. They also give him a lie detector test, but they fail to tell him that lie detector results are inadmissible in Canadian courts. The interviewers also attempt to build up a sense of false trust in the suspect, indicating that if he confesses, he will get psychiatric help for his problem.

The man finally confesses.

What do you think of the man's confession? Should it be allowed as evidence in court? What do you think of the interview? Discuss the case with others, if you have occasion to do so.

We'll return to this situation shortly. First, let's take a look at honesty in policing.

## HONESTY IN POLICING

Throughout this book we have noted the important role that police play in a civil society. That role is well defined in the Canons of Police Ethics, Article 1, where it says that the primary responsibility of the police service and individual officers is the protection of the public through the upholding of the laws of society. These laws include those that limit police actions, ensuring that a civil society does not degenerate into a police state. Officers, as prime defenders of civil society, must not pervert the character of the system. That is, they must uphold the laws that govern all members of society and always work within the parameters of those laws.

Article 4 of the Canons of Police Ethics, "Utilization of Proper Means to Gain Proper Ends," makes the critical point that an officer's use of illegal means to achieve a goal is self-defeating. It is self-defeating because it gives the public the message that you can break the law if you have a good enough reason to do so. The last part of Article 4 makes the fundamental point clearly and concisely. It bears repeating: "The employment of illegal means, no matter how worthy the end, is certain to encourage disrespect for the law and its officers. If the law is to be honoured, it must first be honoured by those who enforce it." The end does not justify just any means. The means must be proper means.

The Code of Conduct of the Ontario Police Services Act, recognizing the proper relationship between the police and society, specifies a number of actions that constitute offences against discipline because they are likely to bring discredit upon the reputation of the police force. Among these offences are a number that are derived from the principle of truth and relate to the truth telling and honesty that we have been discussing. The omission of a necessary entry in any official document or book, for instance, constitutes neglect of duty (1c,ix). Knowingly making or signing a false statement, wilfully making a false statement, and altering or destroying official documents are all deceitful acts, punishable under the Act (1d,i-iii).

Moreover, in our examination of the Law Enforcement Code of Ethics and the Law Enforcement Code of Conduct, we once again saw these professional codes stipulating the key ethical obligations of officers. Among those obligations is one that requires officers to be honest in word and deed, in both their personal and professional lives. Such honesty is essential if officers are to carry out their duties in a manner that respects and protects the constitutional rights of all members of society. In addition, it is officer integrity, we saw above, that will establish and maintain public respect for the police services in a civil society.

It is clear, then, that both the law and police codes of ethics repeatedly emphasize the importance of integrity within individual officers and the police service as an institution of society. Because of many well-publicized cases of police deceit and corruption, honesty in policing has become a very serious concern in contemporary society.

In Situation 9.3 above, the interviewing officers have broken no law. They have, however, repeatedly lied to the suspect, persisting in their interview until they secure a confession. Should the confession be permitted as evidence in court? Isn't it a clear case of a confession secured under duress? Writing in *The Globe and Mail*, Toronto lawyer Clayton Ruby recounts the events that underlie the situation (Ruby, 2000). The evidence was, in fact, accepted in lower courts and eventually confirmed as permissible by the Supreme Court.

Ruby reminds his readers of what the Supreme Court itself says about confessions elicited under pressure, the kind of pressure described in our situation. The Supreme Court *says* it's wrong and unacceptable as evidence because it commonly produces false confessions. That's what the Court *says*, but what did it actually *do* in the case of *Oickle v. The Queen*? As mentioned above, it allowed the confession to stand as evidence.

This judgment, writes Ruby, sends entirely the wrong message to our civil society. He concludes, "Such treatment sets Canada's standards at the lowest common denominator of civilized behaviour. Our values are revealed. They are these: Lie, cheat, mislead if you must. Ignore tears and repeated protestations of innocence. But get a confession from whomever you have in your hands. That's the message the Supreme Court has just sent to police forces across our land. We're playing with fire." (Ruby, 2000).

Before we look at any specific issue, we need to comment on two popular perceptions of the role of police in society, one of which seems to lead to a number of important ethical dilemmas.

## The Role of the Police in a Civil Society

Contemporary, popular culture seems to have two distinctly different perceptions regarding the role of the police in society. One view emphasizes the officer as **public servant**. The other emphasizes the officer as **crime fighter**. Clearly, police officers are both public servants and crime fighters. The crime fighter role, however, carries with it images of war and warfare. It is common, for instance, to hear people speak about the "war on crime." It is the crime fighter perception in particular that seems to generate a number of ethical dilemmas. In contrast, the image of public servant, with its emphasis on the rule of law, seems far less problematic.

Consider the crime fighter and the war on crime. When wars are fought between countries, the usual ethical considerations of peacetime give way to the rule of the jungle, survival of the fittest. Truth, it has been said, is the first casualty in war. Nations at war with one another deliberately and routinely deceive their enemies. Indeed, when the survival of a nation is in question, it is difficult to imagine not using deception as a weapon in one's arsenal. Now, if deliberate deceit can be justified in warfare between nations, can it also be justified in warfare between one segment of society, the police, and another segment, namely criminals?

In a war on crime, as in war between nations, it is often argued that the truth must be the first casualty. In order to stop serious crime in society, deliberate deception must occur. Is this position ethically defensible in a civil society? Is it ethically permissible for police officers, for example, to lie in the course of an investigation or an interrogation? Since the law and police codes of conduct clearly forbid lying, any ethical defence of deception is likely to centre on the utility of deception in achieving a worthy end.

## Does the End Justify the Means?

**Utility**, you will recall from Chapter 3, is another word for usefulness. In any war on crime, when people talk about the utility of deception, they are saying that a certain amount of deliberate deception is useful in winning that war. The *utility of deception argument* says that deliberate deception is an ethically legitimate means to a good end, the defeat of crime. The argument acknowledges that dishonesty is generally wrong (evil), but it goes on to say that this dishonesty is necessary to achieve a worthy end.

This utilitarian argument is also called the *necessary evil argument*, an argument we examined in Chapter 6 in connection with both self-defence and the just war. Above, in connection with Situation 9.2, I asked you to consider whether this argument justifies Constable Tim's adulterous affair. What did you say at that point? What were your reasons?

This justification of deliberate deception is sometimes expressed in terms of choosing the lesser of two evils. When this language is used, people say that a certain amount of a lesser evil, police dishonesty, is justified because it results in the elimination of a greater evil, crime. Lying is wrong and so is dealing drugs, the argument goes, but lying is the lesser of these two evils. Earlier in this chapter, we discussed the matter of good lies and bad lies. You can see, no doubt, a parallel between that discussion and this one. A good lie, it was argued, is one that achieves a good end, one that is neither self-serving nor malicious.

In the sections that follow, the *utility of deception argument* will play an important role in attempts to justify certain questionable police practices. We will examine these attempts to justify certain actions with a view to identifying criteria that can be used to distinguish ethically acceptable justifications from illegitimate ones. We will also emphasize the important distinction between the actions taken by individual officers and those actions authorized by the police service as an agency of government. This distinction is of importance to individual officers and agencies alike. The key to ethical behaviour in policing may well lie in a certain consistency between officer actions and policing policies.

Before going further, consider these words from the Canons of Police Ethics, words that clearly identify the problem with using illegal means to achieve police ends. Does the same argument apply to the use of unethical means that are not illegal? Article 4 reads: "Law enforcement officers shall be mindful of their responsibility to pay strict heed to the selection of means in discharging the duties of their office. Violations of law or disregard for public safety and property on the part of an officer are intrinsically wrong; they are self-defeating in that they instill in the public mind a like disposition. The employment of illegal means, no matter how worthy the end, is certain to encourage disrespect for the law and its officers. If the law is to be honoured, it must first be honoured by those who enforce it."

## OBVIOUS WRONGDOING

In our examination of the principle of truth thus far, we have mentioned a number of practices that are obviously wrong from both legal and moral points of view. The Ontario Police Services Act, for example, includes 11 different categories of offence in the Code of Conduct. Eight of these categories include one or more offences related to the principle of truth. The eight categories are as follows: discreditable conduct, insubordination, neglect of duty, deceit, breach of confidence, corrupt practice, unlawful and unnecessary exercise of authority, and damage to clothing or equipment.

In this chapter I am referring to these offences as "obvious wrongdoing." Perhaps they are not obvious to everyone, but hopefully they are. Calling them obvious in no way suggests that they are unimportant. The theft of money or property, the taking of bribes, lying to superiors, lying while under oath, and the acceptance of gifts and gratuities are extremely serious matters. So, too, is the omission of relevant information in official records and reports, or the alteration of records or reports. Other very serious legal and ethical concerns are, perhaps, not as obvious as those mentioned here. Let's turn to some of them now.

## HONESTY IN POLICE INVESTIGATIONS

The use of stings, fencing operations, informants, and undercover agents in the investigative aspects of the war on crime raises serious questions about honesty in policing. Can those sworn to ethical integrity and the upholding of the law deliberately engage in illegal and unethical practices as they carry out their responsibilities? Can members of a civil society condone such actions if they occur? These actions are, of course, actions that run contrary to one of the principles most important to the welfare of a civil society, the principle of truth.

What does society think when individual officers, investigative teams, and entire police departments conspire to accomplish their goals through actions that are judged to be wrong in the homes, schools, and workplaces of society? What happens to these individual officers, teams, and departments if deliberate deception becomes standard practice for them? What happens when young and impressionable members of society learn that their guardians, the police, can deceive with impunity?

Recently in the United States, the city of Los Angeles and the federal government signed a consent decree on police reform (Wordsworth, 2000). In the wake of a corruption scandal in the Rampart Division's anti-drug squad, the federal government will begin to monitor the performance of police officers in L.A. The corruption has been described as one of North America's most serious police-corruption scandals (Saunders, 2000).

In April of 2000, five officers from the Toronto Police Service were charged with 136 offences, including theft, fraud, forgery, and breach of trust (Duncanson and Rankin, 2000). In November, eight other officers from the Central Drug Squad were charged with 75 criminal offences and 98 charges under the Ontario Police Services Act (Canadian

Press, 2000). The charges include theft and fraud. While these officers have not been found guilty, the sheer number of charges is alarming. The members of a civil society are rightfully concerned when some of their guardians may well be outlaws.

Three important points need to be made in the light of these concerns regarding honesty and integrity in policing.

## Authorizing Deliberate Deception

First of all, individual investigative officers, acting independently of others, must not initiate deliberately deceptive practices. Individuals are not in a position to justify or authorize the use of deliberate deception, and they cannot ethically or morally engage in it without authorization from others. To **justify** a course of action means to provide morally acceptable reasons for the action. To **authorize** means to give official approval to a course of action. The point is very straightforward, but critically important. Individuals can neither justify nor authorize these practices. In a civil society, **justification** and **authorization** must be accomplished through the involvement of others, and not just any others. It must come from those who have legitimate authority.

Second, deliberate deception in investigations cannot be ethically justified or authorized by a group of investigators working independently of their superiors. The same points that were made with respect to individual officers in the preceding paragraph also apply to groups of officers. The justification of practices and their authorization is both a police service and a societal concern, not just the concern of a few. While individuals and groups will carry out the practices, the justification and authorization are everyone's concern.

Third, the authorization of the use of deception must be vested in the leaders of a civil society's police services, the chiefs of police. As suggested in the preceding paragraph, however, the justification of unethical practices must be undertaken by those members of society who have been elected to oversee policing in a community. Police boards, elected by the citizenry, are responsible for ensuring that police practices are ethically defensible. The justification of the limited use of illicit activities within a civil society rests with the people. Renegade individuals and rogue groups, regardless of their rank, will discredit a police service if they act independently of legitimate authority.

Warrants for arrest, search, or seizure, for instance, provide a good example of the legitimate authorization of actions that, without warrant, would be illegal. A magistrate, on behalf of the legal system and the citizenry, issues a writ that authorizes actions that otherwise would be questionable. In this way, among others, a civil society ensures that the police have good reason to take an action. Moreover, it places limits on the police, limits that are justifiable and necessary within a civil society.

## Justifying Deliberate Deception

The preceding section was primarily concerned with the legitimate authorization of police dishonesty. Now we turn to the matter of the ethical justification of police dishonesty. We have already referred to the *utility of deception argument*, and we now turn to the traditional criteria associated with that argument. You will recall that the argument maintains that in certain investigative circumstances the end justifies the means. For example, capturing the drug dealer (the end or goal) justifies or legitimizes a certain amount of police deceit (the means or method).

We should note that the ethical defence of dishonesty has always been a defence of limited deceit. In other words, persons making the argument do not argue for dishonesty in general. Such an argument would be foolish from the start, given the importance of truth in a civil society. The argument is always about a limited use of dishonesty for a particular purpose. The traditional justification of limited dishonesty, then, usually involves *all* of the following criteria:

- The end (goal) must be a good and worthy end.
- The deceitful means must have a high probability of success.
- The deceitful means must be a last resort.
- The deceitful means must not undermine a greater end.

Limited dishonesty is justified, the argument says, only when all four of these criteria are met. Let's illustrate using our example above. First, the capture of the drug dealer is considered to be a good end, a worthy goal. Second, the deliberate deception has a high probability of succeeding. In other words, there must be a strong likelihood that the deception will work. Third, there is no non-deceitful alternative to the dishonest means. Deception is a last resort. Fourth, the use of dishonest practices will not undermine a greater end, such as loss of faith in the police service or the rule of law. Two additional points need to be made.

First, this defence is an ethical defence not because it will persuade everyone or be accepted by everyone. In all likelihood it will not. Some will disagree with it because they will place more value on truth telling than they will on fighting crime in this way. People who object to police dishonesty will argue, no doubt, that the police service will be discredited by such actions, even though the goal seems worthy. Despite the objections of some, the defence is considered an **ethical defence** because it is based on the principles of ethical reasoning, and it provides a rationale for making an exception to the rule, "Don't deceive others." To put it differently, such lies, it is argued, are good lies.

Second, the objection that the police service will be discredited is countered, in large measure, if the justification is a societal one. In other words, if police services personnel, in concert with elected representatives, debate the legitimacy of these practices, then ultimately the people have a say in the matter. This was one of the points we made in the last section. No individual or group within a police service can justify the practice independently of the people they serve. The justification of the practice takes place in a public way, and its authorization and implementation takes place in the normal manner within the police service.

In the light of these remarks, recall Situation 8.1: Justice in the Park? Can the undercover officer's lie to the gay man be justified, ethically speaking? Was the end, in your view, a worthy end? Are the consequences of the public revelation of the man's homosexuality ethically relevant? In a word, did the end justify the means in this case?

Think again of Situation 7.2: Balcony Rapist, the situation based on the Jane Doe case. While a prominent issue in that case was, in the view of the judge, systemic sexism, the matter of means and ends should also command our attention. The end, the capture of the Balcony Rapist, did not justify the means, putting women at risk.

## CODES OF SILENCE WITHIN POLICING

Police officers are sworn to silence on certain aspects of their professional lives. Both the law and their codes of ethics require this silence. Earlier in this chapter, for example, we touched on the importance of confidentiality in policing and other professions. Confidentiality, we said, *is* secrecy. A certain kind of silence or secrecy is essential, if the police are to serve the public effectively.

Police officers, however, are also sworn to speak up when the law is broken. They are sworn to report offenders and that, obviously, is an essential part of an officer's duties. But what if the offenders are fellow officers? Several situations that we have explored in previous chapters should be brought to mind before we proceed. In particular, Situation 5.1: Unruly Prisoner raises questions that pertain to the subject of silence in the police subculture. Will the observing officer remain silent about the actions of his fellow officer, striking the prisoner and tampering with surveillance equipment?

Similarly, Situation 5.2: Shift Partner requires us to question whether silence is an ethical option when one's partner makes racist remarks within the cruiser. Situation 5.4: The Whole Truth, also focuses on police actions and silence in response to them. That case was the one about the theft of cash during the marijuana bust. Also deserving of review, at this point, is Situation 7.1: Important Lessons. The senior officer in that case, you will recall, was intent upon teaching both the native man and you important lessons, lessons on sobering up and keeping silence.

## The Legitimate Code of Silence

The Ontario Police Services Act, in its Code of Conduct, identifies breach of confidence as an offence under the Act. Among several actions that constitute a breach of confidence are the unauthorized divulging of confidential information, the unauthorized release of official documents, the unauthorized communication of a warrant or summons, and unauthorized communication with the media. In each of these cases, one can easily see how silence serves the goals of the police service. Both the Law Enforcement Code of Ethics and the Law Enforcement Code of Conduct address the importance of such confidentiality, keeping silence on certain matters of importance.

## The Illegitimate Code of Silence

Failure to report offenders and failure to report criminal acts are both offences under the Code of Conduct of the Ontario Police Services Act. The Code states that an officer is guilty of neglect of duty if he or she "fails, when knowing where an offender is to be found, to report him or her or to make due exertions for bringing the offender to justice" (1c,v). The Code states further that an officer is guilty of neglect, if he or she "fails to report anything that he or she knows concerning a criminal or other charge ..."

In concert with the Act, both the Law Enforcement Code of Ethics and the Law Enforcement Code of Conduct forbid corruption and the condoning of corruption.

These ethical and legal requirements appear to be ignored in some instances, when the offenders are fellow officers and the criminal or other charges are to be laid against them. An illegitimate code of silence sometimes comes into effect. This "blue wall of silence," as it is sometimes called, goes up as offences go unreported and silence rules the day. While this may occur only occasionally, it is vitally important to discover why this happens. Clearly, this silence is illegitimate by both ethical and legal standards. Why, then, does it occur?

As we consider some possible explanations for this phenomenon, we'll use a clear-cut case of theft as our example. One officer sees another officer steal a large sum of money and a package of cocaine from the cash and drugs ceased in a successful police raid on a drug den. Why would the first officer keep silent in this situation?

## Discretion

Perhaps a police officer's right of discretion, which allows an officer to take different actions when handling offences, might give the officer in our example the idea that he can personally decide whether to report the incident or not. But discretion requires some reasonable course of action on the part of the attending officer. It would be difficult, if not impossible, to defend silence as a reasonable exercise of discretion in a case of theft and possession of an illegal drug. Silence in this situation could not be justified on the grounds of discretionary authority.

## Loyalty

Would an argument based on loyalty provide a legitimate reason for silence? Loyalty to a person or a cause is an important value within society. Remaining faithful to a marriage partner over many years or providing loyal service to one's employer for a lengthy period are examples of such loyalties. Other loyalties, however, are frowned on or condemned. Personal loyalty to an evil person or an evil cause, for example, is considered misguided at best or outright evil at worst. Once again, in our example case, it seems impossible to legitimately defend silence on grounds of loyalty. It might explain one's inaction, but it would not justify it.

## Fear

Could fear of reprisal provide a justification for silence? Perhaps reporting the thieving officer will lead to a reprisal of some sort. One type of reprisal mentioned in popular accounts of the blue wall of silence is refusal to come to the aid of the officer who blows the whistle. Another involves threats to the officer who blows the whistle and to his family. While fear of reprisal along these lines might be a legitimate fear, once again it does not justify silence. If officers yield to such fears, the law of the jungle prevails and civil society loses. If faced with such circumstances, hopefully officers will exhibit the same courage that they exhibit in the face of civilian threats. Keeping the jungle at bay requires "courageous calm in the face of danger, scorn or ridicule."

## Explanation versus Justification

In each instance above, we said that an officer's misunderstanding of discretionary authority, the officer's loyalty, or the officer's fear might explain why the officer keeps silent about the offence committed. Each time we pointed out that the explanation was not a justification. When we say that an officer's fear may **explain** the action, we mean that fear is the motive (**psychological reason**) for the silence. Fear provides an **explanation** for the silence.

In order for something to **justify** an officer's silence, however, it would have to provide a morally defensible reason (**ethical reason**) for the silence. As we said above, none of the three explanations of the silence provides a **justification** for the silence. That's why the silence is illegitimate. If an impartial tribunal heard the facts of the story, surely the silence would be condemned.

Are there any other reasons that can be given to justify silence in these kinds of circumstance? I am not aware of any.

## Justifying Silence with Respect to Minor Offences

Could silence be justified if the thieving officer took only a bottle of whiskey or a single joint of marijuana? Do our duties change, we might ask, when the offences are only minor ones? Is silence morally and legally justified if the consequences of the offence are minor? The actions are still offences and, therefore, wrong. In the case of a minor offence, however, an officer's right of discretion seems like it might be a justification for silence. If the discretion is reasonable and based on the seriousness of the offence, not who committed it, then discretion might be a justification for silence. That would be the case especially if the officer spoke to the offender and discussed the incident with him or her, pointing out that the actions in question are wrong.

Having said this, however, we need to repeat that the proper exercise of discretion always involves a judgment about the offence committed, not the offender's status. Finally, we also need to note the danger of remaining silent when the offence is serious and should be reported. And this last comment, we might add, raises at least two critical questions: At what point does a minor offence become a major offence? and Who decides?

## CHAPTER SUMMARY

This chapter has examined the principle of truth, one of the fundamental principles of a civil society. After citing the Law Enforcement Code of Ethics with respect to statements on truth, we discussed the importance of truthfulness in human relationships. We then stated the principle as both a positive and a negative duty.

We proceeded next to define *truth* as "a statement that accords with reality." An important distinction between false statements and lies was then made. Lies, we continued, are false statements marked by three features. First, they can take the form of statements or actions. Second, they are known falsehoods. Third, they are deliberate deceptions. Lies, we pointed out further, are not simple mistakes.

We then noted that there are good lies and bad lies. Three things can make a lie a bad lie. If a lie is self-serving, deliberately harmful, or disrespectful of the dignity of a person, then it is a bad lie.

Next, we discussed honesty in schools, highlighting the key principle that students must earn their own credits. The principle of merit governs, and all attempts to secure credit without earning it are considered unethical. They are wrong. Marriage, too, is a place for honesty. Beginning with a traditional definition of adultery, we noted that adultery is considered wrong for a number of reasons. First, it involves the breaking of promises. Second, it can produce very harmful consequences for the marriage and family. Third, it is disrespectful of the dignity of the unknowing spouse. We then raised questions about the practice of swinging.

We proceeded then to an examination of dishonesty in policing. We pointed out two popular images of the police, that of public servant and that of crime fighter. The latter image, we maintained, contributes to a number of questionable practices. In the war on crime, deliberate deception plays a key role. We asked whether it can be justified in a civil society committed to the principle of truth. That question led us to an analysis of the *utility of deception argument* that is commonly used to defend deliberate deception in fighting crime. We then raised further questions about the utilitarian approach that argues that the end can justify the means.

After reviewing statements from the Code of Conduct of the Ontario Police Services Act, we turned to the subject of honesty in police investigations. First, we examined the topic of the authorization of deliberate deception, indicating that, in a civil society, this can only occur legitimately between the government and policing agencies. In particular, authorization is vested with the chiefs of police.

Justifying deliberate deception is a closely related but different matter. We looked at the classic justification that is founded on the utilitarian approach to ethics. Four criteria must be met, according to the *utility of deception argument*, if deliberate deception is to prove ethically defensible. First, there must be a good goal. Second, the deception must have a high likelihood of success. Third, deception must be a last resort. Fourth, the deception must not undermine a greater good.

Next, we explored codes of silence in policing, identifying both a legitimate and an illegitimate code. The legitimate code ensures confidentiality, an ethical practice essential for the success of policing in a civil society. The illegitimate code involves the silence associated with officer wrongdoing that goes unreported.

We indicated that officers might remain silent in the face of wrongdoing because they feel that their professional discretion gives them the right to do so. This, we said, was clearly a misunderstanding of discretion. A second explanation for the silence might lie in loyalty to one's fellow officers. This, too, might provide an explanation but not a justification for silence. Last of all, we mentioned the role that fear of reprisal might play in creating a "blue wall of silence." Again, fear might explain silence but it cannot justify it. We concluded with brief remarks and a question about silence in the face of minor offences.

## MASTERING THE MATERIAL

Now that you have read this chapter, use the following guides to ensure that you have mastered the material.

### Introduction

1. Who was Gyges?
2. What is the connection between truth and good relationships?
3. State the truth principle as both a positive and a negative duty.

### Defining Truth

1. Define *truth*.
2. What is a falsehood?
3. Identify the three elements of a lie.
4. What is integrity?

### The Whole Truth

1. Explain deception by distortion and deception by omission.

## Too Much Truth

1. Explain why too much truth can be a problem.
2. Why is confidentiality essential to policing?

## What Makes a Lie a Bad Lie?

1. Identify three things that can make a lie a bad lie.

## Honesty in School

1. What approach to fairness is essential in schooling?
2. Identify three harms that cheating in school can produce.

## Honesty in Marriage

1. Define *adultery* and identify three things that make adultery wrong.

## Do Swingers Commit Adultery?

1. Do swingers commit adultery? If they do, is there anything wrong with it?

## Honesty in Policing

1. Cite sections of policing codes that are concerned with the truth principle.
2. Identify two popular views of the role of the police officer.
3. Define *utility*.
4. State and explain the *utility of deception argument*.

## Obvious Wrongdoing

1. Describe several acts of obvious wrongdoing from the Ontario Police Services Code of Conduct.

## Honesty in Police Investigations

1. Who can authorize deception in police investigations?
2. State the classic ethical defence for deception in policing.
3. Explain the four criteria essential for an ethical defence of police deception.

## Codes of Silence within Policing

1. Describe the legitimate and illegitimate codes of silence within policing.
2. Identify three things that explain but do not justify illegitimate silence.

# CRITICAL THINKING IN POLICING: THE PRINCIPLES MODEL

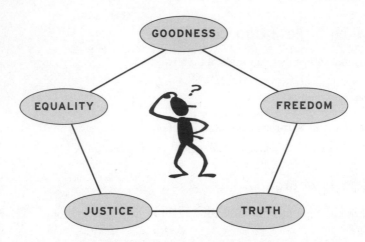

Moral agents act ethically when they tell the truth to others and act with integrity. Lies are justified only when they serve to achieve some greater good for others.

# CRITICAL THINKING IN POLICING:

> Define the issue carefully.

> Employ the equality principle.

> Consider the consequences for all.

> Involve all five principles.

> Decide with integrity.

> Evaluate your decision.

## THE DECIDE PROCESS

**Step #5: Decide with integrity**. This step reminds you to be true to the facts, others, and yourself as you seek to understand ethical issues and as you make your moral choices.

## Police deceit cited as judge lifts woman's murder charge

Canadian Press—OTTAWA After four years in custody, Julia Elliott cried Tuesday as the shackles binding her legs and the second-degree murder charge hanging over her head were removed.

The 39-year-old woman from Barbados wept in an Ottawa courtroom after a judge stayed proceedings against her, stating that the deceit of police and misconduct of Crown attorneys had destroyed her right to a fair trial.

"When the police take the law into their own hands, as in this case, experience shows, and this case proves, that the truth and fairness get trampled under foot," said Justice Paul Cosgrove.

"When the Crown officers employ an exaggerated adversarial stance, as in this case, the trial process becomes so unbalanced that the guaranteed Charter right to a fair trial is undermined."

The judge found that OPP officers were prepared to tailor their evidence under oath and to change their testimony as the need arose.

He cited roughly a dozen Crown prosecutors, as well as an assistant deputy attorney-general for Ontario, for misleading the court and not playing fair with defence lawyers.

In all, Cosgrove found more than 150 examples of Crown and police behaviours that breached Elliott's rights.

The Crown is appealing the decision.

In 1995, Elliott was charged with second-degree murder in the death of Larry Foster, 64, of Kemptville, Ont.

The Crown's case relied upon a police officer's evidence he stopped Elliott in Foster's car. However, Cosgrove found Const. Ron Laderoute made a note of stopping Elliott only after the investigation had begun, then backdated his note. In court, Laderoute admitted to backdating the reference, but he has also denied doing so.

Source: *Kitchener-Waterloo Record*, September 8, 1999, B5.

## A nation of cheaters

The difference between principle and fundamentalism is the element of reality. The federal government is accused of bowing to lawlessness by abandoning the high-tax campaign against tobacco use in an effort to curb tobacco smuggling; so it has, and so, in the circumstances, was it right to do. To insist that principle be defended at all costs, when there is no practical likelihood of success, is the very definition of fundamentalism.

To acknowledge that reality, however, should not blind us to the principles at stake: more explicitly, to the *moral* culpability of those involved. As a matter of policy, there may indeed be a limit on the level of tax rates that can be enforced. But that does not excuse the behaviour of those who have participated in this business, who remain worthy of the heartiest contempt. The repeal of the tobacco tax is not merely the defeat of a particular policy: it is steeped in a peculiarly smelly mix of moral relativism and group politics that has been allowed to ferment for far too long in this country.

Any settling of moral accounts must begin with the cigarette manufacturers. It is not enough that, as a matter of ordinary routine, they knowingly make and market a substance that kills people—a substance that, uniquely among legal products, kills when used exactly as intended. By continuing to ship cigarettes to the U.S. in massive amounts, knowing that almost every last one would be smuggled back into Canada, they have actively colluded in the systematic evasion of the law. Among the guilty, they are scarcely better than the organized crime rings they supply.

The vendors in Quebec who openly sold truckloads of contraband cigarettes under the noses of police, like the shopowners who threatened to break other laws if their demands for lower taxes were not met, are no more to be excused for advertising their defiance. This was not civil disobedience: it was a crime for profit, and blackmail to boot.

Likewise complicit are the native leaders on the border reserves that serve as the smugglers' pipelines. There's no evidence they were directly involved, but by invoking native "sovereignty" at every turn, sometimes accompanied by indirect threats of violence—always to be deplored, of course, but you never know what those young hotheads might do—they have conspired to obstruct police in the enforcement of Canadian law on Canadian land. Unwilling to confront the growing mobocracy on the reserves, they have instead taken the racial demagogue's route: look the other way and blame the white man.

Perhaps it's unfair to link the smuggling issue with native self-government. But given the performance of native leaders to date in this affair, from Ovide Mercredi on down, we're not so sure. And again, there are moral issues beyond the legalities. It may be that natives have the right, under law, to import cigarettes and liquor duty-free. But is it *right* to do so? Is this to be the economic foundation on which native pride and dignity will be rebuilt: bingo, booze and peddling cheap smokes to children?

In the end, however, moral responsibility must rest with those who fuel this foul trade: with the many Canadians who choose to buy illegal cigarettes. We could not but be struck by the number of people prepared to boast to the television cameras of their willingness to break the law, to lie, to sneak about, in effect to steal, for no better reason than that it suits them. But then, this sort of petty cheating has become more or less the accepted standard of behaviour in Canada, hasn't it? It's almost fashionable. Whether it's dodging the GST or fiddling the dole, lying to customs or stealing hotel towels, the rationalization is always the same: well, who's hurt?

Somewhere along the way, a great many people in this country seem to have mislaid their consciences: the notion that a thing is wrong not because you might get caught, nor even because somebody might get hurt, but simply because you know it to be wrong. A sustained act of deceit is not something to boast about. We're all guilty of it from time to time: but the very least we can do is to be ashamed about it. More even than the law, it is conscience that is the final bulwark of a civil society, and it is a civil society that, in ways both large and small, has broken down over much of Canada in recent times.

Society has other sanctions beyond the law. A forgotten contributor to the decline in cigarette consumption, beyond high taxes or even health con-cerns, is the social stigma that now attaches to it; it's considered positively rude to light up at dinner. We hope the stares are just as chilly the next time someone brags of cheating on their taxes.

Source: *Globe and Mail*, February 11, 1994, A22.

## chapter ten

# Freedom: Making Ethical Choices in a Civil Society

## LEARNING OUTCOMES

After completing this chapter, you should be able to

- Define *freedom* and distinguish it from licence
- State the freedom principle as both a positive duty and a negative duty
- Summarize the issue of freedom, determinism, and ethics
- Explain the concept of a moral agent
- Describe the role and limits of freedom in a civil society
- Identify statements on freedom in certain key documents of civil society
- Briefly describe the history of sexual values in the Western world
- Summarize arguments for and against greater sexual freedom
- Distinguish between pornography and erotica
- Identify and explain key ethical issues regarding child pornography
- Identify and explain key ethical issues in dealing with sexual offenders
- Identify and explain key ethical issues with respect to prostitution

## INTRODUCTION

The **principle of freedom**, the subject of this chapter, has been with us from the beginning of our study of ethics. In Chapter 1, for example, we described the nature of a civil society, emphasizing the role of freedom and the rule of law in such societies. The cost of peace and security, we said, was a certain restraint on each individual's freedom. Individuals can't do just what they want when they want. The limitations placed on individual freedom, however, yield a measure of security from threat and a degree of harmony and community. Civil societies limit everyone's freedom but provide the security necessary for individuals to meet their basic needs and the security necessary for individuals to flourish.

Freedom, it must be noted, should not be confused with licence. Many people, it seems, confuse the two. The legendary James Bond, agent 007, had a licence to kill. That meant that Bond could assassinate others without fear of penalty. He had absolute freedom to kill. The word *licence* implies that one has no restrictions whatsoever on one's conduct. Civil societies have never granted licence to anyone. In fact they exist in order to prevent any individual or group, like a dictator or a political party, from having a licence to treat individuals as the dictator or the party wishes.

In this final chapter of our study of ethics in a civil society, we will review a number of key ideas associated with the **freedom principle**. We'll examine its role both in ethics and the law. From an ethical point of view, we will see, the freedom of the individual is never absolute. Individuals make ethical choices only when they consider the impact that their choices will have on others. In effect, that is the essence of morality, to make individual choices, while considering the welfare of everyone affected by those choices.

Before we look at a variety of issues associated with the freedom principle, here's another situation for your consideration.

| SITUATION 10.1 | Licence Application |
| --- | --- |

You are a member of a subcommittee of your city council. You and six others on the committee are responsible for reviewing licence applications for businesses in your city of 225 000 people. Your job is to review applications and objections to applications, and then recommend action to the members of city council. A local businessman has applied for a licence to open a strip club in an area of the city that is zoned commercial. There would be nothing illegal in opening such a business in that part of the city, and the location is not near any residential properties. Some citizens, however, are very much opposed to the development.

A group called the Citizens' Coalition against Live Pornography is opposed to the application and they have sent your committee the following letter, urging you to recommend to city council that they deny the application. They write:

> We oppose the licence application for an adult entertainment lounge (strip club) in the Westbrook commercial zone in our city. We urge you to recommend that the city deny the licence for all of the following reasons: (1) Naked and suggestive dancing is disrespectful of the dignity of the women who will work in the lounge. (2) Naked and suggestive

dancing is disrespectful of the dignity of women in this community. (3) Naked and suggestive dancing is a danger to women of our community as it fosters lustful thoughts that will lead to sexual assaults. (4) Naked and suggestive dancing is destructive of the special bond between marriage partners. (5) Naked and suggestive dancing is destructive of family life in general because it fosters values that are anti-family. (6) Naked and suggestive dancing degrades human sexuality by making it a commercial activity. (7) Naked and suggestive dancing is sick and disgusting, and contrary to the values of our community.

Consider each argument in turn. Which arguments, if any, do you find persuasive? If you have the opportunity, discuss this situation with others. Will you personally recommend that the application be denied or approved? Summarize your reasons.

## ETHICS AND FREEDOM

In Chapter 2 we explored the issue of freedom and determinism. **Hard determinism**, you will recall, maintains that human beings are the products of forces beyond their control and, as such, do not have free will. On this view, the forces of nature and nurture determine the thoughts, feelings, and actions of all human beings. If hard determinism is true, then the concepts of responsibility and accountability make no sense. **Responsibility** is a duty or obligation to do something, and **accountability** is the condition of being answerable to others for one's choices and actions. Those concepts are meaningful only if we assume that humans have free will. Hard determinism denies that humans have free will and, therefore, hard determinism is incompatible with ethics.

Since the concepts of responsibility, accountability, praise, and blame are necessary concepts of ethics, many people take a less stringent view of determinism. **Soft determinism** maintains that humans are, to a large degree, determined by the external forces of nature and nurture, but it holds that humans possess limited free will. This limited free will is what allows humans, then, to make sense of the essential concepts of ethics, the concepts of accountability and responsibility. Our moral language reflects the soft determinist view.

You will recall that a **moral agent** is a human being who can understand the difference between right and wrong and can choose freely to do one or the other. We use the word *moral*, for example, to describe the actions of moral agents who knowingly and freely choose to do what is right. In contrast, we use the word *immoral* to describe the actions of moral agents who knowingly and freely choose to do what is wrong. We praise moral agents who act in an ethical manner and we blame those that do not.

We reserve the word *amoral* to describe the actions of human beings who are incapable of understanding right and wrong or are incapable of choosing freely. Such persons are not moral agents. The actions of the mentally ill, the mentally challenged, and children are best described as "amoral." Non-human animals and things are not moral agents either, and we use the word *non-moral* to describe them (things) or their actions (animals).

### Police Officers as Moral Agents

Sometimes I fear that the expression "moral agent" is an expression that readers find difficult to identify with. The concept, however, is really quite a simple one. In your everyday life, you frequently make ethical choices. These are personal choices that you freely make—nobody forces you to make them—based upon your knowledge of a given situation and basic moral rules. Because you understand the difference between right and wrong, and you choose freely, you are a moral agent who is responsible and accountable for the decisions you make.

Police officers are both moral agents and agents of the government as they carry out their duties. Take, for example, a police officer exercising his duty. In doing so, he must use his professional discretion as he impartially enforces the law in a given situation, handling a speeding violation, for instance. Both discretionary action and impartial treatment of citizens requires that the officer freely make his own informed choices, unhindered and uninfluenced by bias or pressure. Freedom to choose is essential to carrying out one's responsibilities, both personal and professional, as a moral agent.

Too many free lunches at Al's Diner, for example, may create an attachment to Al that will not allow the officer to act freely with respect to Al should the officer ever have to do so. The officer's freedom, we say, may be compromised. Whoever the officer deals with, he needs to be free to exercise his professional judgment in whatever situation he finds himself.

## DEFINING FREEDOM

**Freedom**, then, means making an independent choice. Individuals exercise their free will when they make choices that are independent of external forces of any kind. To make a free choice that is ethical, however, the choice must take the welfare of others into consideration. This is a point that we made above. Moral choices are freely made but they are always made within a context that limits actions. Ethics is a matter of free choice, not licence. In other words, people are always responsible and accountable for their freely chosen actions.

Before we proceed to a closer look at the limitations of freedom, we need to express the principle of freedom as fundamental duties of ethics. First, as a **negative duty**, the principle becomes the rule: "Don't force or intimidate others." As a **positive duty**, it becomes: "Respect the right of others to make choices." When we noted these duties in Chapter 5, we pointed out that one of the greatest signs of respect that we can have for others is to respect their right to make their own choices. Their choices, like ours, however, have ethical limitations. In both cases we are talking about freedom, not licence.

## DEFINING THE LIMITS OF FREEDOM

We now need to be more specific about the limitations placed on the freedom of individuals in a civil society. Since these limitations apply to both ethics and the law, they are extremely important for life in a civil community. In a very important sense we have already taken note of the limitations on individual freedom. The limits of individual freedom are determined by the five basic principles of ethics: goodness, equality, justice, truth, and freedom.

In the **PRINCIPLES Model**, the moral agent is at the centre surrounded by the five principles of ethical reasoning. The moral agent's freedom to choose is limited by consideration of the effects his actions will have on others. These, of course, are moral or ethical considerations. Will anyone be harmed? (Goodness) Will anyone be discriminated against? (Equality) Will anyone be treated unfairly? (Justice) Will the agent be truthful and act with integrity? (Truth) Will anybody's right to choose be infringed upon? (Freedom)

Ethical choices and actions are ones that, first, consider whether the contemplated action will bring good consequences or harmful consequences to those affected by the action. Second, they are ones that treat all others equally, refusing to discriminate for or against anyone on the basis of superficial characteristics, such as skin colour or ethnic origin. Third, they are choices and actions that take into consideration what is just and fair to everyone concerned. Fourth, they are ones that are based on truth and carried out with integrity. Fifth, ethical choices and actions are ones that respect the freedom that others have to make their own choices.

**Libertarians**, you will recall from Chapter 5, claim that the last point is the central point of ethics. They argue that individuals should have maximum freedom to do what they choose, subject only to others having the same degree of liberty. In other words, individuals should never take liberties that they would not grant to others.

One might describe the libertarian approach as a type of golden-rule approach. The golden rule says: "Do unto others as you would have done unto you." The libertarian says: "Act only with the degree of freedom that you are willing to let others exercise." Despite the high value that they place on individual freedom, libertarians argue strongly that there are clear limits to individual freedom.

## FREEDOM AND CIVIL SOCIETIES

Earlier in our studies, we referred to the qualities of the Good Society. In our time, we said, the essence of the Good Society is captured in the ideals set out in United Nations Universal Declaration of Human Rights. Civil societies around the world, including Canada, have patterned their constitutions after those of the Declaration. The fundamental moral premise is set out in Article 1, where it says that all human beings are "born free and equal in dignity and rights." Many specific freedoms, as we saw in Chapter 4, are detailed in a number of articles that follow Article 1 in the Declaration.

These freedoms include all of the following: fundamental liberty (Article 3); freedom from arbitrary arrest, detention, or exile (Article 9); freedom from arbitrary interference with privacy, family, home, and correspondence (Article 12); freedom of movement and residence (Article 13), freedom of thought, conscience, and religion (Article 18); freedom of opinion and expression (Article 19); and freedom of peaceful assembly and association (Article 20).

Canada, in its Charter of Rights and Freedoms, provides a good example of a civil society that has embraced the United Nation's ideal. In Part 1, section 1, the Charter guarantees "the rights and freedoms set out in it subject only to reasonable limits prescribed by law as can be justified in a free and democratic society." In section 2, several specific, fundamental freedoms are identified. These freedoms include freedom of conscience and religion, freedom of thought and expression, freedom of peaceful assembly, and freedom of association.

The Canons of Police Ethics state that the primary responsibility of the police service and its officers is "the protection of the people of Canada through the upholding of our laws." It urges police officers to recognize "the genius of the Canadian system of government which gives to no individual, groups of people, or institutions, absolute power, and they must insure that they, as prime defenders of the system, do not pervert its character." Another way of capturing this critically important point is to say that no individual or group in Canada has absolute freedom. Everyone's freedom is limited for the good of democracy and for the good of all members of our civil society. Police officers play a vital role in protecting that freedom.

We noted earlier in our studies that both the Law Enforcement Code of Ethics and the Law Enforcement Code of Conduct include respect for and the protection of "the constitutional rights of all to *liberty*, equality, and justice" as fundamental duties of an officer. Liberty, of course, is freedom. We can see clearly, then, that the principles of ethical reasoning, and, in particular, the principle of freedom, are at the heart of the constitutions and the laws of civil societies.

## SEXUAL FREEDOM IN A CIVIL SOCIETY

In this section we will look at the issue of sexual freedom and censorship in a civil society. Once we have examined the issue in somewhat general terms, we will turn to two specific issues, pornography and prostitution, in the sections that follow. In both this section and the following one, we will see how some members of society advocate a great deal of sexual freedom within society while others advocate a much more conservative approach.

## Traditional Sexual Values

To better understand the societal debate over sexual freedom in the past and today, we will do well to do a brief historical review of sexual values in Western society. The primary influence on sexual values has been, and to a large degree still is, the Christian church. Other world religions adopt similar views to that of Christianity, it should be noted, without embracing the same beliefs. They, too, are supporters of traditional sexual values. Almost from its beginning, however, Christianity has placed very high value on virginity and celibacy. According to the Christian account, for example, when God set about to save the world, God selected a virgin to bear his son, Jesus.

Many, it would seem, drew the conclusion that virginity is superior to non-virginity. Virginity, they may have thought, is next to godliness. That certainly is the conclusion, it can be argued, that was drawn by the leadership of the church. From its inception to the time of the Reformation, with very few exceptions, the clergy were to take vows of chastity and remain celibate. To this day, that continues to be the official position of the Roman Catholic church.

With sexual abstinence set as the ideal for the clergy, legitimate sexual practices of the laity were limited to sex within marriage. Moreover, since procreation was viewed as the ultimate purpose of sex, only heterosexual relations were considered legitimate. The primary purpose of sex was procreation, and the only legitimate context for sex was that of heterosexual marriage. This particular view of legitimate sexual conduct between lay persons has remained, by and large, the official position of mainstream Christian denominations to this day.

This conservative view of sexual relations was reinforced in the nineteenth century in England and throughout its vast empire under the rule of Queen Victoria. Her reign was a long one—from 1837 to 1901—and her views were conservative ones. Not surprisingly, the **Victorian Era** was a time of very conservative sexual ideals. The ideal described above remained in place throughout her time. Only toward the end of the century do we get the first signs of a change in attitude toward sexuality. The influence for change was modern science.

## Scientific and Social Challenges

Sigmund Freud was one of the first persons to begin to approach sexuality from a scientific point of view. Science, of course, in its pursuit of knowledge, has little reverence for taboos. Quite naturally, later sex researchers, like Alfred Kinsey in the United States, followed in Freud's scientific footsteps and continued to view sex as a legitimate study of science. By the second half of the twentieth century virtually all of the taboos had disappeared. The clinical studies of Masters and Johnson in the 1970s and the survey research of many others, for all intents and purposes, finally banished sexual taboos altogether.

As the scientific revolution progressed, public attitudes were changing as well. The 1960s saw enormous social upheavals in the form of various movements for social change. We mentioned some of these movements in our review of social justice in Chapter 8. Among them were the civil rights movement in the United States, the anti-Viet Nam war movement in the United States and other countries, and the women's liberation movement throughout Western society.

Also part of the general upheaval was the movement for sexual freedom, a movement whose most radical advocates campaigned dramatically under the banner of free sex. A major scientific development, the birth control pill, contributed enormously to new attitudes, as sexual experiences were freed from the fear of pregnancy. Gay and lesbian sex also began to emerge from the closet as homosexuals urged societal acceptance of their lifestyle. The gay rights movement, of course, went well beyond matters of sexual preference, fighting discrimination in all areas of life.

The sexual freedom movement continued to attack the conservative values of the past through the 1960s and 1970s until the AIDS problem brought the attack to a virtual halt in the 1980s. Western sexual values had remained very conservative for centuries, until science and changing social attitudes in the late 1800s and throughout the 1900s opened the door to all kinds of different practices. Today premarital, extramarital, and homosexual practices are engaged in and condoned by many in society. Moreover, specific sexual practices, such as oral and anal sex, are discussed openly in the media. The subject of sex is no longer taboo.

## The Arguments

What are the arguments for and against greater sexual freedom? In the values battle between advocates of greater sexual freedom and the defenders of traditional sexual values, what are the points of debate? Keeping in mind that the ethical battle was mainly a battle about freedom, let's examine some of the arguments for and against greater freedom in matters sexual. Remember, too, that we will look at two specific issues, pornography and prostitution, in later sections of this chapter.

### Arguments for Greater Sexual Freedom

In a very real sense the sexual revolution was a revolution against authority. More and more people, both within the Christian church and outside it, questioned the authority of church leaders to prescribe legitimate sexual practices, even though those leaders claimed to speak for God. The first and fundamental argument of the sexual revolution is the *sexual freedom argument*. It says that freely consenting adults alone should decide what they want to do sexually, provided that their sexual practices don't harm others.

This argument, the basic argument of the sexual freedom movement, implies or includes a second argument for greater sexual freedom. The *anti-authority argument* says that traditional, religiously based sexual values are outdated and should not be imposed upon others by religious authorities. Since modern science has exposed many traditional beliefs as superstitions, the argument goes, neither the Christian church nor any other religious institution has the right to prescribe moral conduct in sexual matters. Adherents of these religions, the argument continues, may choose to follow the prescribed rules, but the prescriptions are not binding on others.

A third argument addresses the challenge to sexual freedom that arises out of the fear of sexually transmitted diseases, especially AIDS. The *safe sex argument* responds to that challenge by maintaining that careful selection of sexual partners, the use of effective protection, and sexual fidelity can prevent the transmission of disease. This concern for safety in sex is, the argument continues, just a natural part of the responsibility that falls to consenting adults who engage in sex.

A fourth argument also responds to a challenge from the defenders of traditional sexual values. Traditionalists argue that greater sexual freedom leads generally to the demise of the family and, more specifically, puts children at risk. The alleged risk to children includes their exposure to sexually explicit materials and the increased possibility of sexual crimes against them. The *legal protections argument* responds by saying that laws can be established to ensure that children cannot access sexually explicit materials. Moreover, the experience of sexually liberal countries from Northern Europe, for example, indicates no higher rates of sexual crimes against children than in sexually restrictive countries.

## Arguments against Greater Sexual Freedom

Several arguments are made in defence of traditional sexual values. The *degradation argument* says that sexual practices other than the traditional ones are degrading or dehumanizing to the participants. They degrade human beings and dehumanize them, lowering them to the level of animals. Traditional sexual ideals, it is argued, elevate humans to a higher level based on love and lasting commitment.

A second argument views greater sexual freedom as an attack on the family. The *demise of the family argument* maintains that liberal sexual practices undermine the special relationship of marriage and contribute to the destruction of the family. The advocates of sexual freedom, the argument continues, promote a self-indulgence that is detrimental to husbands, wives, and children. Unchecked, such self-indulgence will lead to the demise of the traditional family.

The preceding argument leads to a third argument that is closely related. Since the family is the basic unit of society, any undermining of the family is also an undermining of society. The *demise of society argument* makes this point. Greater sexual freedom leads to the demise of the family, and that, in turn, leads to the disintegration of society. In contrast, it is maintained, traditional sexual practices are consistent with strong families and healthy societies.

A fourth argument, the *diseases argument,* emphasizes the point that greater sexual freedom contributes to the spread of sexually transmitted diseases that can cause serious illness and death. Many who have made this argument in defence of traditional sexual values have seen the AIDS crisis as proof of their point and the vindication of their position. There is no doubt that many advocates of greater sexual freedom have had to pause and reconsider their position in the light of the AIDS reality. For many, on both sides of the debate, this is a powerful argument.

In Chapter 6 we first met and explained a type of argument that is called the *slippery slope argument* or the *domino argument*. Defenders of traditional sexual values often make this kind of argument. In this case, the *domino argument* says that greater sexual freedom will lead to an increase in sexual assaults, prostitution, and pornography. All of these will be harmful to individuals and society in general, as the dominoes begin to fall with any abandonment of traditional values.

Before giving thought to the following situation, recall your views regarding Situation 5.5: Neighbourhood Pornography. That situation was presented in Chapter 5 in connection with our introduction to the freedom principle. Here, now, is another situation for your consideration.

| SITUATION 10.2 | Possession of Child Pornography |
| --- | --- |

You are a justice of the Supreme Court of Canada. The Court has been asked to hear an appeal into the case of a man who was charged with possession of child pornography. Lower courts have ruled in favour of the man who has, in each case, defended himself.

Here's how he got to court. In the execution of a search warrant intended to produce evidence of marijuana production and sales, police discovered a quantity of child pornography. Included in the seizure were videotapes and colour photographs of children and adults engaged in various sex acts. Also seized were an artist's sketches of naked children. Each sketch showed one child alone in a sexually suggestive pose. No adults appeared in any of the sketches. The man, an amateur artist, has done all the drawings.

Police charged him with three counts of possession of child pornography. In the lower courts, the man argued that the police action and the existing law violated his right to "freedom of thought, belief, opinion, and expression." In addition, he argued that the material does not pose a harm to society. In fact, he argued, it has therapeutic value, allowing him to relieve his sexual appetites through fantasy, without involving anyone in the real world, including children. The lower courts agreed with him on both points. The Crown has appealed to you and your fellow justices to make a final determination in the matter. They say that the lower court rulings must be overturned.

What will you personally decide? Now, my guess is that most readers are not Supreme Court justices, or even lawyers. Try not to let that fact, if it is one, keep you from wrestling with this issue. The Charter can be found in the appendices at the end of the book, if you wish to refresh your memory on citizen rights and freedoms (s.2(b), in particular). Section 163.1(4) of the Criminal Code of Canada is also relevant to the situation. Now, consider the following questions.

In your view, have the police actions and the law violated the man's Charter rights? In your view, do his statements about the therapeutic value of the material carry any weight? Is there any significant difference, in your view, between the sketches and the other seized material? If you have an opportunity, discuss the situation with others. Remember that you may oppose child pornography but still find the existing law to be a bad one, one that needs to be replaced. What do you think?

# PORNOGRAPHY AND EROTICA

The history of the pornography debate in Canada affords us an excellent opportunity to observe how a civil society has handled a clash between two fundamental principles, the freedom principle and the goodness principle. Both principles, along with equality, justice, and truth, are essential for the proper functioning of a civil society. The debate in Canada has been no different, in a sense, from the debate elsewhere. It has always been a debate between those who advocate freedom and those who advocate goodness. The one side argues for individual freedom of expression and choice. The other argues for the good of society, maintaining that unbridled freedom will only cause harm.

In Canada, the Criminal Code has long outlawed **obscene material**, defining it as "any publication a dominant characteristic of which is the undue exploitation of sex or of sex and any violence." But, we need to ask, in practical terms, what does *obscene* mean? And what constitutes "undue exploitation"? These questions have been answered differently by different Canadians for many years. The problem lies with the terms *obscene* and *undue exploitation*, terms that are open to subjective interpretations.

In court, for example, one side would argue that a particular issue of a magazine seized by the police was obscene. The other side would argue that it was not. Since the word *obscene* is notoriously subjective, the legal battle was often reduced to a battle of tastes, preferences, or opinions. In an attempt to get past the subjective impasse, judges appealed to community standards to settle the matter.

**Community standards** refer to whatever a community in society considers morally acceptable, based on its shared values. A couple of problems immediately arise with this approach. First, what constitutes a particular community? Who, for example, defines the boundaries of a community? A second problem relates to the first. In certain urban areas, for example, it is not an exaggeration to say that on one side of a particular street the community might regard the seized magazine as obscene, while on the other side they might not. Communities, like individuals, can have different tastes. Which side of the street, then, represents the community?

## Pornography

In 1992, the Supreme Court of Canada tried to introduce a measurable degree of objectivity into the pornography debate. Abandoning fruitless, subjective arguments based on individual or community tastes, the Court introduced what it considered to be a more objective standard, namely, the potential harm that a publication may do to a community. Harm, of course, is forbidden by the principle of goodness. The debate now centred on whether an individual's choice to view sexually explicit material constituted a harm or potential harm to other members of the community.

In the Supreme Court ruling, Justice John Sopinka wrote: "Harm, in this context, means that it [the publication] predisposes persons to act in an anti-social manner as, for example, the physical or mental mistreatment of women by men, or, what is perhaps debatable, the reverse" (Cox, 1992). Justice Sopinka acknowledged that it may be difficult to establish a direct link between obscenity and harm to society, but he maintained that pornography can make women feel degraded and that it can have a negative impact on perceptions of women and attitudes toward them.

In its shift from subjective standards of taste to objective standards based on harm, the Supreme Court published guidelines to clarify issues in the courtrooms of the nation.

According to these guidelines, a seized publication would be judged "obscene" and an "undue exploitation" of sex if it included any one or more of the following:

- sex and violence
- degrading or dehumanizing sex
- sex with children

**Pornography**, then, is any sexually explicit material that includes violence, degradation, or children. Sexually explicit material that does not violate these guidelines is not obscene or pornographic.

## Erotica

In movie theatres and video stores today there is a plethora of sexually explicit material. If these movies adhere to the guidelines, then they are not considered to be pornographic. They are, by definition, not obscene. Movies, magazines, and other publications that adhere to the Court's guidelines deserve to be called by another name than "pornography." The term *erotica* is, perhaps, a good choice. Erotica, then, would be sexually explicit material that does not include violence, children, or degrading sexual activities.

More specifically, **erotica** can be defined as the depiction of caring and consensual sex between two or more adults. The caring nature of erotica distinguishes it from the violence associated with pornography, and its consensual nature distinguishes it from the dominance that characterizes pornography. The consensual nature of erotica also implies that it is about adult sexual relationships, as children cannot consent to such matters. Consequently, the portrayal of children in sexual roles is pornographic.

## CHILD PORNOGRAPHY

The legal debate over obscenity in Canada is not over. In 1999, a British Columbia man, Robin Sharpe, was charged with possession of child pornography (Snyder, 1999). He argued, before British Columbia Justice Duncan Shaw, that he had a constitutionally protected right to his thoughts, beliefs, opinion, and expression. He argued, further, that possession of child pornography did not constitute a harm to society. In fact, using the *catharsis argument*, Sharpe argued that his collection was a help to him, providing a cathartic or purifying release for his sexual feelings. He argued, in effect, that the material prevented harm. Apparently, Justice Shaw saw some merit in that argument as well as the first one.

Eventually, the case moved to the Supreme Court of Canada on the question of the violation of Mr. Sharpe's Charter right to freedom of thought, belief, opinion, and expression. The appeal was heard in January of 2000, and in June of that year the Supreme Court reserved judgment. In January 2001, the Supreme Court overturned the lower court decision, upholding the obscenity law. Sharpe now faces four charges of possession.

The consideration of the morality of pornography has to focus on two aspects of the obscenity business, the production of pornography and the consumption of pornography. **Production**, of course, refers to the making of pornography. **Consumption** refers to the possession or use of pornography. This distinction between production and consumption is important for the consideration of all forms of pornography but, especially, for child pornography.

While much, perhaps most, of the debate over pornography focuses on its consumption, the concern regarding child pornography highlights the importance of looking at the production of obscene material. If adults consider getting jobs as performers in the porn trade, they are in a position to choose freely whether they want to do so or not. If adults are forced to perform, that clearly would be wrong. If they choose freely to perform, however, it is difficult to see why their performance would be wrong.

Consider, now, the case of the child who performs in an obscene production. The very fact of being a child precludes the person from giving informed consent. It precludes the person from choosing freely to perform or not. Unlike adults, children don't have this choice. They are not moral agents as adults are. As children, they lack sufficient knowledge and life experience to be able to make an *informed* choice in all kinds of matters, but especially the matter under consideration here. Any child who performs in an obscene production has been forced to perform. That force is wrong when applied to a child just as it is wrong when applied to an adult.

Civil societies are right to outlaw child pornography. A reasonable argument can be made, perhaps, that it is the potential harm to society that justifies the ban. That potential harm may well constitute a good reason for placing a limitation on the freedom of both pornography producers and consumers. An additional and stronger argument, I believe, can and should be made. It is the argument cited above, the argument that says it is wrong to force anyone, adult or child, to perform sexual acts in the *production* of sexually explicit material.

Since the production of obscenity is dependent on its *consumption*, a further argument can be invoked to ban the possession (consumption) of child pornography. In other words, consuming such material compounds the original offence. It is an extension, if you will, of the original offence, an extension that repeats the original offence each time it is viewed. A child is abused in the first instance, the production, and with each and every viewing thereafter, the consumption.

Consider, now, the following situation.

| SITUATION 10.3 | The New Neighbour |
| --- | --- |

As you enter the foyer of your apartment building to check your mail at the end of your workday, you encounter a small but noisy, animated, and angry crowd. "Kill the bastard!" "Throw him out!" "Let me get my hands on him!" A uniformed police officer stands near the front of the crowd where a man cowers beside a woman. The officer urges the crowd to keep back and away from them.

"He won't hurt anybody," says the woman. "We're going to help him and you. He's going to get counselling. You needn't fear. Our church is going to help him."

The man, mustering enough courage to speak, begins, "I'm not going to hurt anybody. I've done my time. I'm gonna get help. This lady's church is gonna help me. I know my problem and I'm gonna get help. Please leave me alone. I've paid my debt. This is my home!"

You ask a guy standing at the back next to you what's going on. He says that the guy's a pedophile who's just been released after serving a seven-year sentence for sexually assaulting a young boy and a young girl.

The shouting continues as the officer asks everyone to keep calm. "Folks," says the officer, "calm down please. The guy's got an apartment here and it's all legal. You're going to have to back off. This is his home now."

"Over my dead body!" "Take him to your place! Let him live in your home!" "Get the pervert out of here now or you'll be responsible for his death!" "Get him out, out, out!!!"

What do you think you would do in this situation? Would you be inclined to join in with the shouts of the crowd? If the crowd were quiet, what would you say to the man? the woman? the officer? What would you ask? What suggestions might you make? How, in your opinion, should a civil society deal with the release of sexual offenders who have done their time? If you have a chance, discuss your thoughts and feelings with others.

## SEXUAL OFFENDERS

In our review of capital punishment, we noted that the recidivism rate among released murderers was very low. The same, we indicated at that time, cannot be said for sexual offenders, child molesters in particular. A 1996 survey of 191 child molesters, for example, found that 77 percent of pedophiles who assaulted boys re-offended between 15 and 30 years of release (Gillis, 1998).

Recently, we have seen situations in our communities that parallel the kinds of events that we find in Situation 10.3. Convicted pedophile Peter Whitmore, released into the community after completing his sentence for two sexual assaults on children, found himself in circumstances similar to our case (Wood, 2000). The Mennonite church attempted to assist him with his reintegration into society. Neighbours in the Toronto community where he found housing were outraged that he would be their new neighbour. They pressured him out.

Within days of going on television to assure the public that he would not re-offend and that he was seeking treatment, he was arrested in a Toronto motel, in the company of a 13-year-old boy. Mr. Whitmore, whose actions violated the terms of his release, was taken into custody. Many, no doubt, breathed a sigh of relief as he was led away. His short-term neighbours may well have felt safer with him in custody. One suspects that Mr. Whitmore, too, felt safer upon arrest.

This case raises many questions for our civil society. Civil societies have always maintained that a person is innocent until proven guilty. Moreover, they have always held that offenders who have served their time are free again to live within the community. They have paid their debt to society. What do we do, though, with the knowledge that the likelihood of re-offending is very high? How can we put our children at risk? Our belief in the released prisoner's right to freedom (freedom principle) comes face to face with the welfare (goodness principle) of our children.

Even before release, matters of treatment in prison are subject to the values of civil society. The prisoner is free, for example, to refuse treatment. He can make the choice to get help or not. Our high valuation of the freedom principle extends beyond the bars and barbed wire into the prison itself. Forced therapy, of course, is not very likely to succeed. For practical reasons, as well as ethical ones, the free choice of the prisoner is honoured. Even when convicted child molesters agree to treatment, however, recidivism seems far too high.

Ethical debate on this important issue is absolutely necessary. Will we be able, in the days ahead, to remain true to the principles of ethical reasoning while ensuring the safety of our children and ourselves? With respect to sex offenders, only time will tell.

## CENSORSHIP

A **censor** is a person who tells others how to behave, what they can or can't do, what they can or can't see and hear. **Censorship** is the act of controlling what others can see, hear, or do. In dictatorships, rulers routinely censor the media so that citizens will hear and see only what the government wants them to see and hear. It is a strategy for maintaining power. In wartime, even democratically elected governments routinely censor the media to ensure that enemies will not receive information that can aid them in the war. In civil societies, where democracy is a fundamental value, censorship is always a threat to the freedom of citizens.

As we have repeatedly noted, free choice depends on having accurate information upon which to make a choice. Democracies deplore censorship, except in emergency situations such as war, because the censor deprives the citizens of their right to make informed choices. That is why democracies place great value on having a free press and other free media. It is the ability to understand and make choices that gives a human being dignity. Censorship is always an affront to that dignity.

Our review of the pornography debate in Canada illustrates how a civil society has dealt with a censorship issue. Because the limitations that have been put on what Canadians can legally see and hear are arrived at through democratic processes, members of society generally respect those limitations. The issue, nevertheless, is a critically important one. By what authority does anyone have the right to decide what others can or cannot see, hear, and do?

In a civil society like Canada, the issue of obscenity is not really different from any other debate about what our society will permit. All our laws are restrictions on what we can do without fear of punishment. They are limitations on our freedom, but, fortunately, ones that are self-imposed through free discussion and debate, according to procedural rules. Once in place, they are binding on all citizens. No individual or group is exempt. This process is, of course, a critical part of the genius of a free and democratic society.

---

| SITUATION 10.4 | **Guest Lecturer** |
|---|---|

You are a rookie constable and you've been assigned to security patrol in a university lecture hall where a guest lecturer from Europe is scheduled to speak to a large audience. Two university security officers have also been assigned to the lecture hall because the speaker has met with some hostility from audiences at other universities where he has spoken. The jammed auditorium becomes quiet as the speaker is introduced and begins his lecture.

He begins by saying that Canadian laws regarding prostitution are outdated, puritanical, and hypocritical. On the first point, he reminds the audience that prostitution is the world's oldest profession. People have been paying for sex for centuries. On the second point, he maintains Canadian laws are puritanical, failing to recognize that we are in the twenty-first century. Our laws, he says, are based on religious values that are passé. The third point he makes is that our laws are hypocritical. They don't outlaw prostitution but they do everything to make it impossible to engage in prostitution.

The audience seems interested in what the speaker has to say and there is no sign of any disruption whatsoever. You continue to keep a keen eye on the audience as you keep a keen ear on the guest lecturer.

To get beyond the outdated past, the puritanical values, and the hypocrisy of the existing situation, he says, Canada needs to change its laws on prostitution. It needs to create "red light districts" where prostitutes can work openly and johns, or "johannas," can buy sexual services without hassle in safe houses. The government can tax the prostitutes and collect from them more easily, enriching the public coffers. The health of prostitutes can be monitored on a regular basis, reducing the possibility of STDs. Crimes related to prostitution, pimping, and drug-dealing, for example, can be eliminated or minimized. The nuisance factors associated with current street solicitation, traffic congestion, for instance, can be eliminated. Furthermore, sex can be bought and sold openly in safety in the districts, and residential communities can be free of hookers.

The lecture eventually ends to mild applause. The question period passes without incident. One questioner says that the guest lecturer's ideas are the "work of the devil" but that is as heated as it gets. Everyone disperses and you take leave of the university and your police colleagues.

When you get off duty and arrive home, your spouse asks you what the lecture was all about and whether you agreed with the speaker. What will you tell your partner? Do you think that the ideas are "the work of the devil?" Why or why not? Do you think that the ideas have any merit? Explain your reasoning.

## PROSTITUTION

Should an individual be free to charge a fee for having sexual intercourse with another person? If we answer the question in the negative, what reasons can we give that might justify our saying no? Putting the second question differently: What is wrong with prostitution? To answer that it is wrong because it is illegal is to miss the point of the question. We are asking the question from a moral or ethical point of view, not a legal one. We are asking, in effect, what, if anything, is wrong with a person charging a fee for providing sexual services to another person?

Many societies believe that there are a number of reasons for banning prostitution. Among these reasons are some that we saw in our review of arguments, earlier in this chapter, against increased sexual freedom in society. Prostitution should be illegal, it is argued, because it undermines family values and contributes to the disintegration of society. Another contention is that prostitution is degrading and dehumanizing. Additional arguments focus on the spread of disease and the spread of crimes that often accompany prostitution, crimes like illegal drug use.

Given this array of arguments against prostitution, why do some civil societies allow people to legally prostitute themselves? Why, for example, is prostitution legal in the Netherlands, where people can purchase sex legally and quite openly, at least in designated areas, the "red light districts"? In societies like the Netherlands that legalize prostitution and permit prostitutes to advertise their services, the reasons for legalization are numerous.

One of these arguments is that adults should be free to choose what they will or will not do with their bodies. Subject to reasonable limitations, people who want to sell their sexual services should be free to do so. A further argument says that where prostitution is illegal, there really are no victims. It is a **victimless crime** because both parties freely consent to have sex for money. For that reason alone, many argue, prostitution should be legal. Another argument addresses the concern for disease, maintaining that legalizing prostitution allows for much greater control of the health of prostitutes. Regarding the spread of crime, it is argued that this, too, is much less likely when prostitution is legal.

In Canada, we have taken a very interesting approach to the world's oldest profession. We have not made prostitution illegal, but we have banned virtually everything necessary to practise prostitution. Section 213 of the Criminal Code of Canada reads as follows:

213. (1) Every person who in a public place or in any place open to public view

    (a) stops or attempts to stop any motor vehicle,

    (b) impedes the free flow of pedestrian or vehicular traffic or ingress to or egress from premises adjacent to that place, or

    (c) stops or attempts to stop any person or in any manner communicates or attempts to communicate with any person

for the purpose of engaging in prostitution or of obtaining the services of a prostitute is guilty of an offence punishable on summary conviction.

The law as it stands clearly addresses public concerns regarding prostitutes and their clients creating a nuisance for other citizens. In many Canadian cities, prostitutes have tied up traffic, inconvenienced residents, and generally disrupted neighbourhood life by their sidewalk solicitations. Sections (a) and (b) are obvious attempts to deal with these disruptive practices. The restrictions on communication in section (c) also address the nuisance problem. The second half of (c), however, has implications that seem to go beyond the problems created by sidewalk solicitations.

An example will serve to make the point. A man at a public telephone on one side of a busy city street calls a woman at a public telephone on the other side of the same street. He asks for a sexual liaison and she agrees, informing him that it will cost $100. Neither of them interferes, in any way, with the pedestrians who are going about their business. They've had what might be described as a private conversation in a public place, a place open to public view. What they will do when they get together at her apartment isn't a criminal offence. Their phone conversation, in contrast, would seem to be a crime.

Section 213. (1) states: "Every person who in a public place or any place open to public view ... in any manner communicates or attempts to communicate with any person for the purpose of engaging in prostitution or of obtaining the services of a prostitute is guilty of an offence punishable on summary conviction." While cigarette and liquor advertising has been restricted by law, those restrictions seem liberal in light of what appears to be an outright ban on advertising one's services as a prostitute. If prostitution is legal, how can a society forbid its practitioners from advertising their services? Perhaps this part of the law will one day be challenged successfully. To date, Charter challenges based on freedom of expression and freedom of association have failed. Nevertheless, from an ethical point of view, it seems unjust to forbid a legal business to advertise.

We raise these questions about the present law because they illustrate once again the role of ethics in civil society. The law is quite clear, but ethical concerns still arise. In this case, the ethical concern stems from a desire for consistency in thought and practice. In Chapter 2, we noted that this desire for consistency is a simple matter of logic. Legal businesses should be free to advertise their products or services. Illegal businesses should not.

It seems logically inconsistent, however, to criminalize the advertising of a service but not the service itself. Logical and legal inconsistencies are never good, and they are especially troublesome when the principle of freedom is in question.

## CHAPTER SUMMARY

We began our study of the freedom principle by pointing out that civil societies attempt to ensure the security of their members by placing certain limits on the freedom of all. Freedom in a civil society does not mean licence. Next, we reviewed the issue of freedom, determinism, and ethics, a subject first examined in Chapter 2. We also reviewed the defining characteristics of a moral agent and used police officers as examples.

We proceeded to define *freedom,* state the freedom principle as positive and negative duties, and review its role in the PRINCIPLES Model. We then noted examples of the principle in basic documents of a civil society and in policing codes of ethics. Next, we looked at the history of traditional sexual values in Western society, identifying scientific and social challenges that eventually led to greater sexual freedom in society. The review summarized the main arguments for and against greater sexual freedom.

After summarizing the historical debate over what constitutes "obscenity," we noted how judges appealed to community standards in an attempt to eliminate subjective interpretations of what is obscene. Then we identified the criteria that the Supreme Court introduced in an attempt to establish a more objective standard, namely, harm done to society. Distinguishing between pornography and erotica, we moved on to discuss child pornography.

Next, we considered the role of freedom both in the treatment of sexual offenders and in their release into society. Noting the high rate of recidivism among such offenders, we drew attention to the critical importance of continued ethical debate on the subject.

After reviewing the issue of censorship in a civil society, we examined certain aspects of prostitution, particularly its legal status. We began by noting how certain other countries approach the matter of prostitution. Turning to Canada, we noted how a perceived ethical inconsistency leads to a questioning of our approach. This questioning, we pointed out, provides yet another example of the important role of ethics in a civil society. Regardless of the law in force, rational debate that employs the principles of ethical reasoning is essential to the welfare of a civil society.

## MASTERING THE MATERIAL

Now that you have read this chapter, use the following guides to ensure that you have mastered the material.

### Introduction

1. How is security achieved in a civil society?
2. What is *licence?* How does licence differ from freedom?

### Ethics and Freedom

1. Describe hard determinism and soft determinism.
2. Why are ethics and soft determinism compatible?
3. Define *moral agent.*

4.  What two aspects of a police officer's role require that the officer be free?
5.  How can the freedom of police officers be compromised?

## Defining Freedom

1.  Define *freedom*.
2.  State the freedom principle as both a positive and a negative duty.

## Defining the Limits of Freedom

1.  What two roles does freedom play within the PRINCIPLES Model?
2.  What makes a choice an ethical choice?
3.  What do libertarians believe?

## Freedom and Civil Societies

1.  Cite parts of the Universal Declaration of Human Rights and the Canadian Charter of Rights and Freedoms that are based on the freedom principle.
2.  Cite parts of two police codes that are based on the freedom principle.

## Sexual Freedom in a Civil Society

1.  Identify the primary source of traditional sexual mores in the Western world.
2.  Identify the two characteristics that define morally acceptable sex in this tradition.
3.  What is the significance of the Victorian era for sexual mores?
4.  Describe the scientific challenges to traditional sexual values.
5.  Give examples of two social movements that challenged traditional sexual values.
6.  State and explain four arguments for greater sexual freedom.
7.  State and explain five arguments against greater sexual freedom.

## Pornography and Erotica

1.  What role do freedom and goodness play in the societal debate about pornography?
2.  Why did judges appeal to community standards in cases involving pornography?
3.  What three criteria did the Supreme Court introduce in 1992 to define pornography?
4.  What is erotica and how does it differ from pornography?

## Child Pornography

1.  Summarize the Supreme Court ruling in the case of Robin Sharpe.
2.  What is the *catharsis argument?*
3.  What two aspects of pornography are essential to the moral debate on the subject?
4.  Why is the production of child pornography wrong? Why is the consumption of it wrong?

## Sexual Offenders

1. Briefly describe the Peter Whitmore case.
2. How does the freedom principle apply in the treatment of imprisoned pedophiles?
3. How does the freedom principle apply to pedophiles upon release?

## Censorship

1. Define *censor* and explain why censorship is a critical issue for civil societies.

## Prostitution

1. Why do some people argue that prostitution should be legal? Why do some others argue that it should be illegal?
2. Why is prostitution called a "victimless crime"?
3. What approach has Canadian law taken with respect to prostitution?
4. Describe the role of ethics in the societal debate about prostitution.

---

## CRITICAL THINKING IN POLICING: THE PRINCIPLES MODEL

Moral agents act ethically when they make personal choices that don't interfere with the right of others to make free choices.

## CRITICAL THINKING IN POLICING: THE DECIDE PROCESS

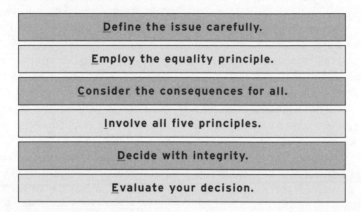

**D**efine the issue carefully.

**E**mploy the equality principle.

**C**onsider the consequences for all.

**I**nvolve all five principles.

**D**ecide with integrity.

**E**valuate your decision.

**Step #6: Evaluate your decision.** This step reminds you to keep an open mind. While the principles of ethical reasoning remain the same, circumstances in your life will constantly change. Your ethical point of view may have to change with them.

---

**Media Watch:
Ethics in the News 10.1**

## The right to offend

Parliament defines obscenity as "the undue exploitation of sex," but who decides what is meant by "undue?" The Supreme Court of Canada says the community does. It set down a test—the community standard of tolerance test—for balancing free speech against society's repugnance at materials that harm women by degrading them. Sensibly, the court said the community now tolerates most depictions of explicit sex, unless these are violent, involve children, or are so dehumanizing that they produce a substantial risk of harm.

In human rights law, however, community standards are irrelevant. A community might well feel there is nothing wrong with discriminating against this or that group; hence human-rights codes and the Canadian Charter of Rights and Freedoms have been developed to hold governments and communities to a standard above local prejudice.

In this context, some of those opposed to pornography, including an unusual alliance of modern feminists and old-style morality crusaders, want to switch the ground on which we talk about the subject. They want to free it from the liberal standard of contemporary Canada as interpreted by the courts under criminal law. By making it a human-rights issue, they hope to remove the need to balance competing rights—instead, the rights of the allegedly harmed individual are unassailable.

In Toronto, two women complained to the Ontario Human Rights Commission that three convenience stores selling magazines such as *Playboy* and *Penthouse* violated their rights by creating a "poisoned environment" for them. The stores apparently met local bylaws requiring the magazines to be behind barriers so that only their titles showed. Even so, the commission agreed the two women had a credible basis for a complaint, and a separate quasi-judicial body struck by the Ontario government has begun an inquiry. The store owners, who must hire counsel at considerable expense to defend themselves, must wonder at this attempt to dress a criminal law in human-rights garb—as the rest of us must wonder.

"If men are leering at the pictures they're going to leer at you," Sandra Nicholson, 45, told reporters after asking for standing at the tribunal to support the two complainants. "As you walk by them they're going to size up how good your legs are and the size of your breasts."

This is dangerous stuff. Ms. Nicholson is asking for censorship of unprecedented breadth: prior restraint on rudeness. If the rude action is to be stopped at all costs, perhaps the rude thought is next; if the milk store today,

maybe the book store tomorrow. (Does Rushdie's *Satanic Verses* "poison the environment" for Muslims? Philip Roth's *Portnoy's Complaint* for Jews?) "I loathe the fact," another woman said, "that men can just buy women as easily as a carton of milk."

We are sexual creatures; we are, for good or bad, sexual objects to one another. Certainly women have suffered from being consistently objectified in this way. One can empathize with those who feel they've been treated in less than their full dimensions as human beings. But free expression also includes sexual expression, within the obvious bounds set by the criminal sanctions against sex with children, assault or exposure. And no magazine is required to portray the full range of human experience.

As the censored (and ultimately murdered) Soviet-Jewish writer Isaac Babel said in 1934, the right to write badly is no small thing; in our context, we might say the right to give offence must not be undervalued. The Ontario Human Rights Commission seeks quasi-constitutional status for a new right: the right to take offence. It should be rejected.

Source: *Globe and Mail*, April 8, 1993, A24.

# Appendix A

# Universal Declaration
# of Human Rights

Adopted and proclaimed by General Assembly resolution 217 A (III) of 10 December 1948

## Preamble

Whereas recognition of the inherent dignity and of the equal and inalienable rights of all members of the human family is the foundation of freedom, justice and peace in the world,

Whereas disregard and contempt for human rights have resulted in barbarous acts which have outraged the conscience of mankind, and the advent of a world in which human beings shall enjoy freedom of speech and belief and freedom from fear and want has been proclaimed as the highest aspiration of the common people,

Whereas it is essential, if man is not to be compelled to have recourse, as a last resort, to rebellion against tyranny and oppression, that human rights should be protected by the rule of law,

Whereas it is essential to promote the development of friendly relations between nations,

Whereas the peoples of the United Nations have in the Charter reaffirmed their faith in fundamental human rights, in the dignity and worth of the human person and in the equal rights of men and women and have determined to promote social progress and better standards of life in larger freedom,

Whereas Member States have pledged themselves to achieve, in co-operation with the United Nations, the promotion of universal respect for and observance of human rights and fundamental freedoms,

Whereas a common understanding of these rights and freedoms is of the greatest importance for the full realization of this pledge,

Now, Therefore THE GENERAL ASSEMBLY proclaims THIS UNIVERSAL DECLARATION OF HUMAN RIGHTS as a common standard of achievement for all peoples and all nations, to the end that every individual and every organ of society, keeping this Declaration constantly in mind, shall strive by teaching and education to promote respect for these rights and freedoms and by progressive measures, national and international, to secure their universal and effective recognition and observance, both among the peoples of Member States themselves and among the peoples of territories under their jurisdiction.

## Article 1.

All human beings are born free and equal in dignity and rights. They are endowed with reason and conscience and should act towards one another in a spirit of brotherhood.

## Article 2.

Everyone is entitled to all the rights and freedoms set forth in this Declaration, without distinction of any kind, such as race, colour, sex, language, religion, political or other opinion, national or social origin, property, birth or other status. Furthermore, no distinction shall be made on the basis of the political, jurisdictional or international status of the country or territory to which a person belongs, whether it be independent, trust, non-self-governing or under any other limitation of sovereignty.

## Article 3.

Everyone has the right to life, liberty and security of person.

## Article 4.

No one shall be held in slavery or servitude; slavery and the slave trade shall be prohibited in all their forms.

## Article 5.

No one shall be subjected to torture or to cruel, inhuman or degrading treatment or punishment.

## Article 6.

Everyone has the right to recognition everywhere as a person before the law.

## Article 7.

All are equal before the law and are entitled without any discrimination to equal protection of the law. All are entitled to equal protection against any discrimination in violation of this Declaration and against any incitement to such discrimination.

## Article 8.

Everyone has the right to an effective remedy by the competent national tribunals for acts violating the fundamental rights granted him by the constitution or by law.

## Article 9.

No one shall be subjected to arbitrary arrest, detention or exile.

## Article 10.

Everyone is entitled in full equality to a fair and public hearing by an independent and impartial tribunal, in the determination of his rights and obligations and of any criminal charge against him.

## Article 11.

(1) Everyone charged with a penal offence has the right to be presumed innocent until proved guilty according to law in a public trial at which he has had all the guarantees necessary for his defence.

(2) No one shall be held guilty of any penal offence on account of any act or omission which did not constitute a penal offence, under national or international law, at the time when it was committed. Nor shall a heavier penalty be imposed than the one that was applicable at the time the penal offence was committed.

## Article 12.

No one shall be subjected to arbitrary interference with his privacy, family, home or correspondence, nor to attacks upon his honour and reputation. Everyone has the right to the protection of the law against such interference or attacks.

## Article 13.

(1) Everyone has the right to freedom of movement and residence within the borders of each state.

(2) Everyone has the right to leave any country, including his own, and to return to his country.

## Article 14.

(1) Everyone has the right to seek and to enjoy in other countries asylum from persecution.

(2) This right may not be invoked in the case of prosecutions genuinely arising from non-political crimes or from acts contrary to the purposes and principles of the United Nations.

## Article 15.

(1) Everyone has the right to a nationality.

(2) No one shall be arbitrarily deprived of his nationality nor denied the right to change his nationality.

## Article 16.

(1) Men and women of full age, without any limitation due to race, nationality or religion, have the right to marry and to found a family. They are entitled to equal rights as to marriage, during marriage and at its dissolution.

(2) Marriage shall be entered into only with the free and full consent of the intending spouses.

(3) The family is the natural and fundamental group unit of society and is entitled to protection by society and the State.

## Article 17.

(1) Everyone has the right to own property alone as well as in association with others.

(2) No one shall be arbitrarily deprived of his property.

## Article 18.

Everyone has the right to freedom of thought, conscience and religion; this right includes freedom to change his religion or belief, and freedom, either alone or in community with others and in public or private, to manifest his religion or belief in teaching, practice, worship and observance.

## Article 19.

Everyone has the right to freedom of opinion and expression; this right includes freedom to hold opinions without interference and to seek, receive and impart information and ideas through any media and regardless of frontiers.

## Article 20.

(1) Everyone has the right to freedom of peaceful assembly and association.

(2) No one may be compelled to belong to an association.

## Article 21.

(1) Everyone has the right to take part in the government of his country, directly or through freely chosen representatives.

(2) Everyone has the right of equal access to public service in his country.

(3) The will of the people shall be the basis of the authority of government; this will shall be expressed in periodic and genuine elections which shall be by universal and equal suffrage and shall be held by secret vote or by equivalent free voting procedures.

## Article 22.

Everyone, as a member of society, has the right to social security and is entitled to realization, through national effort and international co-operation and in accordance with the organization and resources of each State, of the economic, social and cultural rights indispensable for his dignity and the free development of his personality.

## Article 23.

(1) Everyone has the right to work, to free choice of employment, to just and favourable conditions of work and to protection against unemployment.

(2) Everyone, without any discrimination, has the right to equal pay for equal work.

(3) Everyone who works has the right to just and favourable remuneration ensuring for himself and his family an existence worthy of human dignity, and supplemented, if necessary, by other means of social protection.

(4) Everyone has the right to form and to join trade unions for the protection of his interests.

## Article 24.

Everyone has the right to rest and leisure, including reasonable limitation of working hours and periodic holidays with pay.

## Article 25.

(1) Everyone has the right to a standard of living adequate for the health and well-being of himself and of his family, including food, clothing, housing and medical care and necessary social services, and the right to security in the event of unemployment, sickness, disability, widowhood, old age or other lack of livelihood in circumstances beyond his control.

(2) Motherhood and childhood are entitled to special care and assistance. All children, whether born in or out of wedlock, shall enjoy the same social protection.

## Article 26.

(1) Everyone has the right to education. Education shall be free, at least in the elementary and fundamental stages. Elementary education shall be compulsory. Technical and professional education shall be made generally available and higher education shall be equally accessible to all on the basis of merit.

(2) Education shall be directed to the full development of the human personality and to the strengthening of respect for human rights and fundamental freedoms. It shall promote understanding, tolerance and friendship among all nations, racial or religious groups, and shall further the activities of the United Nations for the maintenance of peace.

(3) Parents have a prior right to choose the kind of education that shall be given to their children.

## Article 27.

(1) Everyone has the right freely to participate in the cultural life of the community, to enjoy the arts and to share in scientific advancement and its benefits.

(2) Everyone has the right to the protection of the moral and material interests resulting from any scientific, literary or artistic production of which he is the author.

## Article 28.

Everyone is entitled to a social and international order in which the rights and freedoms set forth in this Declaration can be fully realized.

## Article 29.

(1) Everyone has duties to the community in which alone the free and full development of his personality is possible.

(2) In the exercise of his rights and freedoms, everyone shall be subject only to such limitations as are determined by law solely for the purpose of securing due recognition and respect for the rights and freedoms of others and of meeting the just requirements of morality, public order and the general welfare in a democratic society.

(3) These rights and freedoms may in no case be exercised contrary to the purposes and principles of the United Nations.

## Article 30.

Nothing in this Declaration may be interpreted as implying for any State, group or person any right to engage in any activity or to perform any act aimed at the destruction of any of the rights and freedoms set forth herein.

# Appendix B

# Canadian Charter of Rights and Freedoms

Being Part I of the *Constitution Act,* 1982

[Enacted by the Canada Act 1982 [U.K.] c.11; proclaimed in force April 17, 1982. Amended by the Constitution Amendment Proclamation, 1983, SI/84-102, effective June 21, 1984. Amended by the Constitution Amendment, 1993 [New Brunswick], SI/93-54, *Can. Gaz. Part II*, April 7, 1993, effective March 12, 1993.]

Whereas Canada is founded upon principles that recognize the supremacy of God and the rule of law:

## Guarantee of Rights and Freedoms

1. The *Canadian Charter of Rights and Freedoms* guarantees the rights and freedoms set out in it subject only to such reasonable limits prescribed by law as can be demonstrably justified in a free and democratic society.

## Fundamental Freedoms

2. Everyone has the following fundamental freedoms:
    (a) freedom of conscience and religion;
    (b) freedom of thought, belief, opinion and expression, including freedom of the press and other media of communication;
    (c) freedom of peaceful assembly; and
    (d) freedom of association.

## Democratic Rights

3. Every citizen of Canada has the right to vote in an election of members of the House of Commons or of a legislative assembly and to be qualified for membership therein.

4. (1) No House of Commons and no legislative assembly shall continue for longer than five years from the date fixed for the return of the writs at a general election of its members.
    (2) In time of real or apprehended war, invasion or insurrection, a House of Commons may be continued by Parliament and a legislative assembly may be continued by the legislature beyond five years if such continuation is not opposed by the votes of more than one-third of the members of the House of Commons or the legislative assembly, as the case may be.

5. There shall be a sitting of Parliament and of each legislature at least once every twelve months.

## Mobility Rights

6. (1) Every citizen of Canada has the right to enter, remain in and leave Canada.

   (2) Every citizen of Canada and every person who has the status of a permanent resident of Canada has the right

   (a) to move to and take up residence in any province; and

   (b) to pursue the gaining of a livelihood in any province.

   (3) The rights specified in subsection (2) are subject to

   (a) any laws or practices of general application in force in a province other than those that discriminate among persons primarily on the basis of province of present or previous residence; and

   (b) any laws providing for reasonable residency requirements as a qualification for the receipt of publicly provided social services.

   (4) Subsections (2) and (3) do not preclude any law, program or activity that has as its object the amelioration in a province of conditions of individuals in that province who were socially or economically disadvantaged if the rate of employment in that province is below the rate of employment in Canada.

## Legal Rights

7. Everyone has the right to life, liberty and security of the person and the right not to be deprived thereof except in accordance with the principles of fundamental justice.

8. Everyone has the right to be secure against unreasonable search or seizure.

9. Everyone has the right not to be arbitrarily detained or imprisoned.

10. Everyone has the right on arrest or detention

    (a) to be informed promptly of the reasons therefor;

    (b) to retain and instruct counsel without delay and to be informed of that right; and

    (c) to have the validity of the detention determined by way of habeas corpus and to be released if the detention is not lawful.

11. Any person charged with an offence has the right

    (a) to be informed without unreasonable delay of the specific offence;

    (b) to be tried within a reasonable time;

    (c) not to be compelled to be a witness in proceedings against that person in respect of the offence;

    (d) to be presumed innocent until proven guilty according to law in a fair and public hearing by an independent and impartial tribunal;

    (e) not to be denied reasonable bail without just cause;

    (f)  except in the case of an offence under military law tried before a military tribunal, to the benefit of trial by jury where the maximum punishment for the offence is imprisonment for five years or a more severe punishment;

    (g)  not to be found guilty on account of any act or omission unless, at the time of the act or omission, it constituted an offence under Canadian or international law or was criminal according to the general principles of law recognized by the community of nations;

    (h)  if finally acquitted of the offence, not to be tried for it again and, if finally found guilty and punished for the offence, not to be tried or punished for it again; and

    (i)  if found guilty of the offence and if the punishment for the offence has been varied between the time of commission and the time of sentencing, to the benefit of the lesser punishment.

12. Everyone has the right not to be subjected to any cruel and unusual treatment or punishment.

13. A witness who testifies in any proceedings has the right not to have any incriminating evidence so given used to incriminate that witness in any other proceedings, except in a prosecution for perjury or for the giving of contradictory evidence.

14. A party or witness in any proceedings who does not understand or speak the language in which the proceedings arc conducted or who is deaf has the right to the assistance of an interpreter.

## Equality Rights

15. (1) Every individual is equal before and under the law and has the right to the equal protection and equal benefit of the law without discrimination and, in particular, without discrimination based on race, national or ethnic origin, colour, religion, sex, age or mental or physical disability.

(2) Subsection (1) does not preclude any law, program or activity that has as its object the amelioration of conditions of disadvantaged individuals or groups including those that are disadvantaged because of race, national or ethnic origin, colour, religion, sex, age or mental or physical disability.

## Official Languages of Canada

16. (1) English and French are the official languages of Canada and have equality of status and equal rights and privileges as to their use in all institutions of the Parliament and government of Canada.

(2) English and French are the official languages of New Brunswick and have equality of status and equal rights and privileges as to their use in all institutions of the legislature and government of New Brunswick.

(3) Nothing in this Charter limits the authority of Parliament or a legislature to advance the equality of status or use of English and French.

16.1 (1) The English linguistic community and the French linguistic community in New Brunswick have equality of status and equal rights and privileges, including the right to distinct educational institutions and such distinct cultural institutions as are necessary for the preservation and promotion of those communities.

(2) The role of the legislature and government of New Brunswick to preserve and promote the status, rights and privileges referred to in subsection (1) is affirmed.

17. (1) Everyone has the right to use English or French in any debates and other proceedings of Parliament.

(2) Everyone has the right to use English or French in any debates and other proceedings of the legislature of New Brunswick.

18. (1) The statutes, records and journals of Parliament shall be printed and published in English and French and both language versions are equally authoritative.

(2) The statutes, records and journals of the legislature of New Brunswick shall be printed and published in English and French and both language versions are equally authoritative.

19. (1) Either English or French may be used by any person in, or any pleading in or process issuing from, any court established by Parliament.

(2) Either English or French may be used by any person in, or any pleading in or process issuing from, any court of New Brunswick.

20. (1) Any member of the public in Canada has the right to communicate with, and to receive available services from, any head or central office of an institution of the Parliament or government of Canada in English or French, and has the same right with respect to any other office of any such institution where

   (a) there is a significant demand for communications with and services from that office in such language; or

   (b) due to the nature of the office, it is reasonable that communications with and services from that office be available in both English and French.

(2) Any member of the public in New Brunswick has the right to communicate with, and to receive available services from, any office of an institution of the legislature or government of New Brunswick in English or French.

21. Nothing in sections 16 to 20 abrogates or derogates from any right, privilege or obligation with respect to the English and French languages, or either of them, that exists or is continued by virtue of any other provision of the Constitution of Canada.

22. Nothing in sections 16 to 20 abrogates or derogates from any legal or customary right or privilege acquired or enjoyed either before or after the coming into force of this Charter with respect to any language that is not English or French.

## Minority Language Educational Rights

23. (1) Citizens of Canada

   (a) whose first language learned and still understood is that of the English or French linguistic minority of the province in which they reside, or

(b) who have received their primary school instruction in Canada in English or French and reside in a province where the language in which they received that instruction is the language of the English or French linguistic minority population of the province, have the right to have their children receive primary and secondary school instruction in that language in that province.

(2) Citizens of Canada of whom any child has received or is receiving primary or secondary school instruction in English or French in Canada, have the right to have all their children receive primary and secondary language instruction in the same language.

(3) The right of citizens of Canada under subsections (1) and (2) to have their children receive primary and secondary school instruction in the language of the English or French linguistic minority population of a province

(a) applies wherever in the province the number of children of citizens who have such a right is sufficient to warrant the provision to them out of public funds of minority language instruction; and

(b) includes, where the number of those children so warrants, the right to have them receive that instruction in minority language educational facilities provided out of public funds.

## Enforcement

24. (1) Anyone whose rights or freedoms, as guaranteed by this Charter, have been infringed or denied may apply to a court of competent jurisdiction to obtain such remedy as the court considers appropriate and just in the circumstances.

(2) Where, in proceedings under subsection (1), a court concludes that evidence was obtained in a manner that infringed or denied any rights or freedoms guaranteed by this Charter, the evidence shall be excluded if it is established that, having regard to all the circumstances, the admission of it in the proceedings would bring the administration of justice into disrepute.

## General

25. The guarantee in this Charter of certain rights and freedoms shall not be construed so as to abrogate or derogate from any aboriginal, treaty or other rights or freedoms that pertain to the aboriginal people of Canada including

(a) any rights or freedoms that have been recognized by the Royal Proclamation of October 7, 1763; and

(b) any rights or freedoms that now exist by way of land claims agreements or may be so acquired.

26. The guarantee in this Charter of certain rights and freedoms shall not be construed as denying the existence of any other rights or freedoms that exist in Canada.

27. This Charter shall be interpreted in a manner consistent with the preservation and enhancement of the multicultural heritage of Canadians.

28. Notwithstanding anything in this Charter, the rights and freedoms referred to in it are guaranteed equally to male and female persons.

29. Nothing in this Charter abrogates or derogates from any rights or privileges guaranteed by or under the Constitution of Canada in respect of denominational, separate or dissentient schools.

30. A reference in this Charter to a province or to the legislative assembly or legislature of a province shall be deemed to include a reference to the Yukon Territory and the Northwest Territories, or to the appropriate legislative authority thereof, as the case may be.

31. Nothing in this Charter extends the legislative powers of any body or authority.

## Application of Charter

32. (1) This Charter applies

    (a) to the Parliament and government of Canada in respect of all matters within the authority of Parliament including all matters relating to the Yukon Territory and Northwest Territories; and

    (b) to the legislature and government of each province in respect of all matters within the authority of the legislature of each province.

(2) Notwithstanding subsection (1), section 15 shall not have effect until three years after this section comes into force. [Section 32 came into force on April 17, 1982; therefore, section 15 had effect on April 17, 1985.]

33. (1) Parliament or the legislature of a province may expressly declare in an Act of Parliament or of the legislature, as the case may be, that the Act or a provision thereof shall operate notwithstanding a provision included in section 2 or sections 7 to 15 of this Charter.

(2) An Act or a provision of an Act in respect of which a declaration made under this section is in effect shall have such operation as it would have but for the provision of this Charter referred to in the declaration.

(3) A declaration made under subsection (1) shall cease to have effect five years after it comes into force or on such earlier date as may be specified in the declaration.

(4) Parliament or the legislature of a province may re-enact a declaration made under subsection (1).

(5) Subsection (3) applies in respect of a re-enactment made under subsection (4).

## Citation

34. This Part may be cited as the Canadian Charter of Rights and Freedoms.

# Appendix C

## Police Services Act, Revised Statutes of Ontario, Code of Conduct

14. (1) Any conduct described in the code of conduct, set out in the Schedule, constitutes misconduct for the purposes of section 74 of the Act.

(2) The code of conduct applies to municipal police forces and the Ontario Provincial Police. O.Reg. 123/98.s. 14.

### SCHEDULE

### Code of Conduct

1. In this code of conduct,
   "record" means any record of information, however recorded, whether in printed form, on film, by electronic means or otherwise, and includes correspondence, a memorandum, a book, a plan, a map, a drawing, a diagram, a pictorial or graphic work, a photograph, a film, a microfilm, a sound recording, a videotape, a machine readable record, any other documentary material, regardless of physical form or characteristics, and any copy thereof.

2. (1) Any chief of police or other police officer commits misconduct if he or she engages in,

   (a) DISCREDITABLE CONDUCT, in that he or she,

   (i) fails to treat or protect a person equally without discrimination with respect to police services because of that person's race, ancestry, place of origin, colour, ethnic origin, citizenship, creed, sex, sexual orientation, age, marital status, family status or handicap,

   (ii) uses profane, abusive or insulting language that relates to a person's race, ancestry, place of origin, colour, ethnic origin, citizenship, creed, sex, sexual orientation, age, marital status, family status or handicap,

   (iii) is guilty of oppressive or tyrannical conduct towards an inferior in rank,

   (iv) uses profane, abusive or insulting language to any other member of a police force,

   (v)  uses profane, abusive or insulting language or is otherwise uncivil to a member of the public,

  (vi)  wilfully or negligently makes any false complaint or statement against any member of a police force,

 (vii)  assaults any other member of a police force,

(viii)  withholds or suppresses a complaint or report against a member of a police force or about the policies of or services provided by the police force,

  (ix)  is guilty of an indictable criminal offence or a criminal offence punishable upon summary conviction,

   (x)  contravenes any provision of the Act or the regulations, or

  (xi)  acts in a disorderly manner or in a manner prejudicial to discipline or likely to bring discredit upon the reputation of the police force;

(b) INSUBORDINATION, in that he or she,

   (i)  is insubordinate by word, act or demeanour, or

  (ii)  without lawful excuse, disobeys, omits or neglects to carry out any lawful order;

(c) NEGLECT OF DUTY, in that he or she,

   (i)  without lawful excuse, neglects or omits promptly and diligently to perform a duty as a member of the police force,

  (ii)  fails to work in accordance with orders, or leaves an area, detachment, detail or other place of duty, without due permission or sufficient cause,

 (iii)  by carelessness or neglect permits a prisoner to escape,

 (iv)  fails, when knowing where an offender is to be found, to report him or her or to make due exertions for bringing the offender to justice,

  (v)  fails to report a matter that is his or her duty to report,

 (vi)  fails to report anything that he or she knows concerning a criminal or other charge, or fails to disclose any evidence that he or she, or any person within his or her knowledge, can give for or against any prisoner or defendant,

 (vii)  omits to make any necessary entry in a record,

(viii)  feigns or exaggerates sickness or injury to evade duty,

  (ix)  is absent without leave from or late for any duty, without reasonable excuse, or

   (x)  is improperly dressed, dirty, or untidy in person, clothing or equipment while on duty;

(d) DECEIT, in that he or she,

   (i)  knowingly makes or signs a false statement in a record,

(ii) wilfully or negligently makes a false, misleading or inaccurate statement pertaining to official duties, or

(iii) without lawful excuse, destroys or mutilates a record or alters or erases an entry therein;

(e) BREACH OF CONFIDENCE, in that he or she,

(i) divulges any matter which it is his or her duty to keep secret,

(ii) gives notice, directly or indirectly, to any person against whom any warrant or summons has been or is about to be issued, except in the lawful execution of the warrant or service of the summons,

(iii) without proper authority, communicates to the media or to any unauthorized person any matter connected with the police force,

(iv) without proper authority, shows to any person not a member of the police force or to any unauthorized member of the force any record that is the property of the police force;

(f) CORRUPT PRACTICE, in that he or she,

(i) offers or takes a bribe,

(ii) fails to account for or to make a prompt, true return of money or property received in an official capacity,

(iii) directly or indirectly solicits or receives a gratuity or present without the consent of the chief of police,

(iv) places himself or herself under a pecuniary or other obligation to a licensee concerning the granting or refusing of whose licence a member of the police force may have to report or give evidence, or

(v) improperly uses his or her character and position as a member of the police force for private advantage;

(g) UNLAWFUL OR UNNECESSARY EXERCISE OF AUTHORITY, in that he or she,

(i) without good and sufficient cause makes an unlawful or unnecessary arrest, or

(ii) uses any unnecessary force against a prisoner or other person contacted in the execution of duty;

(h) DAMAGE TO CLOTHING OR EQUIPMENT, in that he or she,

(i) wilfully or carelessly causes loss or damage to any article of clothing or equipment, or to any record or other property of the police force, or

(ii) fails to report loss or damage, however caused, as soon as practicable; or

(i) CONSUMING DRUGS OR ALCOHOL IN A MANNER PREJUDICIAL TO DUTY, in that he or she,

(i) is unfit for duty, while on duty, through consumption of drugs or alcohol,

    (ii) is unfit for duty when he or she reports for duty, through consumption of drugs or alcohol,

    (iii) except with the consent of a superior officer or in the discharge of duty, consumes or receives alcohol from any other person while on duty, or

    (iv) except in the discharge of duty, demands, persuades or attempts to persuade another person to give or purchase or obtain for a member of the police force any alcohol or illegal drugs while on duty.

(2) A police officer does not commit misconduct under subclause (1)(e)(iii) if he or she engages in the described activity in his or her capacity as an authorized representative of an association, as defined in section 2 of the Act.

(3) A police officer does not commit misconduct under subclause (1) (f)(iii) if he or she engages in the described activity in his or her capacity as an authorized representative of an association, as defined in section 2 of the Act, or of a work-related professional organization.

3. Any chief of police or other police officer also commits misconduct if he or she conspires, abets or is knowingly an accessory to any misconduct described in section 2.

O.Reg. 123/98. Sched.

# Appendix D

## IACP Law Enforcement Code of Ethics (1957)

As a Law Enforcement Officer, my fundamental duty is to serve mankind; to safeguard lives and property; to protect the innocent against deception, the weak against oppression or intimidation, and the peaceful against violence or disorder; and to respect the Constitutional rights of all men to liberty, equality, and justice.

I will keep my private life unsullied as an example to all; maintain courageous calm in the face of danger, scorn, or ridicule; develop self-restraint; and be constantly mindful of the welfare of others. Honest in thought and deed in both my personal and official life, I will be exemplary in obeying the laws of the land and the regulations of my department. Whatever I see or hear of a confidential nature or that is confided to me in my official capacity will be kept ever secret, unless revelation is necessary in the performance of my duty.

I will never act officiously or permit personal feelings, prejudices, animosities, or friendships to influence my decisions. With no compromise for crime and with relentless prosecution of criminals, I will enforce the law courteously and appropriately without fear or favour, malice or ill will, never employing unnecessary force or violence, and never accepting gratuities.

I recognize the badge of my office as a symbol of public faith, and I accept it as a public trust to be held so long as I am true to the ethics of the police service. I will constantly strive to achieve these objectives and ideals, dedicating myself before God to my chosen profession ... law enforcement.

# Appendix E

## IACP Law Enforcement Code of Ethics (1991)

As a law enforcement officer, my fundamental duty is to serve the community; to safeguard lives and property; to protect the innocent against deception, the weak against oppression or intimidation and the peaceful against violence or disorder; and to respect the constitutional rights of all to liberty, equality and justice.

I will keep my private life unsullied as an example to all and will behave in a manner that does not bring discredit to me or to my agency. I will maintain courageous calm in the face of danger, scorn or ridicule; develop self-restraint; and be constantly mindful of the welfare of others. Honest in thought and deed both in my personal and official life, I will be exemplary in obeying the law and the regulations of my department. Whatever I see or hear of a confidential nature or that is confided to me in my official capacity will be kept ever secret unless revelation is necessary in the performance of my duty.

I will never act officiously or permit personal feelings, prejudices, political beliefs, aspirations, animosities or friendships to influence my decisions. With no compromise for crime and with relentless prosecution of criminals, I will enforce the law courteously and appropriately without fear or favour, malice or ill will, never employing unnecessary force or violence and never accepting gratuities.

I recognize the badge of my office as a symbol of public faith, and I accept it as a public trust to be held so long as I am true to the ethics of police service. I will never engage in acts of corruption or bribery, nor will I condone such acts by other police officers. I will cooperate with all legally authorized agencies and their representatives in the pursuit of justice.

I know that I alone am responsible for my own standard of professional performance and will take every reasonable opportunity to enhance and improve my level of knowledge and competence.

I will constantly strive to achieve these objectives and ideals, dedicating myself before God to my chosen profession ... law enforcement.

# Appendix F

# IACP Canons of Police Ethics (1957 & 1991)

### ARTICLE 1    Primary Responsibility of Job

The primary responsibility of the police service, and of officers, is the protection of the people of Canada through the upholding of our laws. Law enforcement officers represent the whole of the community and its legally expressed will and are never the arm of any political party or clique.

### ARTICLE 2    Limitations of Authority

The first duty of law enforcement officers, as upholders of the law, is to know its bounds upon them in enforcing it. Because they represent the legal will of the community, be it local, provincial or federal, they must be aware of the limitations which the people, through law, have placed upon them. They must recognize the genius of the Canadian system of government which gives to no individual, groups of people, or institutions, absolute power, and they must insure that they, as prime defenders of that system, do not pervert its character.

### ARTICLE 3    Duty To Be Familiar with the Law and with Responsibilities of Self and Other Public Officials

Law enforcement officers shall assiduously apply themselves to the study of the principles of the laws which they are sworn to uphold. They will make certain of their responsibilities in the particulars of their enforcement, seeking aid from their superiors in matters of technicality or principle when these are not clear to them; including other law enforcement agencies, particularly on matters of jurisdiction, both geographically and substantively.

### ARTICLE 4    Utilization of Proper Means To Gain Proper Ends

Law enforcement officers shall be mindful of their responsibility to pay strict heed to the selection of means in discharging the duties of their office. Violations of law or disregard for public safety and property on the part of an officer are intrinsically wrong; they are self-defeating in that they instill in the public mind a like disposition. The employment of illegal means, no matter how worthy the end, is certain to encourage disrespect for the law and its officers. If the law is to be honoured, it must first be honoured by those who enforce it.

## ARTICLE 5    Cooperation with Public Officials in the Discharge of Their Authorized Duties

Law enforcement officers shall cooperate fully with other public officials in the discharge of authorized duties, regardless of party affiliation or personal prejudice. They shall be meticulous, however, in assuring themselves of the propriety, under the law, of such actions and shall guard against the use of their office or person, whether knowingly or unknowingly, in any improper or illegal action. In any situation open to question, they shall seek authority from their superior officer, while giving a full report of the proposed service or action.

## ARTICLE 6    Private Conduct

Law enforcement officers shall be mindful of their special identification by the public as an upholder of the law. Laxity of conduct or manner in private life, expressing either disrespect for the law or seeking to gain special privilege, cannot but reflect upon the police officer and the police service. The community and the service require that the law enforcement officers lead lives of decent and honourable citizens. Following the career of a police officer gives no individual special perquisites. It does give the satisfaction and pride of following and furthering an unbroken tradition of safeguarding the Canadian public. The officers who reflect upon this tradition will not degrade it. Rather, they will so conduct their private lives that the public will regard them as examples of stability, fidelity and morality.

## ARTICLE 7    Conduct Toward the Public

Law enforcement officers, mindful of their responsibility to the whole community, shall deal with individuals of the community in a manner calculated to instill respect for its laws and its police service. Law enforcement officers shall conduct their official lives in a manner such as will inspire confidence and trust. Thus, they will be neither overbearing nor subservient, as no individual citizen has an obligation to stand in awe of them nor a right to command them. The officers will give service where they can, and require compliance with the law. They will do neither from personal preference nor prejudice but rather as duly appointed officers of the law discharging their sworn obligation.

## ARTICLE 8    Conduct in Arresting and Dealing with Law Violators

Law enforcement officers shall use their powers of arrest strictly in accordance with the law and with due regard to the rights of the citizen concerned. The office gives them no right to prosecute the violator nor to mete out punishment for the offence. They shall, at all times, have a clear appreciation of the responsibilities and limitations regarding detention of the violator; they shall conduct themselves in such a manner as will minimize the possibility of having to use force. To this end they shall cultivate a dedication to the service of the people and the equitable upholding of their laws whether in the handling of law violators or in dealing with the law-abiding.

## ARTICLE 9    Gifts and Favours

Law enforcement officers, representing government, bear the heavy responsibility of maintaining, in their own conduct, the honour and integrity of all government institutions. They shall, therefore, guard against placing themselves in a position in which any person can expect special consideration or in which the public can reasonably assume that special consideration is being given. Thus, they should be firm in refusing gifts, favours, or gratuities, large or small, which can, in the public mind, be interpreted as capable of influencing their judgment in the discharge of duties.

## ARTICLE 10    Presentation of Evidence

Law enforcement officers shall be concerned equally in the prosecution of the wrong-doer and the defence of the innocent. They shall ascertain what constitutes evidence and shall present such evidence impartially and without malice. In so doing, they will ignore social, political, and all other distinctions among the persons involved, strengthening the tradition of the reliability and integrity of an officer's word.

Law enforcement officers shall take special pains to increase their perception and skill of observation, mindful that in many situations they will be the sole impartial testimony to the facts of a case.

## ARTICLE 11    Attitude Toward Profession

Law enforcement officers shall regard the discharge of their duties as a public trust and recognize their responsibility as public servants. By diligent study and sincere attention to self-improvement they shall strive to make the best possible application of science to the solution of crime and, in the field of human relationships, strive for effective leadership and public influence in matters affecting public safety. They shall appreciate the importance and responsibility of their office, and hold police work to be an honourable profession rendering valuable service to the community and to the country.

# Appendix G

## IACP Law Enforcement Code of Conduct (1989)

All law enforcement officers must be fully aware of the ethical responsibilities of their position and must strive constantly to live up to the highest possible standards of professional policing. The International Association of Chiefs of Police believes it important that police officers have clear advice and counsel available to assist them in performing their duties consistent with these standards, and has adopted the following ethical mandates as guidelines to meet these ends.

### PRIMARY RESPONSIBILITIES OF A POLICE OFFICER

A police officer acts as an official representative of government who is required and trusted to work within the law. The officer's powers and duties are conferred by statute. The fundamental duties of a police officer include serving the community, safeguarding lives and property, protecting the innocent, keeping the peace and ensuring the rights of all to liberty, equality and justice.

### PERFORMANCE OF THE DUTIES OF A POLICE OFFICER

A police officer shall perform all duties impartially, without favour or affection or ill will and without regard to status, sex, race, religion, political belief or aspiration. All citizens will be treated equally with courtesy, consideration and dignity.

Officers will never allow personal feelings, animosities or friendships to influence official conduct. Laws will be enforced appropriately and courteously and, in carrying out their responsibilities, officers will strive to obtain maximum cooperation from the public. They will conduct themselves in appearance and deportment in such a manner as to inspire confidence and respect for the position of public trust they hold.

### DISCRETION

A police officer will use responsibly the discretion vested in his position and exercise it within the law. The principle of reasonableness will guide the officer's determinations, and the officer will consider all surrounding circumstances in determining whether any legal action shall be taken.

Consistent and wise use of discretion, based on professional policing competence, will do much to preserve good relationships and retain the confidence of the public. There can be difficulty in choosing between conflicting courses of action. It is important to remember that a timely word of advice rather than arrest—which may be correct in appropriate circumstances—can be a more effective means of achieving a desired end.

## USE OF FORCE

A police officer will never employ unnecessary force or violence and will use only such force in the discharge of duty as is reasonable in all circumstances.

The use of force should be used only with the greatest restraint and only after discussion, negotiation and persuasion have been found to be inappropriate or ineffective. While the use of force is occasionally unavoidable, every police officer will refrain from unnecessary infliction of pain or suffering and will never engage in cruel, degrading or inhuman treatment of any person.

## CONFIDENTIALITY

Whatever a police officer sees, hears or learns of that is of a confidential nature will be kept secret unless the performance of duty or legal provision requires otherwise.

Members of the public have a right to security and privacy, and information obtained about them must not be improperly divulged.

## INTEGRITY

A police officer will not engage in acts of corruption or bribery, nor will an officer condone such acts by other police officers.

The public demands that the integrity of police officers be above reproach. Police officers must, therefore, avoid any conduct that might compromise integrity and thus undercut the public confidence in a law enforcement agency. Officers will refuse to accept any gifts, presents, subscriptions, favours, gratuities or promises that could be interpreted as seeking to cause the officer to refrain from performing official responsibilities honestly and within the law. Police officers must not receive private or special advantage from their official status. Respect from the public cannot be bought; it can only be earned and cultivated.

## COOPERATION WITH OTHER POLICE OFFICERS AND AGENCIES

Police officers will cooperate with all legally authorized agencies and their representatives in the pursuit of justice.

An officer or agency may be one among many organizations that may provide law enforcement services to a jurisdiction. It is imperative that a police officer assist colleagues fully and completely with respect and consideration at all times.

## PERSONAL-PROFESSIONAL CAPABILITIES

Police officers will be responsible for their own standard of professional performance and will take every reasonable opportunity to enhance and improve their level of knowledge and competence.

Through study and experience, a police officer can acquire the high level of knowledge and competence that is essential for the efficient and effective performance of duty. The acquisition of knowledge is a never-ending process of personal and professional development that should be pursued constantly.

## PRIVATE LIFE

Police officers will behave in a manner that does not bring discredit to their agencies or themselves. A police officer's character and conduct while off duty must always be exemplary, thus maintaining a position of respect in the community in which he or she lives and serves. The officer's personal behaviour must be beyond reproach.

# Glossary

**Abortion** The premature ending of a pregnancy. Compare *induced abortion* and *spontaneous abortion*.

**Absolute** A principle or rule that has no exceptions.

**Absolute rule** A rule that has no exceptions.

**Absolutist** A person who holds that a principle or rule has no exceptions.

**Accountability** The condition of being answerable to others for one's actions.

**Achievement** The human need to be successful, to do something or be someone.

**Act of commission** Taking an action to accomplish something. In lying, for example, deceiving by deliberately distorting the truth is an act of commission.

**Act of omission** Deliberately refraining from doing something that it is one's responsibility to do. In lying, for example, refraining from telling the whole truth is an act of omission.

**Active euthanasia** Taking a direct action to kill another person, for mercy's sake, with or without knowing the person's wishes regarding his or her death. If the person wishes to die, then active euthanasia is assisted suicide. If the person's wishes are unknown, then it is mercy killing. Both assisted suicide and mercy killing are illegal in Canada. Active euthanasia is also called *direct euthanasia*.

**Adultery** Sexual intercourse with a person other than one's spouse or long-term partner.

**Advanced directive form** A form used to state one's wishes regarding future treatment that the signer is to receive. It can be a type of living will.

**Affective dimension** The emotional aspect of human nature that includes the experience of feelings and moods.

**Affiliation** The human need for relationships with others. Also called love and belonging needs.

**Affirmative action program** A program designed to assist disadvantaged minority group members to get employment, education, or training.

**Altruism** Generally, concern for others. More specifically, a form of consequentialism that maintains that the right thing to do is always what is in the best interests of others only.

**Altruistic** The quality or tendency of being concerned for the welfare of others.

**Amoral** A word used to describe the actions of humans who are incapable of understanding right and wrong or who act under compulsion, as in a mental disorder.

**Analysis** The process of identifying the component parts of a subject.

**Analytical dimension** The aspect of ethics that defines the meaning of terms and analyzes the logic of arguments. Also called *analytical ethics*.

**Analytical ethics** The aspect of ethics that defines the meaning of terms and analyzes the logic of arguments.

**Appeal to authority** A type of reasoning in which one supports an argument by trusting that someone is knowledgeable about the subject of the argument. If the person consulted is an expert who knows the facts, then the appeal is legitimate. If the person consulted is not, then the appeal is faulty.

**Appeal to public opinion** A type of reasoning in which one supports an argument by trusting public opinion. If the public is right, then the appeal is legitimate. If the public is not, then the appeal is faulty.

**Appeal to status** A type of reasoning in which one supports an argument by invoking one's social rank. Almost always a faulty appeal because the truth is not established by social status.

**Articles** Within a formal document, the parts that state the position that the author of the document takes.

**Assisted suicide** A suicide accomplished with the help of another person. In Canada, assisted suicide is illegal.

**Attacking the person** A type of faulty reasoning in which a person criticizes the character of another person instead of the other person's reasoning.

**Authorize** To give official approval to a course of action.

**Authorization** The act of giving official approval to a course of action.

**Bad lie** A lie that is told for self-serving reasons, or to hurt someone, or that is disrespectful of another. Compare *lie* and *good lie*.

**Behavioural dimension** The actions of human beings that result from the thoughts and feelings that they have. Also called the *psychomotor dimension*.

**Categorical imperative** In the duty ethics approach of Immanuel Kant, the principle that says an act is immoral if the rule authorizing the act cannot be made into a rule for all humans to follow.

**Censor** One who tells others what they can or can't do, see, or hear.

**Censorship** The act of restricting what others can or can't do, see, or hear.

**Circular argument** A form of faulty reasoning in which persons assume the truth of something that they are supposed to prove.

**Civil societies** Societies that are democratic, pluralistic, and committed to the rule of law. Canada is a civil society.

**Civilized way** The approach to societal life that commits to ethics and the rule of law. Civil societies take this approach.

**Code** A set of rules, such as the Criminal Code.

**Cognitive dimension** The rational or thinking aspect of human nature that includes reasoning, decision making, and problem solving.

**Command of God prescription** A religious, non-consequentialist approach to ethics that maintains that the commands of God establish right and wrong.

**Community standards** The ethical standards used by a community to judge what is or is not morally acceptable in that community.

**Compensation approach** An approach to punishment that focuses on the rights of victims. It seeks compensation for the victims of crime.

**Confidentiality** The act of maintaining secrecy in a professional or personal role.

**Consequences** The results, outcomes, or effects of an action.

**Consequentialism** An approach to ethics that maintains that the rightness or wrongness of a proposed action is determined by the results, outcomes, or effects of the action.

**Consumption** The act of using something. With respect to pornography, the act of possessing and making use of obscene material.

**Correctional officers** Those members of society who have been authorized to administer the penalties that society imposes upon offenders. Also called *corrections officers*.

**Corrective justice approach** An approach that sees the primary purpose of punishment as the rehabilita-

tion of the offender. In this approach, punishment is just when it corrects the errant behaviour of the offender. Also called *rehabilitative justice*.

**Courageous** A word used to describe human beings who knowingly face danger without retreating.

**Courts** The institution of society that has responsibility for determining the innocence or guilt of an accused person.

**Crime fighter** A public perception that sees the role of the police as that of warriors in a battle against crime. Compare *public servant*.

**Criminal justice** Generally, societal fairness in criminal matters. More specifically, fairness in (1) the apprehension of suspected offenders, (2) the determination of guilt or innocence of the accused, and (3) in the treatment of those convicted.

**Critical thinking** Thinking that actively seeks to understand, analyze, and evaluate information and arguments.

**Cultural relativism** The view that maintains that ethics is relative to each culture. It holds that there are no universal moral standards and that no culture is entitled to judge another culture.

**Deception by distortion** Lying or deceiving by deliberately misstating the facts of a situation to others who are entitled to know the facts.

**Deception by omission** Lying or deceiving by deliberately choosing to withhold necessary information from others who are entitled to it.

**DECIDE Process** The author's six-step process for understanding moral issues and making ethically defensible choices.

**Deductive reasoning** A type of reasoning that argues from general truths to particular conclusions. Example: If A=B, and B=C, then A=C.

**Democratic** A word used to describe societies in which members elect their leaders.

**Descriptive dimension** That aspect of ethics that concerns itself with the way things actually are in the world. It describes the actual practices of people, not the ideal practices. Also called, *descriptive ethics*.

**Descriptive ethics** That aspect of ethics that concerns itself with the way things actually are in the world. It describes the actual practices of people, not the ideal practices. Also called the *descriptive dimension* of ethics.

**Deserts approach** An approach to distributive justice that says that fairness consists of giving people what they deserve, earn, or merit. Also called the *merit approach*.

**Desire** A want. Something that one wishes to have that is not essential for one's survival.

**Determinism** The view that maintains that human beings do not have free will or freedom of choice.

**Direct euthanasia** Taking an active step to kill another person, for mercy's sake, with or without knowing the person's wishes regarding his or her death. If the person wishes to die, then direct euthanasia is assisted suicide. If the person's wishes are unknown, then it is mercy killing. Both assisted suicide and mercy killing are illegal in Canada. Direct euthanasia is also called *active euthanasia*.

**Discretion** The freedom or authority to exercise reasonable choice in a professional role.

**Discretionary action** An action taken by a professional, after consideration of all reasonable options.

**Discrimination** Unethical actions that stem from prejudice. Persons are discriminated against or favoured on the basis of ethically irrelevant factors such as race, ethnicity, and gender.

**Distributive justice** Fairness in a society's distribution of its benefits and burdens to its members.

**Do-not-resuscitate order (DNR)** An order, usually given by a doctor, that directs others not to revive a person who becomes unconscious.

**Duty ethics** A nonconsequentialist approach to ethics that maintains that the right thing to do is what human reason commands. According to this approach, it is our duty to follow the commands of reason and never to use another person as a means to an end.

**Educational equity** Equality in educational opportunities and standards.

**Egocentric** The condition of being self-centred or exclusively self-interested.

**Egoism** A consequentialist approach to ethics that maintains that the right thing to do in any given situation is whatever is in your own self-interest.

**Emotivist prescription** A nonconsequentialist approach that says that the right thing to do is whatever one feels is right. Also called *intuitionism,* it is a type of subjectivism because it reduces ethics to matters of individual feeling.

**Empathy** Feeling what another person feels, or identifying with the feelings of others. Empathy is the "moral feeling" in that it is essential for moral conduct.

**Employment equity** Equality in the workplace.

**Employment equity programs** Programs put in place to achieve equality in the workplace; that is, equal opportunity to get work and equal pay for equal work.

**Enforcement justice** Fairness in policing. Fairness in enforcing the laws.

**Entrapment** A practice whereby an individual is tricked into committing an offence.

**Equality** Having the same rights and responsibilities as others.

**Equality, negative duty** The equality principle stated in the form of a simple rule: "Don't discriminate."

**Equality, positive duty** The equality principle stated in the form of a simple rule: "Treat others equally."

**Equality of opportunity** An approach to equity issues that seeks to guarantee that everyone has the same chance to compete for available jobs, or seats in education.

**Equality of outcome** An approach to equity issues that seeks to guarantee equality in benefits received. For example, that everyone would be paid exactly the same wage, regardless of their job responsibilities. Also called *equality of results.*

**Equality of results** An approach to equity issues that seeks to guarantee equality in benefits received. For example, that everyone would be paid exactly the same wage, regardless of their job responsibilities. Also called *equality of outcome.*

**Equality principle** The basic moral principle that states that all human beings are of equal moral value and that they have the same moral rights and responsibilities. It is the principle that forbids discrimination on the basis of ethically irrelevant characteristics such as race, ethnicity, and gender. In duty ethics, it is called the *practical imperative.*

**Equity approach** An approach to distributive justice that holds that fairness is achieved by giving equal shares to all concerned.

**Erotica** The depiction of caring and consensual sex between two or more adults. Compare pornography.

**Ethical code** A set of rules that specify what is considered right and wrong behaviour within a group. Also called a *moral code* or *social code.*

**Ethical conduct** Conduct that is consistent with the norms that specify what is right or wrong in human relationships within a civil society.

**Ethical defence** The justification of a course of action based on principles of ethical reasoning. Compare *ethical reason, justify,* and *justification.*

**Ethical norms** The rules that specify what is right or wrong conduct in human relationships in a civil society.

**Ethical principles** The basic concepts or ideas that underlie what is considered right or wrong conduct in a civil society.

**Ethical reason** Justifying a course of action on the basis of principles of ethical reasoning. Lying, for example, in order to surprise a friend with a party (goodness). Compare *psychological reason*.

**Ethical relativism** The view that holds that there are no shared ethical values and principles across differing societies.

**Ethical universalism** The view that holds that there are shared ethical values and principles common to all human societies.

**Ethical values** The values that generate the principles of right and wrong that are applied to human relationships in a civil society.

**Ethical way** The way of the civilized who base their relationships on moral principles and the rule of law. The way of life in a civil society.

**Ethics (formal definition)** The study of the values and principles that generate the norms that specify what is right or wrong conduct in human relationships in a civil society.

**Ethics (informal definition)** The study of right and wrong in human relationships.

**Euthanasia** Literally means good or happy death. Three forms of euthanasia are commonly identified. (1) Natural death involves allowing a person to die, letting nature take its course. (2) Assisted suicide involves killing someone because they have requested you to do so. (3) Mercy killing involves killing someone without knowing whether they want to die or not. Both assisted suicide and mercy killing are illegal in Canada.

**Explain** To provide a reason for an event.

**Explanation** Giving psychological reasons (motives) for taking a particular course of action. Keeping silent, for example, out of fear.

**Extraordinary measures** Using heroic means to save the life of a terminally ill person or to keep them alive. Also called *heroic measures or means*.

**Favouritism** A form of discrimination in which certain people benefit from the actions of the one who discriminates. Discrimination in favour of someone.

**Folkways** The least important norms of a group.

**Freedom** The ability to make an independent choice.

**Freedom, negative duty** The freedom principle stated in the form of a simple rule: "Don't force or intimidate others."

**Freedom, positive duty** The freedom principle stated in the form of a simple rule: "Respect the right of others to make their own choices."

**Freedom principle** The basic moral principle that states that individuals are entitled to make independent choices, choices for which they are both morally responsible and accountable. Also called the *principle of freedom*.

**Good lie** A deliberate distortion or omission of the truth that is done for the sake of a worthy purpose. Compare *lie* and *bad lie*.

**Goodness** The experience of things that are beneficial to one's health and welfare.

**Goodness, negative duty** The goodness principle stated in the form of a simple rule: "Don't harm others."

**Goodness, positive duty** The goodness principle stated in the form of a simple rule: "Do good and prevent harm."

**Goodness principle** The basic moral principle that states that individuals are to do those things that enhance the welfare of oneself and others. Also called the *principle of goodness*.

**Hard determinism** The view that human beings have absolutely no free will or freedom of choice.

**Hasty generalization** An unwarranted conclusion based on insufficient data. One of the causes of stereotypes and stereotypical thinking.

**Heroic measures** Using extraordinary measures or means to save the life of a terminally ill person or to keep them alive. Also called *extraordinary measures or means*.

**Honest** Truthful in word and deed. One of the eight qualities of the ideal police officer.

**Hospice care** Special care provided for the terminally ill. It includes physical, psychological, and spiritual care in an attempt to provide a natural death with dignity. Also called *palliative care*.

**Immoral** A word used to describe the actions of a person who knows the difference between right and wrong and chooses to do what is wrong.

**Impartial** Objective, unbiased, and unprejudiced. One of the eight qualities of the ideal police officer.

**Impartiality** The quality of being objective and fair-minded. One of the eight qualities possessed by the ideal police officer.

**Indirect euthanasia** Allowing nature to take its course in the case of a terminally ill person. Allowing a person to die a natural death. Also called *passive euthanasia*.

**Individual relativism** An approach to ethics that says that there are no objective moral standards and that everything is relative to the individual. Also called *intuitionism, emotivism,* or *subjectivism*.

**Induced abortion** An abortion brought on by intentional human intervention. Compare *abortion* and *spontaneous abortion*.

**Inductive reasoning** A type of reasoning that proceeds from a series of particular truths to a general conclusion. A common approach in scientific research.

**Informed consent** Freely choosing after careful consideration of the facts of a situation.

**Insufficient sampling** Drawing conclusions from a sample that is too small. Associated with a form of faulty reasoning called *hasty generalization*.

**Integrity** Truthful in deeds as well as words.

**Intuitionism** A type of nonconsequentialist approach to ethics that says that the right thing to do is what a person feels or intuits is right. Also called *emotivism* or *subjectivism*.

**"Is-ought" mistake** A form of faulty reasoning in which one argues that people should do something ("ought") because people are doing that thing ("is"). For example, we should drive 120 kph on the 401 because everyone is doing 120.

**Justice** Fairness.

**Justice, negative duty** The justice principle stated in the form of a simple rule: "Don't treat others unjustly or unfairly."

**Justice, positive duty** The justice principle stated in the form of a simple rule: "Be fair to others."

**Justice principle** The basic moral principle that states that individuals are to be fair to one another. Also called the *fairness principle*.

**Justification** The providing of ethically defensible reasons for taking a particular course of action.

**Justify** To provide ethically acceptable reasons for taking a particular course of action. Compare *ethical defence* and *ethical reason*.

**Law** The rules in force in a society at any given time.

**Legal justice** Fairness in the trials of persons charged with offences.

**Legislators** Those who make the laws of a society. In a civil society, elected members of the legislative assembly.

**Libertarian** One who believes that freedom is the primary or sole principle of an ethical system.

**Licence** Unrestricted or absolute freedom.

**Lie** A deliberate distortion or omission of the truth made with the intent to deceive. Compare *good lie* and *bad lie*.

**Living will** A document that is written by a mentally competent person expressing that person's wishes with respect to a future time when the person is no longer mentally competent.

**Logic** The science of correct reasoning.

**Maxim** A brief, moral prescription, such as "Always keep your promises."

**Mercy killing** A form of euthanasia in which someone is killed, for mercy's sake, and the wishes of the person killed are not known. Mercy killing is illegal in Canada.

**Merit approach** An approach to distributive justice that says that fairness consists of giving people what they deserve, earn, or merit. Also called the *deserts approach*.

**Minimal force** The least amount of force necessary to stop an aggressor.

**Mistake** An error. Believing that something is true when it is false, or vice-versa.

**Moral** A word used to describe the actions of a person who understands the difference between right and wrong, and chooses to do what is right.

**Moral agent** A human being who is capable of understanding right and wrong and freely chooses to do one or the other.

**Mores** The most important rules of a group. Pronounced "more-rays."

**Natural death** A type of euthanasia in which a terminally ill person is allowed to die a natural death. Natural death does not involve killing another person, but letting nature take its course. It is commonly practised in Canada, and is not illegal. Also called *passive* or *indirect euthanasia*.

**Need** Anything necessary for survival.

**Needs approach** An approach to distributive justice that says that fairness consists in meeting the special needs of disadvantaged persons.

**Neocortex** The human brain's outer layer of grey matter.

**Nonconsequentialism** An approach to prescriptive ethics that says that the rightness or wrongness of an action is determined by something other than the consequences or outcomes of that action.

**Non-moral** A word used to describe the actions of animals, beings that are not moral agents. Also applied to things.

**Non-voluntary euthanasia** Euthanasia in which the wishes of the terminally ill person are not known. Applies to both natural death and mercy killing. Not to be confused with *involuntary* euthanasia, killing persons against their will, a clear case of murder.

**Norm** A rule. Norms of conduct, for example, are simply rules of conduct.

**Normative ethics** That aspect of ethics devoted to prescribing what is or is not acceptable behaviour, what people should do or should not do. States the ideals of conduct. Also called *prescriptive ethics* or the *prescriptive dimension* of ethics.

**Obedient** A word used to describe persons who comply with the law and the orders of superiors. One of the eight qualities of an ideal police officer.

**Obscene material** The explicit depiction of one or more of the following: sexual violence, sex involving children, or degrading and dehumanizing sex. Pornography. Compare *erotica*.

**Pacifist** A person who believes in non-violence. Pacifists are absolutists in that they allow no exception to the rule "Don't harm."

**Palliative care** Special care provided for the terminally ill. It includes physical, psychological, and spiritual care in an attempt to provide a natural death with dignity. Also called *hospice care*.

**Passive euthanasia** A type of euthanasia in which a terminally ill person is allowed to die a natural death. Natural death does not involve killing another person, but letting nature take its course. It is commonly practised in Canada, and is not illegal. Also called *natural death*.

**Paternalism** An attitude of superiority that leads to the inappropriate treatment of one's peers. Treating adults as though they were children. From the Latin word for father, *pater*.

**Penal justice** Fairness in the treatment of those convicted of offences. Fairness with respect to punishment.

**Physiological needs** Things necessary to sustain life. For example, food is a physiological need. Also called *survival needs*.

**Pluralistic** A word used to describe societies that have a multi-cultural makeup.

**Police** Those members of a society who are authorized to enforce the laws of that society.

**Pornography** The explicit depiction of one or more of the following: sexual violence, sex involving children, or degrading and dehumanizing sex. Compare *erotica*.

**Power** The ability to influence others in a desired direction.

**Practical imperative** In the duty ethics of Immanuel Kant, the principle that says that one is not to use another human being as a means to one's own ends. In simple terms, "Don't use others." More commonly known as the *equality principle*.

**Preamble** In a formal document, the introduction that establishes the context for the articles of the document that follow the introduction.

**Prejudice** Pre-judging a situation or a person. Prejudiced persons make up their minds before they have all the facts. Prejudice, a mental activity, often leads to discrimination, a behavioural one.

**Prescriptive dimension** That aspect of ethics that stipulates what is right or wrong conduct within a group. Also called *prescriptive ethics* or *normative ethics*.

**Prescriptive ethics** That aspect of ethics that stipulates what is right or wrong conduct within a group. Also called the *prescriptive dimension* of ethics or *normative ethics*.

**Principles** The basic concepts or ideas of any field of study. Derived from values, the things most important to a group.

**Principle of equality** One of the five principles of ethical reasoning. The principle that states that all people are of equal moral value. The principle that forbids discrimination on the basis of ethically superficial qualities such as race, ethnicity, and gender. Also called the *equality principle* or *equality*. Compare the *PRINCIPLES Model*.

**Principle of freedom** One of the five principles of ethical reasoning. The principle that states that all moral agents are entitled to exercise their free choice while respecting the choices of others. Also called the *freedom principle* or *freedom*. Compare the *PRINCIPLES Model*.

**Principle of goodness** One of the five principles of ethical reasoning. The principle that states that moral agents are to do good to others and not harm them. Also called the *goodness principle* or *goodness*. Compare the *PRINCIPLES Model*.

**Principle of justice** One of the five principles of ethical reasoning. The principle that states that moral agents are to treat one another fairly. Also called the *justice principle, justice,* or the *fairness principle*. Compare the *PRINCIPLES Model*.

**Principle of truth** One of the five principles of ethical reasoning. The principle that states that moral agents are to tell the truth to one another. Also called the *truth principle* or *truth*. Compare the *PRINCIPLES Model*.

**PRINCIPLES Model** The author's model for ethical decision making that requires a moral agent to consider all five of the basic principles of moral reasoning when attempting to understand a moral issue or make an ethical decision. The five principles are *goodness, equality, justice, truth,* and *freedom.*

**Procedural justice** Fairness in the rules that govern a particular situation. Fairness, for example, in the procedures that govern the arrest and detention of a suspect.

**Production** The creation or making of something. In pornography, the making of obscene materials.

**Professional** A word used to describe persons who strive to achieve the highest standards within their field of work. One of the eight qualities of the ideal police officer.

**Professional code** A set of ethical rules intended for use by the members of a given profession.

**Professional discretion** The freedom or authority that professionals have to make reasonable choices in the exercise of their duties. Discretion involves judgements about the seriousness of an offence, not the offender.

**Professional impartiality** The quality of being objective and fair-minded in the exercise of one's professional duties. Impartiality relates to the treatment of the offender, not the offence committed. Impartiality is one of the eight qualities possessed by the ideal police officer.

**Proportional force** Defensive force that is equivalent to the force exerted by an aggressor.

**Psychological reason** Identifying a motive as the cause of a person's action. Keeping silence, for example, for fear of reprisal. Explains behaviour, but does not justify it. Compare *ethical reason.*

**Psychomotor dimension** The actions of human beings that result from the thoughts and feelings that they have. Also called the *behavioural dimension.*

**Public servant** A public perception that sees the role of the police as that of protectors of the members of society and the rule of law. Compare *crime fighter.*

**Punitive justice** An approach to penal justice that sees the purpose of penalties as punishment of the offender. Also called *retributive justice.*

**Quality of life** The degree of excellence that a life has. Compare *sanctity of life.*

**Racism** Discrimination on the basis of racial characteristics such as skin colour or hair texture.

**Recidivism rate** The rate of re-offending after release from prison.

**Rehabilitation** The correcting or eliminating of errant behaviour.

**Rehabilitative justice** An approach to penal justice that sees the primary purpose of penalties as the correction of errant behaviour. Also called *corrective justice.*

**Religious duties** Obligations that one has to one's god or gods.

**Responsibility** A duty or obligation to do something.

**Retribution** Punishment that balances the harm of the offence committed.

**Retributive justice** An approach to penal justice that sees the purpose of penalties as punishment or retribution, in an attempt to balance the scales of justice. Also called *punitive justice.*

**Ritual duty** Obligations to observe the rites of one's religion.

**Rule of law** A characteristic of civil societies in which no member of society is above the law. The law rules or governs everyone equally. It plays no favourites.

**Sanctity of life** The sacredness or holiness of life. Compare *quality of life.*

**Self-restrained** Having control over one's emotions. Self-controlled or self-disciplined. One of the eight qualities of the ideal police officer.

**Sexism** Discrimination based on gender.

**Sins of commission** In religions, actions that are deliberately hurtful to others.

**Sins of omission** In religions, failing to render help to others when one is able to do so.

**Social disability** A socially created disadvantage. Majority group members, for example, discriminate against minority group members creating a disadvantage for them.

**Social duties** Obligations to others in one's social groupings. Codes of conduct.

**Social justice** Fairness for all members of a large social system such as a society.

**Social needs** Things necessary for healthy relationships and social development. Affiliation, achievement, and power are social needs.

**Societal code** A broad moral code used within a society or very large social group.

**Soft determinism** A view that says that humans have limited free will. Soft determinism is compatible with ethics.

**Spontaneous abortion** The termination of a pregnancy due to natural or accidental causes. A miscarriage. Compare *abortion* and *induced abortion*.

**Stereotype** A false and misleading idea about a group and its individual members.

**Stereotypical thinking** Faulty thinking based on stereotypes.

**Subjectivism** The view that says that there are no objective moral standards and that ethics is relative to each individual. Also called *individual relativism, intuitionism,* or *emotivism*.

**Survival needs** Things necessary to sustain life. For example, the need for food is a basic survival need. Also called *physiological needs.*

**Systemic discrimination** Widespread discrimination within a social system, both in the actions of its members and in the rules of the social system.

**Systemic sexism** Sexism practised by an entire social system or institution of society.

**Trimester** One-third of a normal pregnancy, about 13 weeks.

**Trustworthy** Reliable, worthy of trust. One of the eight qualities of the ideal police officer.

**Truth** A statement that accords with reality or matches reality. A statement of fact.

**Truth, negative duty** The truth principle stated in the form of a simple rule: "Don't lie" or "Don't deceive."

**Truth, positive duty** The truth principle stated in the form of a simple rule: "Tell the truth" or "Be honest."

**Truth principle** The basic moral principle that states that individuals are to be honest with one another and that they are to act with integrity. Also called the *principle of truth.*

**Tunnel vision** An expression used to describe a very narrow mind-set that results in a lack of objectivity and serious errors in judgement.

**Tyrannical behaviour** The actions of a tyrant or despot.

**Tyranny** Oppressive dictatorship. Despotism.

**Tyranny of the majority** A situation in which the good of the majority is achieved at the expense of the minority. The majority function like a dictator or despot who tyrannizes the minority.

**Uncivilized way** The way of those who are unethical. The way of the outlaw. Also called *unethical way.*

**Unethical conduct** Conduct that is inconsistent with the norms that specify what is right or wrong conduct in human relationships in a civil society.

**Unethical way** The way of those who are unethical. The way of the outlaw. Also called *uncivilized way.*

**Universal principles** Principles that are found in all societies. Principles essential to civilized life.

**Unrepresentative sampling** Sampling that does not reflect the characteristics of the group about which one wants to draw a general conclusion. Interviewing only men, for example, when one wants to draw a conclusion about the preferences of women.

**Utilitarian approach** A type of consequentialist approach to ethics that says that the right thing to do is whatever brings about the greatest good for the greatest number of people. It includes a concern for the consequences for both oneself and others.

**Utilitarianism** A type of consequentialist approach to ethics that says that the right thing to do is whatever brings about the greatest good for the greatest number of people. It includes a concern for the consequences for both oneself and others.

**Utility** Usefulness. In ethics, usefulness in bringing about the greatest good for the greatest number. Compare *utilitarianism*.

**Value(s)** Whatever is important to an individual or a group.

**Value system** All the values of an individual or group.

**Vendetta** A blood feud between two parties that involves ongoing reprisals.

**Victimless crime** An expression used to describe criminal offences that have no victims. Prostitution, where it is illegal, is sometimes called a victimless crime as both parties consent to the arrangement.

**Victorian era** A time of very conservative sexual values during the reign of Queen Victoria of England (1837–1901).

**Voluntary euthanasia** Euthanasia in which the person whose life is in question wants to die. Assisted suicide, by definition, is always voluntary euthanasia. Natural death might or might not be voluntary.

# Readings and References

## CHAPTER 1    Origins: Exploring the Role
of Ethics in a Civil Society

Baier, Kurt. 1965. *The Moral Point of View*. New York, NY: Random House.

Canadian Press (Toronto). 2000. "Toronto police union under fire," *Kitchener-Waterloo Record*, January 27. p.A3.

Drews, Elizabeth, and Leslie Lipson. 1971. *Values and Humanity*. New York, NY: St. Martin's.

Facione, P., D. Scherer, and T. Attig. 1978. *Values and Society*. Englewood Cliffs, NJ: Prentice-Hall.

Fraser, Sylvia. 2000. "Straight man." *Toronto Life*, October. p.100.

International Association of Chiefs of Police. 1957 and 1991. *Canons of Police Ethics*. Alexandria, VA.

Gillmor, Don. 2000. "The thick blue line." *Toronto Life*, October. p.126.

Goff, Colin. 2001. *Criminal Justice in Canada*. Toronto, ON: Nelson.

Hayward, Kathryn. 2000. "Good cops." *Toronto Life*, October. p.112.

Hobbes, Thomas. 1962. *Leviathan* (Michael Oakeshott, Ed.). London, UK: Collier-Macmillan Ltd.

MacIntyre, Alasdair. 1966. *A Short History of Ethics*. New York, NY: Macmillan.

Matlin, Margaret. 1999. *Psychology*, 3rd ed. Fort Worth, TX: Harcourt Brace.

Pollock, Joycelyn. 1998. *Ethics in Crime and Justice*. Belmont, CA: West/Wadsworth.

Seagrave, Jayne. 1997. *Introduction to Policing in Canada*. Scarborough, ON: Prentice-Hall.

Wells, Jennifer. 2000. "The watch dogs." *Toronto Life*, October. p.124.

## CHAPTER 2    Analytical Ethics: Thinking Critically
about Ethical Issues in a Civil Society

Cederblom, Jerry, and David Paulsen. 1996. *Critical Reasoning*. Belmont, CA: Wadsworth.

Diestler, Sherry. 1994. *Becoming a Critical Thinker*. New York, NY: Macmillan.

Hick, John H. 1983. *Philosophy of Religion*, 3rd ed. Englewood Cliffs, NJ: Prentice-Hall.

Hospers, John. 1967. *An Introduction to Philosophical Analysis*, 2nd ed. Englewood Cliffs, NJ: Prentice-Hall.

Plato. 1961. "The Republic," in *The Collected Dialogues of Plato*. Edited by Edith Hamilton and Huntington Cairns. New York, NY: Pantheon Books, Random House Inc.

Rasool, Joan, Caroline Banks, and Mary-Jane McCarthy. *Critical Thinking: Reading and Writing in a Diverse World*. Belmont, CA: Wadsworth.

Ruggiero, Vincent. 1995. *Beyond Feelings: A Guide to Critical Thinking*, 4th ed. Mountain View, CA: Mayfield.

Taylor, Paul, ed. 1972. *Problems of Moral Philosophy*, 2nd ed. Belmont, CA: Dickenson.

Wasserstrom, Richard A., ed. 1971. *Morality and the Law*. Belmont, CA: Wadsworth.

## CHAPTER 3    Prescriptive Ethics: Establishing Norms of Conduct in a Civil Society

Bentham, Jeremy. 1967. "The Principles of Morals and Legislations," in *Ethical Theories: A Book of Readings*, 2nd edition. Edited by A.I. Melden. Englewood Cliffs, NJ: Prentice-Hall, Inc.

Fletcher, Joseph. 1966. *Situation Ethics: The New Morality*. Philadelphia, PA: The Westminster Press.

Gauthier, David P., ed. 1970. *Morality and Rational Self-Interest*. Englewood Cliffs, NJ: Prentice-Hall.

Hospers, John. 1982. *Human Conduct*, 2nd ed. New York, NY: Harcourt, Brace, and World.

International Association of Chiefs of Police. 1991. *The Law Enforcement Code of Ethics*. Alexandria, VA.

Kant, Immanuel. 1967. "Foundations of the Metaphysics of Morals," in *Ethical Theories: A Book of Readings*, 2nd edition. Edited by A.I. Melden. Englewood Cliffs, NJ: Prentice-Hall, Inc.

Kinsey, Alfred, Wardell B. Pomeroy, and Clyde E. Martin. 1948. *Sexual Behaviour in the Human Male*. Philadelphia, Penn: Saunders.

Kinsey, Alfred, Wardell B. Pomeroy, Clyde E. Martin, and P. Gebhard. 1953. *Sexual Behaviour in the Human Female*. Philadelphia, Penn: Saunders.

Melden, I., ed. 1967. *Ethical Theories: A Book of Readings*, 2nd ed. Englewood Cliffs, NJ: Prentice-Hall.

Mill, John Stuart. 1967. "Utilitarianism," in *Ethical Theories: A Book of Readings,* 2nd ed. Edited by A. I. Melden. Englewood Cliffs, NJ: Prentice-Hall, Inc.

Narveson, Jan. 1967. *Morality and Utility*. Baltimore, Maryland: Johns Hopkins University Press.

## CHAPTER 4    Codes of Conduct: Examining the Ethical Standards of a Civil Society

Canada, Department of Justice. 1982. *Canadian Charter of Rights and Freedoms*. Ottawa, ON: Queen's Printer for Canada.

Kleinig, John and Yurong Zhang. 1993. *Professional Law Enforcement Codes: A Documentary Collection*. Westport, Conn: Greenwood Press.

Ludwig Theodore M. 1989. *The Sacred Paths: Understanding the Religions of the World*. New York, NY: Macmillan.

International Association of Chiefs of Police. 1957. *The Law Enforcement Code of Ethics*. Alexandria, VA.

International Association of Chiefs of Police. 1957. *Canons of Police Ethics*. Alexandria, VA.

International Association of Chiefs of Police. 1989. *Law Enforcement Code of Conduct*. Alexandria, VA.

International Association of Chiefs of Police. 1991. *The Law Enforcement Code of Ethics*. Alexandria, VA.

International Association of Chiefs of Police. 1991. *Canons of Police Ethics*. Alexandria, VA.

Ontario, Ministry of the Solicitor General. 1998. *Police Services Act*, Revised Statutes of Ontario, 1990. Toronto, ON: Queen's Printer for Ontario.

Smith, Huston. 1958. *The Religions of Man*. New York, NY: Harper and Row.

United Nations High Commissioner for Human Rights. 1998. *Universal Declaration of Human Rights*. Geneva, Switzerland: United Nations Department of Public Information.

## CHAPTER 5    Principles: Identifying the Basic Ethical Concepts of a Civil Society

Canada, Department of Justice. 1982. *Canadian Charter of Rights and Freedoms*. Ottawa, ON: Queen's Printer for Canada.

Canadian Press (Calgary). 2000. "Officer dragged and hit female prisoner, colleague testifies." *Kitchener-Waterloo Record*, January 29, 2000. p.D20.

International Association of Chiefs of Police. 1957. *The Law Enforcement Code of Ethics*. Alexandria, VA.

International Association of Chiefs of Police. 1957. *Canons of Police Ethics*. Alexandria, VA.

International Association of Chiefs of Police. 1989. *Law Enforcement Code of Conduct*. Alexandria, VA.

International Association of Chiefs of Police. 1991. *The Law Enforcement Code of Ethics*. Alexandria, VA.

International Association of Chiefs of Police. 1991. *Canons of Police Ethics*. Alexandria, VA.

Ontario, Ministry of the Solicitor General. 1998. *Police Services Act*, Revised Statutes of Ontario, 1990. Toronto, ON: Queen's Printer for Ontario.

United Nations High Commissioner for Human Rights. 1998. *Universal Declaration of Human Rights*. Geneva, Switzerland: United Nations Department of Public Information.

## CHAPTER 6    Goodness: Preventing Harm and Doing Good in a Civil Society

Andrew, R. David. 1991. "Abortion and the Brain." *The Toronto Star*, July 29. p.A13.

Battin, M. Pabst. 1982. *Ethical Issues in Suicide*. Englewood Cliffs, NJ: Prentice-Hall.

Behnke, John, and Sissela Bok. 1975. *The Dilemmas of Suicide*. Garden City, NY: Anchor Books.

Callahan Daniel, and Sidney Callahan, eds. 1984. *Abortion: Understanding Differences*. New York, NY: Plenum.

Canadian Press (Halifax). 1995. "Woman convicted of aiding suicide." *Kitchener-Waterloo Record*. October 19. p.A3.

Canadian Press (Toronto). 1999. "Abused youth kills mom, sentenced to six months." *Kitchener-Waterloo Record*. October 21. p.A4.

Canadian Press (The Hague). 2000. "Dutch parliament passes bill to make doctor-assisted suicide legal." *Kitchener-Waterloo Record*. November 29. p.A15.

Coyne, Andrew. 1994. "The slippery slope that leads to death." *Globe and Mail*. November 21. p.A14.

Edwards and Mazzuca. 1999. "Three quarters of Canadians support doctor-assisted suicide." Princeton, NJ: *The Gallup Organisation, Gallup Poll Releases*, March 24, http://www.gallup.com/poll/releases.

Hurst, Lynda. 1996. "The last rights." *Toronto Star*, Sept. 28. p.C1.

Jenish, D'Arcy. 1994. "What would you do?" *Maclean's*, November 28. p.18.

Jonas. George. 1997. "Ruling tells women it's OK to kill." *Kitchener-Waterloo Record*. p.A7.

Ramsey, Paul. 1968. *The Just War and Political Responsibility*. New York, NY: Charles Scribner's Sons.

Riley, Susan. 1983. "The nation's new agony over abortion." *Maclean's*. July 25. p.32.

Ross, Val. 1983. "The 'mercy' killers." *Maclean's*. Nov. 21. p.24.

Ross, Val, and Roberta Elliott. 1983. "The cost of compassion." *Maclean's*. Nov. 21. p.29.

Stern, Leonard. 1997. "Mom who shot fetus gets suspended sentence." *Kitchener-Waterloo Record*. February 7. p.A3.

Wood, Chris. 1994. "The legacy of Sue Rodriguez." *Maclean's*. Feb. 28. p.21.

# CHAPTER 7 Equality: Treating Others Impartially in a Civil Society

Aagaard, Christian. 2000. "Rank-and-file closed door on Guelph police chief." *Kitchener-Waterloo Record*. October 12. p.B1.

Canadian Press (Ottawa). 1999. "More women on Canadian police forces in 1999." *Kitchener-Waterloo Record*. December 21. p.A4.

Canadian Press (Saskatoon). 2000. "RCMP investigates police link to freezing deaths of two men." *Kitchener-Waterloo Record*. February 17. p.A3.

Covert, Kim. 1999. "Police sensitivity to rape victims still a problem." *Kitchener-Waterloo Record*. July 13. p.A3.

Cryderman, Brian, Augie Fleras, and Christopher O'Toole. 1992. *Police, Race and Ethnicity*. Toronto, ON: Butterworths.

Editorial. 1996. "Courts should not reinstate bad law." *Kitchener-Waterloo Record*. November 27. p.A10.

Editorial. 1999. "Knock down unfair workplace hurdles." *Kitchener-Waterloo Record*. September 14. p.A6.

Editorial. 1999. "Sexual assault squad needs overhaul." *Toronto Star*, October 27. p.A30.

Gombu, Phinjo. 1999. "The high price of being Jane Doe." *Toronto Star*, p.A4.

Hurka, Thomas. 1999. *Principles: Short Essays on Ethics*, 2nd ed. Toronto, ON: Harcourt Brace.

Hurka, Thomas. 1999. "Affirmative action: giving women an even break at work" in *Principles: Short Essays on Ethics,* 2nd ed., Toronto, ON: Harcourt Brace, p.189.

Hurka, Thomas. 1999. "Patriotism: like family love or racism?" in *Principles: Short Essays on Ethics,* 2nd ed., Toronto, ON: Harcourt Brace. pp.33–36.

Imai, Shin, Katherine Logan, and Gary Stein. 1993. *Aboriginal Law Handbook.* Scarborough, ON: Carswell Thomson.

Jonas, George. 1998. "Ruling about victim of rape goes too far." *Kitchener-Waterloo Record,* July 13. p.A7.

Leiser, Burton M. 1986. *Liberty, Justice, and Morals.* New York, NY: Macmillan.

# CHAPTER 8 Justice: Treating Others Fairly in a Civil Society

Bonner, Raymond, and Ford Fessenden. 2000. "Executions no deterrent, survey finds." *Toronto Star.* September 23. p.A23.

Canadian Press (Toronto). 1995. "Six months enough for some killers, expert says." *Kitchener-Waterloo Record.* February 8, 1995. p.A3.

Canadian Press (Ottawa). 2000a. "Prison population down but costs up." *Kitchener-Waterloo Record.* June 2. p.A3.

Canadian Press (Ottawa). 2000b. "Homicide rates at 30-year low." *Kitchener-Waterloo Record.* October 19. p.A6.

Fennell, Tom, and Danylo Hawaleshka. 1997. "I'm sorry, Paul." *Maclean's.* July 1. p.20.

Gillis, Charlie. 1998. "Many pardoned sex offenders strike again." *National Post.* November 28. p.A1.

Hospers, John. 1982. *Human Conduct,* 2nd ed. New York, NY: Harcourt Brace Jovanovich.

Kaihla, Paul. 1995. "Sex offenders: is there a cure?" *Maclean's,* February 15. p.57.

Leiser, Burton M. 1986. *Liberty, Justice, and Morals.* New York, NY: Macmillan.

Murphy Jeffrie, ed. 1985. *Punishment and Rehabilitation,* 2nd ed. Belmont, CA: Wadsworth.

Wickens, Barbara. 1998. "Final vindication." *Maclean's.* April 20. p.54.

# CHAPTER 9 Truth: Being Honest and Having Integrity in a Civil Society

Bok, Sissela. 1979. *Lying: Moral Choice in Public and Private Life.* New York, NY: Vintage.

Bok, Sissela. 1982. *Secrets: On the Ethics of Concealment and Revelation.* New York, NY: Pantheon Books.

Canadian Press (Toronto). 2000. "Cops charged as money goes missing." *Kitchener-Waterloo Record.* November 23. p.A2.

Duncanson, John, and Jim Rankin. 2000. "5 officers charged in cash probe." *Toronto Star.* April 8. p.A1.

Plato. 1961. *The Collected Dialogues of Plato*. Edited by Edith Hamilton and Huntington Cairns. New York, NY: Random House, p.607, s360b.

Ruby, Clayton. 2000. "Supreme injustice." *Globe and Mail*. October 17. p.A21.

Saunders, Doug. 2000. "U.S. jury convicts LAPD officers." *Globe and Mail*. November 16. p.A3.

St. Clair College. 1997. *Code of Student Rights and Responsibilities* 1997-98. Windsor, ON: College Publication, p.13.

Wilson, John. 1967. *Language and the pursuit of truth*. Cambridge: Cambridge University Press.

Wordsworth, Araminta. 2000. "Washington to monitor police in L.A. for abuse of minorities." *National Post*. November 2. p.A2.

## CHAPTER 10   Freedom: Making Ethical Choices in a Civil Society

Cox, Archibald. 1981. *Freedom of Expression*. Cambridge, Mass.: Harvard University Press.

Cox, Bob. 1992. "Common-sense approach: Supreme Court draws the line at sex that harms people." *Kitchener-Waterloo Record*. March 2. p.A7.

Gillis, Charlie. 1998. "Many pardoned sex offenders strike again." *National Post*. November 26. p.A1.

Hare, R.M. 1963. *Freedom and Reason*. Oxford: Oxford University Press.

Kinsey, Alfred, Wardell B. Pomeroy, and Clyde E. Martin. 1948. *Sexual Behaviour in the Human Male*. Philadelphia, Penn: Saunders.

Kinsey, Alfred, Wardell B. Pomeroy, Clyde E. Martin, and P. Gebhard. 1953. *Sexual Behaviour in the Human Female*. Philadelphia, Penn: Saunders.

Masters, W.H. and V. E. Johnson. 1966. *Human Sexual Response*. Boston, Mass: Little, Brown.

Snyder, Marie. 1999. "Save the children: there is no such thing as harmless possession of kiddie porn." *Kitchener-Waterloo Record*. January 23. p.A17.

Wood, Dianne. 2000. "Pedophile faces parole violation charges." *Kitchener-Waterloo Record*. November 14. p.A3.

# Index